# Dragon NaturallySpeaking™ For Dummies®

W9-CDK-273
Sheet

## Dictating Anywhere

### Capital Letters

**Cap / No Caps / All Caps** *<word>*

**Caps On** *<text>* **Caps Off**

**No Caps On** *<text>* **No Caps Off**

**All Caps On** *<text>* **All Caps Off**

**Cap That**

**No Caps That**

**All Caps That**

### White Space

**New Paragraph**

**New Line**

**Tab Key**

**Spacebar**

### Numbers

Say naturally:

    Numbers

    Dates

    Times

    Fractions

    Dollar amounts

    Phone numbers

**Numeral** *<number>*

**Roman** *<number>*

### Basic Punctuation

**Period, Exclamation Point, Question Mark, Comma, Colon, Hyphen, Dash, Semicolon**

**Open Quote** *<text>* **Close Quote**

**Open Paren** *<text>* **Close Paren**

### Error Handling

**Scratch That**

**Undo That**

**Delete That**

**Correct That** (or **Spell That**)

In the Correction dialog box:

    **Choose** *<number>*

    **Select** *<number>*

    Cursor and deletion commands

    Spelling and punctuation

## Menus and Dialog Boxes

**Click** *<Menu bar choice> <menu item>* …

**Click** *<Name of item or button in dialog box>*

**Press Alt** *<hot key for feature>*

## Desktop and Windows

**Start** *<Any name within Start menu>*

**Click Start, Programs,** …

**Switch to** *<window name in title bar>*

**Switch to Previous / Next Window**

***...For Dummies®: Bestselling Book Series for Beginners***

# Dragon NaturallySpeaking™ 4.0 For Dummies®

## Keystrokes

**Press** (or **Type**) *<key name>*
    (**Alt, Ctrl, Shift** combos allowed)

Spell with ICA letter names:
    a = **Alpha**, b= **Baker**, …

## Keyboard Shortcuts

| | |
|---|---|
| + | Microphone on/off |
| - | Correction dialog box |
| Shift+*<speak>* | Interpret as text |
| Ctrl+*<speak>* | Interpret as command |

## Font Styles Most Places

**Bold That**

*Italicize That*

<u>Underline That</u>

**Restore That**

## Formatting in Selected Applications

**Format That**
    **Arial / Courier / Times**
    *<In Word: other fonts>*
    *<Size in points>*
    *<Any capitalization>*
    **Bold / Italics / Underline**
    **Regular**
    **Left / Right Aligned**
    **Centered**
    *<In Word: styles>*

## Cursor Motion and Selection

**Move Left (Back) / Right (Forward) [*<number>*] [Characters / Words]**

**Move Up (Back) / Down (Forward) [*<number>*] [Lines / Paragraphs]**

**Go To (Move To)**
    **Top (Start, Beginning) / Bottom (End)**
    **of**
    **Line / Paragraph / Document**

**Select Next / Last *<number>* Characters / Words / Lines / Paragraphs**

( ) = terms that mean the same thing

[ ] = terms you can leave off

 / = different words you can use

*…For Dummies®: Bestselling Book Series for Beginners*

TM

# References for the Rest of Us! ®

*Dragon NaturallySpeaking*™ FOR DUMMIES®

by David Kay and Doug Muder

WILEY

Wiley Publishing, Inc.

**Dragon NaturallySpeaking™ For Dummies®**

Published by
**Wiley Publishing, Inc.**
111 River Street
Hoboken, NJ 07030
www.wiley.com

Copyright © 1999 Wiley Publishing, Inc., Indianapolis, Indiana

Published simultaneously in Canada

For general information on our other products and services or to obtain technical support, please contact our Customer Care Department within the U.S. at 800-762-2974, outside the U.S. at 317-572-3993, or fax 317-572-4002.

Wiley also publishes its books in a variety of electronic formats. Some content that appears in print may not be available in electronic books.

*Library of Congress Cataloging-in-Publication Data:*

Library of Congress Control Number: 99-65877

ISBN: 0-7645-0638-2

1B/QX/RQ/ZZ/IN

# About the Authors

**Dave Kay** is a writer, engineer, wildlife tracker, and aspiring artist, combining professions with the same effectiveness as his favorite business establishment, Acton Muffler, Brake, and Ice Cream (now defunct). Dave's computer book efforts include Wiley Publishing Inc.'s *...For Dummies* titles on Microsoft Works, WordPerfect, Web publishing, and VRML, and McGraw-Hill's *Internet: The Complete Reference* and *Graphics File Formats*. In his other life, Dave is the Poo-bah of Brightleaf Communications, where he writes and teaches. He spends his spare time in the woods, playing with molten glass, designing stage scenery, and singing Gilbert and Sullivan choruses in public. He lives in the boondocks of Massachusetts with his wife, Katy, and golden retriever, Alex.

**Doug Muder** is a semi-retired mathematician who has contributed to a number of books about computers and the Internet, including *Internet: The Complete Reference*, *Windows 98: The Complete Reference*, and *VRML For Dummies*. He is also the author of numerous research papers in geometry and information theory. Doug lives with his wife, Deb, in New Hampshire and amuses himself by playing with other people's children, writing fiction, and dabbling in all forms of mysticism. He holds a Ph.D. in mathematics from the University of Chicago.

# Dedication

To Meg, Josh, and Tory, who someday will dimly remember computers you couldn't talk to.

# Acknowledgments

We would like to dictate a rousing cheer of thanks to our wives, friends, and families, especially the Levine-Young "strange attractors" who anchor our chaotic Cabal of authors. Thanks also to Matt Wagner (matzel-tov!), the other folks at Waterside Productions, and the congenial editors at Wiley Publishing, Inc.

The following people were especially important in creating this book, and to them we offer our heartfelt thanks:

- To the knowledgeable and generous mob at Dragon Systems: Kathi "FedEx" Chiango, Renata "Dispeller of Darkness" Aylward, Alessandra Binazzi, Susan Vannini, Valerie Matthews, Alexandra Trudo, Jeff Foley, Carol Gunst, Roger Maddis, and several people whose names we never got straight: Hope we didn't screw up too badly.

- To our project editor, Nate "Sure, Why Not" Holdread: We just need one more week and 24 more pages . . .

- To copy editor Paula Lowell and tech editor Sally Neuman: Thanks for laughing at our jokes!

## Publisher's Acknowledgments

We're proud of this book; please send us your comments through our online registration form located at www.dummies.com/register/.

Some of the people who helped bring this book to market include the following:

*Acquisitions, Editorial, and Media Development*

**Project Editor:** Nate Holdread

**Acquisitions Editor:** David Mayhew

**Copy Editor:** Paula Lowell

**Technical Editor:** Sally Neuman

**Editorial Manager:** Leah P. Cameron

**Editorial Assistant:** Beth Parlon

*Special Help*
Kim Darosett, Stephanie Koutek, Pam Wilson-Wykes

*Production*

**Project Coordinator:** E. Shawn Alysworth

**Layout and Graphics:** Amy M. Adrian, Brian Drumm, Angela F. Hunckler, Jill Piscitelli, Brent Savage, Jacque Schneider, Janet Seib, Michael A. Sullivan, Brian Torwelle, Maggie Ubertini, Mary Jo Weis, Dan Whetstine, Erin Zeltner

**Proofreaders:** Laura Albert, Vickie Broyles, Marianne Santy, John Greenough, Rebecca Senninger, Ethel M. Winslow

**Indexer:** Ann Norcross

---

*Publishing and Editorial for Technology Dummies*
**Richard Swadley,** Vice President and Executive Group Publisher
**Andy Cummings,** Vice President and Publisher
**Mary C. Corder,** Editorial Director

*Publishing for Consumer Dummies*
**Diane Graves Steele,** Vice President and Publisher
**Joyce Pepple,** Acquisitions Director

*Composition Services*
**Gerry Fahey,** Vice President of Production Services
**Debbie Stailey,** Director of Composition Services

◆

The publisher would like to give special thanks to Patrick J. McGovern, without whom this book would not have been possible.

◆

# Contents at a Glance

# Cartoons at a Glance

## By Rich Tennant

"Come on in. I left my new voice recognition system on so you could try it."

**page 57**

"Yeah, these voice recognition systems can be tricky. Let me see if I can open your word processing program."

**page 149**

"I'm using the 'Cab Drivers' edition of Naturally Speaking, so it understands words like '@#*%' and 'NO&#!'."

**page 335**

"For my finale, Rollo here will flawlessly activate my voice recognition system while I empty this bag of marbles into my mouth."

**page 253**

"I ran this Bob Dylan CD through our voice recognition system, and he really is just saying, 'Manaama-manaaabadhaabadha...'"

**page 7**

Fax: 978-546-7747 • E-mail: the5wave@tiac.net

# Table of Contents

# Introduction

*F*ree at last! Finally, someone has freed you from that medieval torture rack, the keyboard, and its contemporary accessory, the mouse. You've been muttering epithets at your computer — now you can actually speak to it. Although it still won't take your epithets to heart, it will now at least write them down for your future convenience.

For those who can't type or spell (or at least, not well) — and for those whose bodies have been punished by keyboarding — Dragon NaturallySpeaking spells relief (and other words, too). NaturallySpeaking gives your lips their job back: being your principal data output device. In fact, with NaturallySpeaking, you may be able to type faster with your lips than with your fingers. At the same time, you can eliminate spelling errors (and spell checking) from your life.

NaturallySpeaking can do great things soon after you open the box, but too often its talents lie hidden under a bushel of complexity. Recognizing speech is one of those human talents that is still very complex to a computer. ("Let's see now," you can hear it saying, "you want to communicate with me by flapping your flesh in a breeze. Right. I'll get right on that. Meanwhile, wouldn't you like a nice keyboard?") Recognizing human speech is as much a miracle for a computer as computing the precise value of Pi is for a human. (Computing the highly abstract value of pie, oddly enough, is much easier for a human.)

NaturallySpeaking borders on being miraculous — but to get really practical results, you have to meet this miracle halfway. Otherwise, you just have an impressive plaything (not that we have anything against playthings). *Dragon NaturallySpeaking For Dummies* is here to help. If you've been wondering what all the excitement is about, either because you're thinking of getting NaturallySpeaking — or because, so far, NaturallySpeaking hasn't been too exciting for you — this book may be what you need.

## About This Book

What's in this book is the stuff you need to know to turn NaturallySpeaking from a technical miracle into a working tool. Following are just a few of the things this book can help you do:

- ✔ Discover what NaturallySpeaking can and can't do.
- ✔ Train NaturallySpeaking to recognize your voice.
- ✔ Run NaturallySpeaking in the best way for your application.

✔ Use voice commands to get the formatting you want.

✔ Correct NaturallySpeaking when it makes a mistake.

✔ Add to or customize NaturallySpeaking's vocabulary.

✔ Speak better for better recognition.

✔ Control your desktop by voice.

✔ Transcribe speech from a portable recorder.

✔ Use playback and text-to-speech tools to help proofread.

✔ Choose hardware for better performance.

✔ Create your own dictation shorthands and custom commands.

# Typographic Weirdness <In> This, Book

Ever try to describe something basically simple and discover that the description made it ridiculously complex, instead? Well, it's that way with describing NaturallySpeaking commands, so we try to simplify the job by using some typographic conventions. We believe you won't really need to think about our typography much (let alone go to any conventions about it), but in case you're wondering about it, here's what it means:

✔ We put NaturallySpeaking commands (the ones you speak, not the menu choices) in bold and initial capitals, such as **Scratch That**.

✔ When part of a NaturallySpeaking command varies according to what you are trying to do, we indicate the variable part in angle brackets (< and >), as in: **Format That _<font>_**. The term _<font>_ here represents one of the many fonts allowed by that command, like Arial.

✔ When part of a NaturallySpeaking command is text from an example we're discussing, we put that part in italics. For example, **Select _we put that part_** is a command telling NaturallySpeaking to select the text "we put that part."

✔ Where we want you to pause slightly in a command, we put a comma. For instance, if we tell you to say, "**Caps On, _The Sands of Barcelona_, Caps Off**", we want you to pause briefly where those commas appear.

# Who Do We Think You Are, Anyway?

We think you are a person of elevated literary taste and acute discernment, who aspires to converse with computers. Beyond that, we have assumed certain things about you, our esteemed reader.

We assume you are a new user of NaturallySpeaking, using (or intending to use) Release 4.0 of some version of NaturallySpeaking. We also assume you are passably familiar with Microsoft Windows.

We figure you're picking up this book for any of the following reasons:

- ✔ You thought it was a book about dragons or natural foods.
- ✔ You've installed NaturallySpeaking and are baffled by it.
- ✔ You're impressed by NaturallySpeaking but wonder if you're getting the full benefit of it.
- ✔ You'd like NaturallySpeaking to work more accurately.
- ✔ You can't get all the NaturallySpeaking features to work.
- ✔ NaturallySpeaking seems to work, but very inconsistently.
- ✔ You don't have NaturallySpeaking, and are wondering if you would like it.

Some users may be looking for a heavy book that helps them squash NaturallySpeaking bugs. We haven't written very much in the bug-squashing line here because: a) bugs tend to be very setup-specific, b) the bugs we would write about today are often fixed tomorrow, c) Dragon's Web site and some of the online user groups are better bug resources, and d) squashing bugs is icky. On the other hand, for squashing real, biological bugs, this book's finely balanced heft and glossy covers make it the perfect desktop solution to entomological angst, and a fine holiday gift.

# How This Book Is Organized

This book is a reference book, which means that you don't have to read it in any particular order. Jump right in wherever something looks good.

This book is organized into lumps, which our editors prefer we call parts. In deference to their good judgment, we have organized this book into the following lumps:

## Part I: Hatching and Launching Your Dragon Software

If you haven't yet installed, trained, and launched NaturallySpeaking, this short part is the place to begin. This part is also the place to go if you have already hatched your dragon but are a bit confused about the way it works.

Chapter 1 helps you know what to expect so that you can tell whether things are working properly or decide whether you have the NaturallySpeaking edition you need. Chapter 2 guides you through various wizards that attend to the mysteries of training your new dragon sidekick. Chapter 3 tells how to start up NaturallySpeaking, points out the tools and options available on the NaturallySpeaking menu, and details the basic word-processing features of the NaturallySpeaking window.

## Part II: Fire-Breathing 101

Part II is where you get down to the nitty-gritty of dictating, editing, and formatting your documents: what to say, how to say it, and how to correct NaturallySpeaking's errors.

Part II also tells you how to use some of the key audio features of NaturallySpeaking Preferred and Professional: how to proofread by playing back — or reading, in a synthesized voice — your dictation and how to set up NaturallySpeaking to handle recorded speech. In this part, you also discover how to record speech on the NaturallyMobile recorder and how to transcribe recorded speech.

## Part III: Giving Your Applications Wings

In Part III, we show you how you can use NaturallySpeaking's basic dictation, editing, and formatting features in virtually any application. Then we show you how specific applications allow you to do nearly anything you can do in the NaturallySpeaking window itself.

Discover how best to use NaturallySpeaking with a variety of applications, from word processing to Web browsing. You can use Dragon's NaturalWord interface in Word or WordPerfect, and your voice commands can control some of those word processors' special features. You can verbally click links in Internet Explorer. Or, with NaturallySpeaking Mobile Organizer, you can dictate memos, e-mail messages, and calendar appointments into the NaturallyMobile recorder and have NaturallySpeaking transcribe them into Microsoft Outlook or other personal information managers.

## Part IV: Precision Flying

The holy grail for companies like Dragon Systems is to get their software to accurately recognize every word you say without becoming intolerably slow. Even with 98% to 99% accuracy, you have, roughly, one word wrong every paragraph. If your accuracy is significantly lower than that, you may begin to wonder where the benefit is.

In Part IV, you embark on your own quest for better accuracy and speed. We play Professor Henry Higgins to your Liza and suggest ways to speak better. You discover how you can train NaturallySpeaking to adapt to your way of speaking and to recognize more words in your vocabulary. You also decide whether you need to beef up your PC hardware for better performance.

Besides dealing with accuracy, Part IV tells you how to handle various changes: upgrading, moving NaturallySpeaking to another computer, and changes in your voice or environment. It also suggests places to go for help or more information.

## Part V: The Part of Tens

Need a quick solution to a problem or a question? The Part of Tens solves the ten most common problems in several different subjects: dictation errors, command errors, and other common mistakes. While you're making errors, though, you might as well have some fun with NaturallySpeaking. We tell you how to make NaturallySpeaking the hit of your parties (if you have rather geeky parties) by having it perform stupid stunts and watching the results.

## Appendix: DragonSpeak: A Glossary

We try to steer you around jargon, but the menus, help files, and dialog boxes of NaturallySpeaking are full of special terms. Here you can discover the difference between NaturalText and NaturalWord, or find out what dictation shorthands are and why you should care about them.

# Icons Used in This Book

Like an ice-cream Blizzard, ...*For Dummies* books are packed full of cool, crunchy tidbits. Accordingly, you'll find the text studded with attractive two-color icons, pointing out tips, warnings, reminders, and the like. (Yes, of course black and white are colors!) Here are the icons you'll find:

Tips are insights and shortcuts that make your life easier, your wit sharper, and your hair more silky and manageable.

You don't have to read paragraphs marked with Technical Stuff, but you'll be a finer, more moral person if you do.

We used to know what this icon was for, but we forget. Oh, it notes a topic that we mentioned previously but which you should remember.

This icon marks things that are likely to blow up in your face or at least may cause problems.

# *Where to Go from Here*

We didn't intend for you to read this book from cover to cover, although you certainly can if you consult your physician first. If you're totally new to NaturallySpeaking, that would be a good, high-fiber, nutritionally balanced way to go. Here are some other suggestions:

- Go to Part I if you are confused about the way NaturallySpeaking works (or ought to work, in your opinion).
- Go to Part II if you need help with dictating, editing, formatting, recording, or transcribing.
- Go to Part III if you want to use NaturallySpeaking with another application, want to verbally control your Windows desktop, or want to use voice commands with your applications.
- Go to Part IV if NaturallySpeaking is not working as accurately as you'd like it to.
- Go to Part V if you need quick answers or a good chuckle.
- Go to the Glossary if Dragon's terms have you baffled.
- Go to the Index if a particular feature or aspect of using NaturallySpeaking has you perplexed.
- Go to the bookstore's cash register if you still haven't bought this book.

You could also go to your e-mail program and dictate us a line. We love to hear from readers. We may not always be able to answer, but we try, if you say nice things to us. Even if we don't reply, you'll get an attractive, ready-to-frame confirmation message from our "gurus" site that we received your message and are even now trying to decipher it.

If you write, please realize that we have absolutely no connection with Dragon Systems, Inc. or any other software or hardware vendor. We're just these two guys, you know? We can't get you upgrades, we probably can't tell you how to fix your bugs (take them to the vet?), and we haven't tested a lot of different hardware. If you still would like to chat or to comment on the book, please write us at dragons@gurus.com.

We hope this book helps you get a lot more out of NaturallySpeaking, or at least gives you a good laugh. Just turn off the microphone before you laugh — it's never a good idea to laugh at a dragon.

# Part I
# Hatching and Launching Your Dragon Software

The 5th Wave    By Rich Tennant

"I ran this Bob Dylan CD through our voice recognition system, and he really is just saying, 'Manaama-manaaabadhaabadha...'"

# In this part . . .

*I*f you have a brand-new dragon companion, this is the place to get your relationship off on the right foot (or wing or claw). In this part, we'll tell you what to expect (and not to expect) from your new pal, how to install it snugly into your PC and get it accustomed to your voice, and then how to launch it for flight.

Chapter 1 tells you what you can expect and what your particular member of the Dragon NaturallySpeaking family can do. How accurate should it be? Can it record meetings? Other people? Does it let you control your desktop by voice? Can it slice, dice, and make julienne fries? Chapter 2 tells you how to get it installed and properly trained. Naturally enough for a mythical creature, it comes with wizards, and Chapter 2 explains how to deal with those. Chapter 3 tells you how to launch NaturallySpeaking and what and where the flight controls are.

If your draconian friend is already trained and ready to go, move on to Part II and start dictating. Otherwise, turn to Chapter 1 and discover what magic is in store for you.

# Chapter 1

# Preparing for Dragons

●　●　●　●　●　●　●　●　●　●　●　●　●　●　●　●　●　●　●　●　●　●　●　●　●　●　●　●　●　●　●　●　●　●　●　●

## In This Chapter

▶ Does voice recognition really work? (Yes.)

▶ What can you reasonably expect to do with NaturallySpeaking?

▶ What can't you do with NaturallySpeaking?

▶ How soon can you expect to start doing the fun stuff?

▶ How are the various editions of NaturallySpeaking different from one other?

▶ Why does NaturallySpeaking need so much training?

●　●　●　●　●　●　●　●　●　●　●　●　●　●　●　●　●　●　●　●　●　●　●　●　●　●　●　●　●　●　●　●　●　●　●　●

*E*ver since we started telling people we were going to write a book about Dragon NaturallySpeaking, a computer program that lets you accomplish things by talking to your computer (rather than just muttering uselessly at it), we've been getting the same two reactions. Almost everybody's first reaction is to light up and exclaim, "That's really cool!" (We know a lot of people who still say things like that.) This initial rush of enthusiasm usually lasts about three seconds. Then people get very serious, look us straight in the eye, and demand: "Does it work?"

It works. (And it *is* really cool.)

We wrote large chunks of this book (including this chapter) by dictating them into NaturallySpeaking, and we had a lot of fun doing it. We predict that you will also find NaturallySpeaking to be both useful and fun — if you approach it with appropriate expectations.

## What Can You Expect NaturallySpeaking to Do for You?

Something about dictating to your computer awakens all kinds of unrealistic expectations in people. We blame *Star Trek*. We can't count the number of times we've heard Captain Picard say something like "Computer, calculate the number of angels that can dance on the head of a pin." The Enterprise computer just goes off and does it, and doesn't even ask what kind of pin it is, whether the angels are slam dancing or ballroom dancing, or whether to reserve any space on the pin for the band. It just produces an answer.

Even if NaturallySpeaking works perfectly for you, it won't do things like that. We didn't write this book by saying "Computer, write a book about NaturallySpeaking." We had to dictate it word for word, just as we would have had to type it word for word if we didn't have NaturallySpeaking.

So what are realistic expectations? You should think of NaturallySpeaking the way that you think of your keyboard and your mouse. It's an input device for your computer, not a brain transplant. It doesn't add any new capabilities to your computer beyond the ability to decipher the words that you're saying into text or ordinary PC commands. If you say "go make me a ham sandwich," NaturallySpeaking will dutifully type "go make me a ham sandwich" into whatever application happens to be open.

*Just because your computer can understand what you say, don't expect it to understand what you mean.* It's still just a computer, you know.

Here are some of the specific things you *can* expect to do with NaturallySpeaking, and where to look for more details about how to do them:

- ✔ **Browse the Web.** If you use Internet Explorer and NaturallySpeaking together, you can cruise around the World Wide Web without ever touching your keyboard or mouse. Pick a Web site from your Favorites menu, follow a link from one Web page to another, or dictate a URL (Web address) into IE's Address box — and leave your hands in your lap the whole time. See Chapter 13 for details.

- ✔ **Control your applications.** If it's on a menu, you can say it and watch it happen — not just in NaturallySpeaking but in all your other applications as well. If your e-mail program has a Check Mail command on its menu, then you can check your e-mail by saying a few words. Anything that your spreadsheet or database program has on a menu becomes a voice command you can use. Ditto for hotkeys; if pressing some combination of keys causes an application to do something you want, just tell NaturallySpeaking to press those keys. See Part III.

- ✔ **Control your desktop.** Not the Formica thing — somebody gave that desktop a "stay" command a long time ago. We're talking about your *Windows* desktop. Applications will start running just because you tell them to. (**"Start FreeCell"** is one of our favorite commands.) Open and close windows, switch from one open window to another, drag and drop stuff from here to there — all by voice. See Chapter 11.

- ✔ **Dictate into a digital recorder and let NaturallySpeaking transcribe it later.** You need the NaturallySpeaking Preferred or Professional edition and a digital (or very good analog) recorder, which you can get packaged together as NaturallySpeaking Mobile edition. See Chapters 8 and 9.

✔ **Write documents.** NaturallySpeaking is darn good at helping you write documents. You talk, it types. If you don't like what you said (or what it typed) you can tell NaturallySpeaking to go back and change it. You can give vocal instructions that make things bold, italic, big, little, or set in some strange font. Chapters 4, 5, and 6 tell you just what you need to know to write documents in the NaturallySpeaking window itself. If you want to dictate into Microsoft Word or Corel WordPerfect, see Chapter 12. For all other word processors, see Chapter 10.

Now, we happen to think that's plenty to get excited about. We can make our own ham sandwiches, thank you. And those smart folks at Dragon Systems are bound to be working on that angel-counting thing.

# What Can't NaturallySpeaking Do?

Even with NaturallySpeaking, your computer's ability to understand English is more limited than what you can reasonably expect from a human being. We humans use a very wide sense of context to figure out what other people are saying. When the teen behind the counter at Burger King says "Wonfryzat?", we know he means "Do you want fries with that?" If he walked up to us at the public library and said "Wonfryzat?", we'd be completely confused.

NaturallySpeaking figures things out from context, too, but only from the *verbal* context — and a fairly small verbal context at that. It knows that "two apples" and "too far" make more sense than "too apples" and "two far." But two- and three-word context seems to be about the extent of its powers. (We can't say exactly how far it looks for context, because Dragon Systems is understandably pretty hush-hush about the inner workings of NaturallySpeaking.) It doesn't understand the content of your document, so it can't know that words like "Republican" and "Democrat" are likely to show up just because you're talking about politics.

Consequently, you can't expect NaturallySpeaking to understand every form of speech that humans understand. In order to work passably well, it needs some advantages like these:

✔ **Familiarity.** Each person who dictates to NaturallySpeaking has to train it individually, so that NaturallySpeaking can build an individualized user model. (See Chapter 2.) So NaturallySpeaking can't transcribe the voice mail that other people leave for you.

✔ **Who is talking?** Each time before you start dictating, you need to identify yourself, so that NaturallySpeaking can load the right user model.

✔ **One user at a time.** NaturallySpeaking only loads one user model at a time, so it can't transcribe a meeting where several people are talking, even if it has user models for each of them.

✔ **Constant volume.** You can't plunk a microphone down in the middle of the room and then pace around while you dictate. A secretary could handle that, but a computer can't. You need to wear a pretty good microphone (like the one that comes with NaturallySpeaking) and position it the same way every time. And it won't understand you if you mumble or let your voice trail off. (It does a pretty good job with accents, though, as long as you're consistent.)

✔ **Reasonable background noise.** Humans may be able to understand you when Metallica is playing or the blow dryer is on. They may be reading your lips at least part of the time, and they can guess that you are probably saying "Turn that thing off!" NaturallySpeaking is sadly lacking in the lip-reading department, as well as in its ability to make obvious situational deductions.

✔ **Reasonable enunciation.** You don't have to start practicing "Moses supposes his toeses are roses," but you do need to realize that NaturallySpeaking can't transcribe sounds that you don't make. See Chapter 17 for an in-depth discussion of this issue.

✔ **Standard turn-of-the-millennium English prose.** If you want to be the next James Joyce, stick to typing. You can have some fun by trying to transcribe Shakespeare or the King James' Bible or things written in other languages (we had a blast in Chapter 27), but it's not going to work very well (unless you do some really extensive training). On the other hand, NaturallySpeaking is just the thing for writing books, essays, reports, short stories, and letters to Mom.

# How Soon Can You Start Doing Stuff?

NaturallySpeaking comes out of the box not knowing anything about you. It has to work as well for Bernadette Peters as for Arnold Schwarzenegger, as well for Buffy the Vampire Slayer as for the Golden Girls, as well for Teddy Kennedy as for Ross Perot. It's going to need some time to figure out how you talk.

How long? If everything goes smoothly — as it probably will if you have compatible hardware and follow the instructions in Chapter 2 — something like an hour or an hour-and-a-half will probably pass between the time you take the shrink-wrap off the box and the time you dictate your first word. Allocate about a half hour of that time for reading to your computer while it analyzes your voice and pronunciation. Dragon has been working to shorten this training, and has succeeded for high-end systems. If you have a Pentium III in your computer, you may only have to spend a few minutes reading out loud.

Even then, you may not be happy with the results. Training continues for as long as you keep using NaturallySpeaking. It makes mistakes, you correct them, it learns — that's the process. It gets better and better the longer you use it.

## But I read in a magazine. . . .

Quite a few magazine and newspaper articles have been written recently about voice recognition in general, and Dragon Systems in particular. Almost all of them contain an example that's something like this: A guy says into a microphone, "Send e-mail to Bob about Friday's meeting. Period. Bob, comma, glad you're going to be there. Period."

As if by magic, an e-mail application opens, a message window appears, Bob's e-mail address is pulled out of an address book somewhere, "Friday's meeting" is entered on the subject line, and the following text is entered into the message body: "Bob, glad you're going to be there." *Star Trek,* here we come.

The example is completely legitimate, as you can see in Chapter 15. But you need to keep a few things in mind: The only edition of NaturallySpeaking that currently has this capability is the $400 Mobile Organizer, and it has

such a close relationship with only a handful of applications, like Outlook and Notes. If you say "Do the numbers on February's revenue receipts," your spreadsheet just sits there.

Finally, like any good magician's trick, more appears to be happening than actually happens. The computer has not suddenly been granted intelligence that rivals that of a human secretary. The Dragon Systems programmers have created a handful of scripts for doing everyday tasks, like generating e-mail messages and entering new events into a calendar program. They've made the commands sound like the instructions you would give a secretary, and they've set things up so that a lot of similar-sounding commands produce the same result. But if you say "Zip a message off to Bob," nothing happens.

Impressive? Yes. Magic? No. It's still just a computer.

The exact error rate you see depends on many factors: how fast your computer is, how much memory it has, how good your microphone is, how quiet the environment is, how well you speak, what sound card your computer has, and so on. Fresh out of General Training, we saw error rates of one or two words per sentence. The first page or two you dictate may be discouraging. Persevere; it gets better — as long as you keep correcting it.

# *Which Version of NaturallySpeaking Should You Own?*

NaturallySpeaking is not just one product; it's a family of products. And like most families, some of the members are much richer than others. Depending on the features you want, you can spend anywhere from about $60 (Essentials edition) to nearly $1,000 (Legal or Medical editions).

In spite of their socioeconomic differences, this family gets along pretty well. The products are all based on the same underlying voice recognition system, so they create the same kinds of user files. This fact has two consequences for you as a user: The products are all about equally accurate at transcribing your speech, and it's easy to upgrade to a better version. You can start out with the inexpensive Essentials edition, test out whether you like this whole idea of dictation, and then move up to a full-featured version without having to go through training all over again. (Dragon Systems even encourages this practice. When we last checked, it was slightly cheaper to start with Essentials and then upgrade to Preferred than it was to buy Preferred directly.)

Which edition is best for you depends on why you're interested in NaturallySpeaking in the first place. Are you a poor typist who wants to be able to create documents more quickly? A good typist who is starting to worry about carpal tunnel syndrome? A person who can't use a mouse and keyboard at all? A traveling salesman or busy executive who wants to be able to dictate into a recorder rather than sit in front of a monitor? Is price an important factor to you? Do you need NaturallySpeaking to recognize a large, specialized vocabulary? Do you want to create macros that let you dictate directly into your company's special forms? The more features you want, the more you should expect to pay.

## NaturalWhat? The Draconian nomenclature

Somebody apparently thought it would be cute (or at least natural) if the major components of NaturallySpeaking had names like NaturalThingamabob. This practice creates some NaturalConfusion at first, but you get used to it. Here are the main NaturalWhatzits you need to know:

- **NaturalText** is the component that lets you dictate into applications other than Word, WordPerfect, Internet Explorer, and NaturallySpeaking itself. When you dictate an e-mail into Eudora or a number into Excel, you're using NaturalText.

- **NaturalWord** provides additional voice commands when you dictate into Word or WordPerfect.

- **NaturalWeb** works with Internet Explorer to let you browse the Web by voice.

Another important piece of terminology is *Select-and-Say*. (For Darwin's sake, we're grateful they didn't call it NaturalSelect.) An application is "Select-and-Say enabled" if, when you are dictating into the application, you can select a piece of text by saying it. For example, suppose you were dictating an e-mail to your mother in Outlook (which is a Select-and-Say-enabled application). You could select the salutation of the e-mail by saying **"Select *Dear Mom*."**

For more natural and unnatural Dragon terminology, see the Glossary at the end of this book.

# *The fourth generation of the NaturallySpeaking family*

The current generation of NaturallySpeaking is the fourth; Version 4.0 was released in the third quarter of 1999. In addition to the usual bug fixes and incremental improvements that you expect in a new version of an application, NaturallySpeaking 4.0 brings the following new features:

- ✔ **NaturalWeb**, a new component that works with Internet Explorer to let you browse the Web using only voice commands.

- ✔ **BestMatch III**, a feature that cuts General Training time from about a half hour to only a few minutes — if you have a Pentium III computer or its equivalent.

- ✔ **Student voice model**, which does a better job of recognizing young voices. This feature debuted in the previous generation's NaturallySpeaking for Teens, but is now offered in all NaturallySpeaking products.

Here is the current lineup of NaturallySpeaking products, with a few comments about their features:

- ✔ **NaturallySpeaking Essentials.** This entry-level edition is perfect for people who just hate to type. (It replaces the earlier entry-level editions Point & Speak and NaturallySpeaking for Teens.) It is just as accurate as the more expensive editions, it allows control of the Windows desktop, it includes NaturalText for dictating into other applications, and it enables you to browse the Web by voice with NaturalWeb. It includes Select-and-Say capability for a small number of applications, not including Word and WordPerfect. It lacks NaturalWord for word processing in Word and WordPerfect, although you can dictate into those applications with NaturalText. Essentials is perfect if you're planning to dictate only the first draft of documents, which you then polish using the mouse and keyboard. Probably not a good choice for the physically challenged.

- ✔ **NaturallySpeaking Standard.** The Standard edition does everything that Essentials does and adds NaturalWord, which extends Select-and-Say capability to Word and WordPerfect, in addition to providing natural language commands in Word.

- ✔ **NaturallySpeaking Preferred.** Preferred includes all the Standard's features, plus a few extras. It lets you select a piece of your document and play back your dictation, a great feature when you're trying to correct a mistake that either you or NaturallySpeaking made 20 minutes ago. It also opens the possibility of dictating into a recorder and letting NaturallySpeaking transcribe it later. See Chapters 8 and 9.

✔ **NaturallySpeaking Preferred USB.** As far as the software goes, this edition is identical to the previous one, but it comes with a much cooler microphone. The Dragon USB microphone has a built-in sound card, eliminating many potential hardware incompatibility problems and providing excellent sound quality. You can also purchase the USB microphone separately for use with any NaturallySpeaking edition, but make sure that your computer has USB connectors before you buy it. See Chapter 19.

✔ **NaturallySpeaking Mobile.** The software is again identical to NaturallySpeaking Preferred, but it comes packaged with Dragon's own mobile recorder.

✔ **NaturallySpeaking Mobile Organizer.** This product is also based on the Preferred edition. You get everything that is in the Mobile edition, plus extra software that works with popular personal information manager programs (like Outlook or Notes) to turn dictation into action. See the "But I read in a magazine . . ." sidebar earlier in this chapter.

✔ **NaturallySpeaking Professional.** This edition is the one to get if someone else is paying for it, or if you're a manager planning to convert your entire office to NaturallySpeaking. The price jumps from about $200 for Preferred to about $700 for Professional, but Professional has two great features: You can build your own specialized vocabularies (see Chapter 18) and create your own voice commands (Chapter 22). Or, more precisely, your office geek can construct specialized vocabularies and commands tailored to match the way your office works, and then you can all use them. This edition doesn't contain the USB microphone or the digital recorder, but you can buy them separately.

✔ **NaturallySpeaking Legal and NaturallySpeaking Medical.** At heart, these two editions are just Professional edition, but Dragon has done some of the work that we assigned to your office geek in the previous bullet. The Medical edition comes out of the box knowing the names of obscure diseases, body parts, and pharmaceuticals. The Legal edition knows *amicus curiae, habeas corpus,* and a bunch of other Latin legal terminology that would make the Professional edition throw up its hands.

What if you want it all? The Professional edition and its Legal and Medical siblings doesn't come with the nifty Mobile Organizer software for updating your personal information manager on the run, and the Mobile Organizer edition doesn't do macros and specialized vocabularies like Professional does. If you want the whole enchilada of capabilities, your best bet is to buy Mobile Organizer (which is based on Preferred) and then order a Preferred-to-Professional (or Legal or Medical) upgrade from the Dragon Systems Web site (`www.dragonsys.com`).

In addition to these off-the-shelf products, you can also have NaturallySpeaking installed on your office network. This option goes beyond the scope of what we cover in this book. If you're interested in this option, contact Dragon Systems directly. Training programs for your staff are also available.

## Orphans

Some products that belong to earlier generations of the Dragon family are not part of the fourth generation and are being phased out. If you have one of these products, you can (at present) get a discount on an upgrade to one of the current family members. See the Dragon Systems Web site (www.dragonsys.com).

- ✔ **Point & Speak.** This entry-level edition wasn't actually thrown out of the family, it just got a facelift, a few more features, and a new name: NaturallySpeaking Essentials. The last version of Point & Speak was 3.52.

- ✔ **NaturallySpeaking for Teens.** The Teen edition grew up. We still see this edition on the shelves, but it is based on the 3.0 release of NaturallySpeaking rather than the current 4.0 release. It was a fine entry-level product in its day, but its student voice model has been absorbed into Essentials, and it lacks features like desktop control and Web-browsing-by-voice. In our opinion, you shouldn't buy it unless you can get it at a very substantial discount.

- ✔ **Dragon Dictate.** NaturallySpeaking's ancestor, Dragon Dictate, is not exactly an orphan, but it is not being sold as actively as NaturallySpeaking. It still has a loyal user community.

- ✔ **WordPerfect Office Voice-Powered.** Dragon made a special version of NaturallySpeaking to be packaged with WordPerfect. It lacks NaturalText and only provides NaturalWord for WordPerfect (not Microsoft Word), so it's mainly useful for creating documents in WordPerfect. The current edition is based on NaturallySpeaking 3.52, and Dragon says it has no plans to upgrade it to 4.0. It's still being sold, but don't bother unless you're planning to buy WordPerfect 2000 anyway. And even then you're probably better off to get a cheaper edition of WordPerfect without NaturallySpeaking, and then buy NaturallySpeaking Standard edition separately.

# Why Do You Have to Train NaturallySpeaking?

We admit it: Training a new piece of software is a strange idea. Other computer programs don't need to be trained. When you get a new word processor, it doesn't have to watch you type for awhile before it catches on. New spreadsheets do their adding and subtracting perfectly well straight out of the box, without any instruction from you. And personally, we're happier knowing that Quicken *didn't* learn how to balance a checkbook by watching us do it.

So why does NaturallySpeaking need to be trained before it understands your speech? The simple answer is that speech recognition is probably one of the hardest things your computer does. We humans may not think speech recognition is hard, but that's because we're good at it. Michael Jordan probably has trouble understanding why the rest of us think it's so hard to dunk a basketball.

The purpose of this section is to explain why deciphering speech is hard for computers and how the training program helps NaturallySpeaking overcome these difficulties. We hope that understanding these issues will give you patience during the training process described in Chapter 2.

## *What's so hard about recognizing speech, anyway?*

If 3-year-olds can recognize and understand speech (other than the phrase "go to bed"), why is it so hard for computers? Aren't computers supposed to be smart?

Well, yes and no. Computers are very smart when it comes to brain-straining things like playing chess and filling out tax returns, so you may think they'd be whizzes at "simple" activities like recognizing faces or understanding speech. But after about 40 years of trying to make computers do these "simple" things, programmers have come to the conclusion that a skill isn't simple just because humans master it easily. In fact, our brains and eyes and ears are chock-full of very sophisticated sensing and processing equipment that still runs rings around anything we can design in silicon and metal.

We humans think it's simple to understand speech because all the really hard work is done before we become conscious of it. To us, it seems as if English words just pop into our heads as soon as people open their mouths. The unconscious (or preconscious) nature of the process makes it doubly hard for computer programmers to mimic — if we don't know exactly what we're doing or how we do it, how can we tell computers how to do it?

To get an idea of why computers have such trouble with speech, think about something they're very good at recognizing and understanding: Touch-Tone phone numbers. Those blips and bloops on the phone lines are much more meaningful to computers than they are to us humans. But several very important features make the phone tones such an easy language for computers, as we discuss in the following list. English, on the other hand, is completely different.

> ✔ **The Touch-Tone "vocabulary" has only twelve "words" in it.** After you know the tones for the ten digits plus * and #, you're in. English, on the other hand, has hundreds of thousands of words.

✔ **None of the words sound the same.** On the Touch-Tone phone, the one tone is distinctly different from the seven tone. But English has homonyms, such as *new* and *gnu,* and near homonyms, like *merrier* and *marry her.* Sometimes entire sentences sound alike: "The sons raise meat" and "The sun's rays meet," for example.

✔ **All "speakers" of the language say the words the same way.** Push the five button on any phone, and you get exactly the same tone. But James Earl Jones and a 10-year-old girl use very different tones when they speak; and Woody Allen, Pat Robertson, and the ambassador from Outer Mongolia may pronounce the same English words in very different ways.

✔ **Context is meaningless.** To the phone, a one is a one is a one. How you interpret the tone doesn't depend on the previous number or the next number. But in English, context is everything. It makes sense to "go to New York." (Well, at least it's correct English.) But it makes much less sense to "go two New York" or "go too New York."

# What's a computer to do?

In order to work effectively for you, a speech-recognition program like NaturallySpeaking needs to combine four very different areas of knowledge. It needs to know a lot about speaking in general, about the spoken English language in general, about the way your voice sounds, and about your word-choice habits.

## How NaturallySpeaking knows about speech and English in general

Dragon NaturallySpeaking gets its general knowledge from the folks at Dragon Systems, some of whom have spent most of their adult lives analyzing how English is spoken. NaturallySpeaking has been programmed to know in general what human voices sound like, how to model the characteristics of a given voice, the basic sounds that make up the English language, and the range of ways that different voices make those sounds. It has also been given a basic English vocabulary and some overall statistics about which words are likely to follow which other words. (For example, the word *medical* is more likely to be followed by *miracle* than by *marigold.*)

## How NaturallySpeaking learns about your voice

NaturallySpeaking learns about your voice by listening to you. During the General Training process, you read out loud some text selections that NaturallySpeaking has stored in its memory. Because it already knows the text that you're reading, NaturallySpeaking can use this time to model your voice and learn how you pronounce words.

NaturallySpeaking goes on learning about your voice every time you use it. When you correct a word or phrase that NaturallySpeaking has guessed wrong, NaturallySpeaking adjusts its settings to make the mistake less likely in the future.

To help NaturallySpeaking learn better, be sure to correct it whenever it's wrong. At times, it may seem simpler just to select the incorrect text, delete it, and start over. But NaturallySpeaking doesn't learn when you do this. It thinks that you have merely changed your mind, not that its interpretation was incorrect.

### How NaturallySpeaking learns about your word-choice habits

Initially NaturallySpeaking learns how you choose words from the Vocabulary Builder phase of training. It may look as if NaturallySpeaking is just learning how you say some unusual words. But, in fact, Vocabulary Builder is worthwhile even if no new words are found, because NaturallySpeaking is analyzing how frequently you use common words and which words are likely to be used in combination.

NaturallySpeaking comes out of the box knowing general facts about the frequency of English words, but from Vocabulary Builder, it learns to sharpen those models for your particular vocabulary.

For example, if you want to use NaturallySpeaking to write letters to your mother and you let it study your previous letters to your mother, then NaturallySpeaking will learn that the names of the other members of your family appear much more frequently than they do in general English text. It is then much less likely to misinterpret your brother Johann's name as *John* or *yawn*.

## Onward to General Training!

By letting you install NaturallySpeaking, your computer has taken on one of the hardest tasks a PC ever faces. It needs your help. If you endure General Training with patience and persistence, and if you gently but firmly correct NaturallySpeaking whenever it makes a mistake, you'll be rewarded with a computer that takes your verbal orders and transcribes your dictation without complaint and even without a coffee break — unless you need one.

# Chapter 2

# Basic Training

✦ ✦ ✦ ✦ ✦ ✦ ✦ ✦ ✦ ✦ ✦ ✦ ✦ ✦ ✦ ✦ ✦ ✦ ✦ ✦ ✦ ✦ ✦ ✦ ✦ ✦ ✦ ✦ ✦ ✦ ✦ ✦ ✦ ✦ ✦ ✦ ✦ ✦ ✦ ✦ ✦ ✦ ✦ ✦ ✦ ✦

## In This Chapter

▶ Installing Dragon NaturallySpeaking

▶ Setting up NaturallySpeaking to work with your hardware

▶ Training NaturallySpeaking to recognize your voice

▶ Training NaturallySpeaking to know your vocabulary and writing style

✦ ✦ ✦ ✦ ✦ ✦ ✦ ✦ ✦ ✦ ✦ ✦ ✦ ✦ ✦ ✦ ✦ ✦ ✦ ✦ ✦ ✦ ✦ ✦ ✦ ✦ ✦ ✦ ✦ ✦ ✦ ✦ ✦ ✦ ✦ ✦ ✦ ✦ ✦ ✦ ✦ ✦ ✦ ✦ ✦ ✦

*B*y now we assume that you have decided which version of Dragon NaturallySpeaking is best for you, that you've concluded that your hardware configuration is appropriate (or that the best way to find out is to try to run NaturallySpeaking and see what happens), and that you've torn the shrink-wrap off the box and are sitting in front of your computer. Are you mere seconds away from starting to dictate your autobiography or a best-selling novel? No, but you're on the right track.

Before you can start doing any useful work (or play) with NaturallySpeaking, you need to do two things: Install the program and train it. Installing NaturallySpeaking is easy — in most cases, you just put the CD into your CD-ROM drive and follow the directions on the screen. Training is straight-forward, but takes anywhere from a half hour to an hour. (Fortunately, a Pause button exists that lets you walk off to get a sandwich or a good, stiff drink.)

The training process can be boring, particularly if you don't like reading out loud, or if you feel silly reading to a computer. But the training's finite, and each user has to do it only once. If your motivation starts to falter, think about how cool it will be to be able to dictate to your computer, or go back to Chapter 1 for an explanation of why you need to do all this training. By the end of this chapter, you really will be ready to start dictating your best-seller, or least a letter to Mom.

# Installing a Dragon in Your Computer

How could a great mythical beast like a dragon wind up in a little beige box like a computer? Clearly only a powerful wizard could perform such magic. In this case, we're talking about the NaturallySpeaking Setup wizard. These instructions are based on installing NaturallySpeaking 4.0, but we've also installed 3.0 and 3.5 on various other occasions, and the process is quite similar. It also makes very little difference whether you're installing for the first time or installing over a previous version of NaturallySpeaking. The wizard probably has to work harder if you're installing from scratch, but he doesn't complain.

1. **Find the envelope that contains the installation CD.**

   The CD is probably in a square white envelope that's sealed with a bar-code strip. The number on the bar code strip is important if you want to register your software, so don't destroy it.

2. **Copy the serial number on the bar-code strip that seals the envelope.**

   You need this number if you want to register your copy of Dragon NaturallySpeaking with Dragon Systems, or if you ever need to call Dragon Systems for help. A few good places to copy it are on the envelope itself, on the inside cover of this book, or on the inside cover of the Dragon NaturallySpeaking manual.

3. **Put the installation CD into your CD-ROM drive.**

   The most likely thing to happen is that the Windows AutoRun feature starts running the installation program automatically, and you see something resembling Figure 2-1. If you wait 30 seconds or so and nothing seems to happen, don't worry. Nothing is wrong; do this instead: Double-click the My Computer icon on the Windows desktop. When the My Computer window opens, find the icon corresponding to your CD-ROM drive and double-click it. Possibly AutoRun will wake up at this point, but if not, find the Setup icon in the CD-ROM window and double-click it. Now you're exactly where you would be if AutoRun had done its job.

4. **Click the Install Dragon NaturallySpeaking button, as shown in Figure 2-1.**

   The Dragon NaturallySpeaking Setup wizard starts.

5. **Click the Next button in the Setup wizard window.**

   The End User License Agreement appears. You have to agree to this piece of legalese if you want to install the software. It's there so that Dragon Systems can sue you if you pirate the software, but you can't sue them if some disaster happens because Dragon NaturallySpeaking misunderstands what you say. Everybody agrees to these licenses, and nobody knows to what extent they stand up in court.

**Figure 2-1:**
Beginning
the
installation
process.

6. **Click Yes to accept the license agreement.**

   You really have no choice. If you click No, you're asked to either reconsider or exit from the Setup wizard.

7. **Choose which components of Dragon NaturallySpeaking to install.**

   The screen displays a list of the components available to you and the number of megabytes each component will take up on your hard drive. This list varies according to which Dragon product you install and what else is on your system. For example, if you don't have WordPerfect installed on your system, NaturalWord for WordPerfect is not on the list. If you are installing NaturallySpeaking Essentials, no form of NaturalWord is on the list.

   You really don't want to do without most of these components, like Help files for example. The main optional components are various forms of BestMatch and NaturalWord, as well as NaturalWeb and (if you have the Preferred edition or higher) the text-to-speech capability. BestMatch makes NaturallySpeaking more accurate, and, in addition, BestMatch III significantly decreases General Training requirements. NaturalWord makes dictating to Word or WordPerfect much easier. NaturalWeb and text-to-speech take up so little space that there's no reason not to choose them.

   The components that the Setup wizard believes will run effectively on your hardware are denoted by a checkmark. All forms of BestMatch and NaturalWord require a lot of RAM, and BestMatch III requires a fast processor. If you really want a component that the wizard doesn't rec-ommend, you should probably upgrade your system. See Chapter 16 for details.

   Unless you're desperate to save disk space, go ahead and accept the Setup wizard's recommendations. But if you want to select or deselect a component, click the checkbox next to its name.

**8. Choose the Destination Directory.**

In other words, in what folder are all the NaturallySpeaking program files going to live? The wizard looks to see whether you already have a previous version of NaturallySpeaking installed somewhere, and if you do, it suggests that you use that same folder. If not, the wizard suggests C:\NatSpeak, which seems as good a choice as any. If you agree, do nothing. If you'd like to choose a different folder, click the Browse button. A Choose Directory window appears to let you find the folder you want. After you select the folder you want, click the OK button in the Choose Directory window.

**9. Click Next.**

A Start Copying Files window appears; its purpose is to make sure you didn't click Next by mistake. You can click No to return to the previous screen (Steps 7 and 8) and change the choices you made there.

**10. Click Yes.**

A little time (approximately 2–5 minutes) passes while your computer copies files from the CD to your hard drive. The length of time varies depending on how many components you install and how fast your hardware is. When all the files are copied, a Setup Complete dialog box appears to ask whether you want to restart your computer.

**11. Remove the CD from your CD-ROM drive.**

Removing the CD before the computer restarts is best, or else AutoRun may start up again.

**12. Click OK in the Setup Complete box.**

Your computer restarts, which is a good thing. Windows does all sorts of bookkeeping during its shutdown and startup phases. Newly installed software seldom works quite right until after you restart the computer. If, for some reason, the Setup wizard doesn't ask you whether you want to restart the computer, do it anyway. Click Start⇨Shut Down from the taskbar menu, and then select Restart from the Shut Down Windows dialog box. Then Click OK.

If you need a break, you can take it now without losing any of your work. (Stopping at any earlier point means starting over from the beginning.) The Setup wizard may ask you whether you want to read the ReadMe file or register your copy of NaturallySpeaking online, but you can always do these things later if you want. Registration and the ReadMe file are two of the choices that exist in the Dragon NaturallySpeaking folder that's now part of your Start⇨Programs menu.

We recommend that you take a moment to congratulate yourself before moving on to the New User wizard (which we discuss in "Training Your Dragon" later in this chapter). You now have a dragon in your computer.

## Should you register your dragon?

Registering is not necessary, but on the other hand, it's pretty easy, so why not? The main benefit is that Dragon Systems may notify you when a new version of NaturallySpeaking comes out and may even give you a discount. We registered our copy, and we haven't noticed any increase in the amount of junk mail we receive.

To register, choose Start⇨Programs⇨ Dragon NaturallySpeaking⇨NaturallySpeaking Registration and fill in the form provided. Remember that you need to fill in only the fields marked with an asterisk. You can submit your registration form via modem, as e-mail, or by printing it out and mailing the paper version.

You can call Dragon Technical Support for help with NaturallySpeaking even if you haven't registered your copy. See Chapter 23 for the details.

# Training Your Dragon

Like a sheep dog or a show horse, your dragon needs some training before it can be of any use to you. In fact, the Dragon NaturallySpeaking program insists that you complete at least the minimum level of training, NaturallySpeaking starts up at the precise point in the training sequence where you left off. Fortunately, you don't have to do the training in one sitting (although you can, and you'll get on to more interesting activities a lot faster if you do).

Training proceeds in several steps:

- ✔ Choosing a user name, so that NaturallySpeaking can set up its filing system for the speech files you will create during the training process
- ✔ Testing and configuring your hardware
- ✔ General training, during which you read your dragon bedtime stories
- ✔ Vocabulary training, in which you give your dragon some of your documents to examine so that it can adjust to your vocabulary

This list may sound daunting — but the New User wizard guides you through the process and keeps track of where you are. If at any point your motivation starts to falter, go back to Chapter 1 and read "Why Do You Have to Train NaturallySpeaking?"

## Running the New User wizard

Training a dragon requires every bit as much magic as capturing it inside a beige box. Thoughtfully, Dragon Systems has provided you with another wizard ally, the New User wizard. You can start the New User wizard in one of the following ways:

- ✔ Automatically the first time you run NaturallySpeaking after installation.
- ✔ Clicking the New button in the Open User dialog box when NaturallySpeaking starts up.
- ✔ Choosing User⇨New from the menu in the NaturallySpeaking window.
- ✔ Choosing Dragon NaturallySpeaking⇨User⇨New from the Microsoft Word or Corel Wordperfect menu when NaturalWord is running.

You may choose to run the New User wizard in the future if other people want to use NaturallySpeaking on your computer, or you may want to set up additional users for your own use. (That seems bizarre right now, but we'll explain it better if and when you need to do it.) Right now we're mainly concerned with setting up the *first* user for your dragon, but the same process happens when you set up subsequent users.

The left column of the New User wizard outlines this process conveniently for you. The green light shows you which part of the process you're currently dealing with.

To start the process of choosing a user name and testing and configuring your hardware:

1. **Click Next on the Welcome screen of the New User wizard.**

   The Create User screen appears. The wizard wants to know three pieces of information:

   - **A user name.** This name will appear on lists and menus in the future so that you can tell NaturallySpeaking which user you are. So pick a name you will recognize as your own. Type it into the textbox near the top of the screen.

   - **A speech model.** The wizard has labeled one choice as "recommended." Choose the recommended model unless you're a child or teenager, in which case you want the Student model that most resembles the recommended model. (For example, if BestMatch is the recommended model, choose Student BestMatch.) Make your choice from the drop-down list.

   - **A vocabulary model.** Again, choose the recommended model from the drop-down list unless you're a student, in which case choose the Student model that most resembles the recommended model.

     At this stage, NaturallySpeaking picks out a generic voice model and vocabulary model for you. These models get modified later on during training, as NaturallySpeaking listens to your voice and analyzes your writings.

2. **After you make your choices, click Next.**

   NaturallySpeaking takes a little time to set up your user files — not long enough to go make a sandwich, but if you do, the User Type screen will be waiting when you come back.

   This screen is pretty boring. All it wants to know is whether you're going to be speaking directly into a microphone or using a tape recorder. Right now we'll assume you're using a microphone. Later on, you may decide you want to dictate into a recorder; you can run the New User wizard again then to set up and train NaturallySpeaking to understand your recorded voice. (See Chapters 8 and 9.)

3. **Click Next to move on to the Adjust Microphone screen.**

   This screen has a single button: Run Audio Setup wizard. This screen has been erratic for us; sometimes it just goes ahead and assumes we pushed the button. If this happens to you, go straight to the Choose Your Sound System dialog box in Step 5, or (if NaturallySpeaking senses that your system has only one sound system to choose) go to the Connect Your Microphone screen in Step 6.

4. **Click the Run Audio Setup wizard button.**

   The Audio Setup wizard is a series of dialog boxes that test and adjust your microphone and sound system. The first of these dialog boxes is called Choose Your Sound System. If your computer has only one sound system available, NaturallySpeaking may skip this screen entirely and take you straight to the Connect Your Microphone screen in Step 6.

   In the Choose Your Sound System dialog box, you're presented with a list of sound systems that your computer has, and asked to choose which of them NaturallySpeaking should listen to in order to hear your voice when you dictate. Quite possibly, you do not recognize what these "sound systems" are, and you may not even have realized that your computer had so many of them. Don't worry — we didn't either, and our systems got set up just fine.

   Fortunately, the wizard has chosen the system it thinks most likely to work — the one that's highlighted when the screen appears. If you happen to forget which item on the list was originally highlighted, click the Default button to highlight it again.

   If you have a voice modem (a modem that lets you talk on the phone through a microphone as well as connect to the Internet), it will show up on this list. Don't choose it.

5. **When you have made your choice in the Choose Your Sound System screen, click OK.**

   The Connect Your Microphone screen is next. This screen is for your instruction only; you don't have to input any information. It simply tells you to make sure your microphone is connected to your computer before you proceed any further.

Unless you have a really good microphone, use the headset that comes with NaturallySpeaking. Those stick microphones that come with most computers these days are not nearly as good. The USB microphone that Dragon makes is excellent if your computer has USB ports. See Chapter 19 for more about microphones and sound cards.

Microphones other than the USB (including the headset microphones that come with all NaturallySpeaking editions except the USB edition) plug into your computer's sound card. That means turning the computer around so that you can see the back where all the cables are. Typically, three jacks line up: microphone, line in, and speaker. In the last few years, computer manufacturers have gotten better about labeling these jacks with icons or abbreviations, but if yours isn't labeled, you will have to check your computer or sound card manual. (Or you can do it the old-fashioned way: by trial and error.)

The red plug from your Dragon headset plugs into the microphone jack, and the black one plugs into the speaker jack. If you like, you can leave the black plug unplugged and continue to use another set of speakers. If the black plug is plugged into your speaker jack, then sound comes out of the earpiece of the headset.

6. **After you read the information in the Connect Your Microphone box, click Next to continue.**

   The Choose Your Input Device screen appears.

   You have a choice of headset microphone, handheld microphone, or electronic device using line input. If you want to use the headset that came with NaturallySpeaking (even if you left another set of speakers connected), then click the headset microphone button.

7. **Choose the radio button corresponding to your input device and click Next.**

   Whichever of the three you chose, you arrive at the Position Your Microphone screen. This is another instructional screen that requires no information from you. It just gives you advice on how to position your microphone and a picture illustrating the approved technique.

   The main idea is that the microphone needs to be near your mouth, but not in front of it. (In front *seems* natural, but you get interference from breathing on the microphone.) It should be far enough to the side that you don't bump it with your mouth when you talk, or scrape a beard or moustache against it. You may need to twist the arm into some funny shape to get the microphone positioned just right.

   The other thing to know about the Dragon microphone is that it has a front and a back side. (Believe it or not, the microphone also listens out the back side so that it can figure out what it should be ignoring. That's what makes it a *noise-canceling* microphone.) The front and back are not labeled very well, so you will probably have to pull the foam piece off the microphone to examine it. The front is louvered like a ventilation duct. You want the front side pointing toward your mouth. Put the foam piece back on when you think you have the microphone positioned correctly.

8. **When your microphone is properly positioned, click Next.**

   It's time to adjust your volume with the Adjust Your Volume screen. This screen is very busy, with all sorts of windows and sliders and things, but you can ignore most of it. Just click the Start Adjusting button and talk at the volume that you plan to use when you dictate. Stop talking when you hear the beep. The screen provides you with some text to read, but that's just to relieve you of the burden of thinking up something to say. The important thing is to keep talking until the wizard is done adjusting the volume. What you say doesn't matter.

   The slider on this screen is the volume adjustment. It starts at full volume, and then adjusts. If it remains at full volume during the entire test, make a note. This could be an indication that NaturallySpeaking isn't really hearing what you say. Or it could mean nothing; don't worry about it unless your system fails the Audio Quality test in the next screen.

9. **Click Next to move on to the Check Your Audio Quality screen.**

   This screen is another where you talk to the computer while it analyzes. Before, it was only listening to the volume. Now it tries to decide whether what it hears sounds enough like a human voice that this whole dictation project has a chance.

10. **When you're ready, click the Start Quality Check button and start talking.**

    You can read the text provided on the screen if you find that easier, but again the important thing is just to keep talking. At this stage, NaturallySpeaking isn't looking for specific words. Speak at the volume that you would like to use when you dictate, and don't stop until you hear the beep.

    After the beep, you're told a speech-to-noise ratio and whether that score is acceptable or not. A higher number is better. Anything under 15 is unacceptable and produces an error message. If you get a score that's unacceptable or on the border, try repositioning your microphone and clicking Start Quality Check to run the test again. You can run it as many times as you want. If you can't get into the acceptable range in several tries, you may need to change your sound card, get a better microphone, or stop using the blow dryer while you dictate. (See Chapter 19 for tips about improving audio input.)

11. **When you're done with the quality check, click the Finish button.**

    Now that the Audio Setup wizard has completed his job, doffed his pointy hat, and said farewell, the New User wizard returns. You now get a choice of either moving on to General Training or declaring partial victory and deciding to come back later. We recommend that you at least get up and walk around a little, especially if you needed several tries to get through the Audio Quality test.

12. **When you're ready to move on, click the Start General Training button. Or you can click Cancel and exit NaturallySpeaking.**

    The next time you start it up, NaturallySpeaking will remember that you made it through Audio Setup and will start you at General Training.

## General training

After NaturallySpeaking has tested and adjusted your speakers and microphone, it's ready to listen to you talk. The New User wizard should be displaying a screen that contains a Run General Training button. Click it.

The first thing you see is the instruction screen for General Training, which tells you that training is in two parts: a simple one to get you started, and a longer one. Click Continue to arrive at the General Training screen.

### The General Training window

The General Training window will be with you through both parts of General Training (about a half hour — much less if you have a high-end computer capable of running the BestMatch III model), so it's worth spending a little time to get acquainted. The white square in the center is the reading window; it contains the text you're supposed to read. As you read, NaturallySpeaking tries to recognize the words. The words it recognizes are in black, and the ones it hasn't recognized yet are in blue. When NaturallySpeaking isn't recognizing the word it's straining to hear, a yellow arrow appears over the word, as if to say "No, no, *this* word."

Below the white window is a measure of how far you've come: the number of paragraphs you've read. The horizontal bar below the white window is a volume meter; the bar is yellow when NaturallySpeaking thinks you aren't talking, and green when it's trying to interpret what you're saying. If the bar turns red, you're too loud. If the bar stays yellow or turns red when you talk, try readjusting the microphone position. The bar *should* turn red when you cough or make some other loud inarticulate noise.

The buttons below the volume meter resemble those of a tape recorder. Click the Record button when you're ready to start reading, and then click Pause when you want to stop. Back Up and Next take you to the previous paragraph or the next one, respectively. The Skip Word button does just what it says: It tells NaturallySpeaking to ignore the current word and move on to the next one. Use it if you can't figure out how to pronounce one of the words, or if NaturallySpeaking refuses to recognize the word no matter how you say it.

After you get through the first part of General Training, you can stop any time you like by clicking Finish. You can stop any time at all by clicking Cancel, though you'll lose the General Training you've done during the current session.

### Dragon Training I: The quick and easy part of General Training

The first stage of training should take only a minute or two. All you need to do is click the Record button in the General Training window and read five short paragraphs out loud. Feeling silly the first time you read to a computer is natural, but try to get over it. After all, the whole point of dictation software is to talk to your computer rather than type into it. People used to feel silly about talking into telephones, but we all got used to it.

After you read the five paragraphs, NaturallySpeaking goes off to think about your voice for a minute or two. When it comes back, it offers you the choice of going on to the longer portion of General Training (represented by the Train Now button) or going off to celebrate another partial victory (Train Later).

### Training later

If you click Train Later, you're asked to reconsider. You may do well to reconsider, because (unlike previous versions of the New User wizard) you'll have to repeat the first part of General Training when you go back. But if you're determined and click OK in the confirmation box, the New User Wizard screen returns.

*Don't click the General Training button.* It just sends you right back to where you were.

Click Next, and the wizard offers you a Quick Tour of NaturallySpeaking. The tour is well worth taking at some point. It requires about 10–15 minutes. See "Taking the Quick Tour" later in this chapter.

Whether or not you take the tour, you wind up at the Setup Complete screen. Click the Finish button and NaturallySpeaking starts up, ready to take dictation. We dictated *The Gettysburg Address* (a bad idea — see Chapter 27) and got "Or score and seven years ago homeowners brought forth on this continent emu nation, conceived in Liberty and dedicated to the proposition that old men are created equal."

## How should you read during training?

In order for training to be effective, you should read the training text the way you plan to dictate. If you read like a Harvard professor, but then dictate like a Combat Zone wino on a bender, the training will not accomplish much.

Try to speak clearly but fluently. Don't slur words together, but be sure to pronounce words the way *you* pronounce them, not the way you think they *should* be pronounced. If I say to-MAY-to and you say to-MAH-to, NaturallySpeaking can

adjust so that neither of us has to call the whole thing off. That's what General Training is for.

It's awfully tempting to rush through training, but you defeat the purpose if you read significantly faster than you plan to dictate. Pace yourself, and pause if you start getting antsy.

For more about how to speak when you dictate, see Chapter 17.

As you can see, NaturallySpeaking without further training is an amusing toy rather than a useful tool. Eventually, you have to do the second part of General Training. Fortunately, NaturallySpeaking doesn't forget that it needs more training, and dragons are well known for their persistence. Every time you open NaturallySpeaking, it gives you the option of continuing with General Training, until you finally give in.

### Dragon Training II: The long and boring part of General Training

The second part of General Training is much like the first part, except that it's longer. (If your computer is spiffy enough to run BestMatch III, you get a break here. You read for a few minutes rather than a half hour.) Proceed as follows:

1. **Start the second part of General Training.**

   If you're continuing from the first part of General Training, the second part begins automatically when you click the Train Now button. Otherwise, you can start the second part by clicking the Start General Training button that Dragon NaturallySpeaking displays at startup. Or you can choose Tools⇨General Training in a Dragon NaturallySpeaking document window. However you start it up, the General Training Instructions screen appears. After you read the instructions, click the Continue button. If you did the first part of General Training in a previous session, you have to repeat it now.

2. **The Select Text window appears with a list of texts that you can read during the training session. Select a text from the list and click the Train Now button.**

   The Select Text window disappears and the General Training window returns.

3. **Click the Record button in the General Training window.**

   You may notice an anomaly in the General Training window: The number of paragraphs left to read seems far larger than you can read in the estimated time. The time isn't to the end of the text, it's to the end of the required training. After you finish the required training, you will be given the option of continuing or choosing another text.

4. **Read the text in the box.**

   In general, you don't need to worry about NaturallySpeaking keeping up with you. If it gets confused, or isn't hearing the word it's listening for, the yellow arrow appears above the word to direct you to start there. Any time you get tired or want to stop for any reason, you can click the Pause button. If you remove your microphone, make sure that when you put it back on, you return the microphone to the same position it was previously in. To start again, click the Record button. You can exit the training session at any time by clicking the Finish button, but if you do so before completing your first text, you will have to start over the next time you run General Training.

5. **When the first text is complete, click Train More if you want to read another text.**

   If the text you chose is longer than is needed for General Training, you may be able to keep reading the same text. You can keep reading new texts to the computer for as long as you like; and the more you read, the better NaturallySpeaking gets at interpreting what you say. If you're ready to be done with this though, you can click Finish and end General Training.

6. **Click Finish.**

   NaturallySpeaking then analyzes the training session and updates your speech files. This process can take several minutes.

When NaturallySpeaking finishes updating your speech files, the New User wizard returns, asking whether you want to run the Vocabulary Builder. If you click the Run Vocabulary Builder button, the next phase of training starts. If not, a document window appears, so that you can begin dictating. Congratulate yourself.

## Building your dragon's vocabulary

The final training stage that the New User wizard takes you through is the Vocabulary Builder. The purpose of the Vocabulary Builder is to give NaturallySpeaking some documents that you have written, so that it can work on its model of your vocabulary. Fortunately, you don't have to read the documents out loud.

You may run Vocabulary Builder again later on (by choosing <u>T</u>ools⇨ Vocabulary <u>B</u>uilder in a NaturallySpeaking window) if you want to improve your dragon's performance (see Chapter 18) or create a specialized vocabulary (in the Professional edition only — see Chapter 21). In this chapter, we assume that you're running Vocabulary Builder for the first time, but the basic steps are the same any time you run it. You can see them listed in the left column of Figure 2-2.

After you click the Run Vocabulary Builder button in the New User wizard, the Vocabulary Builder's Welcome screen appears, as shown in Figure 2-2. Click Next to move on to the first stage in the process, where you are given the option of adding words from a list to NaturallySpeaking's vocabulary.

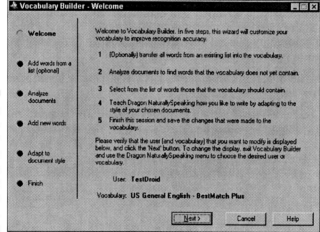

**Figure 2-2:**
The
Vocabulary
Builder lays
out its
agenda as it
welcomes
you.

## Adding words from a list

If you're likely to use terms from some specialized vocabulary in the documents you dictate, you can make a list of such terms and give them all to NaturallySpeaking in one fell swoop. Or better yet, maybe somebody else has already made such a list for you. Or you could skip over this step completely by clicking the Next button.

If you have a list, whether you generated it yourself or got it from someone else, you should store it as a text document on your computer, with one word or phrase per line. Include a specialized phrase even if each of the words in it is common. For example, Queen's Gambit Declined is the name of a chess opening. Each of the three words is surely already in the NaturallySpeaking General English vocabulary, but NaturallySpeaking doesn't know that these three words have a special capitalization pattern when they appear together. If you were likely to dictate documents about chess, you would want to include Queen's Gambit Declined on one line of your list.

---

# What about those words?

The base NaturallySpeaking vocabulary doesn't contain obscenities. You can swear a blue streak into the microphone, and a lot of perfectly harmless English words like *fork* and *shut* appear in your document.

If this crimps your style, you can add a list of obscenities to the vocabulary. Or if such words appear in the documents that you give Vocabulary Builder to analyze, you can select them from the list of words that NaturallySpeaking doesn't recognize.

But you may want to think twice before adding obscenities to your user vocabulary. Being a computer program, NaturallySpeaking has no sense of tact or discretion. There's no way to tell it "Don't transcribe this word unless you're really, really sure that's what I said." So unless you proofread really, really well, unintentional obscenities may start showing up in unfortunate places, like your business letters or your Christmas greetings.

Maybe the people who created the base vocabulary weren't just being prudes. Maybe they had a good idea.

---

To tell NaturallySpeaking where your list is, either type the address into the textbox, or click the Browse button and find the file that way. When the file has been located, click the Add Words From List button. You may add as many lists as you like. When you finish with this, click the Next button to move on to the Analyze Documents screen of the Vocabulary Builder.

## Analyzing documents

At this step, you provide Vocabulary Builder with documents so that it can look at them and pick out any words or capitalized phrases it doesn't recognize. (In essence, it's automatically building a list like the one you may have provided in the previous step.) The more documents you give Vocabulary Builder, the better. In particular, you want to give it documents that resemble the documents you want to dictate — your previous best-seller, for example, or a collection of your office memos.

Spell-check the documents before giving them to Vocabulary Builder. Vocabulary Builder is looking for words it doesn't already know, and it thinks it has found one whenever it runs into a misspelled word. You save yourself some time if you spell-check your documents and correct any misspelled words before giving the documents to Vocabulary Builder.

To give Vocabulary Builder a document to analyze:

1. **Click the Add button in the Vocabulary Builder window.**

   An Add Documents window appears. It behaves like a standard Windows Browsing window.

**2. Use the Add Documents window to select a document you want to add.**

You can select several documents from the same folder by holding down the Control key while you click each of them in succession. Vocabulary Builder recognizes documents in a variety of formats: Word documents (.doc) Version 6.0 or later, WordPerfect documents (.wpd) Version 8.0 or later, rich text format files (.rtf), text files (.txt), or HTML (.htm or .html). The Word and WordPerfect documents can be processed only if you have Word or WordPerfect installed on your computer.

**3. Click the Open button in the Add Documents window.**

The Add Documents window disappears, and the Vocabulary Builder window now includes the added document(s).

**4. Continue adding documents until you have included all the documents you want Vocabulary Builder to process.**

**5. Click the Analyze Documents button.**

Vocabulary Builder goes away and analyzes the documents.

**6. Click Next.**

The Add New Words screen appears, as shown in Figure 2-3. The center of this screen is a list of words that Vocabulary Builder found in the documents but not in its vocabulary. You can list the words either by frequency (how often they appeared in the documents) or alphabetically. You can do a number of tricks with this screen, but we leave that discussion for Chapter 18.

**7. Click the checkbox next to each word that you want to add to the NaturallySpeaking vocabulary.**

Some of the new words will be simple misspellings or one-time coinages that you wouldn't want to see popping up in subsequent documents. Don't bother to check those.

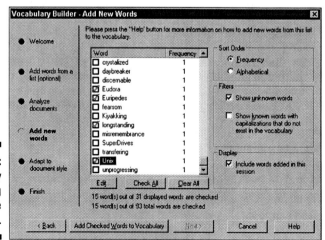

**Figure 2-3:**
Naturally
Speaking
learns some
new words.

8. **Click the Add Checked Words to Vocabulary button.** A confirmation box opens to ask whether you want to train the newly added words.

9. **Click Yes.**

There's no time like the present. The Train Words box appears, as shown in Figure 2-4. Think of Train Words as a small version of General Training.

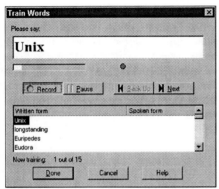

**Figure 2-4:**
Naturally
Speaking
learns how
you
pronounce
the new
words.

10. **Click the Record button in the Train Words box.**

11. **Say the words as they appear in large type at the top of the screen.**

In Figure 2-4, you would say the word *Unix*. Each time you say a word, Vocabulary Builder does a little processing, and then the next word appears. If you feel that you have mispronounced a word, click the Back Up button and say it again.

12. **After you say all the words on the list, click Done.**

You return to the Add New Words box. If you want, you can choose more words and then go back to Step 9.

13. **Click Next.**

You're on to the next phase of Vocabulary Builder's agenda.

### Adapting to document style

NaturallySpeaking learns more from your documents than just some new words. If these documents are typical of the way you write, then NaturallySpeaking can also come to some conclusions about which words you use most frequently, and which words are likely to follow which other words. These conclusions will help NaturallySpeaking interpret some ambiguous utterance. For example, it may learn by analyzing a minister's writings that he is more likely to say "Christmas anthem" than "chrysanthemum," whereas a florist's writings may imply the reverse.

We recommend that you choose Yes on both the questions on this screen, and then click Next. A screen then appears that summarizes all that you have done during this session. Click Finish, and then click Yes in the confirmation box. Now Vocabulary Builder goes off to adjust the NaturallySpeaking vocabulary.

## Taking the Quick Tour

When the Vocabulary Builder has done its thing, the New User wizard returns to invite you to go on the Quick Tour. By all means, you should take it. The tour is 16 screens long, and each screen is a little multimedia presentation demonstrating some aspect of using NaturallySpeaking. (This menu of topics is shown in Figure 2-5.) It's like looking over someone's shoulder while he or she uses the NaturallySpeaking features. You can read all you want in books like this one, but nothing fixes the material in your mind like watching someone apply it.

**Figure 2-5:**
The topics of the Quick Tour. See this list by clicking the Menu button on any Quick Tour screen.

A typical tour screen is shown in Figure 2-6. Control the tour with the Menu button near the top left. Click the left arrow to go back to the previous screen and the right arrow to go forward. Or click Menu and select from a list of all the topics. To start each screen running, click the start button next to the horizontal slider at the bottom of the screen.

Presentation window

Menu button          Results box

**Figure 2-6:**
Part of the
multimedia
Quick Tour:
In this
example,
the Results
box shows
what's being
said, and
the text
below
shows what
Naturally-
Speaking
does in
response.

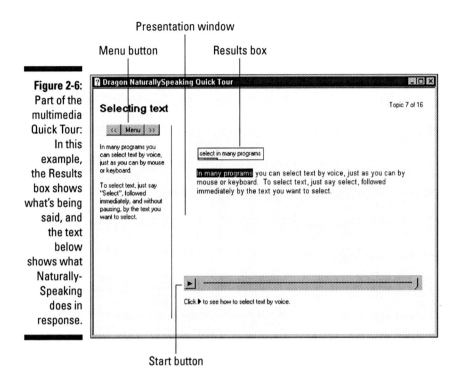

Start button

If you want to take the tour sometime in the future, choose Help⇨Quick Tour
from the NaturallySpeaking menu.

## Setup complete

When the tour is done, the New User wizard returns to tell you that you have
completed the setup process. This is as close to a diploma as you're going
to get from NaturallySpeaking, so it's time to celebrate! You've jumped over
all the hurdles and have completed all the preliminary training. You're now
a fully qualified, dragon-mastering dictator. Click Finish.

The NaturallySpeaking document window now appears. Like Noah's rainbow,
it is a sign that the hardship is over. You can close this window, or move on
to Chapter 3 and start to master NaturallySpeaking itself.

# Chapter 3

# Launching and Controlling Your Dragon

---

## In This Chapter

▶ Launching NaturallySpeaking

▶ Choosing a user

▶ Using the NaturallySpeaking window

▶ Dictating anywhere, using NaturalText

▶ Using voice commands

▶ Understanding the tools and menus of NaturallySpeaking

▶ Customizing the NaturallySpeaking options

---

*Y*ou've hatched, coddled, nurtured, and then educated your draconian friend, and the time has come for it to fly. Now you need to be able to make it do the work you need done, and not accidentally flame your phrases or singe your sentences.

In this chapter, we show you the different ways to launch and control NaturallySpeaking. We also tell you what tools you can use to get better performance and behavior, and where to find them. We refer you to other chapters in this book for the details. If NaturallySpeaking is already up and running on your screen, and you're panting to go and dictate, see Chapter 4!

## Knowing Where to Go for Launch

When you socialize with a dragon, the customary place to go for launch is the Start menu on the Windows taskbar. Use this command:

Start➪Programs➪Dragon NaturallySpeaking *<whatever your edition is>*

This launches the NaturallySpeaking window, where you can dictate documents and control how NaturallySpeaking works. (In NaturallySpeaking Essentials, NaturallySpeaking launches, but its only visible presence is a blue microphone icon on the Windows taskbar.)

You can also launch NaturallySpeaking in a slightly different guise from the menu bar of Word or WordPerfect. In this guise, NaturallySpeaking doesn't pop up a window of its own. Instead, it allows you to dictate documents and control NaturallySpeaking from the Word or WordPerfect window. Choose Dragon NaturallySpeaking⇨Use NaturalWord. You must have installed the NaturalWord option before you can use it. (Also note that NaturalWord doesn't come with NaturallySpeaking Essentials.) Using NaturalWord doesn't restrict you to Word or WordPerfect, though. You can still dictate into other applications (use "NaturalText") when you use NaturalWord.

# *Choosing or Switching "Users"*

When you launch NaturallySpeaking, it may ask you to choose a *user.* If it doesn't ask, don't worry — you probably have only one user: you. You can skip this section if NaturallySpeaking doesn't bring up the subject of a user.

If NaturallySpeaking does ask about a user, here's what's going on. It wants to know who's doing the talking. When you first set up NaturallySpeaking, you created and named a user for yourself and then trained NaturallySpeaking on what that user (you) sounded like. Now, when you launch NaturallySpeaking, you must choose that user so that NaturallySpeaking can recognize you.

When, after launching, NaturallySpeaking displays the Open User dialog box, click the user name you created when you set up NaturallySpeaking and then click the Open button. After a bit of a wait while NaturallySpeaking gets its brains in gear, you're ready to roll.

If you haven't already done the initial setup of NaturallySpeaking, see Chapter 2. If you have only one user (and don't see any good reason to have another), skip the rest of this section and go on to read about the NaturallySpeaking window.

If other people are using this same copy of NaturallySpeaking (or if you have multiple users for yourself), each person must have his or her own user. If you need to add a user, choose User⇨New. This launches the same New User wizard you used to set up NaturallySpeaking for yourself. See Chapter 2 for details on that wizard. For more about multiple users and their vocabularies, see Chapter 21.

You can switch users without restarting NaturallySpeaking:

1. **Choose User⇨Open.**

   NaturallySpeaking may ask whether you want to save your speech files; unless for some reason you don't want to save any corrections you have made to NaturallySpeaking's behavior, click Yes. NaturallySpeaking then displays the Open User dialog box.

2. **Click the user name from the User list, then click the Open button.**

If different people have been making use of NaturallySpeaking, the user names are listed at the bottom of the User menu. Just click a user name to choose it.

# Using the NaturallySpeaking Window

When you launch NaturallySpeaking from Start on the Windows taskbar, you get the NaturallySpeaking window with buttons and menus. (If you're using NaturallySpeaking Essentials, you don't get a window with buttons and menus. You get a blue microphone icon on the Windows taskbar. Right-click the blue microphone icon to get to menus.)

What do you do with the NaturallySpeaking window? It serves two main purposes in your life:

✔ You can dictate your documents into it and later copy them to their final destination. It's a nice, cozy, controlled environment where you can safely get to know all the major features of NaturallySpeaking. You don't have to wonder, "Is that command supported here?" It is. The window is a simple word processor that's very much like the Window WordPad.

✔ You can use its menu bar to access various tools for customizing and improving the performance of NaturallySpeaking. See "Tools and When to Use Them," later in this chapter, for details.

## What's what in the NaturallySpeaking window?

Figure 3-1 shows you what's what in the NaturallySpeaking window. A lot of it will look familiar if you've ever used Windows WordPad. The rest is all special NaturallySpeaking stuff.

Ruler bar
Format bar
Menu bar          Toolbar          Playback bar

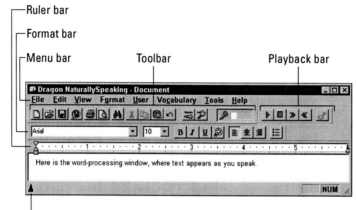

**Figure 3-1:**
The
Naturally-
Speaking
window —
a close
cousin of
WordPad.

Click for history window

NaturallySpeaking doesn't initially display the Format bar and Ruler bar
that Figure 3-1 shows. (The Format bar makes formatting a one- or two-click
process. The Ruler bar helps you set tabs, indentations, and margins visually.)
You display them by choosing View from the Menu bar, and then in the list
that appears, by clicking to place a check mark next to the bar you want.

The toolbar includes many buttons that (unless you're squeaky brand-new
to the world of PCs) you have at least seen, if not used, in other word-
processing programs. Those buttons are New, Open, Save, Print, Print
Preview, Find, Cut, Paste, Copy, and Undo. (As with most toolbars in Windows
programs, pause your mouse cursor over a button to see its name.) The toolbar also contains a few buttons that are unique to NaturallySpeaking, as
shown in Figure 3-2.

# Speech files and users

As part of its definition of a user, NaturallySpeaking
records "speech files." Speech files include an
acoustic model (the way a user's voice sounds
to NaturallySpeaking) and a vocabulary (words
and the way they are used). Speech files
change whenever you change the vocabulary

or correct a recognition error. A user is more
than the sum of its speech files, however.
Besides speech files, a NaturallySpeaking user
definition includes settings in the Options dialog
box and volume settings performed by the Audio
Setup wizard.

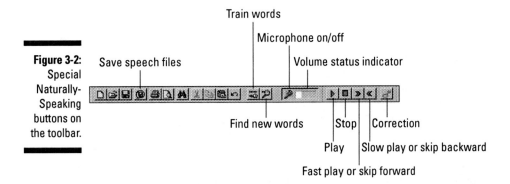

Figure 3-2:
Special
Naturally-
Speaking
buttons on
the toolbar.

Here are the most important special buttons on the toolbar:

✔ The Microphone on/off button is the most critical one. To dictate, click this button so the microphone icon is up at a perky angle, not lying down in a slothful position.

✔ The Save Speech Files button helps you protect your investment in education: It makes sure that any correction or training you have performed gets saved on disk, which lets NaturallySpeaking do better the next time you use it. NaturallySpeaking prompts you to save your speech files when you exit, but manually saving your speech files by clicking this button helps protect you if your system crashes or the power to your PC goes off. The button does the same thing as choosing User⇨Save Speech Files.

✔ The Train Words button pops up a dialog box where you learn words like *choo-choo* and *coal tender*. No, sorry, our tortured brains are shorting out again. This dialog box is where you train NaturallySpeaking to understand a new word or phrase (or your pronunciation of a word or phrase). Clicking the Train Words button does the same thing as choosing Tools⇨Train Words from the menu. See Chapter 18 for more about word training.

✔ The Find New Words button causes NaturallySpeaking to scan your document for any words that aren't in its vocabulary. The Find New Words dialog box that appears is the same one we tell you how to use in Chapter 2, on the vocabulary training of NaturallySpeaking. See Chapter 18 for more about additional vocabulary training.

The Play, Stop, and other buttons on the Playback bar, if they appear in your edition of NaturallySpeaking, are for the groovy 8-track tape player in your NaturallySpeaking window. No, we jest. They are there to help you proofread by listening to your dictation. For the inside scoop on using those buttons, see Chapter 7.

## Using NaturallySpeaking with other applications

After you launch NaturallySpeaking, you can dictate into nearly any Windows application, a feature called NaturalText. Different applications give you different levels of performance, though. See Chapter 10 for the inside story on other applications.

Oh, you're in a rush? Okay, here's the short story: First, minimize the NaturallySpeaking window to a button on the taskbar. (Click the Minimize button with the bar symbol in the far upper-right corner of the window.)

Click the microphone icon on the Windows taskbar to turn the microphone on. (The icon is at the opposite end from the Start button.) Then click in the window of the application you want to use, and talk!

The NaturallySpeaking window lets you review the history of the NaturallySpeaking transcription successes (and errors). To review, click the black up-triangle in the status bar (at the bottom edge of the window). Up pops a list of the most recent transcriptions. You can't do anything about anything you see there; you can only look at stuff. To close the history window, click the triangle again.

"Okay, so now how do you dictate?" you're asking. Easy: Plug in your microphone, put it on, click the Microphone on/off button (also duplicated on the Windows taskbar's system tray), and talk! For the details, see Chapter 4.

## *Why use the NaturallySpeaking window?*

The NaturallySpeaking window is Windows WordPad with ears. That means it's a very simple word processor into which you can dictate or type a document. You then can print the document, copy it to another program window, or save the document as a file that's readable by other programs.

Now you probably know that NaturallySpeaking works with really serious word processors like Word and WordPerfect, and a host of other applications. Why should you give a hoot (or any other utterance) about this simple NaturallySpeaking window, when NaturallySpeaking works with so many other applications?

Here are the main reasons you may want or need to dictate into the NaturallySpeaking window:

- ✔ You don't have Microsoft Word or Corel WordPerfect (or your release of those programs doesn't work with NaturallySpeaking).
- ✔ You do have Word or WordPerfect, but dictating into them with NaturalWord is sluggish or buggy (or sluggy and buggish).

✔ Your PC is tight on memory. Using the NaturallySpeaking window uses less memory than dictating into some other applications.

✔ Your alternative is to use some application in which NaturallySpeaking offers only basic dictation, and not other features. Chapter 10 helps you understand which features you lose with which applications.

✔ You need to transcribe dictation from a recorder (requires the Preferred or Professional edition).

# Tools and When to Use Them

NaturallySpeaking comes with enough tools to make most users nervous. It's like buying a new car, then having the dealer offer to throw in a free, large box of tools. You were sort of hoping that you wouldn't have to use anything like that. Can't you just drive?

Sure, you can "just drive." Dictate away! See Chapter 4. But NaturallySpeaking will never get any better at its job. Tools help you get the most accuracy out of NaturallySpeaking. We'll give you the details of these tools throughout the book, but here's the big picture.

Your toolbox is located in the Tools menu. (Essentials users, right-click your microphone icon.) Following are the tools that we think you're most likely to need, in the order that you're likely to need them:

✔ **Correction dialog box:** Use this tool to educate NaturallySpeaking whenever it makes a recognition error. You may have to use it several times for the same error, but after that, NaturallySpeaking will make the error less often. The Correction dialog box also appears in response to the **Correct That** voice command, the - key on the numeric keypad, or the Correct That icon on the toolbar. (See Chapter 5 for details.)

✔ **Audio Setup wizard:** Run this wizard if NaturallySpeaking seems to be making more errors than it did previously. It adjusts the volume of the microphone input. (See Chapter 2 or 19.)

✔ **Vocabulary Editor:** Use this tool to add specific words to your vocabulary, or train NaturallySpeaking in your pronunciation. It's also useful for creating "shorthands," in which a single spoken phrase like "my address" causes NaturallySpeaking to type some complex text. (See Chapter 17.)

✔ **Word training:** Use this tool to tell NaturallySpeaking how you pronounce a particular word or command. (See Chapter 17.)

Table 3-1 tells you what Dragon tools or technologies to use for what circumstances, and where to read the full details about them.

If you're running NaturallySpeaking but can't see its window, click the NaturallySpeaking button on your Windows taskbar. Then you can access the tools from the NaturallySpeaking menu bar. If you're using Word or WordPerfect with NaturalWord, click Dragon NaturallySpeaking on the Word or WordPerfect menu bar and then find Tools on the menu that appears.

*Note:* Not all capabilities are available in the lower-priced editions of NaturallySpeaking. If, in your edition of NaturallySpeaking, you can't find a particular menu choice listed in Table 3-1, then you don't have that feature.

| Table 3-1 | When to Use Your Tools, and Where They Are | | |
|---|---|---|---|
| **What You Need to Do** | **What Dragon Technology to Use** | **Menu/Toolbar Choice** | **Where to Read More** |
| Correct a NaturallySpeaking error | Correction dialog box | **<lasso>** or - on numeric keypad. | Chapters 4, 5 |
| Adjust for changes in microphone position | Audio Setup wizard | Tools➪Audio Setup Wizard | Chapter 19 |
| Improve recognition of individual words | Word training | Tools➪Train Words or click the Train Words button | Chapter 18 |
| Expand vocabulary, improve recognition. | Vocabulary Builder | Tools➪Vocabulary Builder | Chapter 18 |
| Add words in this document to vocabulary | Find words | Tools➪Find New Words | Chapter 18 |
| Add a specific word to your vocabulary | Vocabulary Editor | Tools➪Vocabulary Editor | Chapter 18 |
| Create a shorthand phrase for long text | Vocabulary Editor | Tools➪Vocabulary Editor | Chapter 18 |
| Add a new user | New User wizard | User➪New | Chapter 2, 21 |
| Switch to new user | Open a new user | User➪Open | Chapter 21 |
| Use another vocabulary for special documents | Use a different vocabulary | Vocabulary➪Open | Chapter 21 |

| What You Need to Do | What Dragon Technology to Use | Menu/Toolbar Choice | Where to Read More |
|---|---|---|---|
| Train NaturallySpeaking for recorded speech | Mobile recorder training | Tools➪Mobile Training | Chapters 8, 9 |
| Record speech to be transcribed later | Sound Recorder | Tools➪Sound Recorder | Chapter 8 |
| Transcribe recorded speech | Transcription | Tools➪Transcribe | Chapter 8 |
| Create custom commands | Develop macros | Tools➪New Command Wizard | Chapter 22 |
| Modify commands | Edit macros | Tools➪Edit Command Wizard | Chapter 22 |

# Choosing Options

Now that you're a dictator, you can order NaturallySpeaking to work your way! Choose Tools➪Options to get the Options dialog box, which has tabs for five different categories of option. Some of the options we have found most useful are

- ✔ Trade-off speed for accuracy: Miscellaneous tab
- ✔ Use one or two spaces after a period: Dictation tab
- ✔ Change microphone on/off, correction hotkeys: Hotkeys tab
- ✔ Double-click to correct in NaturallySpeaking window: Miscellaneous tab
- ✔ Playback on correction: Miscellaneous tab

Each tab has a Restore Defaults button. Click that if you feel you've really mucked something up and want to put things the way they were as NaturallySpeaking came out of the box.

## Results box

The Results box is the tiny box in which NaturallySpeaking lets you watch as it figures out what you said. We've never been particularly bothered by the Results box, but if you are, you can set the following:

✔ **How long it stays on screen:** Move the Auto Hide Delay slider to the left for a shorter stay, right for longer. By default, it stays on-screen 10 seconds.

✔ **Volume meter:** The tiny yellow/green band indicates volume. Make it bigger, smaller, or nonexistent by sliding the Volume Meter Height control.

✔ **Stay in one place:** Click the Anchor checkbox.

## Hotkeys

Hotkeys are things you press on the keyboard to control NaturallySpeaking, like the + key on the numeric keypad to switch the microphone on/off. Here's where you change them. Why change? You may have trouble pressing the key. Or you may need to use the key for something else (like using the numeric keypad + and - keys for calculations).

All the buttons on the Hotkeys tab work the same way: Click the button, and a Set Hot Key dialog box pops up. When it does, don't try to type the names of the keys, just press them. For instance, press the Ctrl key, and {Ctrl} appears. Click OK when done.

Here are the details:

✔ **Microphone on/off:** If you choose a regular typewriter key (like a letter), you must use Ctrl or Alt with it. Otherwise, function keys, arrow keys, and other non-typewriter keys are all fair game either by themselves or in combination with Ctrl or Alt.

✔ **Correction Dialog:** This is a key that pops up the Correction dialog box to correct the last phrase uttered. The rules are the same as for Microphone on/off.

✔ **Force Command Recognition:** This is the key you hold down to try to make NaturallySpeaking interpret what you say as a command, not text. It can only be Ctrl, Alt, Shift, or some combination of them.

✔ **Force Dictation Recognition:** Does the opposite of Force Command Recognition (makes what you say come out as text). Rules for keys are the same as Force Command Recognition.

## Text-to-speech

Text-to-speech is a feature of NaturallySpeaking Preferred and higher. It uses a computer-synthesized voice to read text aloud. It's not very inspirational, but it does great deadpan humor. (Try having it say "I like the nightlife; I love to boogie," sometime. See Chapter 7.)

We find that slowing it down a bit and changing the pitch makes it more intelligible. You can adjust sliders for Volume, Pitch, and Speed; then click the Preview button to hear what the voice sounds like.

# Miscellaneous

Lots of useful stuff hangs out on the Miscellaneous tab (and some less useful stuff, too). Here's what's up with that:

- ✔ **Pause Between Phrases:** This slider tells NaturallySpeaking how long a pause to allow before breaking up a phrase. See the discussion of dictating text and commands in Chapter 4 to understand how it works.

- ✔ **Speed vs. Accuracy:** Slide this guy to the right for fewer recognition errors, or to the left for a quicker, if sloppier job.

- ✔ **Disk Space Reserved for Speech Data:** The larger the amount here, the more of your audio that NaturallySpeaking saves for possible playback.

- ✔ **Backup Every 5 Saves:** Every so many times your speech files are saved, NaturallySpeaking saves a backup copy. If you ever mess up your speech files in some way, you can choose User➪Restore from the menu bar to return the files to an earlier, okay state. If you're paranoid about messing up, use a smaller number here.

- ✔ **Various checkboxes:** A bunch of checkboxes control the truly miscellaneous (the miscellaneous of the Miscellaneous tab).

  - • **Use Active Accessibility:** A technical muddle. Leave it to the Dragon tech support folks.

  - • **Show Microphone In Tray:** (It means "Show it in the system tray on the Windows taskbar.") So what's not to like?

  - • **Enable Double-Click to Correct:** Click this, and when you double-click a word in the NaturallySpeaking window, you launch the Correction dialog box. Nice shortcut, especially useful for correcting transcribed recordings.

  - • **Select Searches Backwards:** Clear this checkmark, and Select and Say looks forward from the cursor location instead of backwards. Clearing this checkmark is not very useful, in our opinion.

  - • **Automatic Playback On Correction:** Check this, and the Correction dialog box plays back your voice for the phrase in question. Useful proofreading tool.

  - • **Microphone On At Startup:** Click this if you want NaturallySpeaking to have the microphone on as soon as it launches. This choice is particularly useful if you're making NaturallySpeaking launch automatically when your PC starts up. (See Chapter 11 for details.)

## Dictation

The Dictation tab controls a few aspects of exactly how NaturallySpeaking translates your mellow, well-modulated dictation into commonplace text. Here's what's happening on this tab:

- ✔ **Two Spaces After Period:** Clear this checkbox to use just a single space after a period; otherwise you get two. In general, documents designed for publication (like this one) should have only one space. Two spaces drive typesetters nuts.

- ✔ **Format Numbers, Telephone Numbers, Currency, and Times Automatically:** Clear this checkbox if you don't like the way NaturallySpeaking automatically handles those various numeric values; you'll also disable the features controlled by the next two checkboxes.

- ✔ **Format Web and E-mail Addresses Automatically:** Grayed out unless the Format Numbers (and so on) checkbox is enabled. Frankly, we're not too impressed with this automatic formatting anyway, so we clear this check mark. (Instead, we add our favorite addresses and shorthand to the vocabulary, like "triple-dub" for www.)

- ✔ **Allow Pauses While Speaking Numbers and Addresses:** A nice feature, because you often pause to check numbers when speaking phone numbers. If you clear this check mark, NaturallySpeaking may put spaces where you pause.

- ✔ **Use Natural Language Commands in Microsoft Word 97:** This check mark is what allows you to use the many special commands for Word that NaturalWord provides. Clear it, and you save memory, but you lose those commands. It's grayed out if NaturalWord isn't installed, or if you have custom commands that you have created.

# Using the Word-Processor Features of the NaturallySpeaking Window

The NaturallySpeaking window's menu and toolbar may seem familiar to you. It is, with the addition of speech features, the same as the menu and toolbar in WordPad (the small-scale word processor that comes with Windows). In fact, the two products are so similar that we suspect Dragon somehow magically and legally hijacks WordPad and gives it an alien-brain implant.

If you're already familiar with WordPad or similar word processors, you can skip this section. Our advice is to move on to Chapter 4.

## Choosing from the menu bar and toolbar

Even if you've never used WordPad, if you've used any word processor, we think you'll find all the choices on the NaturallySpeaking menus and toolbars so familiar (except for the speech-related choices) that you'll hardly need this section. But just in case NaturallySpeaking is among the very first Windows programs you've used, herein lie the details.

You can use the NaturallySpeaking menu bar and toolbar buttons as you would in any Windows program. As with most Windows toolbars, pause your mouse cursor over a button to see the button's name or function.

Because you're running NaturallySpeaking, you can also choose items on the menu bar by using voice commands (as you can in nearly any other application, too). For full details, see the discussion of ordering from the menu in Chapter 10. To choose from the menu bar, use the verbal command, **Click <menu text>**. By *<menu text>*, we mean anything listed on the menu bar, such as File, Edit, or Format. Next, to choose an item from the menu that appears, just say its name. (If you like consistency in your commands, you can instead say **Click** and then its name.) For instance, you can say, **"Click File"** and then say, **"Save."**

## Editing: Cut, paste, and the usual suspects

The Edit menu of NaturallySpeaking holds no surprises for anyone who has used a word processor in Windows (as we assume you have). It has the usual suspects: Copy, Cut, and Paste using the Windows Clipboard; plus Undo, Select All, Find, and Find and Replace.

If you add the Format bar to the NaturallySpeaking window, you can alternatively use the familiar Cut, Copy, and Paste buttons on that bar. The button with the binoculars icon is a shortcut to the Find dialog box.

Choosing Edit⇨Select All (hotkey: Ctrl+A) is useful when you want to copy all the text in the window in preparation for pasting it into a different program. See Chapter 7 if you want details about copying text from NaturallySpeaking by using voice commands.

## Formatting: Fonts, indentations, alignments, bullets, and tabs

The Format menu is (no surprise) where all the fancy formatting stuff hangs out. (Not that NaturallySpeaking offers a lot of "fancy.")

Like the Edit menu, the Format menu is very straightforward if you've used a word processor before. Here's where various formatting lies:

- ✔ **Bullets:** NaturallySpeaking offers only one style of bullets. To turn bullets on, choose Format⇨Bullet Style (or click the Bullets button on the Format bar). Repeat that choice to turn bulleting off again.

- ✔ **Font:** Choose Format⇨Font to get a Font dialog box and make your typeface, style, size, and color choices there. Or add the Format bar to your screen by choosing View⇨Format Bar and choose your font on that toolbar. You can set font styles of bold, italic, or underline in alternative ways, just as in many other programs. Click the B, *I*, or U button on the Format bar; or press Ctrl+B, Ctrl+I, or Ctrl+U, respectively. You can choose font color from the Font dialog box or by clicking the Color button (the palette icon) on the Format bar.

- ✔ **Indents and alignments:** Choose Format⇨Paragraph to get a Paragraph dialog box. Type in an indentation for the left edge, right edge, or just the first line of the paragraph. (For hanging indents, set a Left indent, like 0.5", and then an equal but negative indent, like –0.5", for First Line.) Click Alignment to choose from Left, Center, and Right alignment. Or if the Format bar is on your screen, click the Align Left, Center, or Align Right button.

- ✔ **Tabs:** To set tab stops (where the cursor stops when you press the Tab key), choose Format⇨Tabs. In the Tabs dialog box that appears, type a position (say, 0.8") in the Tab Stop Position box, and then click the Set button. Continue until you've set all your tabs, and then click OK. Click Clear All to restore tabs to the normal half-inch defaults.

You can also set tab stops on the Ruler. (To put the Ruler bar on your screen, choose View⇨Ruler Bar.) Just click wherever you want a tab stop. A tiny L-shaped mark appears; you can drag it to any position you like. To remove it, drag it up or down off the ruler.

## Saving and Opening Documents

You save a NaturallySpeaking document the old-fashioned way: with a menu choice or toolbar button. As in any other application, you can use a voice command to make the menu choice, too, such as saying, **"Click File,"** and then **"Save"** or **"Press Control S."**

The New, Save, Save As, and Open commands in the NaturallySpeaking File menu work as they do in nearly every other Windows application. So do the New, Open, and Save buttons on the toolbar (the first three). In case you forget (or nobody ever told you), here's what they do:

✔ To start a new, blank document, choose File⇨New (or click the New button).

✔ To open an existing document file, choose File⇨Open (or click the Open button).

✔ To save the document as a file, choose File⇨Save (or click the Save button).

✔ To save a new copy of the current document under a new name or in a new location, choose File⇨Save As.

NaturallySpeaking allows you to save your work in one of the following ways (file types), so you can pass your work along to others, or save it for a fun day of editing later on:

✔ **Plain text (.TXT) files:** Text files do not preserve formatting, just the text, plus line or paragraph breaks and tabs. (Tab stop *positions* are not saved, however.) 'Most everything can open a TXT file.

✔ **Rich Text Format (.RTF) files:** Rich Text Format files are rich and creamy, filled with all the formatting you can do in NaturallySpeaking. Nearly all major word processors can open these files, so your formatting survives the translation if you use RTF.

When you choose File⇨Save the first time you save your document (or anytime you choose File⇨Save As), you have to choose which file type to use. A NaturallySpeaking dialog box appears, warning you that saving a text file will lose formatting. It presents you with two buttons to choose between: Rich Text Document or Text Document. (If you simply press the Enter key at this point, NaturallySpeaking will choose RTF.)

Choose Rich Text Format if you want to import your document into a word processor or some other application that allows character formatting (such as bold) and paragraph formatting (such as center-aligned). Choose Text if the application (such as a simple e-mail program) does not support formatting. When you click the button for your choice, NaturallySpeaking presents the typical Save As dialog box you will recognize from other Windows applications. Type a name for the file and choose a folder.

To open an RTF file in your word processor or other application, the usual menu choice is File⇨Open. In the Open dialog box that appears, click the box labeled Files Of Type (or something like that) and look for Rich Text Format (RTF).

If you want to verbally edit documents, you need to load 'em into the NaturallySpeaking window where you can yell at them. In addition to being able to open the RTF and TXT files it writes, NaturallySpeaking can read Microsoft Word 6.0 (.doc files). Most word processors can write Word 6.0, RTF, or TXT files: Using your word processor, check the dialog box that appears when you use the File⇨Save As command. Click the Save As Type box there and choose Word 6.0 (.doc) files, Text (.txt), or Rich Text (.rtf).

# Customizing the Window

Just like most other application windows, your NaturallySpeaking window is a room with a View. That is, you can change the NaturallySpeaking appearance through the View menu. By "appearances," we mean stuff like toolbars, text wrapping in the window, and units of measure on the ruler (metric, English, or typesetting).

To view all the bars in the NaturallySpeaking neighborhood, click View to get a list of available toolbars. (Figure 3-1 shows all the available toolbars.) Click next to a toolbar in that list to put a check mark beside it, and you will turn on whatever toolbar you check. Click again to clear any check mark.

To control how text wraps (continues onto the next line) on your screen, how your mouse selects text, or what units of measure you use, choose View⇨Settings. The Settings dialog box springs into action, where you can fool with any of the following:

✔ NaturallySpeaking normally uses inches for measurement units (used on the ruler and in paragraph formatting). To change measurement units, click the Options tab of the Settings dialog box. You can then choose Inches, Centimeters, Points, or Picas (not to be confused with Pikas, an alpine lagomorph — it's a common mistake, don't feel bad).

✔ When you select with your mouse, NaturallySpeaking (like many Windows programs) normally selects entire words when you stretch the selection highlight to more than one word. If, instead, you want to be able to set the endpoint of your selections in mid-word, click the Options tab, then click to clear the checkbox labeled Automatic Word Selection.

✔ To control how text wraps on your screen, click Rich Text. (Click Text, instead, if you intend to save your file as plain text.) Then click either Wrap To Window (to fill your window with text) or Wrap to Ruler (to force lines to break at the right margin on the ruler). No Wrap simply makes your text hard to read. Choose Wrap to Ruler if you intend to print from the NaturallySpeaking window and want to see exactly how your printed lines of text will break while you type.

None of the wrap settings affects how lines of text break when you print, copy, or save it as a file. NaturallySpeaking always prints according to the page margins you set up, regardless of wrap settings. It never puts line breaks in text that's saved as a file or copied to another program's window. It always leaves the line breaks to that other program, and so avoids any ragged-right margin problems.

# Part II
# Fire-Breathing 101

# In this part . . .

When your new dragon companion is installed and trained, it's time to breathe a little fire into your boring old PC. That's not to say you should incinerate your keyboard quite yet, but in this part, you start setting your fingers free from the tedium of typing.

NaturallySpeaking is a bit like the secretary of old movies who quietly takes dictation and then types it up without a single spelling error. It's also a bit like today's real-life secretary (although sadly lacking any decorative body piercing) who not only types and spells perfectly, but edits and formats your documents, helps you proofread, and transcribes dictation from your portable recorder. As with a human secretary, you do need to give clear instructions to NaturallySpeaking; and in this part, we'll show you exactly what to do, what to say, and how to say it to get the results you want in the NaturallySpeaking window.

# Chapter 4

# Basic Dictating

*I*t seems to us that dictating should be a far easier way to communicate than by wiggling your fingers across a keyboard. And, the basics of dictating are, in fact, pretty easy. You just need to know a few tricks that we'll tell you in this chapter.

The "basics" of NaturallySpeaking are its typewriter-level abilities to turn voice into text. NaturallySpeaking can do lots of other things (edit, format, make tables, launch programs, and more) too, but we cover that elsewhere. The typewriter-like features are the ones you find in even the least expensive version of NaturallySpeaking, NaturallySpeaking Essentials.

This basic typewriter ability works not only in the NaturallySpeaking window, but in any (well, nearly any) Windows application (program). See Part III for using NaturallySpeaking with other applications.

Chapter 5 goes into detail about correcting errors, moving your cursor around verbally, and other fine points of editing using NaturallySpeaking. Chapter 5 also discusses some of the more advanced editing features NaturallySpeaking offers for certain applications.

# *Dictating 101: How to Dictate*

After you have installed NaturallySpeaking on a computer with all the necessary hardware and performed the initial training rites (see Chapter 2), you're on the road to becoming a successful dictator. Take the following steps:

1. **Launch NaturallySpeaking: Choose Start⇨Programs⇨Dragon NaturallySpeaking <your edition >⇨Dragon NaturallySpeaking <your edition >.**

   As Part II points out, you can also use Dragon NaturallySpeaking with a large number of applications. If you're using NaturallySpeaking Essentials, that is the only way you can dictate: into another application's window.

   If you intend to use NaturallySpeaking with another application, you launch that application at this point, too.

2. **Put on your headset, and make sure the microphone is positioned as it was during initial training.**

   The microphone should be positioned about a half inch away from one corner of your mouth, off to the side. It should never be directly in front of your mouth.

3. **Turn the microphone on.**

   The microphone icon in the system tray (the little box full of icons on your Windows taskbar) needs to be pointing up at a jaunty angle, not lying down, in order for you to dictate. If the icon is lying down, click it or press the + key on your keyboard's numeric keypad. (If the icon has little z's next to it, the microphone is disabled, or "asleep," and you either have to say, **"Wake Up"** or else click the icon twice.) If you pause your mouse cursor over the icon, a tiny label tells you what will happen if you click the icon, such as "Turn Microphone On."

   The microphone icon in the toolbar of the NaturallySpeaking window (or the NaturalWord toolbar in Microsoft Word or Corel WordPerfect) works in exactly the same way as the icon on the taskbar.

4. **Click where you want the text to go.**

   Or select (highlight) text that you want to replace with dictated text.

5. **Speak carefully, just as you did when you read stories to NaturallySpeaking during the initial training. Don't rush, and don't speak the words with . . . spaces . . . between . . . them.**

   As you speak, NaturallySpeaking shows you what it thinks you said in a small box in one corner of your screen, called the Results box. Don't panic if what you see doesn't match what you thought you said! Sometimes, NaturallySpeaking changes its mind before it actually records text in your application window.

6. **Speak your punctuation, such as "Period" or "Comma," as you go, and if you want a word capitalized, say the word "Cap" beforehand.**

See the upcoming section, "Capitalization and Punctuation" for details.

If NaturallySpeaking makes errors (and it will), "correct" them rather than edit them. For basic instructions, see "Quick Corrections," later in this chapter. See Chapter 5 for additional details on correction and instructions for editing by voice.

Figure 4-1 is an example of how dictation works in NaturallySpeaking. These paragraphs show the basic "typewriter" input we discuss in this chapter.

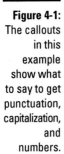

**Figure 4-1:**
The callouts in this example show what to say to get punctuation, capitalization, and numbers.

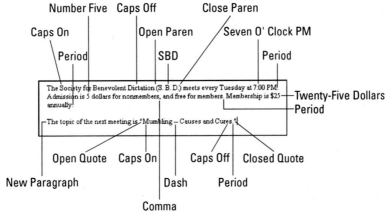

If you don't have a particularly fast computer, NaturallySpeaking may take a while to interpret what you said. You may have to pause once in a while if you want NaturallySpeaking to catch up. You don't have to wait for it, however, after you're confident that it is not making too may errors.

Speak continuously — don't pause between your words (until you come to the end of a phrase)! Dragon NaturallySpeaking is designed to recognize continuous speech. If you deliberately put pauses between your words, Dragon NaturallySpeaking will make more errors, not fewer. (Pausing between phrases is okay, however.)

You can use your keyboard and your mouse just as you would normally — to type, to make menu selections, or use command keys (like Ctrl+Z). Or you can use Dragon NaturallySpeaking to perform keyboard and menu commands. See Chapter 11 for details.

## The results are in. . . .

The results are in . . . in the Results box! The Results box appears somewhere on your screen (usually in a corner) whenever you say something. It's a small, yellowish box, similar to the little label that appears when you pause your mouse cursor over an icon in most programs.

The Results box shows you how Naturally-Speaking is interpreting whatever you said. You can cancel the interpretation process by clicking the tiny red symbol in the corner of the box. You can also drag the Results box anywhere on your screen.

NaturallySpeaking refines its interpretation as you speak, so don't panic if the box initially shows some wildly incorrect guess. It also spells out your commands and punctuation. It displays the word *period*, for example, even though NaturallySpeaking ultimately translates that word into the period symbol on the page.

Along the bottom of the Results box is a little bar showing yellow, green, and gray colors. This bar is a volume indicator, like the one you probably have on a home sound system. You see the indicator fluctuate as you speak. A yellow bar indicates that NaturallySpeaking thinks that it's hearing background noise, not speech. A green bar indicates that NaturallySpeaking thinks that it's hearing your voice. If you're just sitting there not speaking, and the bar is green, run the Audio Setup wizard again. Green doesn't indicate "go." It indicates that NaturallySpeaking is trying to process the sounds it's picking up on the microphone.

If you're dictating directly into the Naturally-Speaking window, you can review your most recent utterances: Click the black up-pointing triangle in the far lower-left corner of that window. A Recognition History box appears; click that triangle again to clear the box.

You can adjust the Results box by choosing Tools⇨Options in the NaturallySpeaking window. Click the Results Box tab in the Options dialog box that appears. To lock the Results box in place in its current location, click the Anchor checkbox. To adjust the amount of time that the Results box remains on your screen, drag the Auto Hide Delay slider — to the left to keep the box on your screen longer, and to the right to have it hang around as briefly as possible. If you're really enamored of the volume indicator, drag the Volume Meter Height slider to the left to make the indicator bar thicker.

# *Distinguishing between Text and Commands*

As you can see in Figure 4-1, NaturallySpeaking lets you mix dictation (words that get converted into text) and commands (instructions to the computer). You don't have to press or click anything to tell NaturallySpeaking, "Here comes a command, don't write this." You just say the command.

Sometimes, however, this scheme runs aground. For instance, **Cap** is a command to capitalize the upcoming word. You may, however, dictate a sentence like, "We want to cap expenditures for this year" and see it come out like this: "We want to Expenditures for this year."

You can use pauses to control the interpretation. Most commands involve two or more words. NaturallySpeaking must hear them together, as a phrase, to interpret them as a command. To convince NaturallySpeaking to take a phrase as text, then, instead of a command, you should pause between two or more of the words.

To have NaturallySpeaking interpret "cap" as text, for instance, you can pause between "cap" and the word it operates on, like "expenditure." For a two- or three-word phrase that sounds like a command (like **Caps On**), you can pause between the words to break up the phrase. ("They put their caps . . . on their heads.") You also need to pause before commands that affect what you just said, as **Scratch That** does. If you don't pause, NaturallySpeaking will lump **Scratch** with the preceding word and consider it all as text. Fortunately, such a pause is natural.

Most people aren't that careful. They speak the phrase and then say, "Oh, nuts" (silently, to ourselves, or else NaturallySpeaking will dutifully type *that* out). Instead of "Oh, nuts," when you see the error, say, **"Scratch That"** to remove the blooper. Then repeat the phrase with the pauses adjusted.

You can adjust the amount of time that NaturallySpeaking considers to be a sufficient pause. See the section on choosing options in NaturallySpeaking, in Chapter 3.

Pausing doesn't help with punctuation and numbers that you want spelled out. For instance, you can't dictate "He typed a comma and continued." You get the comma symbol, not the word. For those problems, use the Vocabulary Editor (described in Chapter 18) to add the written word *comma* with a new spoken form, for example, "word comma." Then you can say, "He typed a word comma and continued."

Although using pauses is the most reliable way to distinguish between text and command, NaturallySpeaking offers an alternative solution. This alternative doesn't work for so-called "dictation commands" that have to do with capitalization, tabs, and line or paragraph breaks, but it does work for many other commands, such as formatting commands. To force your utterance to be taken as text, hold down the Shift key while you speak. To force it to be taken as a command, hold down the Ctrl key.

# Controlling Your (Cough! Sneeze!) Microphone

We find that we constantly switch the microphone off and on to avoid inserting the garbage text that comes from coughing, sneezing, or answering the phone. Dragon NaturallySpeaking gives you several ways to control the microphone:

- ✔ Press the + key on the numeric keypad to switch the microphone between "on" and "off." We find this switch to be the most convenient one.

- ✔ Click the microphone icon that appears either in the toolbar of the program you're using or in the system tray of your Windows taskbar.

- ✔ Say, **"Go to Sleep"** to disable the microphone. The microphone icon lies down, and a string of z's appears next to the microphone icon. To wake up the microphone again, say, **"Wake Up."** (Or click the sleeping microphone icon twice, or press the + key on the numeric keypad twice.) This sleeping and waking stuff is not the same as "off" and "on." What's the difference? When the microphone is asleep, it's still listening for the command, **Wake Up.** If you turn the microphone off, it's not listening at all.

You can change the microphone hotkey (normally the + key on the numeric keypad) by choosing Tools➪Options and clicking the Hotkeys tab in the Options dialog box that appears. Then click the Microphone on/off button in the dialog box, and a tiny Set Hot Key dialog box appears. Now press the key or key combination you would prefer for the hotkey, and then click OK.

# *Tips for New Dictators*

Dictating text, especially if you're used to typing on a computer, can be a little clumsy at first. You need to do things a bit differently than when you type. Following are a few tips to make your dictating easier:

- ✔ Try not to watch the screen as you talk. Seeing text while you dictate is, for some people, like patting their heads while rubbing their stomachs: The two activities are somehow not very compatible. Instead, look out the window or gaze off into the distance to compose and speak your thoughts.

- ✔ Dictate in phrases. You don't have to dictate the entire sentence, with all its punctuation, all at once (although longer utterances may improve accuracy). For instance, as we dictated the preceding sentence, we paused after "the entire sentence" and stood a while in thought. We also paused before and after the commas.

- ✔ Learn to punctuate and capitalize as you speak. Although you can certainly go back and punctuate and capitalize text after you dictate, punctuating as you speak is often easier, after you become accustomed to it.

- ✔ Proofread what you have dictated. Dragon NaturallySpeaking makes mistakes, particularly when you're first getting started with it, and sometimes those mistakes are both potentially embarrassing and so plausible-sounding that they are hard to detect! NaturallySpeaking Preferred Edition or higher provides two tools that can help you address this problem — the playback feature, which plays back a recording of your own voice, and the readback feature, which actually synthesizes a voice from your text. See Chapter 7 for more information on these features.

✔ Many new users are tempted to use unusual, classic, or archaic texts, such as the Gettysburg Address, when trying out NaturallySpeaking, rather than using their normal, day-to-day language. We suggest that you don't do that. See the last chapter of this book if you want to play around with NaturallySpeaking. If you really intend to regularly dictate poetry or something other than contemporary English, use the multiple users or vocabularies described in Chapter 21. As it comes out of the box, NaturallySpeaking is designed for conventional and contemporary English, and using it otherwise can cause many frustrating errors.

✔ Expect dictating to be a bit awkward at first. If, like us, you're used to the modern computer word processor, you may find that composing your thoughts verbally is weird at first.

✔ A compromise between voice and keyboard that we find useful is to keep your hands on the mouse and keyboard for cursor and menu control, and then use Dragon NaturallySpeaking as a fast way to type and format text. For example, you might highlight some text with your mouse and then say, **"Cap That,"** or move your cursor somewhere and dictate.

✔ When just getting started with NaturallySpeaking, don't try to enter text that includes a lot of jargon or acronyms, or that requires a lot of special capitalization. You will get frustrated before you have a chance to really learn and appreciate the product.

✔ To get used to NaturallySpeaking without getting bogged down in it, try typing normally using the keyboard; then, every so often, dictate a bit of text that you find awkward to type.

## Enunciation: Good idea or just a fancy word?

Many people think that the whole idea of "continuous speech recognition" is that you should be able to speak conversationally, as if to a friend, and the computer will take it all down. But the fact of the matter is that your computer isn't as smart as your friends. (Or, at least, we hope that is the case!)

As a result, you may need to help NaturallySpeaking out just a bit by speaking more carefully than you would in casual conversation. Or, you may need to educate NaturallySpeaking in your vocabulary, or even help its "hearing" (sound system) a bit. Part IV gives you various ways to help NaturallySpeaking hear and understand you better.

# Punctuating and Capitalizing

Dictating isn't quite like speaking. Unlike humans, NaturallySpeaking can't interpret the inflections and pauses in our voices as punctuation. (Maybe in the next release, Dragon?) Nor does it know — as we all know, of course — that Laboratory Pancake, Pennsylvania is a town and should be capitalized. (Okay, technically it's two towns, like Minneapolis-St. Paul, but who can resist combining them?)

When you dictate, you'll have to make an effort to help NaturallySpeaking out, although NaturallySpeaking does do some punctuating and capitalization automatically. Here's how to work with NaturallySpeaking to get your pancakes correctly capitalized and your apostrophizing properly punctuated.

## Punctuating your remarks

Speaking punctuation marks as you dictate is annoying but necessary if you want to avoid the tedious process of going back and inserting punctuation. Table 4-1 shows you what words to say to insert punctuation marks as you speak.

| Table 4-1 | PunctuallySpeaking |
|---|---|
| *Punctuation Mark* | *Spoken Form* |
| Single punctuation marks | |
| . | **Period** (or **Dot**, or **Point**) |
| ! | **Exclamation Mark** (or **Exclamation Point**) |
| ? | **Question Mark** |
| , | **Comma** |
| ' | **Apostrophe** |
| 's | **Apostrophe Ess** |
| & | **Ampersand** |
| : | **Colon** |
| ; | **Semicolon** |
| ' | **Open Single Quote** |
| ' | **Close Single Quote** |
| . . . | **Ellipsis** |

| *Punctuation Mark* | *Spoken Form* |
|---|---|
| $ | **Dollar Sign** |
| - | **Hyphen** |
| — | **Dash** |
| Paired punctuation marks | |
| " | **Open Quote** |
| " | **Close Quote** |
| ( | **Open** (or **Left**) **Parenthesis** (or **Paren**) |
| ) | **Close** (or **Right**) **Parenthesis** (or **Paren**) |
| [ | **Open Bracket** |
| ] | **Close Bracket** |
| Symbols often used for math and computers | |
| { | **Open Brace** |
| } | **Close Brace** |
| / | **Slash** |
| \ | **Backslash** |
| @ | **At Sign** |
| ~ | **Tilde** |
| _ | **Underscore** |
| * | **Asterisk** |
| > | **Greater Than** (or **Open Angle Bracket**) |
| < | **Less Than** (or **Close Angle Bracket**) |
| \| | **Vertical Bar** |
| # | **Pound Sign** (or **Number Sign**) |
| - | **Minus Sign** |
| + | **Plus Sign** |
| . | **Point** |
| % | **Percent Sign** |
| ` | **Backquote** |
| , | **Numeric Comma** |
| ^ | **Caret** |

NaturallySpeaking puts no space before an apostrophe, so you can easily make a noun possessive (such as in "Tom's bicycle") by speaking the word ("Tom") and then saying, **"Apostrophe Ess."** Dragon NaturallySpeaking may supply an apostrophe automatically if, from the context, it thinks you're describing a possessive noun or contraction. But it can't always do that accurately. It's more reliable, if more awkward, to speak the word and then add **"Apostrophe Ess."**

NaturallySpeaking uses a double dash character when you say the word **"Dash."** If you would rather use a different character, you can paste that character into your vocabulary list using Dragon's vocabulary editor (described in Chapter 18), and create your own spoken phrase for that character, such as **"Em Dash."**

You can hyphenate any multi-word utterance (such as the phrase, "all encompassing") by saying, **"Hyphenate That"** immediately after speaking the phrase.

If you meant to use a word as text, such as the word "period," and NaturallySpeaking used that word as punctuation instead, you can say, **"Correct That"** and choose the interpretation you prefer. See "Quick Corrections" later in this chapter for instructions.

## Capitalizing on your text

NaturallySpeaking does some capitalization for you, as you dictate. For example, it generally capitalizes the first letter of a sentence. (Its cue to capitalize is that you have started a new paragraph or punctuated the end of a sentence.) It also capitalizes words that it thinks are proper nouns or that it has been taught to capitalize in its vocabulary training or editing. In general, as long as you don't do any manual typing between finishing one sentence and starting the next, NaturallySpeaking automatically takes care of the initial capitalization.

When NaturallySpeaking doesn't capitalize for you, you have several ways to capitalize words yourself. The two best and easiest ways to capitalize are either *before* you speak a word or phrase or *immediately afterward.*

You can also select any text with your mouse or by voice and then apply capitalization and other formatting. See Chapter 5 for more about that technique, which only works in the NaturallySpeaking window and certain other applications.

Here are the basics of capitalizing the initial letters of words:

✔ To capitalize the first letter of any word, before speaking it say, **"Cap"** followed immediately by your word. Don't pause between **Cap** and whatever the word is, or Dragon NaturallySpeaking will type *cap* instead of doing it!

✔ After you say some words and NaturallySpeaking types them in your program window, say, **"Cap That"** or **"All Cap That."** (The words must still be in the tiny, yellowish Results box for this command to work.) **Cap** means the initial letters are capitalized. **All Cap** means all the letters are capitalized.

✔ If you are about to speak a series of words that must be capitalized, say, **"Caps On."** Speak those words (pausing for as long as you like anywhere in this process), and then say, **"Caps Off."** To capitalize *all* the letters in a series of words (LIKE THIS) use the phrases *All* **Caps On** and *All* **Caps Off** instead.

Table 4-2 lists all the various ways to capitalize.

| **Table 4-2** | | **Capital Ideas** |
|---|---|---|
| *To Do This* | *Example* | *Say This* |
| First letter capital | Like This | **"Cap <word>,"** or <phrase> **"Cap That,"** or **"Caps On"** <one or more phrases> **"Caps Off"** |
| All letters capital | LIKE THIS | Use any of the same three approaches listed above for first-letter capitals, but say, **"All Caps"** in place of **Caps**. |
| All letters lowercase | like this | Use any of the same three approaches above, but say, **"No Caps"** in place of **Caps**. |

# What is "That"?

The NaturallySpeaking dictation commands, such as **Cap That,** include the word "that." Just what does **That** mean? It means one of two things.

When you say, **"<some command> That,"** and no text is currently selected in your document, Dragon NaturallySpeaking applies your command to all the words in the last continuous phrase that it recognized. That phrase is the one that appears in the Results box whenever you speak.

If you have selected text in your document, **That** refers to the selection. For example, in the NaturallySpeaking window you can drag your mouse across some text to select it, then say, **"Cap That."** You can't do this trick in all applications, only the NaturallySpeaking window, Select-and-Say applications, and NaturalWord applications. See Chapter 10 for more about limitations in other programs.

NaturallySpeaking has been known occasionally to get stuck in one style of capitalization. If that happens to you and nothing that you do (such as saying, **"Caps Off"**) seems to fix the problem, close and then restart NaturallySpeaking (or Word or WordPerfect, if you're using NaturalWord).

**Caps On** and **Cap That** don't really mean, "Capitalize the first letter of *every* word." A more accurate interpretation would be, "Capitalize the first letter of every *important* word." NaturallySpeaking tends to omit initial capitals for prepositions, articles, and all those other little words whose correct names we (and probably you) forget. Even though NaturallySpeaking is probably being editorially correct according to the *Chicago Manual of Style* or some such authority, such selective capitalization may not be what you have in mind. If you want NaturallySpeaking to capitalize absolutely all the words, you have to say the command, **"Caps"** before each word.

# Getting Properly Spaced-Out

Getting mentally spaced out is pretty easy when you're dictating in NaturallySpeaking. You talk, the words hypnotically appear on the screen. You talk, the words appear. Pretty soon, you are spacey as all heck.

Getting your document spaced out is nearly as easy. NaturallySpeaking does some word, sentence, and paragraph spacing automatically. You can control that spacing, or add space of your own. Spacing — the next frontier.

## Controlling paragraph spacing

NaturallySpeaking has two commands that you can say to create the space that divides paragraphs: **New Paragraph** and **New Line.** What's the difference?

- ✔ **New Paragraph** puts a blank line between paragraphs. It is like pressing the Enter key twice: It inserts two paragraph marks (invisible) into your text. It also makes sure that the first word of the next sentence is capitalized.

- ✔ **New Line** does not put a blank line between paragraphs. It is like pressing the Enter key once. The next line isn't capitalized unless you ended the last line with a period, comma, question mark, or exclamation point.

Dragon's way of doing the **New Paragraph** command is somewhat unfortunate, because it results in two paragraph marks. If you are going to use any kind of paragraph formatting (such as bullets or, in Word, paragraph spacing) you may want to use the **New Line** command instead. Otherwise, in many instances you'll double the effect of the paragraph formatting: You'll get two bullets, or twice the spacing you intended, for instance.

What if you want to actually type out the words "new paragraph" instead of creating a new paragraph? Put a pause between the two words: "new" [pause] "paragraph."

# Controlling spaces and tabs

Dragon NaturallySpeaking does a pretty good job of automatic spacing. It usually deals with spaces around punctuation in the way that you want it to. Occasionally, however, you will want to add a few spaces or a Tab character in your text.

### Automatic spaces

NaturallySpeaking automatically puts spaces between your words. It looks at your punctuation to figure out the rest of the spacing. If, for some reason, you don't want spaces between your words, speak the command **"No-Space On,"** speak your words, and then say, **"No-Space Off."** Or if you anticipate that NaturallySpeaking is about to precede your next word with a space that you don't want, say, **"No-Space"** and then your next word, with no pauses between.

NaturallySpeaking automatically enters two spaces after a period. You can change that to one space. Choose Tools⇨Options in Dragon NaturallySpeaking. Click the Dictation tab in the dialog box that appears, and then click to clear the check mark labeled Two Spaces After Period. Then click OK.

NaturallySpeaking does different amounts of spacing after other punctuation marks. It is done in a way that usually works out. For instance, NaturallySpeaking puts one space after a comma, unless that comma is part of a number, such as 12,000 (whether spoken as "twelve thousand" or "twelve comma zero zero zero"). NaturallySpeaking also offers a so-called "numeric comma" that's never followed by a space.

### Adding spaces and tabs

The quickest way to add a space is to say the word **"Spacebar."** For a tab character, say, **"Tab Key."** Just as NaturallySpeaking does for **Comma** or **Period,** it accepts these words or phrases as a character that it should type.

Another way to do the same thing is to say, **"Press Spacebar"** or **"Press Tab."** In fact, you can tell NaturallySpeaking to press any key on the keyboard by saying the word **"Press"** and then the name of the key. So, to press the spacebar, you can say, **"Press Spacebar."** Or to press the F1 key, you say, **"Press F1."**

When should you use **Press Spacebar** or **Press Tab**? If, like us, you sometimes write about the keyboard, you may end up training NaturallySpeaking to type out the word *spacebar* or *tab* when you speak it, instead of inserting a space character. Sometimes, you may need to use the word *tab* in other contexts. (A bar tab comes to our minds.) In that event, the **Press** command will be the more reliable way to get a space or tab character.

# Entering Different Numbers and Dates

When people speak about numbers and dates, they use so many different forms that it's remarkable that a computer program can figure them out. And yet, NaturallySpeaking can do it. You can say, "eight o'clock" and Dragon NaturallySpeaking types 8:00. Or you can say, "forty-five dollars" and NaturallySpeaking types $45.

Most of the time, NaturallySpeaking types numbers and dates just the way you want them without your doing anything special. The most common correction that you'll have to do is tell NaturallySpeaking to use numerals rather than words for digits zero through nine. To do so, say, "numeral" before speaking the digit. Table 4-3 lists some of the ways you can say numbers and dates.

If a number, date, or time doesn't come out in the form that you want, you may be able to choose the form you want by saying, **"Correct That,"** and then choosing from the list in the Correct That dialog box. For instance, when we spoke the words "seven o'clock," NaturallySpeaking initially typed *seven o'clock*. But, by saying, **"Correct That"** and choosing *7:00,* NaturallySpeaking learned that we preferred the numerical form. See Chapter 5 for more about the **Correct That** command.

| Table 4-3 | Numbers and Dates |
|---|---|
| *To Get* | *Say* |
| .5 | **Point** (or **Period** or **Dot**) **five** |
| 0.45 | **Zero point four five** or **oh point four five** |
| One | **One** |
| 1 | **Numeral one** |
| 42 | **Forty two** or **four two** |
| 192 | **One ninety two, one nine two,** or **one hundred (and) ninety-two** |
| 4627 | **Four thousand six hundred (and) twenty seven, forty-six hundred twenty-seven,** or **four six two seven** |

| To Get | Say |
|--------|-----|
| 4,627 | **Four comma six hundred (and) twenty seven** or **four comma six two seven** |
| $152.07 | **One hundred fifty-two dollars and seven cents** or **dollar sign one five two point zero seven** |
| Aug. 28, 1945 | **August twenty-eight comma nineteen forty-five** |
| May 11, 2010 | **May eleven comma two thousand (and) ten** |
| 2:12 p.m. | **Two twelve pee em** |
| 7:00 | **Seven o'clock** |
| V | **Roman five** |
| XLV | **Roman forty roman five** |
| 842-8996 | **Eight four two hyphen eight nine nine six** |

# Making Quick Corrections

Although making corrections technically falls into the "editing" category, and we discuss editing in Chapter 5, you'll practically always want to make a few corrections the instant you detect an error. Errors fall into two categories:

 ✔ Errors that you make — which we call "bloopers"

 ✔ Errors that that NaturallySpeaking makes in interpreting your utterances

You deal with those errors in two different ways: *scratching* and *correcting*. Read on!

## Scratching your own bloopers

Making a verbal "blooper" is easy to do with speech input. You call across the office to someone or mutter a curse, and NaturallySpeaking dutifully types. If you make a mistake verbally, however, you can also undo it verbally. (On the other hand, if NaturallySpeaking makes the mistake, not you, you should "correct" NaturallySpeaking, not undo the mistake. See the next section for details.) The two verbal commands that are most useful for undoing your bloopers are these:

 ✔ **Scratch That**

 ✔ **Undo That**

The NaturallySpeaking command for undoing your bloopers is **Scratch That.** To use the command, you must not have done any editing with your mouse and keyboard since your last utterance. The command will undo up to ten consecutive utterances, up to the last break in your dictation (where you did some keyboard work).

(We know that we said that the word *that* usually only refers to what's currently in the Results box, but the **Scratch That** command is a bit more forgiving than the other commands. It remembers the last ten non-command contents of the Results box.)

Alternatively, you can say, **"Undo That"** (or **"Undo Last Action"**). That verbal command is the equivalent to the undo command (Edit➪Undo or Ctrl+Z), so it works not only on dictated text but on anything that you could normally undo. For example, if you had just applied bullet style formatting, you could undo that formatting. (In the NaturallySpeaking window, repeating an undo performs a "re-do." In some other applications, you can repeat the command to undo a series of actions.)

Of course, nothing says that you have to use NaturallySpeaking to undo your bloopers. You can use your keyboard or mouse (press Ctrl+Z, for example, press the Backspace key, or select the text and press the Delete key) just as you would if you had typed the mistake.

If physically pressing the Backspace or Delete key is not an option for you, here are two verbal commands you can use for the same purpose:

- ✔ **Backspace** (or **Press Backspace**)
- ✔ **Delete** (or **Press Delete**)

You can backspace or delete several characters by saying, **"Backspace 7"** to backspace seven characters, for instance, or **"Delete 8"** to delete eight characters to the right of the typing cursor. We find the **Backspace** command to be more reliable. (Because the word *delete* is more commonly written out in text than the word *backspace,* NaturallySpeaking sometimes errs on the side of writing out *delete* rather than doing the **Delete** command.)

## *Resuming dictation with an earlier word*

Getting your tang tungled up. . . um, tongue tangled up. . . is easy when dictating. Also, composing sentences on the fly isn't easy, and sometimes you want to change your mind about the phrase you just used.

You can solve both problems (mis-speaking and changing your mind) with the **Resume With <*word*>** command. For **<*word*>**, you substitute the word you want NaturallySpeaking to back up to. That word must be within the last 100 characters you have dictated, and you must have dictated continuously (typed or edited nothing by hand) since that word. (The **Resume With** command only works in the NaturallySpeaking window, not in other applications.)

For instance, following is dictation where someone makes an error in the first line, gives a correction using **Resume With**, and completes the phrase correctly:

1. Speaking the original error: "I keep on getting my tang tungled up. . ."

2. (Brief pause, as the user realizes the error)

3. Backing up: "**Resume With** *my*

4. Correcting from that point: "tongue tangled up"

The resulting text is: Getting my tongue tangled up. . . .

This command is particularly useful when you dictate into a portable recorder. See Chapter 8 for more about using commands when you dictate into a recorder.

# Correcting a NaturallySpeaking error

If NaturallySpeaking has misinterpreted something that you said, you can not only fix that mistake, but also help train NaturallySpeaking if you "correct" the error rather than just typing in the correct text, "scratching" the error, or undoing it. What's the difference?

In Dragon terms, to "correct" something means to tell NaturallySpeaking what you said rather than merely editing the text in the document. When you correct an error, you not only fix the resulting text, but you also educate NaturallySpeaking to your individual speech habits. Correction is one of the main ways in which NaturallySpeaking gets better over time.

We tell you all the different ways of correcting NaturallySpeaking in Chapter 5, but here are two easily remembered ways using the command **Correct That**:

- ✔ If NaturallySpeaking just made the error, say, **"Correct That"** or **"Spell That."** The Correction dialog box appears.

- ✔ If NaturallySpeaking made the error a while back, select the erroneous text and say, **"Correct That"** to get the Correction dialog box.

This second way of correction works only in the NaturallySpeaking window and in what are called "Select and Say" applications. In other applications, you select the text, and then you must speak replacement text. If the new text is also erroneous, say **"Correct That."** See Part III for more tips on using NaturallySpeaking with other applications.

When the Correction dialog box appears, it lists numbered alternatives. Verbally choose one of the alternatives by saying, **"Choose <number>."** For instance, say, **"Choose five."** This approach is our favorite. If none of the alternatives are correct, edit the erroneous text listed in the top box, and then click the OK button. If you prefer not to type, you may verbally spell out the replacement text.

The Correction dialog box has several other useful features, such as the Train and (in most Dragon products) Play Back buttons. For more information about the Correction dialog box, Chapter 5.

# Here Ye!/Hear Ye! Tackling Common Dictation Problems

Following are some common problems users experience with dictation. You can fix many of them by using the Correction dialog box, described earlier in this chapter, or by word or vocabulary training (see Part IV for the details of vocabulary and word training):

- ✔ **Sound-alike words:** When two words normally sound exactly alike, even human speakers make mistakes. The way that humans distinguish one word from the other is by the context. That's how NaturallySpeaking works, too. If it didn't work that way, you couldn't say a sentence like "It was too far for two people to go to purchase two tickets" and have any hope that NaturallySpeaking would get it correct. Vocabulary training and using the Correction dialog box will help this problem to some degree.

- ✔ **Commands as text:** Sometimes, if you say, **"Go To End of Line,"** NaturallySpeaking will type those words instead of performing the command. One solution that may work is to pause very slightly before speaking those words. Another solution is word training, as described in Part IV. A quick fix is to hold down the Ctrl key while speaking a command, which forces NaturallySpeaking to interpret your utterance as a command. Another reason you may experience this problem is if you're trying to use NaturallySpeaking commands that aren't available in the program you're using. For instance, you can't use commands like **"Select** *unicycle*" to select the word *unicycle,* unless you're working within a Select-and-Say application.

✔ **Text as commands:** Sometimes you want to actually type something like "go to end of line," but NaturallySpeaking interprets your utterance as a command, instead. Avoid pausing before and after that phrase, if you can. A quick fix is to hold down the Shift key while dictating, which forces NaturallySpeaking to interpret speech as text.

✔ **Extra words:** If NaturallySpeaking gives you small, extra words in your text, it may be interpreting microphone noises as words. Check to make sure the microphone isn't in front of your mouth, or else it will pick up tiny puffs of breath and interpret them as words. Guys, make sure the microphone cover isn't brushing against your beard or moustache.

✔ **Acronyms and other non-words:** A lot of contemporary English uses acronyms, abbreviations, initials, and other unconventional words. You can add these terms to NaturallySpeaking by using the Vocabulary Editor, described in Chapter 18. You can also add them by speaking them and then correcting the NaturallySpeaking interpretation with the Correction dialog box. The NaturallySpeaking vocabulary already includes many common abbreviations. If NaturallySpeaking thinks it hears initials, and those initials aren't otherwise in its vocabulary, it capitalizes them and puts a period after each letter.

✔ **E-mail addresses:** If you use a particular e-mail or Web address a lot, you can add it to your vocabulary like other "non-words," as the preceding bullet describes. Otherwise, you can say an address, such as person@company.com, much like you would in conversation. To make sure everything is lowercase, say, **"No Caps On,"** then say the e-mail address, and then say, **"No Caps Off."** For the address itself (person@company.com, for instance) you would say, **"person at company dot com."**

✔ **Web addresses:** Use the **No Caps On** and **No Caps Off** commands as suggested in the preceding bullet to prevent capitalization. Speak a Web address in the form, **"w w w dot company dot com."** For a full address (such as http://www.company.com) say, **"h t t p w w w dot company dot com,"** saying nothing about the colon or slashes. NaturallySpeaking adds the colon and slashes and recognizes the terms *com, gov, mil, net, org,* and *sys* just as you would normally say them. If you prefer, you can verbally spell out the letters in those terms.

If NaturallySpeaking insists on capitalizing the *www* portion of a Web address, correct the capitalization by using the Correction dialog box. (NaturallySpeaking has an obsession about capitalizing initials.) Or say, **"No Caps;"** then, without pausing, speak the address. To absolutely, completely suppress all capitals within the address, say, **"No Caps On No Caps w w w dot whatever dot com No Caps Off!"** If you dictate a lot of Web addresses, it might pay to add a special word to your vocabulary for *www* such as "triple-dub." See the discussion of vocabulary editing in Chapter 18.

# Chapter 5

# Selecting, Editing, and Correcting in the NaturallySpeaking Window

● ● ● ● ● ● ● ● ● ● ● ● ● ● ● ● ● ● ● ● ● ● ● ● ● ● ● ● ● ● ● ● ● ● ● ● ● ● ● ● ● ● ● ● ● ● ●

## In This Chapter

▶ Using voice commands to move the cursor

▶ Selecting text

▶ Inserting and deleting text

▶ Undoing actions after you change your mind

▶ Correcting NaturallySpeaking mistakes and training it to do better

● ● ● ● ● ● ● ● ● ● ● ● ● ● ● ● ● ● ● ● ● ● ● ● ● ● ● ● ● ● ● ● ● ● ● ● ● ● ● ● ● ● ● ● ● ● ●

*I*n naïve and optimistic moments, we sometimes imagine that we will write a document (like this chapter) by starting at the beginning and continuing flawlessly to the end. Alas, we have heard tales of such miracles, but never witnessed one ourselves. Whether you write your documents by hand, use a keyboard to enter them into a computer, or dictate them to a pet dragon, from time to time you're probably going to want to insert new text into the middle of the document, delete some text, rearrange a few paragraphs, and rewrite a sentence here and there.

If you like, you can continue using the mouse and keyboard to do this editing, just as if you had never heard of NaturallySpeaking. In fact, dictating your first drafts and editing by keyboard is not a bad way to get your feet wet with NaturallySpeaking. (Just make sure to keep your wet feet away from any plugged-in hardware.) And you can add the editing voice commands to your repertoire as you get more experienced.

Or you can plunge right in and do all your editing by voice, just as if you were dictating your changes to a secretary. Unlike the secretary, your dragon works nights and holidays without complaining and never rolls its eyes when you rewrite a sentence for the tenth time. (It makes a lousy cup of coffee, though.)

In addition to making changes that are a normal part of your creative process, you also want to correct the errors that get into your documents whenever NaturallySpeaking thinks that you said something different than what you intended to say. Occasional mistakes of this sort (known as *recognition errors*) are inevitable, just as occasional typographical errors always manage to sneak into typed documents. (The NaturallySpeaking mistakes tend to be funnier than typos, because they are correct English words that sometimes give your sentences entirely new and unintended meanings. For example, "Quoth the raven, 'Never bore'.")

Although you can just write (or dictate) over these mistakes, NaturallySpeaking has a special correction procedure that teaches it not to make similar mistakes in the future. Just as you teach children to perfect their language skills by correcting their errors, you teach your dragon to understand you better by using the correction procedure.

# Moving Around in a Document

When you're in a cab, you can tell the driver where to go in three ways (excluding the ever-popular "Follow that car").

✔ You can give directions, as in "Turn left and go three blocks."

✔ You can specify a location without saying what's there, as in "Go to Fourth and Madison."

✔ You can name a destination without saying where it is and count on the driver to find it, as in "Take me to the airport."

The same basic ideas work when you tell NaturallySpeaking where to move the cursor in its document window. You have three options:

✔ You can give a directional command like **"Move Up Five Lines."**

✔ You can specify a location in the document by saying, **"Go to End of Paragraph."**

✔ You can say some text and count on NaturallySpeaking to find it by saying, **"Insert After *how are things back home*."**

These commands are summarized in Table 5-1, as well as in the "What Can I Say?" topic of NaturallySpeaking Help. To display this topic, speak the command **"What Can I Say."** The following sections of this chapter provide more detailed instructions for using these commands and their various synonyms.

To see an example of these commands in action, look at the "Moving the Cursor" topic in the multimedia Quick Tour. Select Help➪Quick Tour from the NaturallySpeaking menu, click the Menu button in the Quick Tour window, and click on the title of the topic.

You don't have to use the voice commands if you'd rather not. The mouse and the arrow keys on the keyboard can also move the cursor.

| Table 5-1 | Commands for Moving Around in a Document | | |
|---|---|---|---|
| *First Word* | *Second Word* | *Third Word* | *Fourth Word* |
| Go To | Top, Bottom | | |
| Go To | Top, Bottom | of | Selection, Line, Paragraph |
| Move | Up, Down, Left, Right | 1 – 20 | |
| Move | Back, Forward | 1 – 20 | Words, Paragraphs |
| Insert* | Before, After | That <*text*> | |

## Giving the cursor directions and distances

You can use the **Move** command to move the cursor in different directions: forward or backward a certain number of characters, words, lines, or paragraphs. The short form of the **Move** command uses just three words (as in **Move Down Three**). You can also add a word to specify units (as in **Move Back Two Paragraphs**).

The short, three-word version of the **Move** command imitates the cursor keys on the keyboard. The three words are **Move**, a direction (**Up, Down, Left,** or **Right**), and finally a number from 1 to 20. You don't specify any units. So, for example,

 ✔ **Move Down 12** gives you the same result as if you press the down-arrow key 12 times. In other words, the cursor goes down 12 lines.

 ✔ **Move Right 2** moves the cursor two characters to the right, the same result you get from pressing the right-arrow key twice.

When you want to move a certain number of words or paragraphs, just add **Words** or **Paragraphs** to the command. Use the four-word **Move** command. First you say **Move;** then say a direction (**Back** or **Forward**); then say a number (**1 – 20**); and finally, say a unit (**Words** or **Paragraphs**). For example,

 ✔ **Move Back Six Words**
 ✔ **Move Forward Two Paragraphs**

You can also use the units **Characters** or **Lines** instead of **Words** or **Paragraphs.** When the units are **Words** or **Characters,** you can use **Left/Right** instead of **Back/Forward.** When the units are **Lines** or **Paragraphs,** you can use **Up/Down** instead of **Back/Forward.** For example,

- **Move Left Three Characters** means the same as **Move Back Three Characters** or **Move Left Three.**
- **Move Down Eight Paragraphs** gives the same result as **Move Forward Eight Paragraphs.**

Finally, the word "a" can be used as a synonym for the number 1. **Move Back a Word** is the same as **Move Back One Word.**

If you just want to scroll the text up or down, and you don't care about moving the cursor, say "**Press Page Up**" or "**Press Page Down.**"

## *Going to the head of the line (or paragraph, or . . .)*

Like telling a cab driver to go to the end of a street, you can tell NaturallySpeaking to go the beginning or end of various chunks of a document: the beginning or end of the document, current paragraph, current line, or whatever block of text is selected. (The current line or paragraph is the line or paragraph where the cursor is now.)

The simplest destination commands are

- **Go To Bottom,** which moves the cursor to the end of the document
- **Go To Top,** which moves the cursor to the beginning of the document
- **Go To Top** (or **Bottom**) **of Paragraph** (or **Line** or **Selection**)

NaturallySpeaking understands a number of synonyms for these commands. In particular, you can use **Move To** instead of **Go To** as long as you specify the chunk of text you're moving within. Begin with **Move To** and then use **Start, Beginning,** or **End,** and then specify a **Line, Paragraph, Selection,** or **Document.**

Sometimes NaturallySpeaking understands one form of a command more consistently than another. For example, when I say, "**Go To,**" it often gets interpreted as "due to," "do to," or "good." I'm sure I could eventually train NaturallySpeaking to recognize my (apparently) peculiar pronunciation of "**Go To,**" but I find it easier just to say, "**Move To**" instead.

## *Specifying a destination by quoting text*

Sometimes you want to put the cursor right smack in the middle of a block of text on your screen, not near the beginning or end of anything. And you'd rather not count lines or words or characters. You'd like to tell NaturallySpeaking to put the cursor after this phrase or before that one.

You want the **Insert** command. Suppose you dictated "She sells seashells by the sea shore," and you want to put the cursor between "sells" and "seashells." You can say,

- ✔ **"Insert After *sells*"** or
- ✔ **"Insert Before *seashells*"**

Each of these commands accomplishes the same result.

NaturallySpeaking only searches the text that's currently visible. If "She sells seashells" has scrolled off the screen, NaturallySpeaking reports that it is unable to find the text, and the cursor stays where it was when the command was issued.

If you suspect that the words "sells" or "seashells" appear in several locations, you can use more words to make sure that you specify the right occurrence. For example, **Insert After *She sells*** or **Insert Before *seashells by the sea shore*** each move the cursor between "sells" and "seashells."

If text is already selected, you can move the cursor to the beginning or the end of the selected text by using the commands **Insert Before That** or **Insert After That.** These commands are equivalent to **Go To Beginning of Selection** and **Go To End of Selection,** respectively.

# *Editing by Voice*

Editing a document involves several different activities: inserting new text, deleting text, replacing text by dictating over it, and rearranging the document by cutting text from one place and pasting it into another. All these topics are covered in this section. We discuss reformatting text in Chapter 6.

You can use these techniques to fix the NaturallySpeaking mistakes as well as your own. But in the long run, you'll be happier with your dragon's performance if you teach it to do better by using the Correction commands. See "Spare the Correction, Spoil the Dragon: Fixing NaturallySpeaking's Mistakes" later in this chapter.

Because NaturallySpeaking can only transcribe the words in its vocabulary, both your errors and its own are cleverly disguised as actual English words. They're even correctly spelled. In these circumstances, proofreading becomes an art. Be sure to check out the proofreading tricks in Chapter 7.

## Selecting text

You can select text in three different ways.

- ✔ Select text near the cursor by using commands like **Select Next Two Characters.**
- ✔ Select text by saying it, as in "**Select** *call me Ishmael.*"
- ✔ Select a large block of text by saying the beginning and the end, as in "**Select** *once upon a time* **through** *lived happily ever after."*

Table 5-2 summarizes these commands. To see these commands in action, look at the "Selecting Text" and "Revising Text" topics in the Quick Tour. Select Help⇨Quick Tour from the NaturallySpeaking menu and then click the Menu button in the Quick Tour window and click on the title of the topic.

| Table 5-2 | Commands for Selecting Text | | |
|---|---|---|---|
| *First Word* | *Second Word* | *Third Word* | *Fourth Word* |
| **Select** | **Next Previous** | **1 – 20** | **Characters, Words, Paragraphs** |
| **Select** | **<text>** | | |
| **Select** | **Again** | | |
| **Select** | **<text>** | **Through** | **<text>** |

### Selecting text near the cursor

To select text immediately before or after the current location of the cursor, use the **Select** command in a four-word sentence of this form: **Select,** followed by a direction (**Next** or **Previous**), followed by a number (**1 – 20**), followed by a unit (**Characters, Words,** or **Paragraphs**). For example,

- ✔ **Select Next Seven Words**
- ✔ **Select Previous Three Paragraphs**

If you want to select only one character, word, or paragraph, leave the number out of the sentence, as in **Select Next Character** or **Select Previous Word.**

You can use **Back** or **Last** as synonyms for **Previous,** and **Forward** as a synonym for **Next.**

### Selecting text by saying it

If text is visible on your screen, you can select it by saying, **"Select"** and then saying the text you want to select. For example, suppose Shakespeare is editing the file Hamlet.doc, and the phrase "To be or not to be" is visible. He can select the phrase by saying, **"Select *to be or not to be."***

Sometimes, the phrase you select occurs several times in the current window. Which occurrence gets selected? NaturallySpeaking begins searching at the insertion point (the cursor) and goes backward until it reaches the top of the visible window. Then it starts over at the bottom of the visible window.

If the occurrence NaturallySpeaking selects isn't the one you want to select, just say, **"Select Again"** to select the previous occurrence of the phrase. For example, if Shakespeare said, **"Select *to be,"*** NaturallySpeaking would select the "to be" at the end of "to be or not to be." If he then said, **"Select Again,"** the "to be" at the beginning of the sentence would be selected.

You can choose to have **Select** search the window in the opposite direction: starting at the insertion point and moving forward until it reaches the bottom of the window and then starting over at the top. To do this:

1. **Choose <u>T</u>ools⇨<u>O</u>ptions.**

   The Options dialog box opens.

2. **Click the Miscellaneous tab.**

3. **Uncheck the Se<u>l</u>ect Searches Backwards checkbox.**

To undo this action, so that Select searches backwards again, repeat the process above, but check the box in Step 3.

You can avoid the hassle of repeating **"Select Again"** many times by selecting a larger block of text, which is more likely to be unique. For example, suppose you want to change the phrase "make a choice" to "make your choice." You could try to select "a" and dictate "your" over it, but because you probably use the word "a" many times in your document, **"Select *a"*** is not very likely to get the right "a" on the first try. Try **"Select *make a choice"*** instead, and then dictate "make your choice" over it.

### Selecting more text than you want to say

When you want to select a large block of text, you don't want to have to repeat all of it just to tell NaturallySpeaking where it is. NaturallySpeaking provides a special command for this purpose: **Select. . .Through.** Pick a word or two at the beginning of the selection and a word or two at the end, and then tell

NaturallySpeaking to select everything in between by saying, **"Select <*begin-ning text*> Through <*end text*>."** For example, if your NaturallySpeaking window contains the Pledge of Allegiance, you can select it all by saying, **"Select** *I pledge allegiance* **Through** *justice for all."*

## Deleting text

The simplest way to delete text is to use the **Scratch That** command to delete recently dictated text, as we explain in the previous chapter. You can use **Scratch That** up to ten consecutive times. Another way to delete recently dic-tated text is the **Resume With** command, also covered in the previous chapter.

To delete text that hasn't been recently dictated, use the **Delete** command. If you have learned how to use the **Select** command, you know how to use the **Delete** command. The syntax is exactly the same with one exception: You can't delete text by saying it. You can get the same result, however, if you select the text by saying it (see "Selecting text by saying it" earlier in this chapter) and then say, **"Delete That."** The syntax of **Delete** is summarized in Table 5-3.

 You can see these commands do their stuff by viewing the "Deleting Text" part of the multimedia Quick Tour. Select Help➪Quick Tour from the NaturallySpeaking menu and then click the Menu button in the Quick Tour window and click on the title of the topic.

| Table 5-3 | How to Make a Deleterious Statement | | |
|---|---|---|---|
| *First Word* | *Second Word* | *Third Word* | *Fourth Word* |
| **Delete** | **That** | | |
| **Delete** | **Next, Previous** | **Character, Word, Paragraph** | |
| **Delete** | **Next, Previous** | **1 – 20** | **Characters, Words, Paragraphs** |
| **Backspace** | | | |
| **Backspace** | **1 – 20** | | |

To delete text immediately before or after the current location of the cursor, begin with **Delete** and then give a direction (**Next** or **Previous**), a number (**1 – 20**), and finally a unit (**Characters, Words,** or **Paragraphs**). For example,

> ✔ **Delete Next Seven Words** or
> ✔ **Delete Previous Three Paragraphs**

If you want to delete only one character, word, or paragraph, you can leave the number out of the sentence, as in the following:

> ✔ **Delete Next Character** or
> ✔ **Delete Previous Word**

You can use **Back** or **Last** as synonyms for **Previous**, and **Forward** as a synonym for **Next**.

Saying **"Backspace"** gives the same result as pressing the Backspace key on the keyboard: The character immediately behind the cursor is deleted. To backspace up to 20 characters, say, **"Backspace"** followed by a number between 1 and 20. **Backspace** is a simpler version of the **Delete Previous Character** command. For example, **Backspace Five** produces the same results as **Delete Previous Five Characters.**

## Sharp tongues: Cutting and pasting by voice

To cut or copy text from a document, select it (using the techniques from the "Selecting text" section earlier in this chapter) and then say either **"Cut That"** or **"Copy That."** To copy the entire document (which is useful if you like to compose in a NaturallySpeaking window and then paste the results into an application), say, **"Copy All to Clipboard."**

If something is on the clipboard, you can paste it into your document by saying **"Paste That."**

## Just Undo it

Sometimes the result of editing or dictating something isn't what you pictured. All is not lost; you can still Undo it. Just say, **"Undo That"** or **"Undo Last Action."** These two commands are equivalent.

In the NaturallySpeaking window, **Undo That** is like flipping a switch: If you say it twice, you wind up back where you started. In other words, the second **Undo That** undoes the first **Undo That**. When you use NaturallySpeaking with other applications (see Part III), what you get varies from one application to another. In some applications, saying **Undo That** twice undoes the application's last two actions.

What **Undo That** actually does is type a Ctrl+Z. Different applications handle a Ctrl+Z in different ways, which is why they respond to **Undo That** differently.

If you realize you've made a mistake the instant that the words leave your mouth, you can stop NaturallySpeaking before it executes the command: Just click the red dot in the Results box. (Real life needs a Results box with a red dot in it.) This action also turns off the microphone.

# Spare the Correction, Spoil the Dragon: Fixing NaturallySpeaking's Mistakes

If it's true that "To err is human," then computers are getting more human all the time. NaturallySpeaking sometimes makes hilarious errors, especially if it's still relatively untrained. Because NaturallySpeaking is incapable of a simple typo or misspelling, all of its mistakes are correct English words — just not the words you said or meant to say. Occasionally, you may see something on your screen that resembles a phrase you might hear on the old TV program *Kids Say the Darndest Things.* Our favorite mistake happened during a test in which we dictated Lincoln's Gettysburg Address (see Chapter 27) and found the line "government over the people, buying the people." The NaturallySpeaking manual and Help files refer to these as *recognition errors.*

But cute as some mistakes might be, you don't want to create documents that amuse your readers with unintentional errors. You want those mistakes fixed, preferably in a way that keeps them from happening again the next time you dictate. That's what NaturallySpeaking's **Correct That** and related correction commands are for.

Check out the "Correcting Recognition Errors" topic of the multimedia Quick Tour. Select Help➪Quick Tour from the NaturallySpeaking menu and then click the Menu button in the Quick Tour window and click on the topic.

If you don't care about correcting NaturallySpeaking, and all you want to do is get an error out of the document you're working on, just select the offending text and dictate something else over it. Or, if you catch the error immediately, you can get rid of it by saying **"Scratch That"** or **"Undo That"**, as described in "Editing By Voice" earlier in this chapter. However, just fixing the mistake in the current document is like fixing your daughter's homework without explaining what she did wrong: She gets a better grade, but she doesn't learn from the experience.

NaturallySpeaking learns nothing when you just delete some text or dictate over it. In order for your dragon to mend its ways, you need to tell it firmly that it has made a mistake and how to fix it.

If you have made any corrections during a session, NaturallySpeaking reminds you to save your speech files before exiting. Be sure to choose Yes. Otherwise, all of the lessons NaturallySpeaking learned from these corrections are lost.

## Correcting a NaturallySpeaking recognition error

Depending on how quickly you catch the error, you can correct it in one of the following two ways:

- ✔ If you catch the error as soon as NaturallySpeaking makes it (so that the misinterpretation is still in the tiny, yellowish Results box in one corner of your screen), say, **"Correct That"** or **"Spell That."** See "Casting a spell" later in this chapter for more about **Spell That.**

- ✔ If you don't catch the error immediately, say, **"Correct** *<incorrect text>***."** (You can also select the erroneous text verbally or with your voice and then say, **"Correct That."** )

Table 5-4 summarizes these ways of making a correction. If you would rather not use voice commands at all, select the text and then press the - key on the numeric keypad of your keyboard or click the Correct button (the one with the red lasso) on the NaturallySpeaking toolbar. (You can substitute a different key for the - key; see the discussion of NaturallySpeaking options in Chapter 3.)

| Table 5-4 | Making Your Corrections | | |
|---|---|---|---|
| *First Word* | *Second Word* | *Third Word* | *Fourth Word* |
| Correct | That | | |
| Spell | That | | |
| Correct | *<text>* | | |
| Correct | *<text>* | Through | *<text>* |

No matter how you do it, the Correction dialog box appears, as shown in Figure 5-1.

The dictation error that Figure 5-1 illustrates occurred when I said, "W. S. Gilbert had a flair for puns." What NaturallySpeaking thought I said was, "W. S. Gilbert had a flair for funds." Although that statement may be true, it wasn't what I had intended. (The wonderful plausibility of the

NaturallySpeaking mistakes is what sometimes makes them hard to detect.) When I said **"Correct That,"** the Correction dialog box shown in Figure 5-1 appeared. (If you have NaturallySpeaking Essentials or Standard editions, your Correction box lacks a PlayBack button, but otherwise looks the same.)

List of alternatives

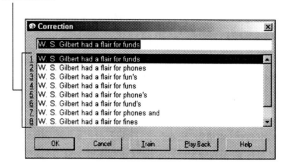

**Figure 5-1:**
Naturally-
Speaking
generates
a list of
alternatives.

When you correct a recognition error, the top line of the Corrections contains the word or phrase being corrected. ("W. S. Gilbert had a flair for funds.") If NaturallySpeaking strongly considered any alternative interpretations of what you said, they are listed in the box below, up to a maximum of ten. Figure 5-1 shows NaturallySpeaking got most of the phrase right, but weighed *funds* against a wide variety of competitors.

If the correct phrase is listed in the Correction dialog box, you need only tell NaturallySpeaking which number it is. If I had said "W. S. Gilbert had a flair for phones," then I could make the correction in Figure 5-1 by saying **"Choose 2."** You can also click the correct version with the mouse or use the **Move Up/Down** voice commands to go up or down the list of choices and then use the Enter key or the OK button to indicate that the currently selected option is correct. However you indicate your choice, the Correction dialog box closes and the correction is made in the text.

If none of the options given by the Correction dialog box is right, but one of them is close, say, **"Select <*number>*"** instead of **"Choose <*number>*".** The selection option moves to the top line, where you can edit it until it is correct.

Sometimes, however, none of the options offered is correct — as is the case in Figure 5-1. At such a point, you need to give NaturallySpeaking a hint. Either start typing the correct version into the top line of the Correction dialog box or start spelling the correct version out loud. (See "Casting a spell" later in this chapter.) With each new letter, more alternatives appear in the box as NaturallySpeaking continues trying to guess what the correct version is. If the correct version appears, you can stop typing or spelling and choose it by number. The Correction dialog box closes and the correction is made in the text.

Here are a few additional reminders and tips for using the Correction dialog box:

✔ Don't use the Correction dialog box to fix *your* errors — use it only to correct the NaturallySpeaking errors. In other words, don't type in text that you didn't actually speak, or you will confuse NaturallySpeaking. Eventually, its accuracy will suffer if you keep this up.

✔ Don't attempt to dictate replacement text in the Correction dialog box. NaturallySpeaking tries to interpret your utterances as letters!

✔ If you're correcting a large block of text, you can say, **"Correct *<beginning of incorrect text>* Through *<end of incorrect text>*."** For example, we could have evoked Figure 5-1 by saying, **"Correct *W* Through *funds*."**

## Casting a spell

One way to correct a simple mistake is to select the mistaken word and spell the correct one. This technique has the advantage of shortening your interaction with the Correction box, though it does get tedious if you're correcting a word like "antidisestablishmentarianism."

Suppose you dictated "New York" and NaturallySpeaking interpreted it as "Newark." You could correct it as follows:

1. **Find the mistaken word "Newark" in the active window.**

2. **Say, "Select Newark."**

   If NaturallySpeaking hears you correctly this time, the mistaken word is selected. If "Newark" occurs several times in the active window, you may need to say, **"Select Again"** to select the occurrence that you want to correct. See "Selecting text by name" earlier in this chapter.

3. **Say the correction: "New York."**

4. **Say, "Spell That Cap N-e-w space bar Cap Y-o-r-k." Or you can use the International Communications Alphabet by saying, "Spell That Cap November Echo Whiskey space bar Cap Yankee Oscar Romeo Kilo."**

   The Correction dialog box appears with the correctly spelled "New York" selected.

5. **Say "Click OK" or "Press Enter." Or you can click the OK button or press the Enter key.**

   NaturallySpeaking replaces the incorrect "Newark" in the text by the correct "New York." Also, NaturallySpeaking makes an invisible little note to remind itself not to be so quick to hear "Newark" instead of "New York." (See the sidebar "Bravo! Charlie tangos with Juliet in November" for more about the International Communications Alphabet.)

If you use a lot of proper nouns (names of people, places, and things), learning the ICA might be worthwhile. You can use the ICA to spell a word even during dictation — not just in the Correction dialog box.

## Recurring errors

The correction process is supposed to prevent the same errors from happening in the future, but sometimes NaturallySpeaking gets stubborn and keeps making some particular error over and over again. In these cases you need something stronger than just correction; you need Word Training.

Begin by identifying the error and typing or dictating the correct version into the Correction dialog box. But instead of clicking the OK button, click Train instead. This opens the Word Training dialog box, where you record both the correct word and the incorrect one that NaturallySpeaking keeps using instead. See Chapter 18 for detailed instructions.

## Playing back an error

The higher-level editions of NaturallySpeaking include a Play Back feature that you can use to listen to your dictation. In particular, when you are correcting a mistake, you can click the Play Back button in the Correction dialog box to hear what you said. You may discover that you aren't dealing with a recognition error at all and that you didn't say what you think you said. See Chapter 7 for more about the playback feature.

---

## Bravo! Charlie tangos with Juliet in November

The problem with dictating letters is that they all sound alike. If you've ever had to spell your name to someone over the telephone, you know how easily d's become t's or m's turn into n's.

This is an old problem, so it's not surprising that someone solved it a long time ago by creating the International Communications Alphabet. In the ICA, the names of the letters all sound different,

so you can spell aloud with confidence — if you know the ICA.

You can find the ICA names of the letters listed in NaturallySpeaking Help. Select Help➪ Help Topics to display Help Topics and then go to the Index tab and look up "Spelling, characters for."

---

# Chapter 6

# Fonts, Alignment, and All That: Formatting Your Document

* * * * * * * * * * * * * * * * * * * * * * * * * * * * * * * * * * * * * * * *

## In This Chapter

▶ Using left and right alignment

▶ Centering a paragraph

▶ Creating numbered or bulleted lists

▶ Using italic, bold, and underlined text

▶ Changing font size and style

* * * * * * * * * * * * * * * * * * * * * * * * * * * * * * * * * * * * * * * *

*T*ext that is all the same font, size, and style can be pretty boring. Formatting commands put some *zing* into your documents and make them *exciting*. Your favorite word processor no doubt provides menus and button bars full of formatting commands and maybe some hot keys on the keyboard as well. You can, of course, continue to use them if you like. But NaturallySpeaking lets you produce many of the same results with voice commands.

In this chapter, we're talking about voice commands especially for formatting, like **Bold That**. As Chapter 11 discusses, you can also choose formatting commands from the menu bar by using general-purpose voice commands, but those take longer. Save those for other applications. In the NaturallySpeaking window (and specific other applications), you can get the job done quickly with formatting commands.

NaturallySpeaking provides several different commands for most actions. These commands fall into two basic types. On the one hand, you can use short, very specific commands for most actions, such as **Underline That** for underlining text or **Center That** for centering a paragraph. Table 6-1 shows the short formatting commands.

## Formatting in other applications besides NaturallySpeaking

The NaturallySpeaking formatting commands in this chapter work only with the Naturally-Speaking word processor and specific other applications: the NaturalWord applications (Word and WordPerfect) and the Select-and -Say applications (WordPad, Notepad, Microsoft Chat 2.1, Microsoft Chat 2.5, Microsoft Outlook, and GoldMine). In other word processors and e-mail programs, the formatting commands are hit-and-miss; they usually don't work, but sometimes you get lucky.

In general, if you want to create or edit a formatted document in some application other than the ones we just listed, you have two choices:

✔ Work in the NaturallySpeaking window and then paste the result into the other application.

✔ Work in the application's own window and get all your formatting commands from the menus. (See Chapter 11.)

Choosing formatting commands from the menus means you can use voice control for *anything* the application can do, not just formatting. For example, if you want to make some selected text bold in Claris Works, you couldn't use the NaturallySpeaking **Bold That** command, but you could access the Bold command on Claris' own Style menu by saying, **"Click Style, Bold."** Specially-supported word processors such as Word and WordPerfect have more formatting features than NaturallySpeaking gives you direct commands for. In these cases, you can access the word processor's own menus by voice as well as by mouse or keyboard. For example, NaturallySpeaking provides no **Footnote That** command for inserting footnotes into Word documents, but you can use the Footnote command on Word's Insert menu by saying, **"Click Insert, Footnote."**

| Table 6-1 | The Short Formatting Commands | |
|---|---|---|
| *To Do This* | *Example* | *Say This* |
| Make selected text bold | **Like This** | **"Bold That"** |
| Italicize selected text | *Like This* | **"Italicize That"** |
| Underline selected text | <u>Like This</u> | **"Underline That"** |
| Make selected text normal | Like This | **"Restore That"** |
| Center current paragraph | Like This | **"Center That"** |
| Right-align current paragraph | Like This | **"Right-Align That"** |
| Left-align current paragraph | Like This | **"Left-Align That"** |

---

## Commands that undo themselves

The commands **Bold That, Underline That, Italicize That,** and **Format That Bullet Style** all share a perverse property: They undo themselves. For example, if you select some regular text and say, **"Bold That,"** the text becomes bold. But if you select some bold text and say, **"Bold That,"** it becomes regular. If you say, **"Bold That"** twice, you wind up back where you started.

What's up with that? In real life, voice commands almost never undo themselves. If my wife says, "Take out the trash" and I've already taken out the trash, I don't go outside and bring the trash back in. What's special about these four voice commands that they should undo themselves?

These commands have something in common: In most word processors, you perform these actions by clicking buttons on a toolbar. The Bold, Italic, Underline, and Bullet buttons on a word processor's toolbar typically work like the power button on a stereo: You push it once to turn the power on, and you push it again to turn the power off.

So the designers at Dragon had a decision to make: Should bold, italic, underline, and bullet commands work like typical voice commands, or should they work like the toolbar buttons that people are used to using? They decided to model the commands after the buttons, and that's why they undo themselves.

---

On the other hand, you can use the slightly longer but more general commands **Format** and **Set** to do almost anything if you know the right syntax. For example, **Format That Bold** and **Format That Centered** bolds or centers text, whereas **Format That Courier 18** changes the font to 18-point Courier. Whether you find it easier to remember a lot of short commands or a general family of longer commands that follow predictable patterns is largely a matter of taste.

# Left, Right, and Center: Getting into Alignment

To change the alignment of a paragraph, move the cursor into the paragraph and use one of the following commands:

- ✔ **Center That**
- ✔ **Left-Align That**
- ✔ **Right-Align That**

(If you're currently dictating a paragraph, you don't have to move the cursor; it's already in the right paragraph. Just speak the command.)

To change the alignment of up to 20 consecutive paragraphs:

1. **Move the cursor to the beginning of the first paragraph.**

2. **Say, "Select Next** *<number>* **Paragraphs," where** *<number>* **is the number of paragraphs you want to realign. For example:** "Select Next Seven Paragraphs."

3. **Say, "Center That," "Left-Align That,"** or "Right-Align That."

To change the alignment of the entire document:

1. **Say,** "Select Document."

2. **Say, "Center That," "Left-Align That,"** or "Right-Align That."

You can use the **Format** command to substitute for any of the alignment commands.

- **Format That Centered** gives the same result as **Center That.**
- **Format That Left Aligned** gives the same result as **Left-Align That.**
- **Format That Right Aligned** gives the same result as **Right-Align That.**

# Using Bullets and Numbered Lists

Clear, concise writing requires more than just simple paragraphs. For example, ...*For Dummies* books just couldn't exist without

- Bullets
- Numbered lists

Or perhaps I should say that these books couldn't get by without

1. Numbered lists

2. Bullets

How can you create bulleted and numbered lists with voice commands? In NaturalWord and Select-and-Say applications, dictate the text that you want a bullet next to and then say, **"Format That Bullet Style."** To get a second bullet, say, **"New Line."**

In this chapter, we are giving commands for dictating in the NaturallySpeaking window. (Although the same commands also work in Select-and-Say applications, including NaturalWord in Word or WordPerfect.) This command doesn't work in all applications. If your document is in an application that's not Select and Say, make the bulleted list in the NaturallySpeaking word processing window and paste it into your document.

The **New Line** command (which you use for doing bullets instead of New Paragraph) doesn't capitalize the first word of the new line unless the previous line ended with a period. You have to speak the **Cap** command at the start of the next bullet.

Like **Bold That** and **Italicize That,** the **Format That Bullet Style** command undoes itself. In other words, you can turn a bulleted paragraph back into regular text by moving the cursor to that paragraph and saying, **"Format That Bullet Style."** You may not think this makes sense — heck, I don't think it makes sense either — but that's the way it works. (See the "Commands that undo themselves" sidebar earlier in this chapter.) Use this technique to end the bulleted list: After the last bulleted paragraph is done, say, **"New Paragraph"** and then, **"Format That Bullet Style."** The new paragraph is now in regular style.

The NaturallySpeaking window doesn't provide a means for generating numbered lists automatically. You have to construct them yourself. For example, say, **"New Line. One period. Cap *this is the first entry on my numbered list.* Period. New Line. Two period. Cap *this is the second entry.* Period."** The result is

1. This is the first entry on my numbered list.

2. This is the second entry.

Microsoft Word users, however, do have a special command for numbered lists, **Format That Numbered**. See Chapter 12 for more about such "natural language commands."

# Changing Font

NaturallySpeaking provides commands like **Bold That** to change the style of a font. You can use the **Set** or **Format** commands to change the size or style of a font, to choose a new font family, or to change everything at the same time.

## What does "That" mean now?

When you use capitalization, spacing, and hyphenation commands (what Dragon refers to as *dictation commands*) such as **Cap That,** the word "that" refers to what you just spoke — text that's still in the Results box. When you use *formatting commands,* however, the word "that" no longer refers to the text in the Results box. It refers only to whatever you have selected! Or if you haven't selected anything, the command affects the current formatting: the format for whatever you dictate next.

So, for instance, if you dictate "I am the master of my fate" and then (not stopping to select anything) say, **"Bold That,"** nothing happens to the text you dictated. However, when you continue,

"and captain of my soul," the text comes out bold. The command simply turned on bold style. The result looks like this:

I am the master of my fate **and captain of my soul.**

The difference in the meaning of "that" sounds like a complicated distinction to remember, but the truth is actually simple. When you say **Bold That, Italicize That, Underline That,** or any of the paragraph alignment commands, NaturallySpeaking is pressing the "command key" (say, Ctrl+B for Bold) assigned to that format.

## *Changing your style: Bold, italic, and underlined text*

The simplest way to create bold, italic, or underlined text is to select the text and then say, **"Bold That," "Italicize That,"** or **"Underline That."**

These three commands are equivalent to clicking the corresponding buttons (**B**, *I*, or U̲) on the toolbar. A perverse effect of making them work like the buttons is that these commands undo themselves. For example, if you select some underlined text and say **"Underline That,"** the underlining is removed. See the "Commands that undo themselves" sidebar earlier in this chapter.

To dictate bold, italic, or underlined text:

1. **Move the cursor to the place in the document where you want the text to be.**

2. **Say, "Bold That," "Italicize That," or "Underline That," depending on what kind of text you want to produce.**

3. **Dictate your text.**

When text is already bold, italic, underlined, or some combination of all three, you can change it back to plain Roman text by selecting it and saying, **"Restore That."**

The **Format** and **Set** commands can substitute for any these commands. For example, the following three commands have the same effect:

- ✔ **Bold That**
- ✔ **Format That Bold**
- ✔ **Set Font Bold**

You can also use **Format That** or **Set Font** with **Italics, Underline,** or **Regular.** For example,

- ✔ **Set Font Regular** and **Format That Regular** are equivalent to **Restore That.**
- ✔ **Set Font Bold** and **Format That Bold** are equivalent to **Bold That.**

## Changing font size

To change the size of a font, you must know the point size that you want. If, for example, you want to change some text to 18 point, you can select it and say,

- ✔ **"Set Size 18"** or
- ✔ **"Format That Size 18"**

Not all point sizes exist for all font families. If you request a nonexistent point size, your command is ignored.

If you want to start dictating in a new font size, move the cursor to the place where you want to begin dictating and give a **Set Size** or **Format That Size** command. For example,

- ✔ **Set Size 10** or
- ✔ **Format That Size 24**

When you begin to dictate, the text appears in the size type that you requested, if that size exists in the current font family.

## Changing font family

NaturallySpeaking recognizes the names of the following font families: Arial, Courier, Courier New, and Times. ("Times" is interpreted as Times New Roman.) You can use the **Set** or **Format** commands to change from one of these font families to another. For example,

- ✔ **Set Font Times**
- ✔ **Format That Times**

both change the font to Times New Roman. Any text that was selected when this command was issued has its font changed to Times New Roman. If no text was selected, any new text dictated at the insertion point will be in Times New Roman font.

If you want to use a font whose name NaturallySpeaking doesn't recognize, you must choose it from the menu, either by voice or using the mouse. See Chapter 11 for a discussion of controlling the menus by voice.

## Changing everything at once

The **Format** and **Set** commands demonstrate their full power when you want to change font, size, and style all with one command. For example,

- ✔ **Format That Courier 14 Italic**
- ✔ **Set Font Courier 14 Italic**

are equivalent commands that change the font to Courier, the font size to 14, and the style to italic. Tables 6-2 and 6-3 tell you how to speak a Format or Set command.

When we put something in angle brackets and italics, like ***<style>,*** it is a placeholder. You don't literally say that word, you replace it with your own particular choice of word from a list of *style*s that we give you.

| Table 6-2 | The Syntax of Format | | |
|-----------|----------------------|----------|----------|
| *Command* | *Then Say* | *Then Say* | *Then Say* |
| Format That | Capitals | | |
| | All Caps | | |
| | Bold | | |
| | Italics | | |
| | Underline | | |
| | Regular | | |
| | Left Aligned | | |
| | Right Aligned | | |
| | Bullet Style | | |
| | Size | 4 – 120 | |
| | *<font family>* | 4 – 120 | *<style>* |

The font family names (*<font family>*) that NaturallySpeaking recognizes are Arial, Courier, Courier New, and Times. The styles (*<style>*) are Bold, Italics, Plain, Plain Text, Regular, and Underline.

Plain, Plain Text, and Regular mean the same thing: not bold, and not italic. They do not remove underlining. To undo underlining, see the earlier section, "Changing your style: Bold, italic, and underlined text."

| Table 6-3 | The Syntax of Set | | | |
|-----------|-------------------|----------|----------|----------|
| *Command* | *Then Say* | *Then Say* | *Then Say* | *Then Say* |
| Set | Size | 4 – 120 | | |
| | Font | *<style>* | | |
| | | *<font family>* | 4 – 120 | |
| | | *<font family>* | 4 – 120 | *<style>* |

You can't change color with the font commands in the NaturallySpeaking window. (You can, however, set font color in Word; see Chapter 12.)

# Chapter 7

# Proofreading and Listening to Your Text

*O*n the one hand, NaturallySpeaking never misspells a word. On the other hand, NaturallySpeaking can make some serious mistakes by choosing the wrong (if perfectly spelled) word. A dairy farmer who writes to the bank "I am growing feeble this year" rather than "I have a growing feed bill this year" is unlikely to get the response he wanted. No computerized grammar checker or other kind of checker is likely to catch that error. Proofreading is the only answer.

Of course, you don't need to hear your text in order to proofread it. But in the Preferred and Professional editions of NaturallySpeaking, you can hear your dictation in one of two ways:

✔ **Playback** of your voice. NaturallySpeaking records your voice as you dictate; it can play it back to help you proofread, and for all we know, it secretly e-mails copies to "America's Funniest Dictations."

✔ **Readback** of the text NaturallySpeaking has generated from your dictation — or of any other text you bring into the NaturallySpeaking window. The NaturallySpeaking text-to-speech feature uses a computer-synthesized voice to convert any text into speech.

(Playback and readback are available not only in the NaturallySpeaking window, but also in Word or WordPerfect if you use NaturalWord.)

What use is playing your own voice back? For one thing, it tends to make the NaturallySpeaking errors stand out. If you read what NaturallySpeaking typed, and as you listen to your voice, the discrepancy between, say, the written word "feeble" and the phrase you spoke, "feed bill," becomes obvious.

For another thing, playback lets you know what you *actually* said, rather than what you *think* you said. Knowing what you actually said is important when you correct NaturallySpeaking. If NaturallySpeaking has typed *fourth-quarter profits are down*, for instance, and you think you said, "in the fourth quarter, profits are down," you should correct NaturallySpeaking — even if you like its phraseology better! If, on the other hand, you really *did* say, "fourth-quarter profits are down," you should *not* correct NaturallySpeaking. Playing back your voice helps you do a better job of correcting NaturallySpeaking.

What about text-to-speech readback? Why listen to synthesized speech, instead of your recorded voice, when you proofread? Text-to-speech, though not a perfect reader, lets you hear what NaturallySpeaking actually typed. The NaturallySpeaking errors (wrong words) are sometimes more obvious when you hear them than when you see them.

Text-to-speech can be useful for other purposes. If you have a visual impairment, for example, you can verbally copy documents or e-mail messages to the NaturallySpeaking window and play them. We have even tried using it to talk on the telephone.

# Voice Commands for Playback

The simplest form of playing back your voice is to speak the command **Play That** (or **Play That Back**) after you dictate some text. The **Play That** command reads back the stored audio for the text that's displayed in the tiny Results box. **Play That Back** is just another form of the same command.

A more practical use of the **Play That** command is to proofread larger blocks of text than just your most recent utterance. You can select the text you want to proofread and then say, **"Play That."** You can use any means you like to select the text: your mouse, your keyboard, or a NaturallySpeaking voice command such as **Select Document, Select Paragraph,** or **Select Line.** (See Chapter 5 for details of various selections.)

Instead of selecting text first and then giving the **Play** command, you can specify what chunks of text are to be played back, right in the command. Use any of the following commands; you can say either **"Play"** or **"Play Back,"** as you prefer (we only show the **Play** form here):

- ✔ Play Line
- ✔ Play Paragraph
- ✔ Play Document
- ✔ Play Window
- ✔ Play Screen
- ✔ Play To Here
- ✔ Play From Here

The **Play To Here** and **Play From Here** commands let you play everything up to the current typing cursor position ("here"), or from that position to the end.

Pressing Ctrl+Shift+S starts the playback from your typing cursor's current position. (It's the same as **Play From Here.**)

NaturallySpeaking stores about a half-hour's worth of dictated text. (Pauses don't count.) Anything you dictated before that point can't be played back.

# Proofreading and Correcting with Playback

Voice playback is a nice feature for proofreading and editing your documents. NaturallySpeaking provides convenient buttons on the toolbar and hot keys on the keyboard for controlling the playback feature as you proofread.

Note that playback doesn't work for text entered in the following ways:

- ✔ Text that has been typed in
- ✔ Text that you didn't dictate in the first place
- ✔ Text that you dictated, but later moved

To hear such text, use the NaturallySpeaking text-to-speech feature instead.

Playback is only available in the Preferred and Professional editions and only within the NaturallySpeaking window or a NaturalWord application such as Word or WordPerfect. In NaturalWord, you don't get the "skip backward" and "skip forward" buttons that you get in the NaturallySpeaking window.

When you're ready to proofread your document and correct the NaturallySpeaking errors, here's how the process works:

1. **Select the text you want to proofread.**

   For instance, say, **"Select Document,"** or select by using your mouse.

   You can select and play in one command by saying a command like **"Play Document"** or **"Play Paragraph"** instead. You can then skip to Step 3.

2. **Say,** "Play That."

   Or press Ctrl+Shift+S or click the Play button on the toolbar shown in Figure 7-1.

Fast play or skip forward

Play | Slower play or skip backward

**Figure 7-1:**
Playback
controls.

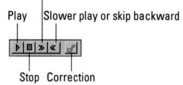

Stop  Correction

3. **Scan the text with your eyes as your dictation plays back.**

   At this point, poise your finger over the minus key on the numeric keypad. (The numeric keypad is usually on the far right end of your keyboard.) You need to strike this key quickly when you hear an error!

   An arrow appears at the start of each of your utterances as NaturallySpeaking plays. If the arrow is yellow, NaturallySpeaking plays the dictation. If the arrow is red, NaturallySpeaking is telling you that it can't play back your dictation — probably because you have edited the text since dictating. Just wait, and NaturallySpeaking will skip that text.

4. **When you come to a NaturallySpeaking error, press the - key (minus key) on the numeric keypad of your keyboard.**

   The playback stops and the Correction dialog box pops up, displaying the last four words spoken. (Clicking the Correction button — the lasso-looking thing on the toolbar — does the same thing as the minus key, but we find the button less convenient.)

   You must press the minus key within four words or punctuation marks of hearing the error, or you will overshoot the error. See the following tips if you do overshoot.

5. **Choose the correct interpretation from the list in the Correction dialog box or type the correct interpretation and then click the OK button.**

(See Chapter 5 if you're not familiar with the Correction dialog box.)

If you type new text into the Correction dialog box, make sure the words you type match the words you hear. Now is *not* the time to change your mind about the text you dictated. Stick with the program here, folks! Just make the text match the speech; otherwise, you'll incorrectly train NaturallySpeaking. See the following sidebar for ways to ensure your corrections are correct. Make any other changes by conventional editing in the document.

When you click OK, the Correction dialog box closes and playback continues immediately. Continue correcting errors as in Steps 4 and 5 until you reach the end of the text to be played.

If you press the minus key too late, you'll overshoot the error. (We do this regularly; age affects the reflexes, we suppose.) That is, the Correction dialog box displays a phrase after the one you want. Here are a few solutions to that and other related problems:

✔ If you realize you have overshot the error, but still haven't pressed the minus key, press the left-arrow key (one of the navigation keys on the keyboard). This backs NaturallySpeaking up by about eight to ten words. Press the left-arrow key repeatedly until you catch the phrase you want. Alternatively, you can click the "Skip Backward" button (with the << symbol) on the toolbar.

✔ If you have already pressed the minus key and the Correction dialog box pops up with the wrong phrase in it, first click Cancel or press the Esc key on your keyboard to exit the Correction dialog box. Then press the left-arrow key to skip backwards.

✔ Keep in mind that when you click the minus key, the Correction dialog box displays only the last four words (or punctuation marks). If playback is already more than three words ahead of the error, press the left-arrow key to skip backwards.

✔ A secret (well, undocumented) alternative to the minus key is the down-arrow key (among the navigation keys on your keyboard). We find this key more convenient, because it's next to the left-arrow key. You can also change the hot key for corrections to any key you like using the Tools⇨Options command in NaturallySpeaking. See Chapter 3 for details.

## Playback in the Corrections dialog box

As we mention earlier, a good reason for playing back your dictation is so that you can correct NaturallySpeaking properly. You want to be sure that the text you type in the Correction dialog box is what you actually said!

One way to ensure that your correction matches your spoken word is to click the Play Back button in the Correction dialog box. NaturallySpeaking then plays your original speech for the phrase being corrected.

If you like this feature, you can tell NaturallySpeaking to play the recorded speech whenever you use the Correction dialog box. Choose Tools⇨Options from the NaturallySpeaking (or NaturalWord) menu. In the Options dialog box that appears, click the Miscellaneous tab and click to place a mark in the Automatic Playback On Correction checkbox. Click OK to close the Options dialog box.

Other playback buttons and hotkeys can help you make corrections more efficiently. Here's what they do:

- ✔ **To stop the playback:** Click the Stop button (with the square) in the toolbar or press the Esc key (or Ctrl+1).

- ✔ **To play back at high speed:** Click the Fast Play button (with the > symbol) once or press the right-arrow key.

- ✔ **To skip forward in your text:** Click the Fast Play button (or press the right-arrow key) a second time.

- ✔ **To resume normal speed when playing fast:** Click the Slower Play button (with the << symbol) or press the left-arrow key. (You cannot play slower than normal by clicking the Slower Play button, although you might think so.)

- ✔ **To skip backward when playing at normal speed:** click the Slower Play (or Skip Backward) button (or press the left-arrow key).

The Fast Play and Slower Play buttons are only available in the NaturallySpeaking window itself. They are not available in Word or WordPerfect.

# Using the Text-to-Speech Feature

The NaturallySpeaking text-to-speech feature is a cute piece of wizardry. It is not perfect; still, with it your PC can do a reasonable job of turning text into speech. (Now we can *sound* like Stephen Hawking — the astrophysicist who uses speech synthesis for all his speaking — even if we can't match his genius!)

Text-to-speech isn't limited to proofreading. It's a general-purpose tool for listening to documents. For instance, you could play a document by copying it into the NaturallySpeaking window. (Text-to-speech is available only in the NaturallySpeaking window, and only in the Preferred and higher editions.) A visually impaired person could do the whole job with the verbal copying and window-switching commands described in Chapter 11.

Its speech takes some getting used to. It has a peculiar accent to our ears, sounding half Asian, half-British. It has a tendency to drop letters like the final *s* of some words, and its emphasis and pacing make it sound like someone not fully familiar with English.

One reason for using text-to-speech is to help proofread your text. But which is better for proofreading — playback of your own voice or readback with text-to-speech?

Playback helps you correct NaturallySpeaking by giving you a single key to interrupt the playback and launch the Correction dialog box to fix the last phrase played. Readback doesn't provide such help. Although you can certainly correct the NaturallySpeaking errors after hearing them read back, you must separately stop the readback process, select the incorrect text, and then launch the Correction dialog box.

Apart from playback's advantage of being linked to the Correction dialog box, it's also usually the best way to find errors. With playback, you hear the correct text and spot errors with your eyes. Because you're comparing the original dictation to the resulting text, playback tends to be a more accurate way of proofreading.

If you tend to be aurally oriented, however — for instance, if you pay better attention to the spoken word than to the written word — you might try text-to-speech readback. With readback, you hear the text that NaturallySpeaking wrote and mentally judge whether that was what you intended. You aren't presented with your original dictation, just the NaturallySpeaking interpretation. A second advantage of readback is that it works even if you edit text manually, whereas playback can't handle manual edits.

To start readback, select some text in the NaturallySpeaking window (using mouse, keyboard, or voice command). Then either give the verbal command **"Read That"** or choose Tools⇨Read That or press Ctrl+Alt+S. (In NaturalWord, in Word or WordPerfect, only the verbal command works.)

Readback verbal commands are the same as playback verbal commands, except instead of saying **"Play"** you say **"Read."** Here are the verbal commands:

- ✔ **Read That** (referring to text you have selected)
- ✔ **Read That Back** (same as **Read That**)

- ✔ **Read Line**
- ✔ **Read Paragraph**
- ✔ **Read Document**
- ✔ **Read Window**
- ✔ **Read Screen**
- ✔ **Read To Here** (where "here" is wherever your typing cursor is)
- ✔ **Read From Here**

You can stop readback in the NaturallySpeaking window by pressing the Esc key, pressing Ctrl+1, or clicking the Stop button on the toolbar. (You may not be able to stop it in Word or WordPerfect, using NaturalWord, so don't select any more text than you want to hear!)

If you hear a NaturallySpeaking error during readback, first stop the readback and then select the erroneous text any way you like (with your mouse or keyboard or verbally). With text selected, launch the Correction dialog box in any of the usual ways, including pressing the minus key on the numeric keypad, clicking the Correction button on the toolbar (the lasso-like symbol), or saying, **"Correct That."**

If you hear an error that you (not NaturallySpeaking) made, stop readback first by pressing the Esc key. Then, select and edit your text any way you like (by speech or by using the keyboard and mouse.)

We find that slowing text-to-speech down a bit improves its intelligibility. You can adjust the speed, volume, and pitch attributes of text-to-speech. Choose Tools⇨Options and then click the Speech-To-Text tab on the Options dialog box that appears. The dialog box sports three sliding adjustments, one for each attribute. Drag the slider to the right for higher speed, volume, or pitch or to the left for lower values. To test the sound at your chosen settings, click the Read Text button. NaturallySpeaking will read the text in the Preview window. To return the values to their original settings, click the Restore Defaults button. Click the OK button when you're done.

# Chapter 8

# Using Recorded Speech

*T*hank Thomas Edison. He's the guy who figured out that you don't have to be standing there talking to your transcriptionist — you can record stuff in the privacy of your own office and then hand it off to your transcriptionist later. Of course, in his day you had to yell into a big horn and your words were recorded on a wax cylinder, but the idea was a good one: Record now, transcribe later.

The idea was so good that Dragon now implements it as a feature of NaturallySpeaking. It's not in all editions of NaturallySpeaking, but it's a feature of the Mobile Edition, Preferred Edition, Professional Edition, and all the other pricier items in Dragon's product list.

For the recording part of this process, you have two options: Record on a high-quality (usually digital) voice recorder or record on your PC (or someone else's PC) using the Sound Recorder utility program that comes with NaturallySpeaking.

If you have NaturallySpeaking Mobile Edition, see Chapter 9. You have special software that makes your life a bit easier. You also have a cute little digital voice recorder that we'll tell you how to use.

# Why Record?

Perhaps the most attractive benefit of recording first and then transcribing later is the same one that Thomas Edison probably had in mind. We suspect that he had no desire to master the manual skill of typewriting, preferring to let his secretary do that job. Likewise, you can simply dictate your text and then let your secretary handle the transcription. That way, you never have to master the intricacies of NaturallySpeaking itself. As with Thomas Edison, however, you still have to master the intricacies of using the recording device.

Even if you don't have a secretary, one of the nice things about recording on a portable recorder is that you don't have to drag your computer around! Even today's low-profile laptop computers are pretty bulky. Sure, you could try to type a document on one of those itty-bitty keyboards or scribble pads that go with a palmtop computer, but life is too short. Much better to sit there talking into a little box in your hand (a recorder). You look just as silly either way, but dictating doesn't strain your eyes or cramp your fingers.

Just don't dictate in an airline seat, an elevator, or other crowded location, or you will be just like those self-important, inconsiderate bozos who talk into their cellular phones two feet from your ear. Besides, do you want the whole world to hear your confidential dictation?

If you don't have a portable recorder, you can still benefit from recording your voice on your PC instead of dictating directly into NaturallySpeaking. NaturallySpeaking requires a significant amount of memory and processor power to operate, and it takes that power away from other applications. Recording doesn't tie up as much of your computer resources. If you don't want to slow down your computer, you can dictate into the NaturallySpeaking Sound Recorder and run the transcription feature while you're out to lunch.

The final advantage of recording first and transcribing later is that, surprisingly, it's often more accurate! If your recorder provides a digital audio file (as does the NaturallySpeaking Sound Recorder), NaturallySpeaking's transcription doesn't have to keep up with your rate of speech. It can take its time and read your speech from the file at its own rate. As a result, it will be more accurate.

You can get the same accuracy that transcription offers even when you dictate directly into NaturallySpeaking — if you don't mind slowness! You can get higher accuracy by allowing NaturallySpeaking to work more slowly. All you have to do is adjust a slider on the Miscellaneous tab of Options dialog box. See Chapter 3 for the details of setting options in the Options dialog box.

The disadvantage of recording first and then transcribing is that you don't get to correct NaturallySpeaking on the fly. As a result, you may find that you have to make the same correction repeatedly throughout your document. Subsequent documents will, however, benefit from your corrections.

One fantasy we should shoot down right now is the one in which you transcribe meetings using your recorder and NaturallySpeaking. One problem is that NaturallySpeaking has to be trained to the voice of each speaker. What's more, the acoustic environment for meetings is invariably far too poor to get a decent recording from even one person. Besides, who really wants everything they said in a meeting to appear in a transcription?!

# Setting Up to Use a Portable Recorder

You need an exceptionally good recorder for NaturallySpeaking. Mr. Edison's wax cylinder device isn't going to do the job. Inexpensive recorders often introduce too much noise and distortion or their microphones are poor. Dragon Systems lists on its Web site (www.dragonsys.com) recorders that they have tested with their products. In general, you need a high-quality digital or mini-disc recorder, preferably one that outputs digital audio files. Dragon NaturallyMobile (see Chapter 9) comes with one of the Dragon-tested recorders, Voice It Technology's digital recorder. For serious remote dictation work, you want a recorder that allows you to store multiple separate recordings. Or — do you feel lucky? You can try using your existing recorder and see how well it does.

You can improve the audio quality of some recorders by plugging a separate microphone into them. Look for a microphone jack on your recorder. Of course, a separate microphone often makes the recorder significantly less convenient and portable. "Stub" microphones (microphones on a short stalk) that do not make the recorder too unwieldy exist for this purpose. Check with a good audio equipment supplier.

You have to do a few things before you can make remotely recorded dictation work, including the following:

- ✔ You must be able to make a physical connection between your recorder and your PC. You can't just let the recorder play into the microphone.

- ✔ If that connection is digital, you need software that transfers the files from the recorder to the PC.

- ✔ You must train NaturallySpeaking to recognize your voice the way it sounds after being altered by the processes of recording and transferring to your PC.

# *Figuring out your connection*

You need a physical connection between recorder and PC that takes one of two forms. Which kind of connection you use depends mostly on whether you have a digital recorder with digital output or an analog recorder.

Digital recorders with digital outputs make the setup process easier. You can skip the Audio Setup wizard part of setup. They also speed up the transfer of dictation from the recorder to the PC.

Don't make the connection yet (you haven't recorded anything), but figure out what kind of connection you need from the following descriptions. You need to know this in order to set up NaturallySpeaking to handle recorded voice.

### *Digital data transfer connection*

If your recorder doesn't use tape, it is almost certainly a digital recorder. It probably supports digital data transfer of some sort to your computer. Digital transfer most commonly takes place through a data cable, running from a connector on a digital recorder to a connector (usually a serial port connector) on your PC. It's possible that your recorder may also make a data connection through an infrared link, through the parallel (printer) port, or through a USB port on your PC. These are all digital connections through which you "copy the data" (your voice recording) to your PC's hard disk drive. Check your recorder's manual for details on how to make this connection.

Other possible ways to transfer digital data include a memory card that you remove from the recorder and place in a slot in your PC (or in a device connected to your PC). Check your PC's manual or your recorder's manual for instructions on copying the data from this memory card to your PC's hard disk drive. Or you may have a mini-disc recorder and a mini-disc drive on your computer.

If you have a digital recorder but it doesn't provide digital data transfer, you need to use the Line In connection (see the next section). Some other reasons that you might use the Line In connection with a digital recorder are: You may not have the digital cable you need; your PC may not have a connector available; or your PC may not be equipped to read the recorder's digital storage medium (such as mini-discs).

### *"Line In" connection*

If your recorder uses tape (or if the recorder is digital but you can't transfer the data for any of the reasons given in the last section), you use the "Line In" connection on your PC. This is also called an "analog" connection (as opposed to digital).

A Line In connection requires a cable from the audio output jack (a round hole) of the recorder to the round Line In jack on your PC. You can use this sort of connection with any recorder that has a "line out" jack or a headphone jack (sometimes marked "ear" or "audio out"). If you use a stereo recorder for a Line In connection, you need a special cable or adapter that creates a monaural (single-channel) output.

## Creating a new user

Most people think their voice sounds pretty terrible after it has been passed through a recorder. So does NaturallySpeaking. In fact, as far as NaturallySpeaking is concerned, your voice is so different that it represents a completely new user. And, for that reason, you must train NaturallySpeaking to recognize the "new user."

Just as when you first start using NaturallySpeaking, you use the New User wizard to train NaturallySpeaking. This time, however, the wizard will guide you to dictate the training text into your mobile recorder instead of into the microphone of your PC.

As wizards are likely to do, the New User wizard takes you through several stages. These stages include naming the user, defining the connection, testing and setting the audio level, and training. We have a section, following, for each of these stages. The wizard does it all in one continuous process, however, so we have numbered our steps in the next few sections continuously. The process will take a little while, so arm yourself with a box of cookies or be prepared to take a few stretch breaks!

### I: Name the user

It's just like having kids. If you're going to create a new being — a new user, in this case — you're going to have to come up with a name for it! The process (referring, now, to the process of creating a software being, not a human one) begins like this:

1. **Choose User⇨New from the NaturallySpeaking window.**

    (If you're using NaturalWord in Microsoft Word or Corel WordPerfect, click Dragon NaturallySpeaking first to access the Users menu.) The Welcome screen appears.

2. **Click Next to move to the New User screen.**

3. **Type a name for this new user.**

    You can name the user something like "My Recorder." Or name it after your grandmother, if you like. She'd be tickled.

If you're a kid, click the Speech Model box and choose Student Bestmatch Model from the list that drops down. No, NaturallySpeaking isn't being condescending, it's just that most kids under 15 just haven't had time to abuse their vocal chords as much. Also, most kids don't speak as ponderously as adults and enjoy the higher speed that a smaller vocabulary offers. Click the Vocabulary box and choose Student General English, – Bestmatch, or – Standard. Choose the Bestmatch version if, in the Speech Model box, Bestmatch is marked *RECOMMENDED*; otherwise, choose Standard.

4. **Click the <u>N</u>ext button.**

   After you click Next, NaturallySpeaking takes a few moments to create a new set of starting speech files for this user. Eventually, the Select User Type screen appears, asking the timeless question pondered by dictators over the ages, "How will you dictate?"

Good work, so far. Reward yourself with a cookie or a good stretch.

### II: Tell NaturallySpeaking about your connection

NaturallySpeaking's question about this new user, "How will you dictate?", actually means, "How will the user's voice get into the computer?" So your next step in the New User wizard is to tell NaturallySpeaking that you will dictate into a recorder and also say how your recorder will connect to your PC.

5. **Click <u>I</u>nto a Recorder.**

   Under "Into a Recorder," the wizard asks, "How will you transfer your recorded data to the computer?" To be able to answer this question, read the earlier section "Figuring out your connection."

6. **Click C<u>o</u>py The Data. . . or <u>C</u>onnect The Recorder. . . (according to your type of connection) and then click the <u>N</u>ext button.**

   If you're using a digital connection, choose the first option (Copy the Data From Recorder Memory. . .). If you're connecting your recorder through the Line In jack, choose the second option (Connect the Recorder To The Line In Jack. . .).

   Click Next, and depending on how your recorder connects to your PC, you go to one of the following:

   - If you connect by copying the data (digital transfer), the New User wizard skips the Audio Setup wizard process and takes you directly to training NaturallySpeaking to your recorded voice. Skip the next section, "Run the Audio Setup wizard," and move on to "Mobile Recorder Training."

   - If you connect through the Line In jack, the New User wizard now invites you to run the Audio Setup wizard. You must run the Audio Setup wizard at some point to finish this new user definition, so you may as well do it now! Move on to the next section of this chapter, "Run the Audio Setup wizard."

If you use a USB microphone to dictate to your PC (a kind of microphone we talk about in Chapter 19), you may at this point get a Choose Your Sound System screen. If so, one of the choices available to you will be USB Audio Device. Choose the other device listed, not the USB Audio Device, and then click OK.

### *III: Run the Audio Setup wizard*

If you're connecting your recorder through the Line In connection, NaturallySpeaking needs to set your PC's volume controls and other audio settings. It also needs to test the quality of the audio that your recorder delivers to your PC. To do all that, NaturallySpeaking now starts the Audio Setup wizard. (If you're using digital data transfer, you skip this part.)

At this point, you're gazing at the Connect Your Recorder screen, which is welcoming you in a friendly and informative fashion to the Audio Setup Wizard. Continue by following these steps:

7. **Click Next to move to the Connect Your Recorder screen, and follow its directions.**

   Unsurprisingly, this screen tells you how to connect your recorder to your PC. Do so! Make sure your recorder's volume is not set to maximum or minimum, and leave it set at the same level throughout all the following steps, unless you're told it's too high or low.

8. **Click Next to move to the Adjust Your Volume screen.**

   This screen displays some text for you to read into your recorder.

9. **Turn on your recorder, start recording, and then read that text into your recorder. Don't click the Start Adjusting button yet!**

10. **Rewind your recording to the beginning, click the Start Adjusting button on the wizard screen, and then play back the recording.**

    You probably will not hear the recording play back, as the sound is going into your PC, not your recorder's speaker. As you play back the recording, you can watch the volume being adjusted. If all goes well, your PC "dings" and the wizard tells you the volume has been successfully adjusted. Otherwise, check that your recorder is properly connected, and try again. If the volume is too high or low, try adjusting the volume control on your recorder.

11. **Click Next to move to the Check Your Audio Quality screen.**

    This screen has yet more fascinating reading material for you!

12. **As you did in Step 9, start recording, and read the text in the box on this screen into your recorder. Don't click the Start Quality Check button yet!**

13. **Rewind your recording to the beginning, click the <u>S</u>tart Quality Check button on the wizard screen, and then play back the recording.**

    As before, you probably will not hear the recording play back. As you play back the recording, the attractive little bar chart on the wizard screen dances suggestively for you.

    If all goes well, the wizard screen now tells you that you have finished the Audio Setup successfully, and the dancing bar chart is replaced by lines giving you a number for "signal to noise ratio" and telling you that your audio quality is acceptable. If the quality is not acceptable, see the section "Getting better sound quality from portable recorders," later in this chapter.

14. **Click <u>F</u>inish.**

    The New User wizard, that relentless taskmaster, now wants you to run Mobile Recorder Training. Have a cookie.

NaturallySpeaking is now trained to expect a certain volume from your recorder. If your recorder playback volume is not set to some fixed volume (and it is not, on most recorders), when you transcribe text, either make sure the volume is set to the same level you used for training or run the Audio Setup wizard again to adjust the volume before transcribing. You may want to put a mark or piece of tape on the volume control to ensure consistency.

## IV: Run Mobile Recorder Training

RCA has a cute logo — a dog ("Nipper") listening with cocked head to an old Victrola record player — captioned with the trademark slogan, "His Master's Voice." Just as Nipper would undoubtedly need training to adapt to recorded commands, NaturallySpeaking needs training to "adapt" to your recorded voice. (The difference is that you, not Nipper, get the cookies as a reward. See how technology improves our lives?)

Training NaturallySpeaking to understand your recorded voice is just like training NaturallySpeaking for direct dictation, with one difference: You read the training material into your recorder, transfer the dictation to your PC, and then have NaturallySpeaking transcribe it.

At this point, the Mobile Recorder Training Wizard screen is welcoming you with the usual sort of welcome blurbage. Yeah, yeah, yadda, yadda, yadda. Here's how to proceed:

15. **Click <u>N</u>ext to move to the Recording Your Speech screen.**

    The wizard displays a selection of fine, edifying reading material to choose from in order to train your recorder. We, ourselves, prefer the selections marked "Easier Reading." They are intended for young children, we suspect, but then, we are Sesame Street fans when not writing computer books.

16. **Click a selection and then click View.**

    Unexpectedly, a window (usually Windows Notepad) appears with your chosen text.

17. **Turn on your recorder and start dictating the displayed text into your recorder.**

    (If your recorder is still connected to your PC from running the Audio Setup wizard, you can disconnect it while you record, if you like.) Make sure to hold the microphone off to the side of your mouth, at a consistent distance of about ½ inch, and don't shuffle your fingers on the recorder (it makes noise).

18. **When done dictating, click whatever button you need to stop recording on your recorder, and then close the window that is displaying the text (click the X in the upper-right corner).**

19. **Click the Next button in the Mobile Recorder Training Wizard window to move to the Transferring Recorded Speech screen.**

    The wizard now needs to know (in Step 1 on the wizard's screen) whether you will be using an analog Line In connection (Connect Recorder To Line In Jack...) or digital transfer (Copy The Recording From Recorder Memory...). Click the proper selection for your kind of connection.

    If you're using digital transfer, you now have to make that transfer happen. Exactly how it happens is up to you and the vendor of your digital recorder, so see the instructions with your recorder. After you transfer the file according to those instructions, click the Browse button in Step 2 of that same wizard screen. In the Select Wave Input File dialog box that appears, select the file you have transferred.

20. **Click Next to move to the next screen.**

    Where you go from here depends on what you selected in the last screen. If you chose digital transfer, you move to the Adapting Your User screen. Click Start Adapting.

    If you chose analog transfer, you move to the Playing Your Voice to the Computer screen. Reconnect your recorder to your PC if it's not already connected. (If you think you may have paused more than five seconds while recording the training material, increase the number in the Assume Recording Is Done After 5 Seconds of Silence setting.) Rewind to the beginning of your recording and then click the Start Recording button on the wizard. Press the Play button on your recorder.

You now have time to take a nap, perhaps eat the rest of the box of cookies, take Nipper, the dog, for a walk, or whatever. You can use your computer for other purposes while NaturallySpeaking is adapting, but you will find that it runs a bit slower. Don't do anything with NaturallySpeaking until the adapting is done.

Eventually, the Mobile Recorder Training wizard lets you know that adapting is finished. Click the Next button, and then on the Congratulations screen that appears, click the Finish button and wait.

But are you finished? Nooooo. Now the New User wizard wants you to run the Vocabulary Builder. It's cookie time again.

### V: Vocabulary Training: Build or import?

The final step in training NaturallySpeaking to recognize this "new user" (you, processed through a voice recorder) is to tell NaturallySpeaking what sort of vocabulary this user has. Vocabulary building is when NaturallySpeaking reads some of your writing or previous dictation to find out what words you're likely to use and how.

If you have never before done vocabulary building for NaturallySpeaking, it is something you should do. Click the Run Vocabulary Builder button and see Chapter 2 for basic instructions on the Builder. Or, if you're feeling tired of this whole setup process, defer the Vocabulary Builder until later. Click to clear the Remind Me To Run The Vocabulary Builder Later checkbox.

If you have already done vocabulary building for NaturallySpeaking, you may be thinking, "Wow, this is one stupid wizard. I'm the same person, fer cryin' out loud, and I have the same vocabulary whether I talk into a recorder or not!" For you, irritated reader, NaturallySpeaking has just the salve you need: vocabulary importing — that is, assuming you have the Professional Edition. If you have the Preferred Edition, you don't have the importing option, and you will have to run the Vocabulary Builder. If you do have the Professional Edition and want to import a vocabulary, click to clear the Remind Me To Run The Vocabulary Builder Later checkbox.

When you have either completed the vocabulary building or deferred it until later, click the Next button on this wizard screen. This takes you to the Quick Tour screen, where, if you have never taken the tour, you should: Click the View Quick Tour button there.

If you have already taken the tour or don't care about it, click to clear the tour reminder check mark. Click the Next button, and on the final wizard screen that appears, click the Finish button.

You're done creating your new user! Celebrate by eating your last few cookies, or go take a couple of victory laps around the block. (If you decided to import a vocabulary in NaturallySpeaking Professional, however, now's the time to go do it. See Chapter 21.) Now you can record your own dictation instead of reading stories.

# Getting better sound quality from portable recorders

For lots of reasons, you're more likely to have sound quality problems when you use a mobile recorder than you are when you dictate into your PC. Here are some tips to avoid problems:

- ✔ Use a high-quality digital or mini-disc recorder. Most tape recorders won't do the job.

- ✔ Avoid noisy environments: moving cars, traffic, machinery, wind, surf, discotheques, car washes, rock concerts, or active airport runways.

- ✔ Don't move your fingers around on your recorder while recording, because this causes noise.

- ✔ Don't speak so directly into the microphone that it records puffs of breath when you speak. Keep the microphone of your recorder off to one side of your mouth. Keep the microphone a constant distance from your mouth.

- ✔ If your recorder has different microphone sensitivity settings (or a microphone volume control), use the lowest sensitivity that still gives you a strong, clear recording. (Too high a sensitivity picks up background noise and sometimes distorts your voice.)

- ✔ Make sure your recorder is set for the highest quality of recording, if it offers different quality levels. Check your recorder's instructions. Highest quality usually comes at the expense of maximum recording time, so choose the setting that gives the shortest recording time if quality is not mentioned.

# Recording Your Dictation

When you record text for NaturallySpeaking to transcribe, speak that text just as if you were dictating into NaturallySpeaking directly. Chapter 4 tells you how to do it.

Certain aspects of recording, however, make that process a little different than dictating directly to NaturallySpeaking. Using commands, for instance, is tricky because you can't see the transcription in progress. (It's sort of like telling your spouse how to program the VCR over the phone.) In addition, dictating into a portable recorder introduces some new issues that affect sound quality. Finally, you may want to record your dictation on your PC, using Dragon's Sound Recorder utility. Read on for details.

## *Using commands while recording*

Because you can't see the result of NaturallySpeaking's transcription as you dictate, using certain commands in recorded speech is risky. NaturallySpeaking might, for instance, edit or delete the wrong text in response to a command, and you wouldn't know until you see your text on the screen.

Because of that risk, NaturallySpeaking ignores most editing commands it encounters while transcribing your recording. (You can tell it not to ignore them, if necessary, when you transcribe the recording. See the section "Transcribing your recording" for more details.)

NaturallySpeaking does, however, accept dictation commands in your recorded text — the ones that control capitals and spaces. The safest procedure is to use commands that apply only to the following word, such as **Cap** *<word>*. Even though NaturallySpeaking allows you to use the dictation commands that turn something "on," such as **Caps On,** NaturallySpeaking may occasionally miss the concluding **Caps Off** or other "off" command. You may end up making more work for yourself (or whoever does the final cleanup) by using those on/off commands.

Following are some of the commands that, in addition to punctuation, we think work most reliably in recorded speech:

- ✔ **All Caps** *<word>*
- ✔ **Cap** *<word>*
- ✔ **New Line**
- ✔ **New Paragraph**
- ✔ **No Caps** *<word>*
- ✔ **No Space** *<word>*
- ✔ **Spacebar**
- ✔ **Tab Key**

If you're careful, you can also use **Scratch That** (which deletes back to the last time you paused) if you make a mistake. Use it only if you're sure when you last paused, or you'll delete more or less than you intended! You can repeat the **Scratch That** command to back up through multiple pauses if your memory for pauses is very good.

To avoid having to remember your pauses, a better command for amending recorded dictation is **Resume With <*word*>.** This command allows you to back up to a specific word within the last 100 characters and then dictate new text beginning from that point. (Of course, it only works if NaturallySpeaking got your word right in the first place!)

See Chapter 4 for more about **Scratch That** and **Resume With.** Both commands are allowed when you transcribe from a recording.

## *Recording on your PC with Sound Recorder*

If your objective is to record dictation on the road, you need a high-quality portable recorder. (See "Using a Portable Recorder," earlier in this chapter.) If, however, your objective is simply to record now and transcribe later (or have someone else transcribe), try the NaturallySpeaking Sound Recorder.

Don't confuse the NaturallySpeaking Sound Recorder program with the one that comes with Windows. You can certainly use the Windows Sound Recorder, if you like. Its operation is similar, but you must set the resulting file's properties to the format NaturallySpeaking wants. Follow the instructions beginning with Step 3, "Choose File➪Properties," in the sidebar "WAVing to NaturallySpeaking," later in this chapter.

All versions of NaturallySpeaking from the Preferred Edition on up come with a utility program called the Sound Recorder. The NaturallySpeaking Sound Recorder creates a digital voice (audio) file as you speak into the microphone and also allows you to make changes to your dictated audio file before giving it to NaturallySpeaking to transcribe. You can launch the sound recorder in either of two ways:

- ✔ From the NaturallySpeaking menu, choose Tools➪Sound Recorder. (Sound Recorder is not available from Tools on the NaturalWord menu.)

- ✔ From the Windows taskbar, choose Start➪Programs, choose whatever edition of NaturallySpeaking you're using (say, Dragon NaturallySpeaking Preferred), and then choose Sound Recorder.

You get a Sound Recorder window like the one in Figure 8-1. A series of buttons provides the same record, rewind, and playback features that you find on any VCR or voice recorder, and they are marked with similar symbols. (If you prefer, you can use the function keys shown in Figure 8-1 to operate the Sound Recorder.)

Adjust record/playback position

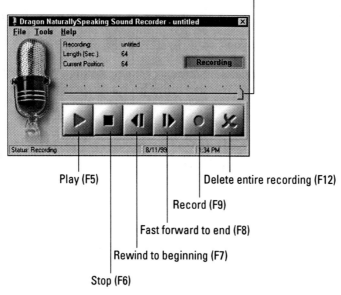

**Figure 8-1:**
The Sound
Recorder
window —
very much
like any
recorder,
but flatter.

Play (F5)

Delete entire recording (F12)

Record (F9)

Fast forward to end (F8)

Rewind to beginning (F7)

Stop (F6)

### Making a recording

With the Sound Recorder on your screen, here are the steps to take to record:

1. **Run the Audio Setup wizard if you have never dictated into NaturallySpeaking — or for best results if you have just put your microphone headset on your head.**

   If you have already set up your PC and microphone to dictate to NaturallySpeaking, you can skip this step. For optimal performance, however, just in case you have put your microphone on your head in a slightly different position today, you may want to run the Audio Setup wizard to adjust microphone volume. Choose Tools➪ Run Audio Setup Wizard. Click the Next button and follow the instructions that appear.

   If you haven't dictated at all into NaturallySpeaking on your PC, choose Tools➪Run Audio Setup Wizard. Then follow the instructions for running a complete setup in the Audio Setup section of Chapter 2.

2. **Click to switch the NaturallySpeaking microphone icon (at the end of the Windows taskbar, farthest from the Start button) to the off (lying down) position, if it's currently on (erect at an angle).**

   Or you can press the + key on the numeric keypad of your keyboard (at the far right end of the keyboard, usually) to switch the microphone icon between on and off.

(The physical microphone can only serve one application at a time, and you want it to serve the Sound Recorder now, not NaturallySpeaking. Turning the NaturallySpeaking microphone icon to the off position allows the microphone to serve the Sound Recorder.)

3. **Click the Record button (the one with the red dot).**

   Or press F9, or choose Tools⇨Record. If you skipped Step 2 and left the NaturallySpeaking microphone icon in the "on" position, you may get an error message from the Sound Recorder ("SoundRec") at this point, to the effect that "all wave devices that can record in this format are in use." If so, click OK and return to Step 2.

4. **Speak!**

   Dictate just as you would to NaturallySpeaking. See Chapter 4 for instructions on speaking, punctuation, capitalization, numbers, dates, and other special text. See the tips that begin this section, "Recording Your Dictation," for additional instructions when recording speech.

5. **When you pause, click the Stop button (the one with the black square). To resume speaking, click the Record button again.**

   Sound Recorder resumes where you left off when you stopped. If you stopped because you mis-spoke, you can delete that error at this point. See the upcoming section, "Playing back and editing your recording."

6. **Save your dictation by choosing File⇨Save As.**

   A dialog box appears, with the usual controls that most Save As dialog boxes have. Type a filename in the File Name box (you don't need to type .WAV at the end, but you may), and then click the Save button. The Sound Recorder saves a file (of the WAV type) with your dictation in it.

## Playing back and editing your recording

Sound Recorder allows you to rewind and play back your dictation as you would on any other recorder. It doesn't make that cool, old-fashioned zipping noise as it rewinds, but it does allow you to do the following edits:

✔ Insert new dictation anywhere in the recording

✔ Erase from any point to the end of the recording

You can edit the recording that's currently in the Sound Recorder, or you can open a previously recorded file and edit that. Here are the details of playing back and editing:

- ✔ To play back your recording from the start, click the Rewind button (see Figure 8-1) and then the Play button (with the green triangle).

- ✔ To play back your recording from any point, move the position slider that runs the length of the Sound Recorder, just above the buttons. The slider indicates where in the recording you are. You can drag the slider with your mouse to any position from the start (far left) to the end (far right). Click the Play button to play from that point.

- ✔ To insert text into your recording, play the recording to find the place you want, and then click the Stop button (the black square). Click the Record button to begin recording the text you want to insert. Click the Stop button when you're done. (The new recording doesn't overwrite the old.)

- ✔ To add text to the end of your recording, click the Fast Forward button to move the slider to the far right, and then record as usual.

- ✔ To chop a piece off the end of your recording, position the slider at the chopping point and click the Delete button (the red X).

- ✔ To edit a previously recorded file, choose File⇨Open and choose that file from the Open dialog box. You can edit any WAV file, whether or not it was recorded by Sound Recorder.

- ✔ Save your edits by pressing Ctrl+S or choosing File⇨Save.

Now you have a recording. The next step is to have NaturallySpeaking transcribe it. See the section "Transcribing Your Recording" later in this chapter.

# Transferring Files from a Digital Recorder

If you have a digital recorder that can output digital audio files, you'll need instructions from the recorder manufacturer for transferring files to your PC. The Dragon NaturallyMobile recorder, for instance, comes with a special utility program, VoiceIt, designed to handle the transfer from that specific recorder. See Chapter 9 on NaturallyMobile for instructions.

If you have a different digital recorder, it may have its own program for handling file transfer that you need to install on your PC. Check your recorder manual for instructions.

Where on your PC's hard drive should you put the digital audio (.WAV) files from your recorder? You can put them anywhere, but the NaturallySpeaking transcription feature looks first in the Program folder in the NatSpeak folder on your hard (C:) drive, where NaturallySpeaking is normally installed. For convenience, put them in that Program folder.

TECHNICAL STUFF

---

# WAVing to NaturallySpeaking

The kind of digital files that NaturallySpeaking can transcribe are digital audio files of the WAV type (the file ends in .WAV). For Naturally-Speaking to use them, the WAV files must be in a specific format called "PCM 11,025 Hz, 16 Bit Mono."

To see whether your WAV file is in that format (and fix it if it's not), use the Sound Recorder program that Windows provides (not the NaturallySpeaking Sound Recorder program). To do so:

1. **Click the Windows taskbar's Start button and choose Programs⇨ Accessories⇨Entertainment⇨Sound recorder. (In Windows 95, choose Multimedia instead of Entertainment.) Or on most PCs, double-click your WAV file to open the Sound Recorder.**

2. **In Sound Recorder, open your WAV file with File⇨Open.**

3. **Choose File⇨Properties.**

   The Properties dialog box that appears lists Audio Format in the fourth line. Naturally-Speaking needs "PCM 11,025 Hz, 16 Bit Mono" in this line.

4. **To change the format, click the Convert Now button.**

5. **In the Sound Selection dialog box, click the Format box and choose PCM, and then click the Attributes box and choose 11,025 Hz, 16 Bit, Mono.**

6. **Click the Save As button, and in the Save As box that appears, type "Dragon."**

7. **Click OK in the Sound Selection dialog box and then in the Properties for Sound dialog box.**

8. **Save your converted file by choosing File⇨ Save.**

When, in the future, you want to convert a file to Dragon format, repeat the procedure, but when the Sound Selection dialog box appears, simply choose Dragon by clicking the Name box instead of setting the Format and Attributes.

---

If you have a digital recorder but it doesn't offer digital output or you do not have the necessary cable or software to make a digital transfer, you may be able to make an analog connection instead. See "Figuring out your connection," earlier in this chapter. Bring your recorder to an electronics store and ask for a cable to connect its audio output jack to a PC's audio line-in jack.

# *Transcribing Your Recording*

Watching NaturallySpeaking transcribe a recording is kind of magical. You sit there and your words (or something like them) appear on the screen.

NaturallySpeaking transcribes recorded speech from one of two possible sources, depending on your recorder. (See "Figuring out your connection," if you don't know which one you use.) Those two sources are the following:

- ✔ It listens as your recorder plays sound through a cable from the recorder's Line Out jack (or "headphone," or "audio output" jack) to your PC's Line In connector (also called the "input jack").

- ✔ It transcribes a sound file (a file with a .WAV extension), created by a digital recorder or the NaturallySpeaking Sound Recorder utility, which you have stored on your PC's hard drive. (Oh, you haven't? See "Transferring Files from a Digital Recorder" earlier in this chapter.)

To transcribe a recording from a portable recorder, NaturallySpeaking must be set up with a special "new user" specifically trained to handle recorded speech from that recorder. (See the section "Setting Up to Use a Portable Recorder.") You don't need to choose a special user to transcribe files from the NaturallySpeaking Sound Recorder (assuming the files were created on your PC); use the same user that you use for dictating directly to NaturallySpeaking.

Launch NaturallySpeaking if you haven't already, and take the following steps to transcribe:

1. **Open the new user you created especially for recorder input by choosing U̲ser(s)⇨O̲pen from the NaturallySpeaking menu, clicking the special "user" that you named and set up for recorded speech (My Recorder, for instance), and then clicking the Open button.**

If your portable recorder uses the analog (Line In) connection, NaturallySpeaking will be expecting a certain volume from your recorder. When you transcribe text, either make sure the volume is set to the same level you used for training or run the Audio Setup wizard again at this point. To run the Audio Setup wizard, choose Tools⇨ Audio Setup Wizard and choose the Adjust Volume Only selection.

2. **In NaturallySpeaking, choose T̲ools⇨Transcri̲be.**

   The Transcribe Recording dialog box appears.

3. **Click either W̲ave File or T̲hrough the Input Jack to tell NaturallySpeaking where to look for the recording.**

   If you choose Through the Input Jack, NaturallySpeaking will, unless you tell it otherwise, stop transcribing when it encounters a ten-second silence in your recording. To tell it otherwise, double-click the "10" in the line Stop Transcribing After 10 Seconds of Silence and type a new number. If you record multiple documents on your recorder by leaving a pause between different recordings, you can ensure that NaturallySpeaking will stop at the end of a recording.

If you choose Wave File, click the Browse button to select the file you want to transcribe from your hard drive. NaturallySpeaking looks first in the Programs folder within the folder where NaturallySpeaking is installed (typically, C:\NatSpeak).

4. **In the Destination area of that same dialog box, choose where you want the transcribed text to appear: <u>N</u>aturallySpeaking Window or Into Ne<u>x</u>t Window.**

   If you choose Into Next Window, NaturallySpeaking transcribes into the next window you click in after you click OK in the Transcribe Recording dialog box. Open that window (say, for instance, Microsoft Word) now.

5. **Click OK.**

   (If you chose to transcribe Into Next Window, now's the time to click in the window where you want the text typed.) NaturallySpeaking now begins to transcribe your document into text as you watch!

If you want to restrict or expand the variety of commands that the transcription process heeds, you can change the selection in the Commands area of the dialog box. The NaturallySpeaking transcription feature is initially set up to heed only "restricted" commands: those that control capitalization, spaces, tabs, line and paragraph endings, plus **Scratch That** and **Resume With.** If you don't intend to use **Scratch That** and **Resume With** in your dictation, choose Dictation Only. If, on the other hand, you're feeling brave and want to use lots of commands, you can choose All Commands.

# Chapter 9

# Mobile Edition and NaturallyMobile Recorder

* * * * * * * * * * * * * * * * * * * * * * * * * * * * * * * * * * * * *

* * * * * * * * * * * * * * * * * * * * * * * * * * * * * * * * * * * * *

*W*e think the whole idea of being able to dictate into a pocket recorder and have your PC transcribe it is, well, just too Star Wars–cool — even for George Lucas. In fact, the promise of being able to dictate notes from the field was the first thing that sucked us into the world of NaturallySpeaking.

Amazingly, it works. The NaturallySpeaking Mobile digital recorder (called NaturallyMobile, naturally enough) is the mobile part of the package. It gives you about 40 minutes of recording time, and you can add memory modules for up to 80 minutes more.

The rest of the package is NaturallySpeaking Preferred, which gives you the ability to transcribe recordings, plus Voice It Link, which connects the recorder to the PC and transfers files. You could cobble together your own recorder and transfer software and use NaturallySpeaking Preferred, but Dragon's solutions are tested and comparatively slick.

The system is not perfect, however. You can't use the recorder in noisy environments, and you have to avoid sliding your fingers around on it (they make noise). Also, you have to go back and clean up the transcribed text for the punctuation you forgot or correct NaturallySpeaking's mistakes. Surprisingly, if you get a clean recording, NaturallySpeaking can be more accurate on recorded speech than on live speech! It does better because it can take its time with recorded speech.

# Turning on the Recorder

To turn on the recorder, press the POWER button, hold it down for about a second, and release. (At first, we thought our recorder was broken. We pressed the Power button too quickly, and nothing happened. We suspect this feature was designed to keep the recorder from turning on accidentally in your pocket!)

Do the same press, hold, and release action to turn the recorder off. You can just leave the recorder on, too — it will turn itself off in a few minutes. Battery level is indicated by a tiny battery icon in the upper-right corner of the display. The icon's outline is filled when the batteries are fresh and gradually becomes empty as the batteries poop out.

The recorder makes a series of cute noises as you do stuff. We call the higher-pitched tones "beeps" and the lower-pitched tones "boops." Beeps usually indicate "Okay, I did that." Boops usually indicate "No, I don't think so." (Don't like these beeps and boops? You can turn 'em off. See "Changing Settings," later in this chapter.)

The very first time you turn on the recorder, you'll have to set the clock. (The recorder stamps all of your recordings with a date and time.) Here's how to set the clock:

✔ Press the Fast-Forward button (▶▶) to increase any setting, such as the hour. Press the Rewind (◀◀) button to decrease any setting. Press and release the button to increase/decrease by 1; hold the button down to change more quickly. (Notice that the clock keeps track of AM and PM. There is no special button for that; just keep advancing the time to change between AM. and PM. If you prefer 24-hour time, press the Folder button.)

✔ Press and release the Play (▶)button to move forward from one setting to the next (from hours to minutes to day, month, and year). You can't move backwards from, say, minutes to hours. Just repeatedly press the Play button until you return to the earlier setting.

✔ Press and release the POWER button when you're done to proceed to the regular mode of operation.

You can use your recorder for a pocket watch. Press and release the POWER button quickly to see the date and time for a few seconds.

# Recording

Okay, Mr. or Ms. Busy Executive, you want to get right down to it and dictate? Here's what to do:

1. **Press and release the RECORD button.**

   The recorder chirps in an upbeat way and displays RECORD VT. No, VT does not stand for Vermont or Verb Transitive. It means the recorder speed is set to Voice-to-Text. If your recorder doesn't display VT, it's set to the wrong speed. See "Changing Settings," later in this chapter.

   To minimize stray noise, cup your hand and grasp the recorder along the dark gray edges only, using the thumb, fingertips, and palm of one hand. Leave a gap between your palm and the recorder. Then press the buttons with your other hand. Otherwise, if you try to press buttons with the thumb of your grasping hand, you will make noises in the recording. Keep your grasping hand still and don't slide or move your fingers while dictating. Now, while standing on your head, put your left kneecap up to your right ear and . . .

2. **Speak into the recorder.**

   A no-brainer, right? Well . . . as with the NaturallySpeaking headset microphone, it's best not to speak directly into the microphone, but hold it to one side of your mouth, about two inches away. The microphone is under a series of three holes, on the left, just under the display panel. Hold the microphone roughly the same distance from your mouth each time you use it.

4. **Press and release PAUSE when you get stuck for words. Do it again when inspiration returns.**

   The recorder double-beeps in a friendly way (like R2D2 in *Star Wars*) when you press PAUSE.

5. **Press and release RECORD again to stop recording.**

   The recorder chirps a conclusive, two-tone note.

Those steps give you one file, and the display indicates the file number and the folder number the file is in, such as FOLDER 1 FILE 1. Repeat those steps and you have another file. (A file is a lump of dictation. When you transcribe, you transcribe one file at a time, although you can transcribe several files into one document if you like.)

You may not want to make a bunch of separate files but instead pick up where you left off at the end of the last recording. To do that, see the "Editing File Content" section later in this chapter.

As you record files, the recorder's memory fills up. You can get a rough idea of how full the memory is by looking at the gauge, which is in square brackets at the top left of the display. As you use memory, the brackets fill up with as many as eight black squares, like this: [■ ■ ■ ■]. When memory is nearly full, the squares flash. To know exactly how much memory is left, repeatedly press and release the MENU button until you see SETUP PRESS ▶. Press the ▶ (Play) button, and the remaining recording time is displayed like this: 35:19 (35 minutes and 19 seconds, in this example). Press and release the POWER button to clear this display.

You can use an external microphone or headphone (or microphone-headset) with the recorder, if you like. Using a headphone lets you play back your dictation in privacy. Using an external microphone can improve the quality of your recordings and so improve the accuracy of transcription. The headset that comes with NaturallySpeaking serves both functions nicely. Plug the microphone jack into the hole labeled MIC and the headphone jack into the hole labeled EAR. If you plan to use an external microphone, make sure you use it when you perform the user training for NaturallySpeaking (see "Training NaturallySpeaking," later in this chapter). If you plan to switch between internal and external microphones, you need to train two "users" for NaturallySpeaking.

If you buy an external microphone, ask for one that's an "electret" type with an "impedance" (im-peá-dense) of about "2.2 K ohms" (kay omes).

# Listening

To hear something you've just recorded, press and release the ▶ (Play) button. (To quickly move to the end of the file and stop playback, press and release the Play button again.)

Want to hear the file again? Press and release the ◀◀ (Rewind) button first, and then press the ▶ (Play) button.

To hear the next file, press and release the ▶ (Play) button. If the recorder boops disapprovingly instead of playing back, the recorder has no more files to play for you (in the current folder).

The recorder displays a little you-are-here marker: a dot that appears just before or after the FILE *N* display. (*N* represents a file number here). The dot must be just before FILE *N* for you to be able play that file. If the dot appears after FILE *N*, you are at the end of the file and must press the Rewind button before you can play it again.

To play a specific file, press and release the ▶▶ (Fast-Forward) button to advance to a higher-numbered file, or press and release the ◀◀ (Rewind) button to move to a lower-numbered file. Then press and release the ▶ (Play) button.

To adjust volume, find the thumbwheel recessed into the right edge of the recorder. For higher volume, push the thumbwheel up; for lower, push it down. (The volume control is for listening volume only; it doesn't affect recording volume.)

To listen at high speed, in which you sound like a hyperactive chipmunk, press and release the ▶▶ (Fast-Forward) button while playing back. Press and release the button again to return to normal speed. Likewise, to listen more slowly (in which you can sound like a moose on Valium), press and release the ◀◀ (Rewind) button while playing. Besides being fun, these settings are actually useful when you're reviewing or editing the content of files. See "Editing File Content" for more.

# Moving Around, Between, and Within Files

The Rewind and Fast-Forward buttons are your navigation keys. They move you around, both between and within files.

## Moving from file to file

To move around from one file to another, first make sure you're not playing a file. (No sound is coming out!) Then press and release either the ◀◀ (Rewind) or ▶▶ (Fast-Forward) button.

The Rewind button moves the little you-are-here dot back one file; the Fast-Forward button moves it forward. (See the preceding section's Tip for a description of the you-are-here dot.) If the dot appears after the file number, you're at the end of a file and will have to press Rewind twice to move to the preceding file.

## Moving within a file

You can move around within a file either when the recorder is playing the file or when the recorder is paused. (To pause the recorder, press and release the PAUSE button. The display then reads PLAY PAUSE.)

Now press *and hold* either the ◄◄ (Rewind) or ►► (Fast-Forward) button to move back or forward in time. To play from that point, press and release the ► (Play) button.

Your recorder keeps track of how many seconds or minutes you are into a file. It displays that information, analogous to a tape counter, in the lower-right corner of the display when you play or pause. For instance, a display of 1:36 would mean you're listening to the recording at 1 minute, 36 seconds into the file.

## Bookmarking sections for later reference

You can bookmark, or "index," your recordings to make it easier to find sections later. While recording or playing a file, press and hold the MENU button until it double-beeps and INDEX SET appears on the display.

To move quickly between indexed points while playing a recording, press and release the MENU button. INDEX appears on the display. Then press either the ◄◄ (Rewind) or ►► (Fast-Forward) button to move to the previous or next bookmark, respectively.

# Using Folders

To help you stay organized, the recorder lets you keep your dictation files in different categories, called folders. Each folder is numbered, 1–4. Initially, you record and play back files in Folder 1. You can add more folders — up to 99, if you need them. (See "Changing Settings" in this chapter.) You can also give the folders names instead of numbers by using the Voice It Link software described in the section "Going from Recorder to PC."

The current folder number appears at the top of the display. Whenever you record or play back your dictation, you are using this "current" folder.

To advance from one folder to the next, press and release the FOLDER button. Repeat that action and eventually you will return to Folder 1.

If you have extra memory in your recorder, the recorder keeps the folders in the extra memory separate from the folders in the main memory. If you want to use a folder in the extra memory, press and hold the FOLDER button. Repeat to return to the folders in the main memory.

To move a file from one folder to another, do the following:

1. **Go to the folder where the file currently resides.**

   Press and release the FOLDER button if you need to change folders.

2. **Go to the file you want to move by pressing ▶▶ to move to a higher-numbered file or ◀◀ to move to a lower-numbered file.**

3. **Press and release the MENU button until the display shows MOVE FILE PRESS ▶.**

4. **Press and release the ▶ (Play) button.**

   The display briefly reads GO TO DEST PRESS MENU. A tiny illegible symbol also flashes on the top of the display. (Actually, it's a ◀◀ ▶▶ symbol.)

5. **Go to the folder where you want to put the file by pressing and releasing the FOLDERS button repeatedly.**

6. **Press and release the MENU button.**

   The display briefly shows MOVING . . . , and then you're done.

If you "move" a file from a folder in main memory to a folder in expanded memory, the file is actually copied. The original remains where it was.

# Editing File Content

One very nice feature of a digital recorder is that you can edit your recording. By "edit," we mean you can do the following:

✔ Insert new material anywhere in an existing file

✔ Add new material to the end of a file

✔ Delete ("cut") a chunk from an existing file

✔ Delete an entire file

So you can be more precise and efficient in your editing, you can use the Rewind and Fast-Forward buttons to slow down or speed up the playback as you review the file. See "Listening" for details.

## Inserting new material mid-file

Sometimes the insertion of even a single word (like "not") can make all the difference! To insert new material in a file, do this:

1. **Play the file up to the point where you want to change it.**

2. **Press and release the PAUSE button.**

   The recorder displays PAUSE. If you're poised and ready to speak, you can skip this step if you like and just go to Step 3. It takes us a few seconds to gather our wits before speaking.

3. **Press and release the INSERT button, speak your new material, and then press and release the INSERT button again.**

4. **Press and release the PAUSE button.**

    The recorder continues playing the file.

We think of the procedure as a kind of sandwich, with the new material as the filling: PAUSE, INSERT, speak, INSERT, PAUSE. Just remember to keep your "paws" on the outside of the sandwich when you insert.

You must rewind before you can play your edited file. The you-are-here dot we tell you about in the "Listening" section will help you figure out whether you need to rewind before you can play.

## Adding new material to the end of a file

If, like us, you dictate in spurts of inspiration (or something), you'll be constantly appending new dictation to a file. To add new material to the end of a file, do this:

1. **Begin playing the file.**

2. **Press and release the RECORD button.**

    The recorder skips to the end of the recording and begins to record your new material.

3. **Speak your additional dictation.**

4. **Press and release the RECORD button again.**

Like inserting, this procedure is another sandwich, but without the lettuce or mayo: RECORD, speak, RECORD.

## Cutting out material from a file

If brevity is the soul of wit, editing is the soul of writing (or the bluebird of happiness, or something). It's a good idea, anyway. Here's how to trim material from a file:

1. **Play the file up to where the offending part begins.**

    If you don't want to play through a long file to find the segment you want to delete, you can move around within the file. See the section "Moving Around, Between, and Within Files" to do that.

2. **Press and release the PAUSE button to pause the playback.**

3. **Press and release the DELETE button to mark the start of the segment to be removed.**

   The display briefly shows START CUT, and then leaves the tiny word CUT blinking at the top of the display to show you that it's in a cutting mood.

   Don't hold the DELETE button down unless you want to cut everything from here to the end of the file.

   If you do want to delete to the end of the file, you must keep the button down, not release it as Step 3 says; in a moment, the recorder displays CUT TO END? and then double-boops. Keep the button down. Finally, it displays DELETED SEGMENT, and then it displays AT END. Release the DELETE button and press the ▶ (Play) button. You're done — skip the rest of the steps that follow.

4. **Press and release the ▶ (Play) button and listen to the offending piece.**

5. **When you get to the end of the offending part, press and release the PAUSE button again.**

6. **Press and hold the DELETE button until it double-boops.**

   The recorder displays DELETE?/SEGMENT. (At this point, if you change your mind about deleting the segment, you may release the button to cancel the cut.) Keep holding the button down until the recorder double-boops and displays DELETED SEGMENT. You may release the button at any point now. The recorder displays PLAY PAUSE.

7. **Press and release the ▶ (Play) button.**

   The recorder plays the rest of the file (unless you have cut to the end).

This procedure is kind of a double-decker club sandwich. It goes: PAUSE, DELETE, Play (the offending piece), PAUSE, DELETE, and Play again.

## Deleting a file

To delete a file, first move to that file so that it's displayed as the current file. (Make sure it's not playing. No sound should be coming out of the recorder.)

Then press and hold the Delete key until you hear a double-boop. The display also flashes DELETED and shows the FILE number that was deleted.

## Checking file date and length

If you have a lot of files on the recorder, you can easily get confused about which is which. One way to tell them apart is by their creation date and length.

To examine the creation date and length of the file currently displayed on the recorder, press and release the MENU button. The display reads FILE INFO PRESS ▶.

Now, press and release the ▶ (Play) button. Each time you do, you see additional information about the file. In order, you see

 ✔ The length of the file in minutes and seconds. For example, 14:32 indicates a file 14 minutes and 32 seconds long.

 ✔ Which number file this is, of how many files in the folder.

 ✔ The creation date and time.

Press and release the ▶ (Play) button one more time to return to regular operation of the recorder.

# Changing Settings

The recorder works pretty well for most people the way it comes out of the box. However, you may want to make the following changes:

 ✔ Adjust the date and time

 ✔ Turn beeps on or off

 ✔ Add or remove folders

To adjust the date and time, keep pressing and releasing the MENU button until you see CLOCK SET PRESS ▶. Press the ▶ (Play) button, and then see the first section of this chapter for instructions on setting date and time.

To turn beeps on or off, keep pressing and releasing the MENU button until you see SETUP PRESS ▶. Then do the following:

1. **Press the ▶ (Play) button.**

2. **Press and release the MENU button twice more, until the display reads BEEPS ON or BEEPS OFF, with ON or OFF flashing.**

3. **Press the ▶▶ (Fast-Forward) or ◀◀ (Rewind) button to change between ON and OFF.**

4. **Press the POWER button to return the recorder to the normal mode of operation.**

To add or remove folders, keep pressing and releasing the MENU button until you see SETUP PRESS ▶. Then do this:

1. **Press the ▶ (Play) button.**

2. **Press and release the MENU button three more times, until the display reads FOLDERS, with the current number of folders flashing.**

3. **Press the ▶▶ (Fast-Forward) to increase the number of folders or the ◀◀ (Rewind) button to decrease the number.**

   If you increase folders, the display will briefly read ADDED FOLDER and, flashing, the number of the new folder. If you decrease folders, it will read DELETED FOLDER and show the folder number deleted. You can't delete a folder that has files in it. The recorder will say FOLDER IN USE. You must delete the files first.

4. **Press the POWER button to return the recorder to the normal mode of operation.**

You can use similar steps to change the recording speed from VT (Voice to Text) or recording volume ("microphone mode") from Dictation, but those changes are not recommended for dictating to NaturallySpeaking.

A nice, easy way to change some settings is by using the Voice It Link software that comes with NaturallySpeaking Mobile. See the sidebar "Changing recorder settings from Voice It Link" in the next section.

# Going from Recorder to PC

After you have your dynamic dictation on your recorder, it's time to transcribe it into titillating text. Part of the trick is to get those voice files over to your PC's hard drive. For that, you need a cable and some special software. You also need to train NaturallySpeaking to recognize your recorded voice, which is not exactly Dolby Surround-Sound theater quality.

The data comes over a cable included with the NaturallyMobile recorder. Your PC needs to have a serial port available with the right kind of connector for this cable. Look on the back of your PC for a connector with a D-shaped (okay, trapezoidal) outline and 9 pins. It's about a half inch by a quarter inch. It might be labeled "data," "serial," "101010," or not at all, depending on how cute your PC vendor gets. You may have a serial port that is otherwise okay but uses a 25-pin D-shaped connector. In that case, jog on down to Radio Shack or a computer store with your recorder's cable and ask for a DB-25 to DB-9 adapter. You may have to unplug some other device, most likely a modem, to free up a serial port.

Turn off your recorder and turn on your PC. Plug one end of the cable into your PC and the other into the bottom of your Naturally Mobile recorder.

The software you use to transfer files is separate from NaturallySpeaking. It's called Voice It Link, and it's installed with NaturallySpeaking Mobile.

Before you can transcribe text, however, you must have trained NaturallySpeaking to understand your recorded speech. This is called creating a new user for your recorder. If you have already trained NaturallySpeaking to your recorded voice (not just to your voice when dictating directly into the PC), jump ahead to the section at the end of this chapter called "Transcribing Your Files." Otherwise, read on.

## *Training NaturallySpeaking*

You may have already created a user in NaturallySpeaking so NaturallySpeaking can recognize your voice. Unfortunately, your recorded voice sounds so different that you have to train a new user.

When you train a new user for your NaturallyMobile recorder, you don't actually have to record anything! Instead, you plug the recorder into your PC by the cable that comes with it, and then you use the recorder as a microphone, talking directly into it when the wizard prompts you.

The procedure is almost exactly the same as when you first set up NaturallySpeaking. Only the first steps are different, and here they are:

1. **Connect your NaturallyMobile recorder to a serial port on your PC, using the cable that came with it.**

2. **Launch NaturallySpeaking Mobile: choose Start⇨Programs⇨ NaturallySpeaking Mobile⇨NaturallySpeaking Mobile.**

   If you have never created a user before, a Welcome screen appears for the New User wizard. If so, click <u>N</u>ext to move to the Create User screen.

   If you have created just one user previously, NaturallySpeaking opens with that user chosen. Choose User⇨New from the NaturallySpeaking window.

   If you have created several users previously, NaturallySpeaking displays an Open User dialog box. Click the New button there.

3. **Type a clever name for this new user, like *Recorder*.**

   Leave the Speech Model and Vocabulary settings alone unless you're under age 15, in which case you should probably choose settings beginning with "Student."

4. **Click the Next button.**

   After a bit of a wait while NaturallySpeaking assembles a set of brains for the new user, a User Type screen appears, asking "How Will You Dictate?"

5. **Click Into a Recorder.**

   Under "Into a Recorder," the wizard now asks, "How will you transfer your recorded data to the computer?" and provides three possible answers.

6. **Click Use The Dragon NaturallyMobile Recorder and then click the Next button.**

   The General Training Instructions screen appears.

7. **Click the Continue button.**

   The General Training screen welcomes you.

At this point, training goes exactly the same way it did when you first set up NaturallySpeaking. Turn to the section on General Training in Chapter 2 and continue from there.

# Using your recorder for a microphone

One cute trick of NaturallySpeaking Mobile (Release 4) that is easy to miss is that your recorder can now be a microphone for your PC! Whenever you use the user that you trained for your NaturallyMobile recorder and you plug your NaturallyMobile recorder into your PC, you can dictate directly into your PC or verbally control your Windows desktop from that recorder.

Click the NaturallySpeaking microphone icon on the toolbar or Windows taskbar to the "on" position, and in a few seconds the recorder turns on and displays PC LINK LINE ON. Dictate into the recorder as you would a regular microphone. (Don't forget to hold it to one side of your mouth, not directly in front.)

This recorder/microphone has two advantages over your regular microphone. One advantage is that you can use the same user to dictate to and control your PC that you use to transcribe your recordings. No need to switch users. The other advantage is that your recorder acts as a digital microphone, not unlike the USB microphone we speak so highly of in Chapter 19. A digital microphone removes all the variables of connecting through an audio card and generally gives you more reliable peformance, especially if you're using a notebook or laptop computer.

The recorder/microphone also has disadvantages. You can't use it as a microphone when you're transcribing files with Voice It Link, the transcription software we're about to discuss. You'll have to use your mouse or keyboard.

It also is rather sensitive to noise from your fingers moving on the recorder, and, unlike a headset microphone, the mouth-to-microphone distance can vary as your hand moves.

## Transcribing your files

Transcribing in NaturallySpeaking Mobile is slick. You can transfer your files and transcribe them in one fell swoop by using the Voice It Link software that comes with NaturallySpeaking Mobile. The process takes just the following five steps:

1. **From the Windows taskbar, choose Start⇨Programs⇨ NaturallySpeaking Mobile⇨Voice It Link.**

   If you're already running NaturallySpeaking and using the recorder as a microphone, click to turn the microphone icon off again, or else when you do Step 2, the Voice It Link will complain that "the communications port cannot be opened."

   Whether you use mouse or voice, the Voice It Link window of Figure 9-1 now appears. (The window is empty, at first, however.)

2. **From the Voice It Link menu, choose Link⇨Link to Recorder.**

   Your PC wakes up the recorder and begins to communicate with it. The Voice It Link window then shows you what folders are on your recorder, as in the left-hand panel in Figure 9-1.

Make link to recorder

Break link to recorder

Commands for recorder settings and links

Transcribe

**Figure 9-1:**
Voice It Link lets you peer into your recorder, transfer files, and change settings.

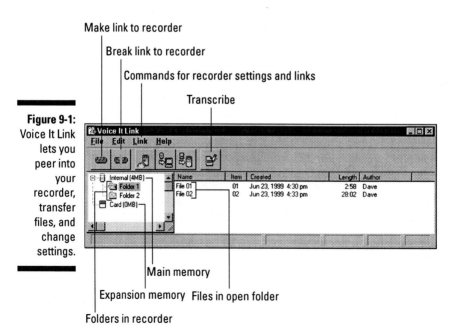

Main memory

Expansion memory   Files in open folder

Folders in recorder

3. **Click to open the folder containing the file or files you want.**

4. **In the larger, right-hand panel of the window, click to select the file to be transcribed.**

   You can transcribe multiple files if you want them to follow each other in order of file number in the same document. Hold down the Ctrl key while you click to select multiple files, or press Ctrl+A to select all files in the folder.

5. **Choose File⇨Transcribe or click the Transcribe button shown in Figure 9-1.**

   Voice It Link exports the file to your PC and then launches NaturallySpeaking (or opens its window if it's already running).

If the Open User dialog box appears, click the name you assigned as the user when you trained NaturallySpeaking to your recorded voice. (For instance, Recorder.) Click Open, and NaturallySpeaking begins transferring and transcribing your file! (If you have NaturallySpeaking set up to display tips at startup, you will first have to click Close in the Tip of The Day dialog box.)

At this point, it's best to just sit back and watch or take a nap. Don't use other windows on your PC while transcription is going on, or NaturallySpeaking will start trying to type into the wrong window! If you need to cancel transcription, look on the Windows taskbar for the button NatLink Transcribing Your Recordings. Click that button and then click the Cancel button in the window that appears.

To transfer control back to your recorder from Voice It Link, break the link. Either click the button with the broken-chain icon or choose Link⇨ Disconnect from Recorder.

The steps we just gave you do file transfer and transcription all in one lump. If you like, you can transfer recording files to the PC now, and transcribe them later by choosing Tools⇨Transcribe from the NaturallySpeaking menu bar. See the end of Chapter 8 for details about transcription. Or you may want to just transfer the files (not transcribe them) so you can e-mail someone a sound file.

To transfer a sound file, use Steps 1–4 of the preceding steps, and then instead of Step 5, choose File⇨Copy to PC As Wave File. An Export File As dialog box appears, where you can enter a filename and choose a folder for the file. Click Save to transfer the file, which you will find has a file type (an extension) of .WAV on the computer.

In the File menu of the Voice It Link program, you'll see other choices for ways to transfer files to the PC, too. The Copy To PC choice copies the file in the special format used by the NaturallyMobile recorder (SRI, or SR Image file). That format isn't particularly useful on the PC, however, because hardly any program besides Voice It Link can read it. Any reference to "compressed" files is about those kinds of files. You can also transfer files from the PC to the recorder by choosing Copy to Recorder (for files in the recorder's own compressed file format) or Copy Wave File To Recorder (for .WAV files).

After your text is transcribed, close the link between Voice It Link and your recorder: Either click the button with the broken-chain icon or choose Link⇨Disconnect from Recorder. In fact, we suggest you close Voice It Link (choose File⇨Exit), and turn the recorder off. This saves battery power and avoids picking up any stray sounds from the recorder.

Make corrections to any NaturallySpeaking recognition errors in the usual way. For instance, select a phrase containing an error and click the Correction button on the toolbar (the lasso-like icon). Use regular text editing (or dictation, if you like) to change text that was properly recognized but that you no longer like. See Chapter 5 for all the details.

## Changing recorder settings from Voice It Link

Voice It Link gives you an easier way to change some recorder settings than using the recorder buttons. (See "Changing Settings" for that procedure.)

To give folders names, add folders, or delete folders, first establish a link between PC and recorder. Choose Link⇨Link To Recorder or click the Link button (with the chain icon.) When the folders appear in the skinny left-hand panel, right-click a folder, choose Rename from the menu that appears, and type a name. To delete a folder, right-click it and choose Delete File from the menu. To add a folder, right-click anywhere in the panel where the folders are, and then choose New Folder from the menu.

To set the date and time to match your PC's date and time, choose Link⇨Set Recorder Clock. In the dialog box that appears, click OK.

To turn beeps on or off or change the clock display between 12-hour and 24-hour time, choose Link⇨Recorder Properties, and the Recorder Setup dialog box appears. Here, you'll find controls for those settings and others. (Two of the settings, Microphone and Speed, you shouldn't change if you're doing transcription with NaturallySpeaking. Leave Microphone set to Dictation and Speed to VT.)

Are you using your recorder as a microphone? As of this writing, the ability to use your recorder as a microphone immediately after transcribing is a bit unreliable. If it doesn't seem to work after clicking the microphone icon to the on position (and waiting a few seconds), change to the original user you trained on NaturallySpeaking. (Choose User⇨Open, and in the Open User dialog box that appears, double-click that original user.) Then, either use the original microphone that goes with that user or switch back to the user that goes with the recorder.

To make correction easier, you can set up NaturallySpeaking to open the correction box when you double-click improperly transcribed text in the NaturallySpeaking window. In NaturallySpeaking, do the following:

1. **Choose Tools⇨Options.**

   The Options dialog box appears.

2. **Click the Miscellaneous tab, and click to put a check mark in the option Enable Double-Click To Correct.**

3. **Click OK.**

4. **Now, in the NaturallySpeaking window, double-click the first word of any three-word utterance you want to correct.**

   The Correction dialog box appears with those words displayed. (If fewer than three words appear, they were not spoken as a continuous phrase.)

# Part III
# Giving Your Applications Wings

The 5th Wave — By Rich Tennant

"Yeah, these voice recognition systems can be tricky. Let me see if I can open your word processing program."

# In this part . . .

*L*ike many of us, NaturallySpeaking does some of its best work in its own cubicle — the NaturallySpeaking window. (Okay, okay, so it's a cubicle with a window; report us to the Metaphor Police.)

But NaturallySpeaking is also a good team player that can lend its wings to lots of different applications. It gives basic dictation to any application on your PC, and it also lets you take voice control of menus, your mouse, and the Windows desktop.

Certain programs get special attention from Dragon, so they can work as well as — or better than — NaturallySpeaking's own window. If you team NaturallySpeaking up with Word or WordPerfect by using NaturalWord, those applications get all the powers of the NaturallySpeaking window. In Microsoft Word, you also get special voice commands for its word-processing features, like fonts, paragraph alignments, or tables. Run NaturallySpeaking with Internet Explorer, and you can browse the Web by voice. With an e-mail or chat program, you can dictate your messages to people any-where in the world.

Here's the part where you discover the practical ins and outs of using NaturallySpeaking with your favorite applications. (And even if they are not your favorites, NaturallySpeaking may at least make them more interesting!)

# Chapter 10

# Dictating into Other Applications

● ● ● ● ● ● ● ● ● ● ● ● ● ● ● ● ● ● ● ● ● ● ● ● ● ● ● ● ● ● ● ● ● ● ● ● ● ● ● ● ● ● ● ● ● ● ● ●

*In This Chapter*

▶ Dictating into any application

▶ Using NaturalText applications

▶ Using Select-and-Say applications

▶ Using menus in other applications

● ● ● ● ● ● ● ● ● ● ● ● ● ● ● ● ● ● ● ● ● ● ● ● ● ● ● ● ● ● ● ● ● ● ● ● ● ● ● ● ● ● ● ● ● ● ● ●

*Y*ou can get quite a bit done just by dictating into the NaturallySpeaking window and then using cut-and-paste techniques to move the text into documents belonging to other applications. But you haven't seen the full potential of NaturallySpeaking until you've used it to dictate directly into other applications. At that point, NaturallySpeaking stops being just another program that does a cute trick with the microphone and becomes an essential component of your computer, like the keyboard or the mouse.

In addition to entering text into another application's windows, NaturallySpeaking voice commands can also control another application's menus. When you combine these techniques with the desktop control commands and dialog box techniques of Chapter 11, you can have a true no-hands computer experience.

In this chapter we focus on general techniques that you will use with many applications — NaturalText and Select-and-Say in the NaturallySpeaking terminology. Subsequent chapters in this part cover special sets of commands that work only with specific applications: NaturalWord for Word and WordPerfect (Chapter 12), NaturalWeb for Internet Explorer (Chapter 13), and NaturallySpeaking Mobile Organizer for personal information managers (Chapter 15).

The bottom line in using NaturallySpeaking with other applications is that basic dictation works pretty much the same, but your abilities to do other tasks varies widely. Keeping track of what works where is — quite frankly — very confusing. In this chapter, we tell you about the abilities you can expect in different sets of applications, plus the details of what you can expect to work where. Our hope is that, when you get confused by the way NaturallySpeaking is working, you can turn here to at least find out what's supposed to work. But don't try to get it all straight in your head at once!

# Levels of Power

One of the most frequently asked questions about NaturallySpeaking is "Does it work with *<name of application>*?" The answer is Yes. If the application has menus, dialog boxes, or a window into which you can type text, then you can use NaturallySpeaking with it. The more interesting question isn't *whether* NaturallySpeaking voice commands work with some application, but *which* commands work with which applications.

If you've been spending much time around children during the past decade, chances are you've seen *Power Rangers* at least once. Once is enough to grasp the basic formula: In every episode, the Rangers access higher and higher levels of power to deal with greater and greater threats until they finally join their super-powered robots together to form the awesome Megazord. (Sorry if we've ruined the plot for you.)

NaturallySpeaking has different levels of power, too, depending on what application you dictate to. Commands that work in some applications don't work in others. You'll save yourself a lot of frustration if you keep track of the level of power you have in whatever application you dictate to.

Here are the basic power levels, from weakest to strongest:

- ✔ **Desktop.** Even if you have no applications (other than NaturallySpeaking) open at all, you still have a few dictatorial powers: You can open files and applications on the desktop or the Start menu. You can switch from one open window to another. You can use the mouse commands. See Chapter 11 for details.

- ✔ **NaturalText.** Certain powers and abilities are with you in any application. You retain all the desktop powers. You can enter text by dictating. You can use the application's hot keys and menus. You can move around in a document by using the **Move** and **Go** commands. You have a limited amount of selection and correction capabilities. See "Creating Documents with NaturalText" later in this chapter.

- ✔ **Select-and-Say.** You have all the NaturalText abilities, plus the ability to select or correct text by saying it. In other words, editing and correcting work exactly the way they do in the NaturallySpeaking document window. The formatting commands work in some Select-and-Say applications but not others. In WordPad you have all the formatting power of the NaturallySpeaking window, while in Notepad you have only the NaturalText formatting. See "Select-and-Say Applications" later in this chapter.

✔ **NaturalWord.** You have the full editing, correcting, and formatting powers of the NaturallySpeaking window, plus a Dragon NaturallySpeaking menu is added to the application's menu bar. Using this menu, you can do virtually anything that you could do in the NaturallySpeaking window: define new users, run the Vocabulary Builder or Audio Setup wizard, open NaturallySpeaking Help, play back your dictation, and so on. You can rise to this level only in Microsoft Word or Corel WordPerfect. See Chapter 12.

✔ **Natural Language Commands.** This is the Megazord level, where you have awesome powers that surpass even those of the NaturallySpeaking window itself. Only Microsoft Word achieves this level, though if you have the Mobile Organizer edition, some natural language commands work with Outlook, Notes, and a few other personal information managers.

A few applications are special and don't fit into this list. NaturallySpeaking's NaturalWeb component (see Chapter 13) gives Internet Explorer unique Web browsing powers in all editions, and the NaturallyMobile edition (Chapter 15) has a special relationship with certain personal information managers.

| Table 10-1: | NaturallySpeaking in different applications |
|---|---|
| *When You Use . . .* | *NaturallySpeaking Gives You . . .* |
| Windows desktop | Commands for launching applications, controlling windows, and using the clipboard |
| Nearly any Windows application | All the above, plus basic menu control, dictation, navigation |
| Select-and-Say applications | All the above, plus Select-and-Say and additional formatting |
| NaturallySpeaking window | All of the above plus NaturallySpeaking toolbars and menus |
| Word and WordPerfect | All the above plus special commands (Standard edition and higher) |

# Getting Started

The hardest part of flying is leaving the nest. You may already be comfortable dictating into the NaturallySpeaking window, and you may have developed confidence that you can create documents there. If so, then you have already

mastered the techniques that allow you to dictate to other applications —
you just need to know which commands you can use in which situations. If
you're not already familiar with dictating in the NaturallySpeaking window,
the next sections will tell you what you need to know.

## Dictating your first words

The first step in achieving dictatorial mastery of other applications is to
make the words you say appear in a window controlled by the other application. (We can worry later about whether those words are correct or what you
should do if they aren't.) To get those first words to show up in the correct
window, do the following:

1. **Open NaturallySpeaking and the other application.**

   In the figures, we're dictating into WordPad, but you can use any application you want. It doesn't matter whether you open NaturallySpeaking or
   the other application first.

   At this point you need to notice two icons that NaturallySpeaking puts
   into the Windows System Tray on the right end of the taskbar: the
   speech bubble and the microphone icon. (See Figure 10-1.) They're there
   whenever NaturallySpeaking is running, but you don't need to pay attention to them until you start using NaturallySpeaking with other
   applications.

**Figure 10-1:**
These two
icons on the
System Tray
help you
control
Naturally-
Speaking
without
using the
Naturally-
Speaking
window.

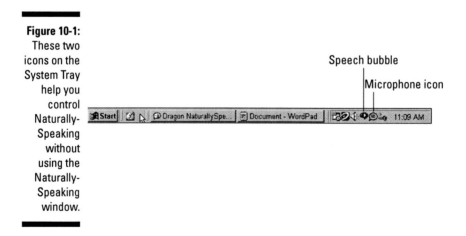

Speech bubble

Microphone icon

2. **Click the microphone icon on the Systems Tray to turn the microphone on.**

This microphone icon works just like the one in the NaturallySpeaking window: If the icon is elevated, the microphone is on; if the icon is lying flat, the microphone is off. Change from one state to the other by clicking the microphone.

By default, the microphone is off at startup and the speech bubble is on. If for some reason the speech bubble is off — it's gray and has *z*s in it — turn it on by clicking it.

3. **Activate the window of the other application.**

   Either click in the other application's window or click the other application's button on the taskbar. You can even do this by voice command: Say, **"Switch To WordPad"** or **"Switch To *<application name>*."** See Chapter 11 for more about the **Switch To** command.

4. **Start dictating.**

   We said, "Dictating into other applications really works. Period." Our WordPad window then looked like Figure 10-2.

**Figure 10-2:** WordPad takes dictation from Naturally Speaking.

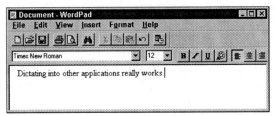

If you're not going to be using the NaturallySpeaking window for awhile, minimize it. A minimized window uses less of your computer's resources for display and leaves more for the really difficult problems, like figuring out what you just said. But don't *close* the NaturallySpeaking window. If you do, you'll instantly lose your dictating capabilities.

## Points to ponder

NaturallySpeaking may strike you as kind of peculiar. Normally, you launch an application, you get an application window, and you work in that window. End of story. Not NaturallySpeaking and for good reason: You want to be able to use voice input in lots of different places, not just in a single window.

The real core of NaturallySpeaking — the basic program that turns your speech into text or actions — actually runs in the background, or hidden. This hidden program puts its text into whichever application window you are using at any given moment. If you give a menu command, say, **Click File**, the command goes to that application's window, too.

To be technically precise, NaturallySpeaking works with whichever application is active at the time. An application is active if its title bar is colored. Click on a application's title bar, or anywhere in its window, to make it active.

# *NaturallySpeaking elements that follow you around*

When you dictate into another application, the other application's window is active, so you lose immediate access to the NaturallySpeaking window's buttons and menus. (If you need them, you can switch back to the NaturallySpeaking window by clicking the NaturallySpeaking button on the taskbar or saying, **"Switch to NaturallySpeaking."**)

But two items from the NaturallySpeaking window come with you to provide some simple dictation controls. They are the two icons following:

 The microphone icon is in the up position (at a slight angle) when it's on, as shown at the left of this paragraph. Click it to switch between on and off. If you prefer, you can use the + key on the numeric keypad (at the far right end of your keyboard) as a microphone on/off button.

 You can turn NaturalText dictation on and off. Look for an icon on the Windows taskbar that looks like a speech bubble from a cartoon, as shown at the left of this paragraph. When the speech bubble is on, it's colored and two scribbly lines appear in it. When it's off, it's gray and has cute little snoozing ZZZs in it. Click it to change between on and off.

 The speech bubble only turns off NaturalText. You can still dictate to

   ✔ The NaturallySpeaking window itself

   ✔ Any Select-and-Say application

   ✔ Word or WordPerfect if NaturalWord is running

   ✔ Internet Explorer

   ✔ The Windows desktop

## Powers you have in any application

No matter what application you find yourself working in, you can do the following (as long as NaturallySpeaking is running as well):

   ✔ **Use menus.** See "Ordering from the Menu" later in this chapter.

   ✔ **Use hot keys.** In any application, that has hot keys, you can use them with the **Press** command. See the "These keys are hot" sidebar later in this chapter.

   ✔ **Dictate text.** In most applications, you have to accept some limitations on selecting, editing, and formatting commands, as we describe in "Creating Documents in NaturalText" later in this chapter. But the simple ability to dictate a phrase (including capitalization, punctuation, and hyphenation) and see it appear on the screen is never lost.

   ✔ **Undo your last action.** The **Undo That** command works in all applications.

   ✔ **Move the cursor around in a document with the Move and Go commands.** The **Move** and **Go** commands work in any application the same way they work in the NaturallySpeaking window. See Chapter 5.

   ✔ **Use the mouse commands.** See the section about mice understanding English in Chapter 11.

   ✔ **Control windows.** You can open and close windows, start applications, and switch from one window to another. See Chapter 11.

# Creating Documents in NaturalText

When you work at the NaturalText level and you are not in a Select-and-Say application, you give up a lot of handy capabilities. In general, you will find that dictating a few lines at the NaturalText level is a reasonable thing to do, but dictating several paragraphs or pages is not. For long dictations, you are better off to dictate in the NaturallySpeaking window and then paste that dictation into the other application.

## *Powers you lose in NaturalText*

When you dictate into an application where only NaturalText applies, you lose several capabilities that you would have in a Select-and-Say application, a NaturalWord application, or the NaturallySpeaking window:

✔ **You can't select, correct, or move the cursor to text in a document by saying it.**

✔ **You can't select a block of text and then refer to it as "That."** In NaturalText, the term "That" only refers to the phrase most recently in the Results box. So you can say, **"Correct That"** to fix what you just said, but not to fix text that you select.

✔ **You lose the formatting commands.** Commands like **Bold That** or **Center That** are gone, as well as any form of **Format** or **Set**. The only formatting commands you have left are the ones having to do with capitalization, hypenation, and spaces — stuff you could do on a typewriter, in other words. See Chapter 4.

You can use the application's menus and hot keys to work around some of these limitations. For example, you can't use the **Italicize That** command in Claris Works, but that doesn't mean that you can't use voice commands to italicize a selected phrase. You can still use the menu (**Click Style, Italic**) or a hot key (**Press Control I**) to get what you want.

---

## Dictating to a nearsighted scribe

When you're dictating in a NaturalText application and can't use Select-and-Say, it's all very well to have a list of commands that work and another list of commands that don't work, but we find it useful to have a metaphor to help you remember which is which.

Picture a nearsighted scribe. He can write down the words you dictate to him, but after they are down on paper, he can't read them back. The words just look like little blobs to him. If you say, **"Move Up Five Lines"** or **"Go Back Four Words,"** he can do that because he can count lines and words. But if you say, **"Go Back To friends, Romans, countrymen,"** he's lost, because he can only count the words, not read them back. Even if you select some words for him and say, **"Italicize That"** or **"Correct That,"** he can't read them to copy them over.

When NaturallySpeaking works with an application at the NaturalText level, it behaves like that nearsighted scribe. Commands like **Select Next Three Paragraphs** work fine, but it can't handle commands like **Select Ask not what your country can do for you.** It can't see well enough to look through your document and find specific words.

Like the scribe, NaturalText has a little bit of memory; it can recall the phrase that was most recently in the Results box. So you can use commands like **Scratch That** or **Correct That** to alter what you just said. But if you say, **"Correct Austin Red Sox,"** it has no idea what to do.

## *Moving around in a document*

The **Move** and **Go** commands work the same way in NaturalText as they do in the NaturallySpeaking window, but the **Insert Before/After** commands don't work. See Chapter 5. You can also use the mouse commands to position the cursor. See Chapter 11.

If you are just reading a document and don't care where the cursor is, use **Press Page Up** and **Press Page Down**.

## *Selecting and editing text*

You feel the limitations of NaturalText most when you edit a document. The basic idea of editing text remains the same: You select any text you want to change and dictate the new text over it. But carrying out that mission is more difficult, because you can't select text by saying it.

Consequently, you end up doing a lot of counting, because you have to tell NaturallySpeaking how many characters, words, lines, or paragraphs to select. These uses of the **Select** command — **Select Next Four Words**, for example — work just as they do in the NaturallySpeaking window. See Chapter 5.

If an editing job turns out to require more work than you feel like doing in a NaturalText application, take it "back to the shop." In other words, cut the text out of the application window and paste it into the NaturallySpeaking window, where you have more tools to work with. After you get the text the way you want it, cut-and-paste it back to the original application.

## *Deleting text*

You can delete text in a NaturalText application just as you do in the NaturallySpeaking window (see Chapter 5), with two exceptions:

- ✔ You lose the **Delete That** command. It's no big loss, considering that you can get the same result by saying, **"Press Delete."** The other uses of the **Delete** command, such as **Delete Previous Three Words**, are unchanged.
- ✔ The **Resume With** command doesn't work in NaturalText.

## Making corrections

Your ability to make corrections at the NaturalText level is limited to correcting the phrase you just dictated, the one that was most recently in the Results box. If you spot a NaturallySpeaking mistake immediately after it happens, you can say, "**Correct That**" to invoke the Corrections dialog box.

To correct a NaturallySpeaking error that happened a while ago, select the text with your mouse and then dictate new text. If the new text is still wrong, say, "**Correct That**." The Corrections dialog box itself always works the same way, no matter what application you call it from. See Chapter 5.

## Formatting

You can use all the capitalization, hyphenation, and spacing commands from Chapter 4. You can't, however, change capitalization, hyphenation, or spacing, except to change the phrase you just spoke (the phrase currently in the Results box). For example, if you dictate "no, exclamation point, **All Caps That**," NaturallySpeaking transcribes "NO!"

A good general rule is that the formatting commands available in NaturalText let you do the kind of formatting you could do on a typewriter. To do any more complex formatting in a NaturalText application, you have to use the application's menus and hot keys.

### What if it doesn't work?

So there you are, dictating into an application. You aren't sure whether the command you want (say, **Set Font Arial**) will work here or not, so you try it once and it doesn't. Does that mean it just doesn't work and you should never try it again? No.

Maybe NaturallySpeaking didn't understand you properly. So try the command again, and watch the Results box this time to see what NaturallySpeaking thinks you said. If "set phone to aerial" appears, then the jury is still out on whether the command works here or not. Keep trying.

On the other hand, if **Set Font Arial** shows up in the Results box, or as text on your screen, but still nothing happens font-wise, then you can reasonably conclude that the command isn't going to work.

# Select-and-Say Applications

In some applications, NaturallySpeaking gives you the ability to select, correct, or move the cursor to text in a document by saying the text. This capability is called Select and Say, and the applications in which you have this capability are called Select-and-Say applications.

The following applications have the Select-and-Say capability:

- ✔ **Notepad**
- ✔ **WordPad**
- ✔ **Microsoft Chat 2.1 and 2.5**
- ✔ **Outlook.** When you use Word to edit Outlook's e-mail messages, the Word windows are also Select-and-Say.
- ✔ **GoldMine 4.0**
- ✔ **Internet Explorer 4.0 and higher.** Internet Explorer's Select-and-Say capability only applies to Web pages that expect your input, such as online forms or Web e-mail interfaces.

Dictating in these applications is very similar to dictating in the NaturallySpeaking window. The commands for moving the cursor, selecting text, or making corrections work in exactly the same way as they do in the NaturallySpeaking window. (See Chapter 5.) You lose the ability to play back text while you proofread, but the Play Back button in the Corrections dialog box still works if you have NaturallySpeaking Preferred or higher.

The cut-and-paste commands like **Cut That** or **Copy That** work in some Select-and-Say applications but not others. In the applications where they don't work, you can easily accomplish the same purpose with menu commands. For example, use **Click Edit, Cut** instead of **Cut That**.

The formatting commands described in Chapter 6 all work in WordPad, but not in some of the other Select-and-Say applications. (You wouldn't expect them to work in Notepad, for example, because Notepad doesn't allow formatting in any case.) We know of no case in which a formatting command works differently in a Select-and-Say application than it does in the NaturallySpeaking window: Either it works in exactly the same way, or it doesn't work at all.

Dictation only works if NaturallySpeaking is running. You can minimize the NaturallySpeaking window while you dictate into another window, but if you close NaturallySpeaking, you won't be able to dictate.

# Ordering from the Menu

The folks at Dragon can't anticipate every command that any stray application could possibly use, and so they've done the next best thing: They made the **Click** command work in such a way as to turn an application's own menus into voice commands.

Say, **"Click <*menu name*>"** to expand a menu. Any title that appears on an application's menu bar will work: **Click File, Click Edit,** and so on. After the menu expands, an entry on the menu becomes a voice command. For example, after you say, **"Click Edit,"** you can say, **"Paste"** if Paste appears on the Edit menu. The result is the same as if you had clicked Edit⇨Paste.

Be patient when you use menu commands. In most situations, it doesn't matter how far ahead of NaturallySpeaking your dictation gets. Theoretically, you could say, **"Click File, Save"** and then be off dictating something else before NaturallySpeaking had finished interpreting the **"Click."** In practice, though, waiting for NaturallySpeaking to catch up with you before giving it a menu command is best. Recognition errors in dictation are a nuisance, but they are easily fixed. Recognition errors in menu commands can delete your file. So to be safe, say, **"Click File,"** and then wait to see whether the File menu really does drop down. Then say, **"Save."**

If a menu has submenus, saying the name of the submenu causes it to expand as well. Then any command on the submenu is fair game. For example, if you have the My Computer window open and want to display the text labels for the buttons on its toolbar, say, **"Click View, Toolbars, Text Labels."** (Don't say "comma"; just pause in your speech where a comma appears.)

Menus in applications that were written for Windows 3.1 or MS-DOS may not respond to voice commands.

# Chapter 11

# Controlling Your Desktop and Windows by Voice

* * * * * * * * * * * * * * * * * * * * * * * * * * * * * * * * * * * * * * * * * * * * *

## In This Chapter

▶ Controlling the Start menu

▶ Starting NaturallySpeaking automatically

▶ Running applications by name

▶ Opening files and folders by name

▶ Switching from one window to another

▶ Talking to your mouse

▶ Dealing with dialog boxes

* * * * * * * * * * * * * * * * * * * * * * * * * * * * * * * * * * * * * * * * * * * * *

*P*eople have been talking to their operating systems since the very early days of computing, but most of what they've been saying is not repeatable in polite company. Finally, though, you can talk to your operating system and have it *do* something in response: run an application, switch to another window, move the mouse pointer, or choose a command from a menu.

You're probably used to controlling Windows's windows and applications through the keyboard and/or the mouse. You can easily imitate keyboard commands with the voice command **Press — Press Right-Arrow**, for example. You can also imitate mouse actions that click buttons or choose items from a menu with the voice command **Click** — for example, **Click OK**, or **Click File, Save.** (Unfortunately, this technique doesn't apply to toolbar buttons like Back. See Table 11-1 later in this chapter for keyboard and menu equivalents for the My Computer and Windows Explorer toolbar buttons.)

By contrast, mouse actions that involve maneuvering the mouse pointer to click some tiny, nameless object (like the +/- boxes in Windows Explorer or the arrow that drops a drop-down list box) are less convenient to do by voice. You *can* maneuver the mouse pointer by voice (see "Do Mice Understand English?" later in this chapter), but doing so is seldom the most efficient way to accomplish your purpose. Fortunately, these difficult mouse actions almost always have some keyboard equivalent that you can use with the **Press** command.

And so, in addition to the obvious theme of this chapter — learning voice commands to control Windows — a secondary theme appears: learning keyboard commands to do tasks that you may be used to doing with the mouse.

# Talking to Your Desktop

Plenty of people talk to their desktops, particularly when they are under great stress or have stayed too late at the office Christmas party. Unfortunately, up until now, most of that talk has been unproductive; the desktops have seldom responded, and those that did respond came up with very few ideas that were worth putting into practice.

Enter the Dragon (apologies to Bruce Lee fans). NaturallySpeaking lets you talk to your desktop and actually see results. Now your desktop responds to your commands by starting applications, opening windows, and giving you access to menus, including the Start menu.

However, as far as we know, pounding your head against your desktop is *still* unproductive. We recommend against it.

# Ya Wanna Start Something?

You can start applications running or open files or folders by saying, **"Start *<name of application, file, or folder>*."** For example, say, **"Start WordPad,"** to open the WordPad application. You can also use voice commands to access anything on the Start menu — Favorites, Documents, the Control Panel, or anything else.

## Starting applications by voice

Dictating text is nice, but the first feeling of real power we got from NaturallySpeaking was when we said, **"Start Word."** The screen blinked, the hard drive ground, angels sang hosannas (okay, maybe we imagined that part), and the Word window appeared in all its glory.

You can use the **Start** command to open any application whose name appears in one of the following places:

✔ **The desktop.** For example, if a Microsoft Paint shortcut is on your desktop, you can start it up by saying, **"Start Microsoft Paint."**

✔ **The top of the Start menu.** If you see the name of an application when you click the Start button, you can run it with the **Start** command.

> ✔ **In the Programs folder on the Start menu, or in any of the subfolders
> of the Programs folder.** For example, **"Start FreeCell"** opens the
> FreeCell game, even though FreeCell lies deep inside the Programs folder
> hierarchy (in Programs/Accessories/Games — unless you've moved it).

In general, you should use whatever name is on the menu or shortcut. If the
entry on the Programs menu is Adobe PhotoDeluxe 2.0, then you should say,
**"Start Adobe PhotoDeluxe 2.0."** NaturallySpeaking does recognize a few
nicknames, though. If you say, **"Start Word,"** for example, it runs Microsoft
Word. However, saying **"Start Works"** doesn't run Microsoft Works (unless
you've renamed the shortcut "Works").

If you don't like saying these long program names, you can create your own
shortcuts and name them whatever you like. For example, if you use
Netscape Messenger to get your e-mail, you can create a shortcut to
Netscape Message, put it on your desktop, and rename it "Mail." Then you
can start Netscape Messenger by saying, **"Start Mail."**

You also aren't stuck with the names on the Programs menu. You probably
didn't create most of those entries yourself; some of them have been there
since you unpacked your computer, while others have been created by the
setup wizards that installed your applications. Nuke 'em. If, like me, you have
a long-winded, hard-to-remember entry on your Programs menu — something
like "WinZip 6.2 32-bit" — you can change it to something catchy like "Zip," so
that you can start it by saying, **"Start Zip."** Here's how:

1. **Click Start⇨Settings⇨Taskbar & Start Menu.**

   You can do this by voice if you like; say, **"Click Start, Settings, Taskbar
   and Start Menu."** In either case, the Taskbar Properties dialog box opens.

2. **Click the Start Menu Properties tab, or say,** "Click Start Menu
   Properties."

3. **Click the Advanced button, or say,** "Click Advanced."

   An Exploring window opens to allow you to edit the entries on the
   Programs menu. Exploring windows behave a lot like Windows
   Explorer, which is discussed in "Giving orders to Windows Explorer"
   later in this chapter.

4. **Find and select the entry you want to rename in the right-hand pane
   of the Explorer window.**

   If you do this step by voice, move the cursor from the left-hand pane of
   the window to the right-hand pane by saying, **"Press Tab."** Select the
   appropriate folder in the right-hand pane with the **Move Up/Down** commands. Open folders as necessary by saying, **"Press Enter."**

5. **Click File⇨Rename or say,** "Click File, Rename."

6. **Say or type the new name that you want to appear on the Programs
   menu.**

7. **Close the Explorer window. You can do this by saying,** "Click Close."

8. **Click OK in the Taskbar Properties dialog box, or say,** "Click OK."

## *Starting NaturallySpeaking automatically*

Sure, NaturallySpeaking can start applications by voice, but how do you start NaturallySpeaking? Aren't you stuck using the keyboard or mouse then? Not necessarily.

It stands to reason that you aren't going to get anywhere by saying, **"Start NaturallySpeaking,"** because if NaturallySpeaking isn't running already, who's listening to you? But that's not the only trick you have up your sleeve: You can set Windows up so that NaturallySpeaking starts automatically whenever you turn on your computer. (Note: NaturallySpeaking uses a lot of memory, so if you only use NaturallySpeaking occasionally, or if your computer is short of memory, you shouldn't set up NaturallySpeaking to run automatically.)

If you want NaturallySpeaking to run automatically whenever you turn on your computer, follow these steps:

1. **Click Start⇨Settings⇨Taskbar & Start Menu. The Taskbar Properties dialog box opens.**

2. **Click the Start Menu Programs tab of the Taskbar Properties dialog box.**

3. **Click the A̲dvanced button.**

   A Windows Explorer window opens to let you edit the Start Menu folder.

4. **Expand the Programs folder by clicking the "+" next to its icon in the left-hand side of the Windows Explorer window.**

   This is one of those mouse actions that is difficult to do by voice unless you use the keyboard equivalent: Use the **Move Down** command to highlight the Programs folder and then say, **"Press Right Arrow"** to expand the folder.

5. **Select the Dragon NaturallySpeaking folder.**

   You can either click it with the mouse or you can use a **Move Down** *<some number of steps>* command. However you do it, the contents of this folder appear in the right-hand side of Windows Explorer window.

6. **Right-click the Dragon NaturallySpeaking program shortcut in the right-hand side of the Windows Explorer window.**

   Doing this step by voice takes three separate commands: Say, **"Press Tab"** to move the cursor to the right-hand pane; then **"Move Down *<number of steps>*"** to select the DNS shortcut. Say, **"Right Click"** to complete the job.

   This shortcut is the one that you choose on the Start⇨Programs⇨Dragon NaturallySpeaking menu whenever you start up NaturallySpeaking. The context menu drops down.

7. **Select Copy from the context menu.**

8. **Click the StartUp folder in the left-hand side of the Windows Explorer window.**

    Two steps are required to do this by voice: **Press Shift Tab** moves the cursor back to the left-hand pane of the window. Then you find the Start Up folder with a **Move Down** command. The right-hand side of the Windows Explorer window now shows the programs that run automatically when you start your computer.

9. **Select Edit⇨Paste from the Windows Explorer menu bar.**

10. **Close the Windows Explorer window and the Taskbar Properties dialog box.**

To undo this process, so that NaturallySpeaking no longer starts automatically, repeat Steps 1 through 4, and then click the StartUp folder and delete the NaturallySpeaking icon from the right-hand side of the Windows Explorer window.

There's only one catch: NaturallySpeaking starts with the microphone off. You still have to press the + key to turn the microphone on. This also can be fixed, as follows:

1. **Select Tools⇨Options from the NaturallySpeaking menu bar, or say,** "Click Tools, Options."

    The Options dialog box appears.

2. **Click the Miscellaneous tab or say,** "Click Miscellaneous."

3. **Click the Microphone On at Start Up checkbox, or say,** "Press Alt M."

The next time you start your computer after making these changes, NaturallySpeaking starts automatically with the microphone on but asleep. If you are the only user, your user files load automatically and you can start dictating by saying, **"Wake Up."** If your copy of NaturallySpeaking has more than one user, then you'll still have to make it past the Open User dialog box by hand before you can dictate.

## Using the Start menu

Anytime that NaturallySpeaking is running, you can say, **"Click Start,"** to pull up the Start menu. You can then say the name of any object on the Start menu: Shut Down, Log Off, Run, Help, Settings, Documents, Favorites, Programs, or any individual applications, files, or folders that you have added to the top of the menu. The resulting action is the same as if you had clicked the mouse on that entry in the Start menu:

✔ If the object is itself a menu (that is, if it has a little arrow next to it like Find, Settings, Documents, Favorites, and Programs do), it expands. (For example, Find expands to this list: People, On the Internet, Computer, and Files or Folders.) You may then select any of those objects by saying its name. If the object is another menu, it expands, and so on.

✔ If the object is an application, it runs. (You can run the application more easily just by saying, **"Start <*application name*>."** See "Starting applications by voice" earlier in this chapter.)

✔ If the object is a file or folder, it opens. The files could be documents or even Web pages.

For example, if "Favorites" appears on your Start menu, and if you have a Favorite named "Bank" that points to the Web address of your Internet bank account, then you can access your account online by saying, **"Click Start, Favorites, Bank."** (The commas represent short pauses; don't say, "comma.") To open the Control Panel, say, **"Click Start, Settings, Control Panel."**

We recommend against shutting down the computer by voice, unless you have handicaps that prevent you from doing it any other way. In general, we have found that shutting down Windows with a lot of applications running (especially complicated applications like NaturallySpeaking) is a good way to crash the system, or at the very least to cause one of the applications to do something illegal that makes Windows shut it down in an unnatural way — possibly losing some data in the process. Of course, Windows runs better on some systems than on others (and during certain phases of the moon), so you may get lucky. But why take the chance if you don't have to?

# Does It Do Windows?

Yes, NaturallySpeaking does do windows. You can open them, close them, move them, resize them, switch from one window to another, use their menus, and interact with their dialog boxes — all without taking your hands out of your lap.

## Closing and resizing windows

To close the active window, say, **"Click Close."** To maximize, minimize, or restore the active window, say, **"Click Control Menu,"** and then say, **"Maximize," "Minimize,"** or **"Restore."**

If you want to do something to a window that isn't the active window (the one on top), you first have to make it the active window by switching to it. Switch to any open application window (even if the window is minimized) by looking at the text displayed on its taskbar button and saying, **"Switch To *<text>*."** You can cycle through the open application windows by saying, **"Press Alt Tab."** See "Switching from one application to another" later in this chapter.

The simplest way to resize a window by voice is to drag-and-drop the lower right-hand corner of the window. See "Drag until you drop" later in this chapter.

## Opening My Computer and other folder windows

You can open My Computer or any other folder on your desktop with the **Start** command. Just say, **"Start My Computer,"** or, more generally, **"Start *<folder name>*."** The My Computer folder opens in a window, just as if you had double-clicked its icon on your desktop.

After a folder window is open, you can select any visible object inside the window by saying its name. You can then act on the object by using the menus. For example, you can open the Dial-Up Networking folder as follows:

1. **Say,** "Start My Computer."

   The My Computer window opens.

2. **Say,** "Dial Up Networking."

   The Dial Up Networking folder is selected.

3. **Say,** "Click File."

   The File menu drops down.

4. **Say,** "Open."

After you have a folder window open, you can use the commands off its menu. (See "Ordering from the Menu" later in this chapter.) You can also drag and drop within a folder window or from one window to another. (See "Drag until you drop" later in this chapter.) Unfortunately, no direct way exists to use the toolbar buttons other than to maneuver the mouse pointer over one and say, **"Click."** The toolbar buttons in My Computer or Windows Explorer have keyboard and menu equivalents that you can access by voice. You can duplicate the toolbar button functions with the keyboard and menu commands shown in Table 11-1.

| Table 11-1 | Voice Commands for Toolbar Button Functions | |
|---|---|---|
| *Toolbar Button* | *Voice Menu Command* | *Voice Key Combination* |
| Back | **Click Go, Back** | **Press Alt Left Arrow** |
| Forward | **Click Go, Forward** | **Press Alt Right Arrow** |
| Up | **Click Go, Up One Level** | **Press Backspace** |
| Cut* | **Click Edit, Cut** | **Press Control X** |
| Copy* | **Click Edit, Copy** | **Press Control C** |
| Paste* | **Click Edit, Paste** | **Press Control V** |
| Undo | **Click Edit, Undo** | **Press Control Z** |
| Delete* | **Click File, Delete** | **Press Delete** |
| Properties* | **Click File, Properties** | <none>* |
| Views* | **Click View** | **Press Alt V** |

*Commands marked with an * are also on the right-click menu.*

## Giving orders to Windows Explorer

Windows Explorer is an obedient little application. If you say, **"Start Windows Explorer,"** it pops up, ready to take your orders. As with My Computer, the Windows Explorer menus are available to your voice commands, but the toolbar buttons are not. (See "Ordering from the Menu" later in this chapter and Table 11-1.)

Windows Explorer has three main components, which are shown in Figure 11-1: The Explorer bar, the Contents window, and the Address box. How Windows Explorer responds to your commands depends on what component the cursor is in.

### Moving the cursor from component to component

Windows Explorer opens with the cursor in the Explorer bar, the left pane of the main window, the one that displays the overall structure of your file-and-folder system. Pressing the Tab key (or saying, **"Press Tab"**) cycles the cursor through the following three components of the Windows Explorer window:

✔ **Contents window,** the right pane of the main window, which displays the contents of the folder selected in the left pane

> ✔ **Address box,** which displays the address of whatever file or folder is currently selected
>
> ✔ **Explorer bar,** the left pane of the main window that can contain a variety of things, depending on your choice in View⇨Explorer Bar

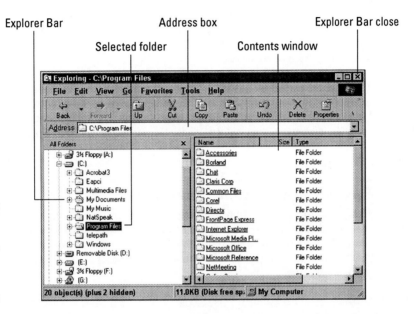

Explorer Bar   Address box   Explorer Bar close

Selected folder   Contents window

**Figure 11-1:**
Exploring
the parts of
Windows
Explorer.

Depending on how Windows is set up on your system, a fourth component may exist — the Explorer bar close button, that little X in the upper-right corner of the Explorer bar. (It's kind of a silly thing to make a component out of, but what can we say — it's Windows.) When the Explorer bar close button is selected, you can make the Explorer bar go away by saying, **"Press Enter."** To get the Explorer bar back, say, **"Click View, Explorer Bar, All Folders."**

The Shift+Tab key combination moves the cursor through these components in the opposite order. Say, **"Press Shift Tab."**

### Selecting and opening files and folders

The Explorer bar and the Contents window are each a list of folders and files. You can select an item from the list by saying its name. That sounds great, but a few complications exist: You have to say the complete name, and if the file extension is displayed, you have to say it as well. Also, if the name of the item is not an English word that's in the NaturallySpeaking active vocabulary, the name won't be recognized unless you spell it.

We must also tell you about one particularly strange and frustrating bug: After Windows Explorer fails to recognize a folder name in the Explorer bar, it gets depressed and gives up on itself (at least that's how it appears to us amateur software psychologists). After that first failure, anything you say takes you to your C: drive; or if you have several hard drives, it cycles among them.

Fortunately, you can also select items by using the **Move Up/Down/Left/Right** commands. The Explorer bar is treated as if it were one long vertical list. If you want to select the folder that's three lines below the currently selected folder, say, **"Move Down 3."**

The Contents window has both lines and columns. Use **Move Left/Right** to move from one column to another, and **Move Up/Down** to move within a column. So, for example, if the file you want is two columns to the right and three lines up from the currently selected item, say, **"Move Right 2, Move Up 3."**

After you select an item, open it by saying, **"Press Enter."**

### Expanding and contracting lists of folders

Those "+" and "-" signs in little boxes next to the folders on the Explorer bar control whether a folder's subfolders appear on the list. You may be accustomed to clicking these little boxes with the mouse, but you *don't* want to try that technique with the vocal mouse commands; it's possible, but much too time-consuming.

Instead, select a folder on the Explorer bar, and then use the right/left arrow keys to expand and contract the list of subfolders. If the folder is contracted (that is, the "+" is showing), say,**"Press Right Arrow,"** to expand it. If it's expanded ("-" is showing), say, **"Press Left Arrow,"** to contract it.

## Switching from one application to another

If you have several application windows active on your desktop, you can switch from one to another just by saying so. You can do this in four ways:

- ✔ If the window represents an application or a folder, you can call it by the name of the application or the folder. For example, **"Switch To Word"** or **"Switch To My Documents."** (Windows Explorer is an exception; switch to an open Windows Explorer window by saying, **"Switch to Exploring."**)

- ✔ You can return to the previously active window by saying, **"Switch To Previous Window."** This command is equivalent to pressing Alt+Tab. Repeating this command several times switches back and forth between two windows.

- ✔ You can cycle through all the active windows (even the ones that are minimized) by repeating, **"Switch To Next Window."** This command is equivalent to pressing Shift+Alt+Tab on the keyboard.

✔ If the name of the document appears on the title bar, you can use the name of that document in a **Switch To** command. For example, if you're using Microsoft Word to edit a document called My Diary, the title bar of the window says "Microsoft Word — My Diary." (The block on the taskbar corresponding to this window says the same thing, though the block may not be large enough to accommodate the full title.) You can switch to this window either by saying, **"Switch To Word,"** or by saying, **"Switch To *My Diary*."**

 Switching to documents by name is simpler when the file extensions aren't shown. For example, **"Switch To *My Diary*"** is easier to say than **"Switch To *My Diary dot doc*,"** and other file extensions may be even more difficult. You must, however, say the name as it appears on the title bar. You can make sure Windows 98 doesn't display file extensions on the title bar as follows:

1. **Select Start⇨Settings⇨Folder Options.**

   (In Windows 95, open Windows Explorer and select View⇨Options. You get the Options dialog box instead of the Folder Options dialog box.)

2. **Click the View tab on the Folder Options dialog box.**

3. **Make sure that the Hide File Extensions For Known File Types box is checked.**

   (In Windows 95, click Hide MS-DOS File Extensions For File Types That Are Registered.)

4. **Click OK to make the Folder Options dialog box go away.**

You can also use the mouse commands to switch to a window, either by clicking the window itself or by clicking the corresponding entry on the Windows taskbar at the bottom of your screen. Usually, this technique takes longer than **Switch To,** but having an alternative technique handy in case of mental block is a good idea. See "Do Mice Understand English?" later in this chapter.

## Switching from one document to another

The **Switch To** command switches between the windows of different applications, corresponding to different entries on the Windows taskbar. To switch among different windows in the same application, for example, two Word documents or five open message windows in Eudora Pro, use the hot key Ctrl+F6. Say, **"Press Control Function 6."** Repeat this command to cycle through all the open windows associated with the active application.

If you have trouble remembering F6 (all function keys look alike to me), you can use the Window menu of the application. The trick here is remembering that the underlined numbers next to the document names are actually hot keys. So, for example, if you have three document windows open in Microsoft Word, you can switch to the third document on the Window menu by saying, **"Click Window, Press 3.**

# Do Mice Understand English?

Once you had to go to Disney World to find a mouse that understood English. Now you have one attached to your computer. The NaturallySpeaking voice commands let you move the mouse pointer anywhere on your screen and give you access to the full range of mouse clicks: right, left, and double. You can even drag and drop objects within a window, or from one window to another.

## Telling your mouse where to go

NaturallySpeaking gives you two methods for moving the mouse pointer. **MouseGrid** breaks up the screen (or the active window) into a series of squares, letting you zero in on the location you want to move the pointer to, whereas the mouse pointer commands let you make small adjustments by saying things like **Mouse Up 5.**

How does it work? Surprisingly well, after you get used to it. Naturally, you have to adjust your expectations: Voice commands are not a high-performance way to move the mouse, so you won't be breaking any speed records the next time you play Minesweeper or Solitaire. But your virtual, voice-commanded mouse, like the physical mouse attached to your computer, is remarkably intuitive. It makes a good backup system for those times when you can't remember the right hot key or voice command.

### Making your move with MouseGrid

In days of yore, before the invention of GameBoy, children used to amuse themselves on long driving trips with number-guessing games. Here's a simple one: One kid picks a number and another makes guesses. The number-picker responds to each guess by saying "higher" or "lower." The guesser tries to narrow down the range where the number can be until eventually he knows what the number is.

MouseGrid is like that, but in two dimensions. You have picked a point on the screen where you want the mouse pointer to go, and NaturallySpeaking is trying to guess where it is. You start the game by saying, **"MouseGrid."**

NaturallySpeaking's first guess is that you want the mouse pointer to be in the center of the screen. But just in case it's wrong, it turns your screen into the *Hollywood Squares*, as in Figure 11-2. The nine squares are numbered like the keypad of a touch-tone phone: The square on the upper left is 1, and the square on the lower right is 9. The pointer is sitting right on 5. If you look very closely, you can see the numbers in the centers of the squares.

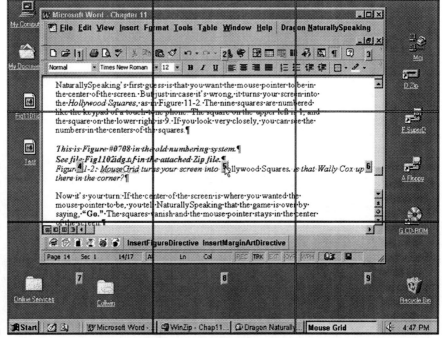

**Figure 11-2:** MouseGrid turns your screen into *Hollywood Squares.* Is that Wally Cox up there in the corner?

Now it's your turn: If the center of the screen is where you wanted the mouse pointer to be, you tell NaturallySpeaking that the game is over by saying, **"Go."** The squares vanish and the mouse pointer stays in the center of the screen.

If the center was not the point you had in mind, you say a number to tell NaturallySpeaking which square your chosen point is in. For example, you may say, **"Nine,"** indicating that the point is in the lower- right part of the screen. NaturallySpeaking responds by making all the squares go away other than the one you chose. Now it guesses that you want the mouse pointer to be in the center of that square. But just in case it's wrong, it breaks that square into nine smaller squares, as in Figure 11-3. These squares are numbered 1 – 9, just like the larger squares were.

Again, you either say, **"Go"** to accept NaturallySpeaking's guess and end the game, or you say a number to tell it which of the smaller squares you want the mouse pointer to be in. It then breaks that square up into nine really tiny squares, and the game continues until the pointer is where you want it.

This description makes it sound as if you'll be old and gray before the mouse arrives at the point you had in mind, but, in fact, this process happens very quickly after you get comfortable with it. If you're aiming for something like a button on a toolbar, two or three numbers usually suffice. You say, **"MouseGrid 2, 6, 3, Go,"** and the mouse pointer is where you want it.

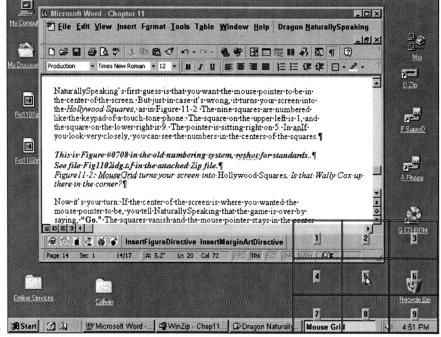

**Figure 11-3:**
Naturally-
Speaking
closes
in on the
destination
you have
chosen for
the mouse
pointer.

You can use **Cancel** as a synonym for **Go**. (This situation may be the only one in human history where "cancel" and "go" are synonyms.) We choose between them according to our mood: If we succeed in putting the mouse pointer where we want it, we say, **"Go,"** and if we just want out of the game we say, **"Cancel."** It makes no practical difference.

If you want to move the mouse pointer to a place within the active window, you can restrict MouseGrid to that window by saying, **"MouseGrid Window,"** instead of **"MouseGrid."** Now only the active window is broken up into *Hollywood Squares*. The process of zeroing in on the chosen location is the same as before — for example, **"MouseGrid Window 2, 7, Go."**

You can also get out of MouseGrid by giving a click command (which is probably why you were moving the mouse pointer to begin with). So rather than saying, **"MouseGrid 5, 9, Go"** and then **"Click,"** you can say, **"MouseGrid 5, 9, Click."** This trick works with any of the click commands, and also with **MouseGrid Window.** See "Clicking Right and Left" later in this chapter.

### Nudging the mouse pointer just a little

If the mouse pointer is *almost* where you want it and just needs to be nudged a smidgen, use the mouse pointer commands **Mouse Up**, **Mouse Down**, **Mouse Left**, and **Mouse Right.** You need to attach a number between one and ten to the command in order to tell the mouse how far to move. So, for example, say, **"Mouse Up Four,"** and the mouse pointer dutifully goes up four.

"Four what?" we hear you ask. Four smidgens, or four somethings, anyway. NaturallySpeaking Help rather unhelpfully calls them *units*. Ten minutes of experimentation has convinced us that a *unit* is about three pixels, if that helps. (Your computer screen is hundreds of pixels wide.)

Never mind all that. All you really need to know about units is

- They're small, so **Mouse Right Six** isn't going to move the pointer very far. (For big motions, use MouseGrid.)
- They're all the same size, so **Mouse Down Three** is going to move the pointer three times as far as **Mouse Down One.**

As with MouseGrid, you can combine the mouse-pointer commands with the click commands. Instead of saying, **"Mouse Left Ten"** and then **"Double Click,"** you can say, **"Mouse Left Ten Double Click."**

## Clicking right and left

You don't usually move the mouse pointer just so that you can have a little arrow displayed on your screen in an aesthetically pleasing location. You move the mouse pointer so that you can *do* something, and doing something usually involves clicking one of the mouse buttons.

NaturallySpeaking gives you a full squadron of click commands:

- **Click** or **Left-Click,** which presses the left mouse button
- **Right-Click,** which presses the right mouse button
- **Double-Click,** which presses the left mouse button twice

If NaturallySpeaking is having trouble understanding your **Click** commands, add the word **Mouse** to the command: **Mouse Click, Mouse Double-Click,** and so on. The longer command is easier to recognize.

## Dragging until you drop

When you know how to maneuver the mouse pointer and click, you're ready to drag and drop. Drag-and-drop voice commands allow you to do almost everything that you can do with hand-and-mouse commands: Move objects from one window to another, rearrange objects within a window, select a number of objects within a window, resize windows, or move windows around on the desktop.

You perform all of these actions with the **Mark** and **Drag** commands, as follows:

1. **Move the mouse pointer until it's over the object that you want to drag.**

   This object could be an icon on your desktop or in a window, the title bar of a window that you want to move, or the lower-right corner of a window that you want to resize. It could even be an empty place in a window or on the desktop that you're using as one corner of a selection rectangle.

2. **Say, "Mark."**

3. **Move the mouse pointer until it's at the point where you want to drop the object.**

4. **Say, "Drag."**

You can combine **Mark** and **Drag** with the **MouseGrid** command. For example, instead of saying, **"MouseGrid 4, 5, Go"** and then **"Mark,"** you can just say, **"MouseGrid 4, 5, Mark."**

For example, suppose that your My Computer icon is in the top-left corner of your desktop, and you want to move it to the bottom-right corner of your desktop. Do this:

1. **Say, "MouseGrid 1, 1, Mark."**

   On my screen, **MouseGrid 1,1** was sufficient to get the mouse pointer over the My Computer icon. Depending on your screen settings, you may need to say more than two numbers. For fine control, use mouse-pointer commands like **Mouse Up Two.**

2. **Say, "MouseGrid 9, 9, Drag."**

   The My Computer icon disappears from its old location and reappears at the 9, 9 location, which is in the lower-right corner of the screen.

The **Mark. . .Drag** combination mimics certain familiar mouse actions, but isn't precisely equivalent to any of them. For example, selecting an icon (with either a mouse click or by saying its name) doesn't mark it. Also, a marked object stays marked until something else is marked. You can, for example, mark an object on your desktop, go off and edit a document in your word processor, and then go back to your desktop to complete the drag-and-drop. The object is still marked, so all you have to do when you return to the desktop is move the mouse pointer to the appropriate location, and say, **"Drag."** Dragging and dropping by hand is not nearly so flexible.

**Mark. . .Drag** doesn't drag-and-drop text or illustrations within a word processing document. Use **Cut That. . .Paste That** instead. (See Chapter 5.) Another deficiency of the **Mark** command is that it doesn't mark collections of objects. For example, if you have selected four objects inside a folder window (possibly by using **Mark. . .Drag** to drag a selection rectangle over them), you cannot now move them all by marking them as a group and dragging them elsewhere. Instead, choose Edit⇨Cut from the folder window, and then Paste from the Edit menu of the window where you want them (or Paste from the context menu of the desktop).

# "Dialoging" with a Box

After you start talking to your desktop, it's only a matter of time before you find yourself having a dialog with a box. In fact, you may have been talking to NaturallySpeaking dialog boxes even before you started dictating to other applications. Don't fight it; dialog boxes are where Windows does its dirty work. Put an old copy of "I Talk to the Trees (But They Don't Listen)" on the record player and prepare to get down to business.

Dialog boxes are more difficult to deal with than menus, because they can contain almost anything: radio buttons, drop-down lists, textboxes, checkboxes, tabs, browsing windows — sometimes all in the same dialog box. How the dialog box responds to a voice command depends on where the cursor is: If the cursor is in a text box, the dialog box interprets as text utterances that otherwise might select a file or change a radio button. Consequently, you must always pay attention to where the cursor is in a dialog box. The cursor location tells you what kind of input the dialog box is expecting, which determines how it will deal with any commands you give it.

## These keys are hot!

People who don't have voice-recognition software (you may have been one of them until quite recently) use the mouse a lot when they are confronted with dialog boxes. Click here, click there, type something, double-click somewhere else, then click OK, and it's over.

NaturallySpeaking has mouse commands (see "Do Mice Understand English?" in this chapter), but moving the mouse pointer around by voice is not as quick as moving it by hand. And hitting a tiny target like the down-arrow on a drop-down list requires some patience.

Fortunately, you don't have to do things that way. Most actions that are performed with a mouse can also be done through the keyboard, by using what are called "hot keys." The Tab and Shift+Tab keys, for example, cycle the cursor through the various components of a dialog box.

The Alt key is used in most hot-key combinations. The Alt+↓ key combination makes a drop-down list drop down, whereas Alt+↑ retracts a drop-down list. The **Press** command lets you use these key combinations by voice, as in **"Press Alt Down Arrow."**

Buttons and checkboxes have hot keys as well. You can find the hot key by looking for the underlined letter in the accompanying text. In the Settings dialog box of Figure 11-4, for example, the text next to the Status Bar checkbox isn't really "Status Bar," it's "Status Bar." So you could check or uncheck the box by saying, **"Press Alt S."**

## *Moving the cursor around a dialog box*

A dialog box may have any number of windows, textboxes, buttons, and so on. Before you can deal with any particular component, you usually have to get the cursor into its window. (Buttons are an exception. If the box has a Cancel button, for example, **Click Cancel** closes the box no matter where the cursor is.)

When you're working by hand, the simplest way to put the cursor where you want it is to move the mouse pointer there and click. You can do the same thing by voice if you want (see "Do Mice Understand English?" earlier in this chapter), but often you will find it simpler to cycle through the components of the dialog window with the Tab key. Say, **"Press Tab"** to move from one component of a dialog window to another. Repeat the command to cycle through all the components of the box, and say, **"Press Shift Tab"** to cycle in the opposite direction.

To see exactly how this works, go through some of the examples in "Looking at a few of the most useful dialog boxes" later in this chapter.

## *Dealing with dialog box features*

Many menu commands lead directly to dialog boxes. For example, in the NaturallySpeaking window itself, the menu selection View⇨Settings opens the Settings dialog box (shown in Figure 11-4), which illustrates a number of the simpler standard features of dialog boxes: buttons, radio buttons, checkboxes, and tabs.

**Figure 11-4:**
The
Naturally-
Speaking
Settings
dialog box.

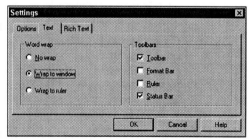

▸ **Buttons.** You can click a button by saying, **"Click *<button name>*."** You could make the dialog box in Figure 11-4 go away by saying, **"Click Cancel."** You can also use the command **Press Enter** as an alternative way to click the OK button or whatever button is currently selected (has the darkest outline).

✔ **Radio buttons.** Choose an option by saying its text label. In Figure 11-4, saying, **"No Wrap"** would change the word wrap to No Wrap from Wrap To Window. In general, this technique works when you have a single set of radio buttons (that is, a setup in which selecting one button deselects the others). In more complicated radio-button configurations (like the Date tab of the Find dialog box discussed in "Finding files and folders" later in this chapter) a **Click** command is necessary: **"Click No Wrap."**

✔ **Checkboxes.** Checkboxes are on if they are checked and off if not. Change from on to off or off to on by saying the text label. In Figure 11-4, saying, **"Format Bar"** puts a check in the Format Bar checkbox, while saying, **"Status Bar"** removes the check from the Status Bar checkbox.

✔ **Tabs.** Switch to another tab by saying its name. In Figure 11-4, you could say, **"Click Options,"** to switch to the Options tab.

Notice that the radio buttons and the checkboxes all have hot keys associated with them. (See the "These keys are hot" sidebar.) So, for example, you could check or uncheck the Toolbar checkbox by saying, **"Press Alt T."**

The Open dialog box shown in Figure 11-5 has a more complex set of features: drop-down lists, a textbox, toolbar buttons, and a list of files and folders. Although we obtained this dialog box by selecting File⇨Open from the NaturallySpeaking window, it's typical of a type of Windows dialog box. It also illustrates a standard problem: The Open dialog box first appears with the cursor in the File Name textbox. Any text you say other than **"Click"** or **"Press"** or **"MouseGrid"** will be interpreted as the name of a file. Deal as follows with the features exemplified in this box.

**Figure 11-5:**
The Open dialog box illustrates a common problem: How do you get the cursor out of the File Name text box?

✔ **Drop-down lists.** The Open dialog box has two drop-down lists: Look In and Files of Type. You can recognize them as drop-down lists because of the little down-arrow at the right edge of the text. To bring the cursor into the list say, **"Click <text label>."** For example, say, **"Click Look In."**

In some cases, this command also causes the list to drop down, but if it doesn't, say, **"Press Alt Down Arrow"** to display the list. After the list drops, change the selected item on the list either by saying its name or by using the **Move Up/Down** command. Say, **"Move Down 5,"** for example. To retract the list — and lock in the new selection — say, **"Press Alt Up Arrow."**

✔ **Textboxes.** The Open dialog box opens with the cursor in the File Name textbox. Enter text into this box by saying it. To get the cursor out of this box, use the **Click** command to click a button or a drop-down menu; or use the **MouseGrid** command to click the mouse inside some other part of the dialog box; or say, **"Press Tab"** or **"Press Shift Tab,"** to move the cursor into Files of Type or the file and folder list in the main window, respectively.

✔ **Toolbar buttons.** Unlike the big buttons (OK, Cancel, and so on) toolbar buttons in dialog boxes usually don't respond to their names. If you want to use them, you must click them with the mouse.

✔ **Lists of files and folders.** The tricky thing about using the list of files and folders is getting the cursor into its window, because there is no **Click** command that puts it there unless you maneuver the mouse pointer into the window. Instead, say, **"Press Shift Tab,"** if the cursor is just below the window in the File Name textbox, or **"Press Tab"** if the cursor is just above the window in the Look In drop-down list. After the cursor is in the main window, select files and folders either by name or by using the **Move Up/Down/Right/Left** commands. Open a selected file or folder by saying either, **"Click Open"** or **"Press Enter."**

When you open a folder from a list of files and folders in a dialog box, either **Click Open** or **Press Enter** does the job. But **Click Open** returns the cursor to the File Name textbox, whereas **Press Enter** leaves the cursor in the main window, which now displays the contents of the opened folder. We prefer **Press Enter.**

For a detailed example using a similar dialog box (Save As) see "Open, Save, and Save As" later in this chapter.

## Looking at a few of the most useful dialog boxes

Now we get down and dirty and slug it out with a few of the dialog boxes that you're going to run into again and again. These are "look Ma, no hands" examples, where everything is done with voice commands. Naturally, sometimes you can accomplish the task faster by pecking a key or moving your mouse — but we assume you know how to do that already. Over time, you'll work out your own set of compromises between voice commands and mouse-and-keyboard commands. By giving these pure-vocal examples, we leave the compromising to you.

### Finding files and folders

Suppose that a couple days ago you found a great article about aardvarks somewhere on the Web, and you know you saved it somewhere. Probably you used "aardvark" somewhere in the filename, but in the heat of the moment, you're not sure you spelled it right. You know you got the "aa" right, though, and it's bound to be somewhere on your C: drive. Do this:

1. **Say,** "Click Start, Find, Files or Folders."

   The Find: All Files dialog box, shown in Figure 11-6, opens. The cursor starts out in the Named textbox. This box is where you want the "aa" to go.

**Figure 11-6:**
The Find:
All Files
dialog box.

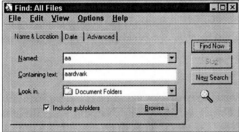

2. **Say,** "Press A, Press A."

   The "aa" appears in the <u>N</u>amed textbox.

3. **Say,** "Press Tab."

   The cursor moves into the <u>C</u>ontaining Text box. What text would an article about aardvarks be sure to contain?

4. **Say,** "aardvark."

   Unless you regularly talk about aardvarks, NaturallySpeaking may interpret this as "art park," or some similar-sounding phrase. Use **Spell That** or some other correction command (described in Chapter 5) to get it right.

5. **Say,** "Click Browse."

   A Browse for Folder window opens, so that you can tell Find to limit its search to the C: drive. (You could also have done this through the Look In textbox.) The window remembers whatever folder you chose the last time you did a search. For us, it opened with My Computer selected. The C: drive is two places lower on the list. (If it's a different number of places lower on your machine, adjust the number in Step 6.)

6. **Say,** "Move Down <number>" **or** "Move Up <number>" **to chose the C drive.**

   You may wonder what to do if you want to specify a folder inside the C: drive. If you were doing this by hand, you would click the "+" box on the line with C, and the subfolders of C would appear in the Browse for

Folder window, but hitting that target with the vocal mouse commands isn't the best way. Say, **"Press Right Arrow,"** to expose the subfolders of any selected folder, and **"Press Left Arrow"** to make them go away.

**7. Say,** "Press Enter."

The Browse for Folder window goes away. Now C: is in the Look In textbox.

**8. Say,** "Click Date."

This command shifts you to the Date tab of the dialog box. Probably you've already given Find enough information to zero in on the file you want, but let's really nail it down by limiting the search to files created in the last three days.

**9. Say,** "Click *Find All Files.*"

The Find All Files radio button only responds to the **Click** command, rather than just saying its text label "Find All Files."

**10. Say,** "Press Tab."

The cursor moves into the drop-down list next to the Find All Files radio button. The default choice is "Modified," but you want the next item down the list, which is "Created." This drop-down list works slightly differently than the one described in "Dealing with dialog box features." The down-arrow key moves down the list without dropping the list down.

**11. Say,** "Press Down Arrow."

"Modified" replaces "Created" in the text window next to Find All Files.

**12. Say,** "Press Alt D."

Notice that the bottom two radio buttons have the same text label: "during the previous." If you had said **"Click *during the previous,*"** you might have clicked the wrong one. But (as you can tell from the underlining) the two radio buttons have different hot keys. This command has chosen the bottom radio button, not the one above it.

**13. Say,** "Press Tab."

The cursor moves to the number box next to the bottom radio button.

**14. Say,** "Move Up 2."

The number in the box changes from 1 to 3. Now we have input all the information we know.

**15. Say,** "Click Find Now."

The search begins. After a short wait, a window appears at the bottom of the dialog box, listing all the files that satisfy the criteria of the search. Suppose the article you want is the third item on the list.

**16. Say,** "Move Down 3."

The article on aardvarks is now selected.

**17. Say,** "Press Enter."

The article opens.

### Finding and replacing text

Suppose your daughter has used the NaturallySpeaking window to dictate a report for Show-and-Tell about your new dog Spot. The report is excellent, except for one small problem: She believes that Spot is a cat. How can she repair this error in her report?

**1. Say,** "Click Edit, Replace."

The Replace dialog box opens, as shown in Figure 11-7. The cursor starts in the Find What textbox.

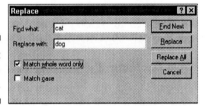

**Figure 11-7:**
The Replace
dialog box.

**2. Say,** "cat."

**3. Say,** "Press Tab."

The cursor moves to the Replace With textbox.

**4. Say,** "dog."

You're almost done. But unless you want the word "category" replaced with "dogegory," you need to do one more thing.

**5. Say,** "Click *Match Whole Word Only.*"

The corresponding checkbox is checked.

**6. Say,** "Click Replace All."

### Changing fonts

NaturallySpeaking recognizes the names of the following fonts: Arial Courier, Courier New, and Times. (It recognizes many more fonts in Microsoft Word when NaturalWord is running. See Chapter 12.) But if you want to use an obscure font like Wingdings or Copperplate Gothic Bold in any application other than Word, you have to work with the that application's version of the Font dialog box. NaturallySpeaking's Font dialog box is shown in Figure 11-8.

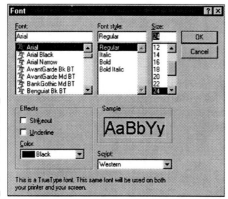

**Figure 11-8:**
The Font
dialog box in
Naturally-
Speaking.

This example shows how to switch from 12-point Arial font to 24-point Mistral font in NaturallySpeaking. The same general issues occur for any font other than the ones explicitly recognized by the NaturallySpeaking **Set Font** command.

1. **Open the Fonts dialog box from the NaturallySpeaking window by saying,** "Click Format, Font."

   The cursor starts out in the Font textbox with the name of the current font (Arial) selected. If you wanted a font whose name was a word in the NaturallySpeaking active vocabulary, like Times or Impact or Symbol, you could just say it. But "Mistral" isn't in the active vocabulary (unless you put it there), so if you say "Mistral," it is be interpreted as "missed role" or some other phrase that sounds like "Mistral" but isn't. You could start spelling it, or you could try something clever.

2. **Say,** "mist."

   "Mist" is a perfectly good English word, which is bound to be in any active vocabulary. If NaturallySpeaking misinterprets it, you can say, **"Correct That"** and have a reasonable chance of seeing "mist" as one of the options. After "mist" is in the Font textbox, "Mistral" should appear in the alphabetical list below the Font textbox. When we tried it, "Mistral" was at the top of the list.

3. **Say,** "Move Down One."

   If Mistral isn't at the top of the alphabetical list, count how far down it is and say that number instead of one. Mistral is now selected in the Font textbox.

4. **Say,** "Click Size."

   The cursor moves to the Size textbox.

5. **Say,** "Twenty-four."

   You could also say "2, 4," but "twenty-four" is less likely to be misunderstood.

**6. Say,** "Click OK."

The Font box, defeated, vanishes. You can now start dictating in 24-point Mistral.

### Open, Save, and Save As

The Open, Save, and Save As dialog boxes are all quite similar. In all three cases, you use the dialog box to specify a folder in your file system and the name of a file. When you use the Open dialog box, the file is already contained in the folder, and you want to open it. When you use Save or Save As, you want to save the current document as that filename in that folder.

Suppose you want to save the current, untitled NaturallySpeaking document as Pointless Drivel.rtf in the Useless Stuff folder on a floppy disk in your A: drive.

**1. Say,** "Click File, Save As."

A box appears asking whether you want to save the file as a Rich Text Document or as a Text Document.

**2. Say,** "Click Rich Text Document."

Welcome to the Save As dialog box, which you can see in Figure 11-9. The cursor starts in the File Name text window.

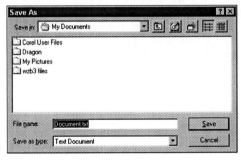

**Figure 11-9:**
The Save As dialog box.

**3. Say,** "Cap Pointless, Cap Drivel."

Now the file has a name: Pointless Drivel. It needs a file type.

**4. Say,** "Press Tab."

The cursor moves to the Save As Type drop-down list. The default (in spite of Step 2) is Text Document. You want the list to drop down, so that you can see the other choices.

**5. Say,** "Press Alt Down Arrow."

The list drops. You see that Rich Text Format is just above Text Document on the list.

6. **Say,** "Move Up 1."

   Now Rich Text Document is selected.

7. **Say,** "Click Save In."

   The cursor moves to the Save In drop-down list. Again, you want the list to drop down, so that you can see where the A: drive is on the list.

8. **Say,** "Press Alt Down Arrow."

   The Save In list drops, revealing that the My Documents folder is currently selected, and the A: drive is two places below My Documents on the list.

9. **Say,** "Move Down 2."

   Now the A: drive is selected.

10. **Say,** "Press Enter."

    The list retracts. The contents of the A: drive appear in the main window, including the Useless Stuff folder.

11. **Say,** "Press Tab."

    The cursor moves into the main window.

12. **Say,** "Useless Stuff."

    The folder is selected. You could also have selected it with **Move Up/Down/Left/Right** commands.

13. **Say,** "Click Open."

    The Useless Stuff folder opens.

14. **Say,** "Click Save."

    The file is saved.

# Chapter 12

# Using NaturalWord for Word and WordPerfect

*T*wo word processors get special treatment from Dragon: Microsoft Word and Corel WordPerfect. That special (all-natural) treatment is called NaturalWord. (Probably organically grown. Very natural, in any event.) NaturalWord is a way of running NaturallySpeaking, but you launch it from the Word or WordPerfect menu bar instead of from the Windows taskbar Start button and get a bunch of highly organic features.

Being the most popular word processor, however, Word not only gets asked to all the best parties, but it also gets some extra natural (supernatural?) features called natural-language commands. Natural-language commands are part of NaturalWord — but only for Word, not for WordPerfect.

## *NaturalWord for Word and WordPerfect*

The simplest way to think about NaturalWord is that it gives you almost all the features you get in the NaturallySpeaking window, so that you can work with your favorite documents in their natural setting. For instance, it gives you Select and Say ability, and formatting commands like **Format That Bullet Style.**

NaturalWord also duplicates nearly all of the Dragon NaturallySpeaking menu, putting those commands under NaturalWord in Word or WordPerfect's menu bar. From that menu, you can train words, add to the vocabulary, or change users, for example. You don't need to launch the NaturallySpeaking window in order to get access to those tools.

NaturalWord does occupy significantly more memory than NaturallySpeaking alone (at least 16MB more). As a result, it may run more slowly on your PC than NaturallySpeaking alone would do.

You don't have to run NaturalWord when you use Word or WordPerfect. You can run NaturallySpeaking in the background and use basic NaturalText dictation and dictation commands in Word or WordPerfect, as you might in any other application. (See Chapter 11 for more about dictating using NaturalText.) If you don't run NaturalWord, however, you don't get Select-and-Say capability. If you choose not to run NaturalWord, you don't need this chapter to dictate into Word or WordPerfect.

## *Installing NaturalWord*

NaturalWord is a component that you can install at the same time as the other NaturallySpeaking components, or you can install it later. In NaturallySpeaking 4.0, you can use it with Word 97 or Word 2000 and with WordPerfect 8 or 9.

The choice to install NaturalWord is made on the Component Selection screen of the NaturallySpeaking Setup wizard, shown in Figure 12-1. The only options you're offered are the versions of NaturalWord corresponding to the word processors installed on your machine. So, for example, the computer in Figure 12-1 has WordPerfect 9 installed, and no version of Word. Consequently, only NaturalWord for use with WordPerfect 9 is listed in the Component Selection screen.

To install NaturalWord at the same time as you install NaturallySpeaking, go through the installation procedure described in Chapter 2, and make sure to check the NaturalWord box (or boxes) offered to you in the Component Selection screen, along with whatever other NaturallySpeaking components you desire.

To install NaturalWord later (as you will need to do if you install a new version of Word or WordPerfect after NaturallySpeaking is installed), go through the installation process in Chapter 2, but *only* check the NaturalWord components in the Component Selection screen. (Do *not* go through the New User wizard again. When the Setup wizard is done, so are you.)

**Figure 12-1:**
The Setup
wizard lists
only the
versions of
Natural
Word that
go with the
word
processors
already
installed on
your
machine.

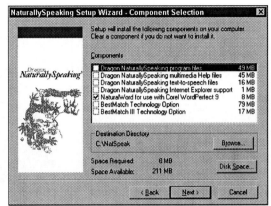

**Figure 12-1:**
The Setup
wizard lists
only the
versions of
Natural
Word that
go with the
word
processors
already
installed on
your
machine.

# *Launching NaturalWord*

You launch NaturalWord from the Word or WordPerfect menu bar. Here are
the all-natural details:

1. **Launch Word or WordPerfect.**

    We assume you know how to launch your word processor.

    You should find Dragon NaturallySpeaking on the menu bar, as Figure
    12-2 shows. If that choice isn't there, see the sidebar, "Voice-powered
    WordPerfect"

    If NaturallySpeaking is already running, just launch Word, and
    NaturalWord will start up automatically.

2. **Choose Dragon NaturallySpeaking⇨Use NaturalWord on the word
   processor's menu bar.**

    (If you have several editions of NaturallySpeaking installed with
    NaturalWord, you will be presented with a choice of which edition
    to use.)

3. **If the Open User dialog box appears, click a user, click Open, and
   you're ready to roll.**

    If you get the New User wizard at this step instead of the Open User
    dialog box, it's because you haven't defined a "user" yet. See Chapter 2.

The buttons of Figure 12-2 may be arranged differently in your word proces-
sor, or some buttons may be absent, depending upon which edition of
NaturallySpeaking, and which word processor, you use. For instance, only the
Preferred and Professional editions come with the playback controls.

---

# Voice-powered WordPerfect

Another way to combine WordPerfect and NaturallySpeaking is to get the voice-powered edition of WordPerfect Office 2000. NaturallySpeaking is part of the package (for only about $50 more than the standard edition of WordPerfect Office 2000), but it comes without NaturalText. So you can dictate in the NaturallySpeaking window, in WordPerfect, and in the Quattro Pro spreadsheet — but nothing else.

In addition, this product seems to be dead-end. The current version contains NaturallySpeaking 3.52, not 4.0, and there appears to be no plans to upgrade it.

If you're a dyed-in-the-wool WordPerfect user who was going to buy Office 2000 anyway, then by all means spend the extra $50 and get the voice-powered edition. But if you want to be able to dictate into a wide variety of applications, stick with the standard edition of WordPerfect Office 2000 and spend $60 for NaturallySpeaking Essentials (without NaturalWord) or $100 for NaturallySpeaking Standard (with NaturalWord).

---

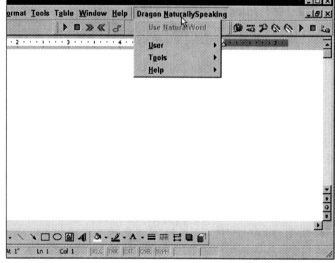

**Figure 12-2:** The Word menu and toolbars, with NaturalWord installed. You may not have all these buttons.

In WordPerfect, the playback buttons are more limited, and the microphone on/off control is in the Windows system tray, where the NaturalText microphone control is. You also don't have buttons for the Vocabulary Editor or Builder, although you can launch either tool from the NaturallySpeaking Tools menu.

With NaturalWord, you have most of the same features you get when you use the NaturallySpeaking window. You have access to the NaturallySpeaking User, Vocabulary, Tools, and Help menus by clicking Dragon NaturallySpeaking on the menu bar. Word has the same toolbar buttons as the NaturallySpeaking window for correction (see Chapter 5), playback (see Chapter 7), and training (see Chapters 2 and 18).

If you have problems with launching NaturalWord or finding it on the Word or WordPerfect menu bar, you may find yourself provoked into uttering a few other natural words. The problem may be as simple as this: You haven't installed NaturalWord yet for this word processor. Go back to "Installing NaturalWord" earlier in this chapter.

Not only can you dictate in the Word or WordPerfect window at this point, but you can also dictate in any other application window. (NaturalText, which runs in the background, handles that job. Chapter 3 provides an introduction to what NaturalText is, and Chapter 4 describes the basic dictation you can do with it. )

You can't do anything until the microphone is on! Check either of the microphone icons: the one on the NaturallySpeaking toolbar in Word or the one at the end of the Windows taskbar farthest from the Start button. (WordPerfect has only the latter.) The microphone should be up at a jaunty angle, not lying down. Click it to make it stand up.

To exit NaturalWord, you have to exit the word processor from whence it launched. (Choose File⇨Exit or use the **Click Close** command.) When you exit, NaturallySpeaking asks whether you want to save your speech files now. If you have made corrections or done any other training, click Yes in order to save your speech files.

As of this writing, Dragon doesn't give you any way to exit NaturalWord while leaving Word or WordPerfect running. (And for you more technical types, no, we don't recommend ending the NatSpeak task with Ctrl+Alt+Del. Word doesn't exit reliably after that.)

## Dictating text

For simply dictating text, NaturalWord gives you exactly the same all-natural, organic dictation features you get in any other application. (We discuss these features in Chapter 4.) NaturallySpeaking uses the exact same software to handle basic dictation, no matter what application you're using. Same vocabulary, same voice model, same everything, because it's using the same user files.

The recognition accuracy of NaturallySpeaking varies enough from one session to the next that it's tempting to imagine that NaturalWord makes it either better or worse. (NaturallySpeaking users, like indigenous farmers who depend on the weather, develop many such superstitions.) But trust us on this one. You may be tempted to turn NaturalWord on or off to improve the accuracy, but unless your computer is running out of memory (a problem marked by long delays and grinding noises from your hard drive) you would do just as well (or better!) to sacrifice a chocolate-chip cookie to the voice-recognition gods.

Although dictation in NaturalWord works exactly as it does elsewhere with NaturallySpeaking, some behaviors may seem a bit peculiar to the regular Word or WordPerfect user. Here are a few points to remember about dictating:

- Don't panic if **Undo That** doesn't seem to completely restore an error. Speak the command again. You may have to repeat the command several times to restore things as they were. Why? Many of the NaturallySpeaking commands are actually multiple commands as far as your word processor is concerned, and **Undo That** only undoes one Word or WordPerfect command at a time.

- NaturallySpeaking's idea of a paragraph isn't exactly the same as Word's or WordPerfect's idea. When you create a paragraph with the **New Paragraph** command, NaturallySpeaking (in effect) presses the Enter key twice. That action creates two paragraphs! (In Word, click the ¶ button on the toolbar to see the paragraph marks.) To get a single Word or WordPerfect paragraph, you must use the command **New Line.**

- After a New Paragraph command, Dragon capitalizes the first letter of the next sentence. After a **New Line** command, Dragon does the same, but only if the last sentence ended in a period, comma, or question mark.

## Editing and formatting text

NaturalWord brings to Word and WordPerfect all the editing and formatting features of the NaturallySpeaking window (described in Chapters 5 and 6). See those chapters for the picky details. Here's an overview of those features, and a couple of examples of the verbal commands each uses:

- Ordinary cursor control commands (**Go To Top** or **Move Back Three Words**)

- Ordinary selection (**Select Paragraph** or **Select Previous Three Words**)

- Select and Say (**Select <*text*>** or **Select <*beginning text*> Through <*end text*>**)

- Correction, without or with Select and Say (**Correct That** or **Correct <*text*>**)

- Insertion with Select and Say (**Insert Before <*text*>** or **Insert After <*text*>**)

- Cut and paste (**Copy That** or **Paste That**)

- Deletion (**Delete That** or **Delete Previous Character**)

In addition, NaturalWord gives Word an added benefit that WordPerfect users will have to get along without: natural-language commands. This chapter explains those commands a bit later.

---

## Bugs, crashes, and other large-scale failures

Like any more-or-less leading-edge product, NaturalWord has been known to do funky and unpleasant things, or to fail to work at all under some circumstances. Such problems can result from weird installations, strange Windows configurations, and even such innocuous things as having a particular version of Internet Explorer installed. Also, NaturalWord has some plain old bugs. (For instance, we find it works poorly if you're using the Change Tracking or "revision marks" feature of Word.)

One of the first things to consider in that case is to make sure you have the latest Service Release (SR) for Microsoft Word. Or at least that you have the last SR that was in existence before your copy of NaturallySpeaking came out. Check Microsoft's Web site at www.microsoft.com for information on service releases for Microsoft Office products — specifically, for Word.

---

When you refer to "paragraphs" while editing in Word or WordPerfect, as in **Select Previous Three Paragraphs,** NaturallySpeaking properly interprets the command no matter whether you have used NaturallySpeaking "paragraphs" (two presses of the Enter key), or true paragraphs (a single press, which NaturallySpeaking calls a "line"). If you have both "lines" and "paragraphs" in your document NaturallySpeaking sometimes doesn't appear to count correctly. You can make sense out of its behavior by thinking about it this way: NaturallySpeaking interprets two consecutive paragraph marks exactly as it does one mark.

In addition to the commands available through menus and dialog boxes, NaturalWord for Word gives you much power and flexibility with its natural-language commands.

## *Playback and readback*

Playback lets you play back a recording of your voice to help you proofread. Readback is the NaturallySpeaking text-to-speech feature. Chapter 7 provides the details of both playback and readback, including the Playback toolbar that now appears in Microsoft Word. These features come only with the Preferred and Professional editions.

You can play back your text by menu command and voice command, as well as with the toolbar. First, select the text you want to hear. The menu command for playback is then Dragon NaturallySpeaking➪Tools➪Play That Back.

You can have NaturallySpeaking read your selected text out loud by using the **Read That** (or **Read That Back**) command. Oddly, NaturalWord gives you no menu command for text-to-speech, so voice command is your only option.

## *AutoCorrecting — not*

Dragon suggests that you turn off AutoCorrect, mainly because doing so saves memory and processing time better used for dictation. AutoCorrect, AutoComplete, and AutoFormat are three features that are really of no use when you use NaturallySpeaking. (One reason they are useless is that NaturallySpeaking enters text into Word in a way that bypasses these automated adjudicators: They never even see what NaturallySpeaking types.)

To turn off these features in Word, first choose Tools⇨Autocorrect. To turn off AutoCorrect, click the AutoCorrect tab, and then click to clear the checkbox, Replace Text As You Type. To turn off AutoComplete, click the AutoText tab, and then click to clear the checkbox, Show AutoComplete Tip for AutoText and Dates. To turn off AutoFormat, click the AutoFormat tab, then clear all the checkmarks.

In WordPerfect, select Tools⇨QuickCorrect, and go through each tab of the QuickCorrect dialog box, unchecking all checked options. Then select Tools⇨Proofread⇨Off.

You really shouldn't need any automatic correction. NaturallySpeaking doesn't make the typos or spelling errors that AutoCorrect is designed to fix. (It makes bigger, sneakier mistakes, but that's another problem!) AutoComplete is designed to allow you to save keystrokes by just typing a few of the first letters of a word or phrase. But if you dictate, saving keystrokes is not an issue.

# *Natural Language Commands for Microsoft Word*

The worst thing about dealing with computers is that you have to learn their language. Sure, NaturallySpeaking takes dictation, but when you want to tell it what to do with that dictation, you're back in the same old situation, right? If you don't like a 10-point font, you have to say something geeky like **"Format That Size 12."**

If there were an actual human being setting type for you, you wouldn't say anything remotely like **"Format That Size 12,"** would you? You'd say **"Make It a Little Bigger,"** and the human would know what to do.

That's what a Natural Language command is. It's a command that sounds like something you would naturally say, in your own language, rather than being something you would only say because you're talking to a computer. So far, NaturallySpeaking has Natural Language commands for only one application: Microsoft Word.

One application isn't going to change the entire human/computer relationship, but it's a start. And who knows, maybe in the course of time Dragon Systems will make that number a little bigger, too.

You only get Natural Language commands in Word if you use NaturalWord. If you launch NaturallySpeaking separately and dictate into Word (a process that uses NaturalText), you don't get Natural Language commands.

# What you can say using Natural Language commands

The engineers who built NaturalWord for Word believe in freedom of speech. They tried to anticipate any way in which you might want to command Word. We think this task is Herculian, given that we may say anything from **Bold that sucker** to **Slice this turkey into two columns.** (You're probably more restrained, presuming you're not a crazed computer book author.)

Nonetheless, Dragon engineers do succeed in giving you a lot of flexibility in giving Word commands. Consider, for example, all the following perfectly acceptable commands for indentation in Word:

- ✔ **Indent that**
- ✔ **Indent the page two point five inch**
- ✔ **Make indentation two and a half inches**
- ✔ **Decrease indentation for the last three lines**
- ✔ **Set indentation to zero**

Wow! Now, that's flexible!

We would be nuts to try to document all the thousands of different ways you can give commands, and you wouldn't be any better off. Instead, we're mainly going to tell you what you can talk about, and tell you the best verbal commands to use.

Natural Language commands don't cover everything. You still need to use menus for some functions. You can use either your mouse or voice commands for those menu choices, however. You can verbally "click" menu and dialog box selections. Say, **"Click,"** followed immediately by one of the menu bar choices, and then say any choice on the menu that appears.

How do you know what to say? NaturallySpeaking accepts commands in so many different forms that Dragon suggests you just try speaking a command and see whether it works.

Clever as NaturallySpeaking is, accidentally coming up with a "command" that doesn't work is still quite possible. And, to add injury to insult, if you have selected text in your document when you speak a "command" that NaturallySpeaking doesn't recognize, that text is replaced by the text of your "command"! If that happens to you, make sure you undo the error by saying, **"Undo That"** or pressing Ctrl+Z. You may have to repeat that command to totally undo the error.

Dragon's "try and see approach" is okay if you don't mind experimenting. The *...For Dummies* approach is to give you a few memorable ways of doing something, and also tell you what things can't be done. For instance, we bet that rather than beating your head against the wall guessing at a command for inserting a textbox, you would prefer to know that no command exists!

If NaturallySpeaking doesn't perform your command, either NaturallySpeaking doesn't recognize it as a command, or the command can't be accomplished because the context where you're trying to use it is incorrect. If NaturallySpeaking recognizes your utterance as a command, the text in the Results box will be initial-capped (except for small words).

The next sections tell you how to do many Word commands by using the NaturalWord Natural Language commands. We've organized the sections roughly like the menu bar in Word, for your convenience: File, Edit, View, Insert, Format, and so forth.

## Natural Language commands for file operations and page margins

Word's file opening, closing, and page setup features such as paper orientation have no special Natural Language commands. Use the "click" commands described in Chapter 11, such as **Click File** then **Open.**

NaturalWord does, however, have commands for margins, which are on the File menu. State your marginal commands in either of these ways:

- ✔ **Make <Left Right Top Bottom> Margin <*distance*> <*units*>**
- ✔ **Set <Left Right Top Bottom> Margin To <*distance*> <*units*>**

For example, you can say, **"Make Top Margin One Point Two Inches."** The <*distance*> in this example is 1.2 and the <*units*> are inches. Allowable units are inches, centimeters, points, and picas.

The verb **Set** works as **Make** does, but you have to set something "to" a distance. For instance, you would say, **"Set Top Margin to One Point Two Inches."** We find the **Make** command more reliable.

# Natural Language commands for printing

NaturalWord for Word does offer some commands for printing. You can print any number of pages, the current page, or selected text, and you can use Print Preview.

Say **"Print,"** then one of the following terms (substituting your chosen page numbers for *<page number>*):

- ✔ **Preview/Preview Off**
- ✔ **Document**
- ✔ **Selection**
- ✔ **Page**
- ✔ **Page** *<page number>*
- ✔ **Pages** *<page number>* **Through** *<page number>*

So, for instance, say, **"Print Preview"** or **"Print Page."** You can say, **"Print This Page"** or **"Print The Current Page,"** too, if you like.

# Natural Language commands for editing

Natural Language commands for editing in Word (meaning, mainly, the stuff in the Edit menu of Word) are spotty. Sometimes NaturalWord for Word gives you a Natural Language command, sometimes not. Here's what you have:

- ✔ **Undo/Redo:** You have the same **Undo That** command in Word that you have anywhere with NaturallySpeaking. (You don't have a Redo command, but you can always say, **"Press Ctrl+Y,"** instead.)

- ✔ **Selection:** Selection in Word is through Select and Say. (Chapter 10 describes Select and Say in more detail, but the basic form of the command is **Select** *<text>*, where *<text>* is some text you can see.) You can also use **Select All** to select the whole document.

- ✔ **Cut, Copy, and Paste:** You enjoy the same **Cut That**, **Copy That**, and **Paste That** commands you do elsewhere with NaturallySpeaking. Likewise, you have the **Copy All** command for copying the whole document.

- ✔ **Find and Replace:** No special commands exist for **Find** or **Replace**. You have to use the **Click** command and the Edit menu for those functions, or else verbally press the hotkey: **Press Control F** (for Find) or **Press Control H** (for Replace).

✔ **Go To:** You can "go to" places (move the cursor) just as you can in any other application served by NaturallySpeaking. See Chapter 5 for the commands, which include such favorites as **Go To Top, Go To Bottom,** or **Go Back Three Paragraphs.** (Or, as we prefer because Naturally-Speaking gets it right more often, you can use **Move** in place of **Go** for everything except **Go To Top** or **Go To Bottom.**)

A convenient way to "go to" a specific phrase is to use Select and Say. (The phrase must be in the Word window, somewhere before your current cursor position, because Select and Say normally searches backwards and only in the window.) First, say, **"Select < *phrase*>,"** (substituting your word or phrase for < *phrase*>) then say **Move Right One.** Your cursor is now positioned just after that phrase.

One of the best editing features of NaturalWord has nothing to do with the Edit menu. It's the **Move That** command. With **Move That,** you can select some text and then say, **"Move That Down Two Paragraphs,"** for instance.

You can replace the word **That** with a reference to any number of words, lines, paragraphs, pages, or sections. For instance, you can say, **"Move Next Three Paragraphs To Bottom of Document,"** or **"Move Previous Three Lines Up One Paragraph."**

## Natural Language commands for viewing

NaturalWord provides no Natural Language commands for the various ways of viewing your document, toolbars, or anything else on the View menu. If you want to verbally control those views, you must use the **Click View** command and choose from the View menu. For example, you can say, **"Click View, Page Layout."**

## Natural Language commands for inserting

NaturalWord doesn't give you commands for most items on the Insert menu of Word. That is, it gives you no Natural Language commands for inserting page numbers, date or time, symbols, or most of the other interesting objects. For those, you have to use the **Click Insert** command and choose from the menu.

You *can* use the Natural Language **Insert <*something*>** command for page and section breaks, however, which are on the Insert menu. You can also use the command for other whitespace features like lines, tables, and columns. (*Whitespace* refers to stuff that doesn't actually put ink on paper.)

Say the word **Insert,** and then immediately say one of the terms in the following list of whitespace <*somethings*>:

## What, which way, how much, and where

The objects that you can talk to NaturalWord about are the Character, Word, Line, Sentence, Paragraph, Section, Page, Column, Row, Cell, Table, or Document. (You can also talk about the Whole or Entire Document, or "All.") You can move any number of these objects Up, Down, Left, Right, Ahead, Back, Backwards, or Forwards.

You can move some number of the Next, Last, Forward, Following, Back or Previous objects. You can move them a distance, measured in some number of objects. "Huh?" you say. Okay, for instance, you can **Move the Next Three Words up Two Paragraphs**. Or you can move an object to a destination: the Top or Bottom, Start, Beginning, or End of another object.

✔ **Space**

✔ **Line** or **Blank Line** (both mean the same thing)

✔ **Paragraph**

✔ **Section Break** or **Section** (both mean the same thing)

✔ **Row** (referring to rows in a table)

✔ **Column** (meaning columnar formatting, or columns within a table)

✔ **Page Break** or **Page** (both mean the same thing)

✔ **Table** (see the section on creating tables, coming up soon)

To insert just one of any in this list, use the singular form, as in **Insert Line.** To insert several, use the plural form and tell NaturallySpeaking how many you want. For instance, say, **"Insert Ten Lines."**

NaturallySpeaking makes a paragraph with two presses of the Enter key; a line is one press. In Word, that makes two paragraphs! If you want a single Word paragraph, use **Line** instead of **Paragraph**.

The verbs **Make, Add, Create,** and **Start** do the same thing as **Insert,** and may feel more natural. Saying, **"Start Two Columns,"** for instance, feels more correct than saying, **"Insert Two Columns,"** because the two-column formatting starts where the cursor is. You can also interject the article "a" after any of the verbs, if it seems more natural, for instance, to say, **"Make A Page Break."**

The verb **Insert** can also be used for formatting borders, numbers, and bullets. See the section "Formatting paragraphs," coming up soon.

# Natural Language commands for formatting

Formatting is where Natural Language commands for Word really start to get interesting, mainly because there is so much more to talk about. ("Interesting" in a relative sense, anyway; if conversing with your date, we recommend leaving formatting out of the conversation entirely.) You can make things bigger or smaller, or indent them more or less.

## Formatting characters

In Word, you can format characters (choose basic fonts and styles, like bold) using the same commands you would use in any other Select-and-Say application. See Chapter 6 for instructions.

NaturalWord gives you additional options for Word, however. We just give a few examples here using our favorite **Format That** command, and point out where NaturalWord adds flexibility.

✔ **Font faces:** You can say **Format That** *Arial,* for instance. NaturalWord recognizes a peculiar selection of typefaces. (We suspect it was simply the list of typefaces that happened to be installed in the computer of a Dragon engineer. Who the heck has Albertus font?!) In other applications, NaturallySpeaking only recognizes Times, Times New Roman, Courier, Courier New, and Arial. But in NaturalWord, you say **Format That** and then immediately follow with any of the following faces:

| | |
|---|---|
| • Albertus Extra Bold | • Albertus Medium |
| • **Antique Olive** | • Arial |
| • **Arial Black** | • Arial Narrow |
| • Book Antiqua | • **Bookman Old Style** |
| • Century Gothic | • **Clarendon Condensed** |
| • COPPERPLATE GOTHIC BOLD | • COPPERPLATE GOTHIC LIGHT |
| • Coronet | • Courier |
| • Courier New | • **Garamond** |
| • **Impact** | • Letter Gothic |
| • Lucida Console | • Lucida Handwriting |
| • Marigold | • Συμβολ *(Symbol)* |
| • Tahoma | • Times |
| • Times New Roman | • **Univers** |
| • **Univers Condensed** | • ✠✣■⅋⌂✣■⅋◆ *(Wingdings)* |

✔ **Font sizes:** Just as in the NaturallySpeaking window, or in WordPerfect with NaturalWord, you can say, **"Format That *Size 14,*"** or you can add the font size to a font family by saying, **"Format That *Arial 14.*"** You can't, however, say, **"Format That 14"** (without the font name or the word size). Sizes are limited to the ones Word lists in the toolbar and dialog box. (So, for example, you can't use odd-numbered sizes in the 20- to 30-point range. NaturallySpeaking types your command as text, if you try.)

✔ **Font styles, colors, and effects:** Say **Format That *<style>***, where *<style>* is anything in the following list. You can apply a style by itself with, for example, **Format That *Italics,*** or add the style at the end of a longer font command, as in **Format That *Courier Italics.*** Say, **"Format That,"** and then immediately follow with any of the following terms:

- **Black**
- **Blue**
- **Bright Green**
- **Dark Blue**
- **Dark Red**
- **Dark Yellow**
- **Gray**
- **Green**
- **Pink**
- **Red**
- **Teal**
- **Turquoise**
- **Violet**
- **White**
- **Yellow**
- **No Highlight**
- **Bold** or **Bolded** or **Bolding**
- **Italics** or **Italicized**
- **Double Strike Through**
- **Embossed**
- **Engraved**

- **Hidden**
- **Shadowed**
- **Superscript**
- **Subscript**
- **Underline** or **Underlined**
- **Double Underlined**
- **Wavy Underlined**
- **Thick Underlined**
- **Strike Through**
- **Bigger** or **Larger**
- **a Little Smaller**
- **Smaller**
- **Much Smaller** or **a Lot Smaller**
- **a Little Bigger** or **a Little Larger**
- **Much Bigger** or **Much Larger** or **a Lot Bigger** or **A Lot Larger**
- **With Hyphens**
- **Lowercase** or **No Caps**

- **Normal**
- **Default** (which means the default style of the template you're using)
- **Plain** or **Plain Text** (which means Courier)
- **Regular** (which means no style)

- **Caps** or **Initial Caps** or **Capitals** or **Capitalized**
- **All Caps** or **Uppercase**
- **Small Caps**

You can use an imperative verb form of command for certain styles. (Remember imperative verbs from English class? No, us neither, but that's what they are!) The imperatives for fonts are a short list, as follows:

- ✔ **Capitalize That**
- ✔ **Italicize That**
- ✔ **Bold That**
- ✔ **Underline That**

When you format something, **That** refers to text you have selected. You can say things other than **That** if you like. See the upcoming bullets that talk about equivalent terms.

As with most commands in NaturalWord, you can say them in different ways. Here are a few of the variations NaturalWord allows you for font commands:

- ✔ **Turn, Make,** and **Set** are all equivalent to **Format.** For instance, you may say, **"Turn That Blue,"** or **"Make That Arial Twelve Point."**

- ✔ You can use **Selection** or **It** instead of **That,** as in **Format Selection Normal.** You can also substitute for **That** phrases like **Next Three Words** or **Previous Two Paragraphs** to avoid having to select the text first. You can direct your font commands to the previous or next 1–20 **Words, Lines, Paragraphs, Pages, Sections, Columns, Tables, Rows, Cells,** or to the **Document.**

- ✔ You can use the term **Font** in place of **It** or **That.** You can use **Format Font Blue,** for instance. To help NaturallySpeaking recognize your command more reliably, you can add the word *the,* and use **the Font** or **the Selection.**

### *Formatting paragraphs*

For formatting paragraphs in Word, we prefer (you guessed it) the **Format That** *<some formatting>* command. Because you can use **Format That** no matter whether you're formatting paragraphs, fonts, or anything else, it's easiest for our poor brains to remember.

When you go to format paragraphs, however, you have two other types of commands you can use. Table 12-1 gives the gory details. The top three rows give the conventional commands that work anywhere (left-, right-, and center-align). The remaining rows list commands that NaturalWord gives you.

NaturallySpeaking gives you no Natural Language command for setting tabs. For most purposes, though, you can use indentation or table commands instead.

| Table 12-1 | Three Ways to Format Paragraphs in Word | | |
|---|---|---|---|
| *Say, "Format That" and Then* | *Or Just Say* | *Or Say, "Turn On" and Then* | *Notes* |
| **Left Aligned** | **Left Align That** | **Left Alignment** | |
| **Right Aligned** | **Right Align That** | **Right Alignment** | |
| **Center Aligned** or **Centered** | **Center That** | **Center Alignment** | |
| **Justified** | **Justify That** | **Justification** | Means no ragged right edge. |
| **Indented** Also **Outdented** | **Indent That** Also **Outdent That** | **Indentation** Also **Outdenting** | Means increase indentation to the next default or user-added tab stop. (Outdenting decreases indentation.) |
| *(nothing)* | **Indent That** *<distance>* | *(nothing)* | *For indenting a specific amount; for example, 1.5 inches. Substitute your indentation distance for <distance>.* |

*(continued)*

**Table 12-1** *(continued)*

| Say, "Format That" and Then | Or Just Say | Or Say, "Turn On" and Then | Notes |
|---|---|---|---|
| **Bulleted** *or* **Bullet Style** *or* **A Bulleted List** | **Bullet That** | **Bulleting** *or* **Bullets** | *Repeat this command to turn off bullets.* |
| **Numbered** or **A Numbered List** | **Number** (or **Unnumber**) **That** | **Numbering** or **Numbers** | Repeat this command to turn off numbering. |
| **Double Spaced** | **Double Space That** | (nothing) | |
| Also **Single Spaced** | Also **Single-Space That** | | |

*For most work, we suggest our favorite command, **Format That** <whatever>, shown in the first column.*

**That** refers to paragraphs you have selected, or where your blinking cursor is. See the bullets that follow for other words you can use instead of **That**.

As with font formatting, NaturalWord lets you say paragraph formatting commands in different ways. Here are a few of the variations NaturalWord allows you:

- You can substitute **Justified** for **Aligned**. (And, as you may suspect, you can also substitute **Justify** for **Align**, or **Justification** for **Alignment**.)

- You can use the terms **Selection** or **It** for the word **That**.

- You can use the term **Paragraph** in place of **That**. You can also substitute phrases like **Next Three Paragraphs** or **Previous Two Pages** to avoid having to select the text first. You can direct your paragraph commands to the previous or next 1–20 **Paragraphs, Pages, Sections, Columns, Tables, Rows, Cells,** or to the **Document**.

- In NaturalWord, the verbs **Turn** and **Make** work just as well as **Set** or **Format** (described in Chapter 6), for changing the formatting of a font or paragraph.

### Formatting headings and other styles

Using the same sort of command you would use for paragraph formatting, such as **Format That** *<some style>* (see Table 12-1), you can apply many of the Word built-in named styles to your text. You can even redefine styles verbally with the command **Remember That As <*some style*>**. We think Dragon should call this feature Speak A Style. (Dragon doesn't call it that, however. Yet. Dragon, we'll tell you where to send the royalty checks.)

Want a top-level heading? Say, **"Format That Heading 1."** Want to redefine what Heading 1 is? Format a paragraph (by voice or by hand), then say, **"Remember That As Heading 1."**

(If you aren't familiar with styles, here's the story in brief: Styles are combinations of font and paragraph formatting that go by a certain name, such as Heading 1. Word comes with certain predetermined styles. You, however, can change what font and paragraph formatting goes with any of the named styles.)

You can't use verbal commands for style names that you create. For example, if you create a style called Indented Quote, you can't say, **"Format That Indented Quote."** Instead, try using the **Remember That As** command to redefine the standard Word styles, like Block Text. Then use those redefined styles. (Your new definition applies only to the current document. To apply it to other documents, you use the Word Style Organizer, but that's a whole 'nother discussion!)

To apply a style, first click in a paragraph or select some text. Then say **"Format That"** followed immediately by any of the following phrases:

- **Normal Text** (same as Normal)
- **Text** (same as Body Text)
- **Body Text**
- **Body Text 2**
- **Body Text 3**
- **Plain Text** (Courier)
- **a Quote** (same as Block Text)
- **Quoted Text** (same as Block Text)
- **a Caption**
- **a Heading** (same as Heading 2)
- **Heading 1**
- **Heading 2**
- **Heading 3**
- **a Heading 1**
- **a Heading 2**
- **a Heading 3**
- **a Major Heading** (same as Heading 1)

- ✔ **a Minor Heading**(same as Heading 3)
- ✔ **a List**
- ✔ **List 2**
- ✔ **List 3**
- ✔ **Bulleted List 2**
- ✔ **Bulleted List 3**
- ✔ **a Title**
- ✔ **a Subtitle**
- ✔ **Numbered List 2**
- ✔ **Numbered List 3**

Note that NaturalWord doesn't do all the Word styles, just the ones we list.

To see what these styles are like, choose Format⇨Style, and the Style dialog box appears. In that dialog box, click in the box marked List, and then choose All Styles. The area marked Paragraph Preview shows you what the current paragraph formatting for that style looks like; the Character Preview area shows you the font currently in use. The Description section lists exactly what font and paragraph formatting the style contains. Many style descriptions begin "Normal+", which means the style is based on (uses the same settings as) Normal style, then modifies the settings from there. If you change the Normal style, all the styles based on Normal will change.

Some of the style commands, like the ones for numbered and bulleted styles, sound very much like the paragraph formatting commands, but they really refer to named styles. The number **2** or **3** at the end of certain commands refers to how much the line is indented. A **3** is more indented than a **2**.

To change a style, first format the text the way you want it. Then use the command **Remember That As *<some style>***, substituting any of the terms in the bulleted list for *<some style>*.

As with paragraph or font commands, NaturalWord lets you say it your way. Here are some other ways you can say things:

- ✔ If the term **Format** doesn't seem natural to you, you can use **Turn, Make,** or **Set.** For instance you can say, **"Turn That Into A Quote."**
- ✔ You can use the terms **Selection** or **It** for the word **That.**
- ✔ You can use the term **Paragraph** in place of **That.** You can also substitute phrases like **Next Three Paragraphs** or **Previous Two Pages** to avoid having to select the text first. You can apply your style commands to up to twenty of the previous or next **Paragraphs, Pages, Sections, Columns, Tables, Rows, Cells,** or to the **Document.**

### Formatting columns

Just say the word, and you can format your Word document into columns. (If you want to get picky about the width and spacing of your columns, however, you can't use Natural Language commands. You can use the **Click** command to choose Format⇨Columns if you like, and set the formatting in the Columns dialog box that appears.)

Click just before the area you want to format, and then speak the command. The basic command is

**Format That** *<number of columns>* **Column(s)**

Substitute **1** to **5** for *<number of columns>*. You can say either **Column** or **Columns.** As with other formatting commands you can use **Turn, Make,** or **Set** instead of **Format,** if you like.

If you want columns only in a specific area, you may be tempted to try selecting the area before giving the command. The command doesn't work that way, however. Instead, you have to give the command twice: once to turn on columns before that area and once to change it back after that area. Use **Format That 1 Column** to return to no-columns.

You can make columns begin at some specific point *before* your current cursor position by saying things like "**Format Last Three Paragraphs Two Columns.**" The same trick doesn't work for positions *after* your current cursor position.

## Tool time: spelling and grammar

When we writers use tools, certain Natural Language phrases come automatically to our lips, such as: "Get the @#$*& in there" or "What the *&^#$ is wrong with this drill?" The Natural Language commands for the *Word* tools, fortunately, are much more printable and useful. Following are the commands for the two Microsoft Word tools for which NaturalWord provides Natural Language commands: spelling and grammar.

Say **Run** followed immediately by any of these phrases:

 ✔ **Spell Checker**
 ✔ **Spelling Checker**
 ✔ **Spell Check**
 ✔ **Spelling Check**
 ✔ **Grammar Checker**
 ✔ **Grammar Check**

You can say **"Do A"** instead of **"Run."** For instance, you may say, **"Do A Spell Check."**

On the other hand, if you truly are dictating everything in your document using NaturallySpeaking, you should never need to run the spelling checker! The one kind of mistake that NaturallySpeaking never makes is a spelling error (unless you added a misspelled word to your NaturallySpeaking vocabulary).

Keep in mind that when you run the Word spell checker, it may not recognize words that are in your NaturallySpeaking vocabulary. The two programs maintain their own lists of what words are acceptable.

## Tables

NaturalWord lets you create Word tables with up to 20 rows or columns using Natural Language commands. You can use the commands **Insert, Make, Add,** or **Create,** as you prefer. We tend to prefer **Insert** because it's the same command we use for other whitespace insertions like spaces, paragraphs, or page breaks. Here are the different forms of commands you can use (using **Insert** as our example):

- ✔ **Insert Table <*n*> Rows By <*m*> Columns**
- ✔ **Insert <*n*> Row By <*m*> Column Table**
- ✔ **Insert Table With <*n*> Rows And <*m*> Columns**

Substitute numbers between 1 and 20 for <*n*> and <*m*>. In any of these commands, you can say the columns first and then the rows, or vice versa.

You can leave out either the rows or the columns in any of these commands and then add them later. For instance, **Insert Three Column Table** leaves out any discussion of rows, and so creates a three-column table with one row.

After you have a table, you can verbally move your cursor around in the table, referring to rows, columns, or cells. Commands use either **Move** or **Go** and take forms like these examples:

- ✔ **Move Right One Column**
- ✔ **Move to Next Row**
- ✔ **Go Down Three Cells**

You can move **Left, Right, Up, Down, Back, Backward, Ahead,** or **Forward.**

You can add rows or columns using exactly the same sort of command you used to create the table: **Insert, Add, Make,** or **Create.** Place the insertion point where you want to add stuff, and speak the command.

As usual, we prefer **Insert** because we are curmudgeonly, old stick-in-the muds. Also, we have lousy memories and hate learning new terms. You can insert a number of rows or columns or insert "a new" row or column. Here are a few examples, using our favorite command, **Insert:**

- ✔ **Insert a New Row**
- ✔ **Insert Five Rows**
- ✔ **Insert Two Columns**

You can select, delete, cut, or copy rows, columns, or cells just as you would words in regular text. For instance, you can use **Select Row** to select the row your cursor is in, or use **Select Next Five Rows.** You can also use **Delete Row** or **Copy Row.** Deleting rows only removes the data from the row, not the row itself. To paste a row, column, or cell you have copied, just use **Paste That;** don't refer to a row, column, or cell in the command.

Inserting, deleting, and pasting by voice works just as it does when you insert, delete, or paste by hand. That is, rows are inserted above the current row; columns are inserted to the left of the current column.

# Windows

NaturalWord doesn't give you any special commands for document windows in Word. If you want to do anything in the Word Window menu, you have to do it manually or with the **Click Window** command. You can, however, make use of the key combination Ctrl+F6 to switch document windows (say, **"Press Control F6"**) or Ctrl+F4 to close a document window (say, **"Press Control F4"**).

This isn't to say you can't switch between the Word window and other program windows. As in any application, you can say, **"Switch to *<Program Name>*"** (if that program is running) or **"Switch to Previous Window."**

# Help

If you want help with Word, you have to go through the Word Help menu, either manually or with the **Click Help** command. You can get help on NaturallySpeaking at any time, though, by using the NaturallySpeaking usual **What Can I Say** command or the **Give Me Help** command.

As of this writing, however, the NaturallySpeaking help files give you very little information on Natural Language commands. The official Dragon position appears to be that these commands are so comprehensive that most commands you can think of will work, and so who needs documentation?

# Chapter 13

# A Dragon Online

*W*ord processing may be the first and most obvious application of speech recognition, but chances are it's not the only thing you do with your computer. If you're like us, you spend more time than you care to admit on the Internet — browsing Web pages, exchanging e-mail, and chatting.

NaturallySpeaking provides an entire component — NaturalWeb — for Web browsing. Natural Web is new with version 4.0, and it makes no-hands Web browsing practical for the first time.

There are no special NaturallySpeaking commands for e-mail or online chat, but we predict that you'll hardly notice. The menu commands of the e-mail and chat applications provide all the specialized commands you need, and the rest is basically just word processing and window management. Nonetheless, we've assembled a few tricks that we think are worth knowing.

Using AOL with NaturallySpeaking presents special challenges, because the AOL interface is so mouse-oriented, and NaturallySpeaking's mouse commands are inefficient. Knowing the right hotkey combinations, however, makes all the difference.

## Browsing the Web

In our opinion, the most important new feature of NaturallySpeaking 4.0 is NaturalWeb. Using NaturalWeb with Internet Explorer lets you do all your Web browsing by voice, pleasantly and efficiently, without touching the mouse or keyboard.

The only problem we've found with NaturalWeb is that it works only with Internet Explorer. If you're a religious user of Netscape Navigator or some other browser, you have to choose between your browser and NaturalWeb. See "Choosing Navigator over NaturalWeb" later in this chapter.

## Getting started

To start browsing the Web with NaturalWeb, follow these instructions:

1. **Start NaturallySpeaking.**

2. **Start Internet Explorer.**

   It doesn't matter how you start Internet Explorer. You can start it with the **Start** command (see Chapter 10), by selecting a Favorite from the Start menu, or by clicking its desktop icon with the mouse.

That's all there is to it. If everything is set up correctly, a blue NaturalWeb startup screen appears briefly as Internet Explorer is starting up, and you can start dictating to Internet Explorer immediately.

If you don't see the blue NaturalWeb startup screen, and if a little experimentation convinces you that NaturalWeb is not working, you are probably in one of the following situations:

- ✔ **NaturalWeb is turned off.** Turn it on by using the Start menu: Select Start⇨Programs⇨Dragon NaturallySpeaking⇨NaturalWeb⇨ Turn on NaturalWeb.

- ✔ **NaturalWeb isn't installed.** If you don't see a NaturalWeb entry in the Dragon NaturallySpeaking folder on your Start⇨Programs menu, NaturalWeb probably isn't installed. Put the NaturallySpeaking CD into your CD-ROM drive and run the Setup wizard again. This time be sure to check NaturalWeb when the wizard asks which components to install. See Chapter 2 for details on the Setup wizard.

## Giving orders to Internet Explorer

You can give Internet Explorer its marching orders in three ways:

- ✔ **NaturalWeb commands.**

- ✔ **Keyboard commands.** See Chapter 11 for a discussion of hotkeys.

- ✔ **Menu commands.** See Chapter 10.

In addition, you can use the same **Move** and **Go** commands that work in the NaturallySpeaking window, like **Go To Top/Bottom** or **Move Down Three Paragraphs.** You can also use the mouse voice commands (see Chapter 11) to click toolbar buttons or links on Web pages, but usually one of the other techniques achieves the same result more easily. Table 13-1 shows how to replace the Internet Explorer toolbar buttons with NaturalWeb, keyboard, or menu voice commands.

### Table 13-1 Voice Commands that Substitute for the Toolbar Buttons

| Toolbar Button | NaturalWeb | Menu | Key Combination |
|---|---|---|---|
| Back | Go Back | Click View, Go To, Back | Press Alt Left arrow |
| Forward | Go Forward | Click View, Go To, Forward | Press Alt Right arrow |
| Stop | Stop Loading | Click View, Stop | Press Escape |
| Refresh | Refresh | Click View, Refresh | Press F5 |
| Home | Go Home | Click View, Go To, Home Page | Press Alt Home |
| Search | <none> | Click View, Explorer Bar, Search | Press Ctrl + E |
| Favorites | <none> | Click View, Explorer Bar, Favorites | Press Ctrl + I |
| History | <none> | Click View, Explorer Bar, History | Press Ctrl + H |
| Mail | <none> | Click Tools, Mail and News | <none> |
| Print | <none> | Click File —> Print | Press Control P |
| Edit | <none> | Click File —> Edit | <none> |

## Telling Internet Explorer where to go

Web browsers provide a large number of ways to open a Web page or to get from one Web page to another. Your start page opens when you start Internet Explorer (unless you started it by selecting an entry from the Start⇨Favorites menu), and from there you can move around on the Web by choosing links; with toolbar buttons (whose menu and keyboard equivalents are listed in Table 13-1); entering a Web address into the Address box; or by jumping to a page whose location you have stored on the Favorites menu.

### Linking from one Web page to another

The most important new feature that NaturalWeb provides is the ability to select a link on a Web page by saying its text label, or part of its text label.

For example, suppose that you are viewing the Web page of Figure 13-1 — the News and Events page of the Dragon Systems Web site — and you want to follow the link labeled Wordwide Schedule. All you have to do is say, **"worldwide schedule."** NaturalWeb searches the links visible in the Internet Explorer window to see if any of them contain *worldwide schedule.* Because one and only one such link appears on the page in Figure 13-1, a red arrow appears under the link, and a few seconds later the linked page appears.

**Figure 13-1.**
NaturalWeb waits to be told whether the first occurrence of "Press" in a link is the one we wanted.

In Figure 13-1, we have said **"press."** Several different visible links contain the word *press,* so NaturalWeb doesn't know which one to go to. Consequently, it displays a red arrow and a yellow question mark under the first such link, Press Releases. Unlike the previous case, it waits for input before proceeding. Say, **"That One"** to open the link it has selected, or **"Next"** to select the next link containing *press.* You may say, **"Next"** as often as you like; NaturalWeb cycles through the matching links. To back up to the previous selection, say, **"Previous."**

Pick out whatever part of the link's text label is easiest to say. For example, if you want to link to a news story "1331 injured in Ulan Bator earthquake," say, **"injured"** or **"earthquake."** Either should be sufficient to tell NaturalWeb which link you want.

If the link is an image, say, **"Image."** NaturalWeb selects the first image visible in your viewing window. If that's not the one you want, keep saying, **"Next"** until NaturalWeb finds the image you want. Then say, **"That One."** If you know the text label of the image (which is displayed while the image is loading) you can select it by name, just as you would any text link.

Unfortunately, NaturalWeb doesn't know what to do with images that contain several links, like those maps that link different places to different pages. In those cases, you must use the mouse or the mouse voice commands.

### Dictating to the Address box

The Address box is the textbox at the bottom of the browser's toolbar, the one that shows the Web address of the current page. Say, **"Go To Address"** to move the cursor into the Address box. Then dictate the address you want and say, **"Go There."**

You can start a Web search by dictating, **"Question mark *<search terms>*"** into the Address box and then saying, **"Go There."** For example, if you are looking for articles about McDonalds franchises in Antarctica, say, **"Question mark, McDonalds, comma, Antarctica."** When you see "?McDonald's, Antarctica" appear in the Address box, say, **"Go There."**

Our tongues tie in knots whenever we try to say, "Double-you, double-you, double-you," so we came up with the following trick: We used the Vocabulary Editor to introduce the word "http://www" into the NaturallySpeaking vocabulary, and defined its spoken form to be **"Dubdubdub."** (or a second alias we created, **Triple-Dub**). (See Chapter 18 for a detailed description of Vocabulary Editor tricks like this one.) So if we want NaturallySpeaking to type "http://www.yahoo.com," we just say, **"Dubdubdub dot yahoo dot com."**

The last 25 Web addresses that were typed or dictated into your Address box are kept on a list that drops down from the Address box. To make it drop down, get the cursor into the Address box, and then say, **"Press Alt Down Arrow."** Naturally, **"Press Alt Up Arrow"** makes the list retract again. Move up or down the list with the **Move Up/Down** commands, like **Move Down Three**. After you select an address from the list, say, **"Press Enter"** to tell your browser to go there.

### Using the Favorites menu

By far, the easiest way to connect to a Web page is to have its location stored on the Favorites menu. Using this menu is also the simplest, quickest way to keep track of Web sites and return to them by voice commands. You can use voice commands to go to a Web site on the Favorites menu in three ways.

✔ If Internet Explorer and NaturalWeb are running in the active window, say, **"Go To Favorite <*favorite name*>,"** where <*favorite name*> is the name that you have given the Web page on the Favorites menu. It doesn't matter where on the menu the favorite is. If, for example, you have a favorite called CNN in a folder called News Sites on the Favorites menu, you just have to say, **"Go To Favorite CNN."** You don't have to say the name of the News Sites folder.

✔ Whether Internet Explorer is running or not, you can select a Web page from the Start⇨Favorites menu. Now you do have to say all the intermediate folders. For example: **"Click Start, Favorites, News Sites, CNN."**

✔ You can use the Favorites menu on the Internet Explorer menu bar just as you use the Start⇨Favorites menu. If Internet Explorer is the active window, say, **"Click Start, Favorites, News Sites, CNN."**

**TIP**

When you create favorites, give them short names that are easy for you to pronounce and easy for NaturallySpeaking to recognize. If the names of the favorites you already have are too long or too difficult, you can change them as follows:

1. **Select the folder containing the favorite on the Start⇨Favorites menu.**

   Don't select the favorite itself, because you don't want to open it right now. In the CNN example earlier in this section, you would say, **"Click Start, Favorites, News Sites."** The menu expands so that you can see the CNN favorite, but it is not selected.

2. **Use the Move Up/Down commands to highlight the favorite.**

   If CNN is the fifth entry in the News Sites folder, say, **"Move Down Five."**

3. **Say** "Right Click, Rename."

   A Rename dialog box appears.

4. **Dictate the new name.**

5. **Say,** "Click OK."

## *Reading a Web page*

NaturalWeb provides an automatic scrolling feature that we find very convenient for reading long articles. Just say, **"Start Scrolling Down"** and the text of the current Web page starts moving up your screen like the credits at the end of a movie. Adjust the scrolling speed by saying, **"Speed Up"** or **"Slow Down."** (We love it — no computerese nonsense like "Set Scrolling Speed Up Five," or something equally obscure.) The **Stop Scrolling** command — we bet you've figured this out already — stops the scrolling. To go backwards, say, **"Start Scrolling Up."**

If automatic scrolling makes you feel like you're in a speed-reading test, you have other options for moving through a Web page. You may be accustomed to using the scroll bar on the right edge of your browser's window to move through a Web page, but as always, mouse-oriented techniques don't translate to speech as well as keyboard-oriented techniques do. The simplest way to scroll through a Web page by voice is to say, **"Press Page Down"** when you want to display the next screen's worth of text.

The **Move** and **Go** commands from Chapter 5 also work with a browser, but predicting what they're going to do is sometimes hard. The "lines" that NaturallySpeaking moves when you say, **"Move Down 4 Lines"** don't precisely correspond to the lines of text that you see on your screen. (They're usually a little bit larger than the lines of text. Don't ask me why.) And on Web pages that have several frames, images, animations, or other advanced features, what a "paragraph" means is anybody's guess. "Top" and "bottom" are still meaningful terms, though, and you will find that **Go To Top** and **Go To Bottom** are good commands to remember when you're reading long documents on the Web.

# *Entering information on a Web page*

Many Web pages contain forms for you to fill out, or textboxes into which you can dictate longer messages. NaturalWeb has special commands for entering such information or messages.

Before you can dictate text into a textbox, you must first move the cursor there. You can, of course, move the cursor by clicking the mouse in the box, just as you would if you weren't using NaturallySpeaking. But you can also say **"Type Text"** to move the cursor to the first textbox on the page. Once the cursor is in the box, you can dictate, edit, and correct just as you would in any Select-and-Say application. (See Chapter 10.) When you finish with the first textbox, say, **"Next"** to move on to the second, and so on. Go back to an earlier textbox by saying, **"Previous."**

To move the cursor to radio buttons or checkboxes on a Web page, just say, **"Radio Button"** or **"Check Box."** The cursor moves to the first such object on the page. Say, **"Next"** to go to the next one or **"Previous"** to return to the one before. (NaturallySpeaking figures out from context what kind of object **"Next"** refers to.) To change the state of a radio button or checkbox, say **"Click That."**

To cycle through the objects on a Web page, say, **"Press Tab."** Say, **"Press Shift Tab"** to cycle in the opposite direction. This technique is useful when you want to go from an object (like a textbox) to a different kind of object (like a radio button).

## *Choosing Navigator over NaturalWeb*

If you like Netscape Navigator (or some other browser) better than Internet Explorer, the Dragon Systems folks haven't served you very well. NaturalWeb doesn't work with any browser but Internet Explorer, so you can't select links by saying them in Navigator. This is a major disadvantage, because trying to click links with the MouseGrid commands is clumsy and time-consuming. Adding insult to injury, NaturallySpeaking doesn't handle the Navigator Bookmarks menu well — it doesn't recognize items on the Bookmarks menu by name, so you have to use the **Move Up/Down** commands to maneuver through the list of bookmarks.

If you want to use Navigator with NaturallySpeaking, you can recover most of this capability by doing the following two things:

✔ **Declare Navigator to be the Windows default browser, so that the Start⇨Favorites menu works with Navigator.** How difficult this is depends on which version of Windows you have and which version of Navigator. (Microsoft wants it to be difficult and Netscape wants it to be easy, so they battle back and forth with each new version of their software.) Look for instructions at the Netscape Web site at home. netscape.com/download/netscape_now.html.

✔ **Buy the Web Keyboard utility.** Web Keyboard pre-processes the Web pages you open and numbers all the links on a page, so that you can jump to a link by just saying the number. The net result is almost as good as being able to select links by saying them. You can download Web Keyboard from the Adynware Web site at www.adyn.com/web_key for a free 30-day trial. A permanent license cost $27.95 the last time we checked.

# *Dragonmail*

In fantasy novels, a dragon's "mail" consists of its interlocking armored scales. But NaturallySpeaking is a dragon whose mail weighs nothing in any kind of scale, armored or not. Naturally, I'm speaking about e-mail — that novel and fantastic interlocking system of messages and replies and forwards.

Unlike NaturalWeb for Web browsing, NaturallySpeaking has no special e-mail commands. Of course, it doesn't need a **Mail That** or **Reply To That** command, because those commands already exist in the menus of the e-mail applications themselves.

Using NaturallySpeaking and your e-mail application together in the most effective, least tedious way involves a subtle change of style, particularly if you're used to operating your e-mail application by using the mouse to click buttons. Some buttons respond to a **Click** *<button name>* command, and some don't. Those that don't are best replaced with a keyboard or menu command, rather than using the vocal mouse commands to track down the button, especially if it's small.

## Using the three-pane e-mail application window

The most popular e-mail applications (Eudora, Netscape Messenger, and Outlook Express) all have the same basic three-pane window shown in Figure 13-2:

- ✔ **The folder list:** A vertical pane on the left displaying message folders or mailboxes
- ✔ **The message list**: A horizontal pane in the upper right listing the messages contained in the selected message folder
- ✔ **The reading pane:** A horizontal pane in the lower left displaying the contents of the selected message

Microsoft Outlook, the only Select-and-Say e-mail application (other than GoldMine, a contact-management tool aimed at sales and service organizations) can be put into the three-panel form by choosing to display the Folder List but not the Outlook bar. We recommend this configuration because the Outlook bar is a mouse-oriented tool that is less convenient to use with voice commands. (Use the <u>V</u>iew menu to choose which Outlook components to display.)

**Figure 13-2:**
The three-pane window of Outlook Express has the same general structure as all the popular e-mail applications.

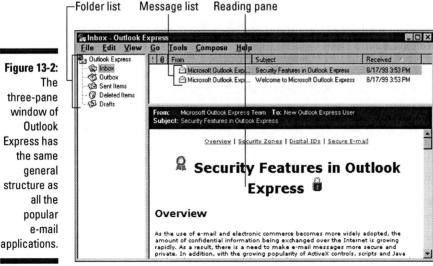

Move from one pane to another by pressing the Tab key or saying, **"Press Tab."** Move in the opposite direction with Shift+Tab. In Messenger and Outlook Express, you can reach all three panes by this technique. In Eudora, the Tab key moves the cursor back and forth between the message list and the reading window. To move the cursor to the folder list in Eudora, use the Tools⇨Mailboxes menu command or say, **"Click Tools, Mailboxes."**

### The folder list

The folder list in an e-mail application behaves like the folder list in Windows Explorer. (See Chapter 11.) When the cursor is in this pane, use the **Move Up/Down** commands to select a folder or mailbox. For example, **Move Down Five** selects the folder or mailbox five places below the currently selected folder or mailbox. Folders that contain subfolders or mailboxes have a +/- checkbox next to their folder icons. To display the subfolders or mailboxes, select the containing folder and say, **"Press Right Arrow."** To hide the subfolders or mailboxes again, say, **"Press Left Arrow."**

Eudora makes a distinction between highlighting a folder and selecting it. Even after a folder or mailbox has been highlighted in the folder list, its messages don't display in the message list until you select the folder or mailbox. Select the highlighted item in the folder list by pressing the Enter key or saying, **"Press Enter."** In Outlook Express and Messenger, a folder is selected automatically when it's highlighted in the folder list.

### The message list

The message list is, first and foremost, a list. When the cursor is in the message list pane of the e-mail application window, you can select messages in the list by using the **Move Up/Down** commands. To select the message three places above the currently selected message, say, **"Move Up Three."**

### Reading messages

You can read a message in the reading pane of the application window, or you can get a little more reading room by opening a message window. Open a message window in Messenger or Outlook Express by selecting a message in the message list and selecting File⇨Open from the menu (or saying, **"Click File, Open"**). In Eudora, select the message and say, **"Double Click."**

In Outlook Express and Messenger, the message window is outside the application window and has its own button on the Windows taskbar. In Eudora, the message window covers the two right-hand panes of the application window (the message list and reading window), and has its own button on the Eudora taskbar at the bottom of the Eudora application window.

Whether the cursor is in the reading window or in a message window, the **Move** and **Go** commands from Table 13-1 move the cursor through the message. However, the most useful command when you're reading a message is **"Press Page Down,"** which displays the next window-full of text.

### *Switching between open mailboxes and messages*

In Eudora, a mailbox or message that you've opened remains open until you close it or exit the program. The various open mailboxes are represented by a taskbar just beneath the reading window. In both form and function, this taskbar resembles the taskbar on the Windows desktop, except that the items on the taskbar are open Eudora mailboxes and messages rather than open application windows.

Switch from one open mailbox to another by pressing Ctrl+F6 or saying, **"Press Control F6."** Alternately, you may use the numbered hotkeys on Eudora's Window menu.

In Outlook Express and Messenger, open message windows have their own buttons on the Windows taskbar. Say, **"Press Alt Tab"** to cycle through the items on the taskbar. Switch to a new mailbox by selecting it in the folder list.

## Dictating messages

At present, the only Select-and-Say e-mail application is Outlook (not Outlook Express). If you use Outlook, dictating messages is just like dictating text in a Select-and-Say word processor. (See Chapter 10.)

For all other e-mail applications, we recommend using the menu commands (Reply, Reply to All, Forward, or New Message) to open a message composition window, and that you address the messages using the e-mail application's address book or by dictating or typing the address into the appropriate line of the message composition window. (If you used a Reply or Reply to All command to generate the composition window, the address is filled in automatically.) But you should dictate the text of the message either in the NaturallySpeaking window or in a Select-and-Say or NaturalWord word processor. When you have the text the way you want it, cut and paste it into the message composition window.

A message composition window consists of a number of textboxes: several one-line boxes corresponding to the various parts of a message header, and one large textbox for the body of the message. Move the cursor from one textbox to another by using the Tab key or saying, **"Press Tab."** Move in the opposite direction with Shift+Tab.

Send your messages by using your e-mail application's menu commands.

## Getting your mail read to you

In the Preferred or Professional editions of NaturallySpeaking you can use the text-to-speech feature to have your mail read to you. Just copy the text of the

message from the reading pane of your e-mail application to the
NaturallySpeaking window and say, **"Read Document."** The Naturally Speaking
voice and diction isn't going to compete with James Earl Jones anytime soon,
but if you listen closely you should be able to understand what it's saying.

# Dragon Tricks for AOL

On the surface, America Online appears to be as mouse-oriented as a feline
hunting expedition. Everywhere you look, AOL confronts you with things to
click: channel buttons, hyperlinks, and those tiny heart-shaped Favorite
Places icons, just to mention a few. Even the Help files are full of instructions
to click here and click there — which isn't very helpful when you're relying
on voice commands to get you where you want to go. No one looks forward
to long hours of saying things like **"MouseGrid 7, 3, 8, 1 Click"** over and over
again.

But, to use a metaphor that only a mouse could love, there are many ways to
skin a cat — even on AOL. Lurking deep within AOL's menus are commands
that duplicate many of the buttons, links, and other clickabilia that fill the
AOL window. And did we mention hotkeys? User-defined hotkeys? They exist.

But we don't want to raise false expectations. AOL was designed with the
mouse in mind, and even if you know all the tricks, you will probably not be
able to have a full, rich AOL experience without using your mouse or the
mouse voice commands from time to time.

NaturalWeb doesn't work with AOL's embedded copy of Internet Explorer. See
"Opening a separate copy of Internet Explorer" later in this chapter for a
workaround.

# Signing on

If AOL is on your Start or Programs menu, or if you have an AOL shortcut on
your desktop, you can start AOL by saying, **"Start America Online."** You
have to use the exact name that's on the entry in the menu or on the shortcut. You can name these entries whatever you want, but we've had better
recognition with "America Online" than "AOL."

When AOL starts, the first thing you see is the Sign On dialog box. The cursor
begins in the Select Screen Name box. Use the **Press Up Arrow** and **Press
Down Arrow** commands to choose among your screen names. When you
have the screen name right, say, **"Press Tab"** if you need to choose a different
entry on the Select Location list. Again, use the **Press Up/Down Arrow** commands to get the entry you want.

When you have the screen name and location you want, say, **"Click Sign On."** The automatic sign-on process takes it from there.

# Channels

The first thing you see when you log in to AOL is the array of Channels buttons. These buttons don't respond to the Click command directly, but all the same entries are on the Channels menu, which does respond. So instead of clicking the News channel button, for example, pick it off the menu by saying, **"Click Channels, News."**

# Keywords

One advantage that AOL's universe has over the Web is that keywords are easier to remember than Web addresses. If you're trying to find the score of last night's game while you wait for your morning coffee and worry about being late for work, would you rather try to remember "sports," the keyword of AOL's sports channel, or "http://espnet.sportzone.com," the URL of ESPN's Web site? The answer seems obvious to us.

But how do you use that keyword by voice? As is so often the case, the tricky part is getting the cursor into the right textbox. And as is so often the case, the solution is a hotkey.

1. **Say,** "Press Control K."

   A keyword textbox opens right in the middle of the screen.

2. **Dictate the keyword into the textbox.**

   In our example, you would say, ***"sports."***

3. **Say,** "Press Enter."

# Controlling window proliferation

AOL's windows are like a toddler's toys; more and more of them keep getting opened, and they never put themselves away. Eventually, you have to pretend to be a grown-up and do some housekeeping, or else your computer's entire memory will be swamped by the window clutter.

Fortunately, you can close windows without MouseGriding your way down to those tiny little X's in the upper-right corners. To close the current window, say, **"Press Control F4."** This is a case where you have to get it right: Alt+F4 closes the entire AOL application window and logs you out — do not pass Go, do not ask for confirmation.

Hoover up vast quantities of windows in a hurry by saying, **"Click Window, Close All Except Front."** Or if that's too much of a mouthful, use the hotkey and say, **"Click Window, Press A."** This command does just what it says — closes all the windows except the one on top.

A numbered list of the currently open windows appears in the Window menu. To switch to window number three, for example, say, **"Click Window, Three."** To move to the next window in the sequence, say, **"Press Control Tab."** To move back, say, **"Press Control Shift Tab."**

If a window has several tabs (like the Mailbox window for example, which has tabs for New Mail, Old Mail, and Sent Mail), you can move one tab to the right by saying, **"Press Control Right Arrow"** and one tab to the left by saying, **"Press Control Left Arrow."**

## Opening a separate copy of Internet Explorer

AOL's embedded Web browser is Internet Explorer, but NaturalWeb doesn't know that and doesn't work with it. (We hope Dragon fixes this in future versions.)

But all the advantages of NaturalWeb are not lost. You can open up Internet Explorer outside of the AOL application window and still have it use the AOL Internet connection: Just open AOL, sign in, and then open Internet Explorer in a separate window. NaturalWeb will work with the separate copy of Internet Explorer, even as it continues to ignore the embedded copy of Internet Explorer inside AOL.

## AOL Mail and Instant Messaging

The Read Mail and Write Mail buttons on the AOL toolbar don't respond to **Click** by name, but **Press Control R** is equivalent to clicking Read Mail, and **Press Control M** is equivalent to clicking Write Mail. To start composing an instant message, say, **"Press Control I."** To send a message (either an instant message or a piece of e-mail) that you have composed in the current window, say, **"Press Control Enter."** Table 13-2 lists the AOL hotkeys related to mail and messaging.

The AOL mailbox has three tabs: New Mail, Old Mail, and Sent Mail. Move from one tab to the next by saying, **"Press Control Right Arrow"** or **"Press Control Left Arrow."**

| Table 13-2 | Mail and Messaging Hotkeys in AOL | |
|---|---|---|
| *This Key Combo* | *Said Like This* | *Opens This Search Window* |
| Ctrl+R | Press Control R | Your mailbox |
| Ctrl+M | Press Control M | A Write Mail window |
| Ctrl+I | Press Control I | An Instant Message window |
| Ctrl+Enter | Press Control Enter | Sends the mail or instant message in the current window |

## Defining your own hotkeys

The key combinations Ctrl+0, Ctrl+1, . . . Ctrl+9 are yours to define. You may assign any AOL keyword or Web address to these key combinations, and then whenever you either press the keys or tell NaturallySpeaking to press them, AOL opens a window displaying the corresponding content.

To define your keys, or just to see the default definitions that AOL has made on your behalf, say, **"Click Favorites, My Shortcuts, Edit Shortcuts."** An Edit Shortcut Keys window similar to Figure 13-3 appears.

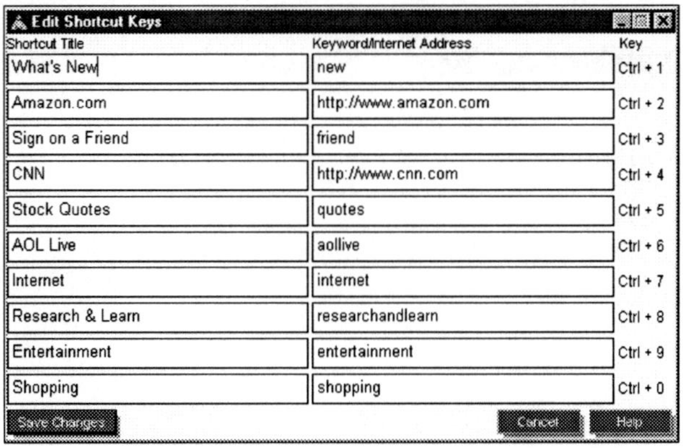

**Figure 13-3:** Type Web addresses or AOL keywords into the columns, and then click the Save Changes button.

| Shortcut Title | Keyword/Internet Address | Key |
|---|---|---|
| What's New | new | Ctrl + 1 |
| Amazon.com | http://www.amazon.com | Ctrl + 2 |
| Sign on a Friend | friend | Ctrl + 3 |
| CNN | http://www.cnn.com | Ctrl + 4 |
| Stock Quotes | quotes | Ctrl + 5 |
| AOL Live | aollive | Ctrl + 6 |
| Internet | internet | Ctrl + 7 |
| Research & Learn | researchandlearn | Ctrl + 8 |
| Entertainment | entertainment | Ctrl + 9 |
| Shopping | shopping | Ctrl + 0 |

The Edit Shortcut Keys window consists of 20 textboxes — ten for the titles of the shortcuts, and ten for the keywords or Web addresses they point to. Move the cursor from box to box either by saying, **"Press Tab"** or by clicking the mouse on the box you want to edit.

When you find a key that you want to redefine, type the title of the new short-cut in the left-hand box, and the Web address or keyword in the right. When you have made all the changes you want to make, say, **"Click Save Changes."**

After you have a hotkey defined, you can use it either as a menu or keyboard command. For example, given the definitions in Figure 13-3, I could access the CNN Web site by saying either, **"Press Control 4"** or **"Click Favorites, My Shortcuts, CNN."** The title that you give the shortcut serves as its menu entry.

## Accessing your favorite places

AOL's version of a Favorites menu is called Favorite Places. Unfortunately, it's designed to be used with the mouse and lacks some essential keyboard or menu equivalents. You won't be able to use this feature fully without employ-ing the vocal mouse commands. (See Chapter 11.)

Your ten *most* favorite places belong on your user-defined hotkeys, which you *can* easily access by voice. See "Defining your own hotkeys" earlier in this chapter.)

Open the Favorite Places window (shown in Figure 13-4) by saying, **"Click Favorites, Favorite Places."** This window is an expandable list arranged into a hierarchy of folders, much like the left pane of the Windows Explorer window.

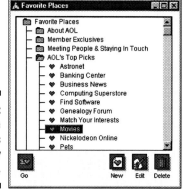

**Figure 13-4:**
The Favorite
Places
window
in AOL.

Like the Navigator Bookmarks window, Favorite Places doesn't let you choose an item by naming it. Use **Move Up/Down** to highlight items on the list.

You need your mouse or mouse commands to open and close folders. They appear not to open for the Enter key or any other. You must double-click them. We recommend opening all the folders once and then leaving them open. (AOL remembers which of the folders are open when you come back to the window.) After all the folders are open, you can select favorite places with the **Move Up/Down** commands. To go to a selected place, say, **"Press Enter."**

To add the currently active window to the Favorite Places list:

1. **Say,** "Click Favorites, Add Top Window to Favorite Places." **(Or you can use one of the short versions —** "Click Favorites, Press A" **or** "Press Control Plus.")

2. **When the confirmation box appears, say, "Click Add to Favorites."**

To delete an item from Favorite Places:

1. **First open the Favorite Places window (refer to Figure 13-4) by saying,** "Click Favorites, Favorite Places."

2. **Find the item you want to delete in the same way you would if you wanted to select that item. (Refer to earlier in this section.)**

3. **After you select the item, say,** "Press Delete."

## Searching for places and people

AOL provides a number of tools that help you search for Web sites, for AOL keywords, and for information on your fellow AOL members. Better yet, use the hotkeys listed in Table 13-3 to get the ball rolling on all these processes.

| Table 13-3 | AOL Hotkeys That Help You Look for Information | |
|---|---|---|
| *This Key Combo* | *Said Like This* | *Opens This Search Window* |
| Alt+D | Press Alt D | Find |
| Control + L | Press Control L | Locate Member |
| Control + G | Press Control G | Get a Member's Profile |
| Control + F | Press Control F | AOL Search |

## Taking notes

If you want to jot down some ideas without leaving the AOL window, and maybe eventually turn the document into an e-mail or instant message, say, **"Press Control N"** to open a document window. You can dictate into the document window, but it isn't Select and Say.

# *Chat*

Basically, we all want two things out of a chat application: We want to get our messages out quickly, so that the conversation doesn't pass us by, and we want to get the messages out right, so that we avoid creating unnecessary misunderstandings.

NaturallySpeaking is a great help in getting a message out quickly, especially if you don't type fast. But you have to proofread carefully to avoid sending out the wrong message, because the NaturallySpeaking mistakes are correct English words that aren't obviously typos. If you're trying to tell somebody to chill, you don't want it to come out "kill" instead.

Given all that, why you want your chat application to be Select and Say is obvious: You want to be able to pick out and correct mistakes quickly, so that your message gets out before the conversation moves on to some other topic. At the moment, that consideration limits your choice of chat applications down to one: Microsoft Chat, Versions 2.1 or higher.

## *Using Microsoft Chat*

If you don't have Microsoft Chat, don't panic — it's free. You can download it at the Microsoft Web site at `www.microsoft.com/windows/ie/chat`. The download-and-install process is remarkably simple, and the instructions at the Web site are good. The whole process may take as long as 15 minutes, unless you have a really slow modem or the Web is clogged that day.

### *Starting and connecting*

The Chat installation process puts a Microsoft Chat entry on the Start⇨ Programs menu, so you can start the program running by saying, **"Start Microsoft Chat."**

The first thing you see when Chat starts is the Chat Connection dialog box. This box has two tabs: Connect (which starts out on top) and Personal Info. Change from one to the other by saying, **"Click Connect"** or **"Click Personal Info."** The Connect tab is where you describe the chat room or server that you want to connect to. The Personal Info tab lists the information about yourself that you want to offer the other chatters.

Every textbox or radio button on either tab has a hotkey, denoted by the underlined letter in the text label. For example, to move the cursor into the textbox labeled "Server," say, **"Press Alt S."** After the cursor is inside a text box, you can dictate text into that box.

When you have the Chat Connection box the way you want it, say, **"Click OK."** Now Chat goes off to find the chat server and chat room that you have specified.

## Chatting

Microsoft Chat is another three-pane window, resembling the e-mail window of Figure 13-2, except that the vertical window is on the right rather than the left. The three panes are

- The dialog window (above left), where all the chat in the room displays
- The input window (below left), where you dictate what you want to say
- The participant list (right), where the participants in the current chat room are listed

Cycle the cursor through the three windows by saying, **"Press Tab."**

When the cursor is in the input window, dictate what you want to say. Because Microsoft Chat is Select and Say, you can use any of the selection and correction features described in the Chapter 5. In particular, you can correct text by saying it. For example, if NaturallySpeaking misinterpreted "Go back" as "Go bad," you can say, **"Correct *bad*."**

On the right side of the input window are five buttons modifying how your input will be displayed. The options are Say, Think, Whisper, Action, or Play Sound. Choose among them by saying, **"Press *<hotkey combination>*,"** where the hotkeys are given in Table 13-4. When you click one of these buttons or press the corresponding key combination, your input is transmitted to the chat room in the manner corresponding to the button.

| Table 13-4 | The Hotkeys Corresponding to the Five Actions in Microsoft Chat | |
|---|---|---|
| *Action* | *Key Combination* | *Voice Command* |
| Say | Ctrl+Y | Press Control Y |
| Think | Ctrl+T | Press Control T |
| Whisper | Ctrl+W | Press Control W |
| Action | Ctrl+J | Press Control J |
| Play Sound | Ctrl+H | Press Control H |

For example, suppose your character is named TestDroid, and you want the other participants in the chat to know that TestDroid is thinking "Test. Test. Test." Dictate, **"test period test period test period"** into the input window, and then say, **"Press Control T."** The result of this action is that your dialog window (and everyone else's dialog window) now contains the line "TestDroid thinks: Test. Test. Test."

## *Web-based chat*

Many Web sites have their own chat rooms, in which you participate by typing text into a textbox in your browser window. Treat these Web pages as you would any other Web pages with textboxes. See "Entering information on a Web page" earlier in this chapter.

# Chapter 14

# Dragon Your Data Around

● ● ● ● ● ● ● ● ● ● ● ● ● ● ● ● ● ● ● ● ● ● ● ● ● ● ● ● ● ● ● ● ● ● ● ● ● ● ● ● ● ● ● ● ● ● ● ● ●

## In This Chapter

▶ Using NaturallySpeaking with spreadsheets

▶ Using NaturallySpeaking with databases

▶ Using NaturallySpeaking with personal information management applications

▶ Using NaturallySpeaking with contact management applications

● ● ● ● ● ● ● ● ● ● ● ● ● ● ● ● ● ● ● ● ● ● ● ● ● ● ● ● ● ● ● ● ● ● ● ● ● ● ● ● ● ● ● ● ● ● ● ● ●

*I*n previous chapters, you find out what NaturallySpeaking has to offer word-oriented people, but what about number-oriented people, people who have a lot of data to enter into the computer, to keep track of, and to process? Not quite so much. NaturallySpeaking does allow you to work with spreadsheets and databases, but doesn't give you any special tools. NaturalWord helps you with Microsoft Word or Corel WordPerfect, but Dragon hasn't yet seen fit to come out with a NaturalNumber to help you with Microsoft Excel or Access, or Corel Quattro Pro. Still, we can save you a little time by explaining a few simple tricks to get you started.

The situation is somewhat better for personal information management and contact management. Microsoft Outlook, whose e-mail capabilities we discuss in Chapter 13, is a Select-and-Say application that lets you keep track of your appointments, acquaintances, and business contacts. GoldMine is a Select-and-Say contact manager designed for sales and service organizations.

The top-of-the-line combination of voice recognition with contact management is Dragon NaturallyOrganized, which combines NaturallySpeaking Preferred, Dragon's NaturallyMobile recorder, and a special interface for Symantec's ACT! 4.0 contact management database.

# Doing Excel-lent Works with Spreadsheets

The fundamental problem of using NaturallySpeaking with spreadsheets is that NaturallySpeaking itself doesn't know the names of the cells. You'd like to say something like, **"Go To A5"** or **"Select Column C"** — no dice, your dragon has no idea what you're talking about.

You can, of course, use the mouse for these sorts of operations, and dictate only the text that goes into the cells. Or you can use **MouseGrid,** but even here the inability to drag a selection rectangle limits what you can do.

Fortunately, you have another option. Spreadsheets are designed by and for geeky types who regard using a mouse as a sign of weakness, so for their sakes most popular spreadsheet applications contain (at last count) bazillions of hotkey combinations that do just about anything you would ever want to do. If you know the right hotkeys, you can use **Press <*keyname*>** voice commands to have a reasonably pleasant and efficient no-hands experience with your spreadsheets.

Unfortunately hotkeys, like menus, are only partially standardized from one application to another. Some of the basic spreadsheet hotkeys, like Ctrl+G (Go To), Ctrl+R (Fill Right), or Ctrl+D (Fill Down) work on most spreadsheets, but many commands have hotkeys only in some spreadsheets or are assigned to different keys in different spreadsheets. The Help files of your spreadsheet application should have a list of hotkeys and what they do; look in the index under *keyboard.*

We tested the examples in this section on the most popular spreadsheet application, Microsoft Excel. Our point isn't to endorse Excel, or even to teach you how to use Excel, but just to show you the kinds of activities that are possible when you combine the **Press** command with a spreadsheet's hotkeys. (Excel has a bunch of hotkeys we don't even mention.) Entire books have been written about spreadsheet applications, and if you plan to use your spreadsheet for anything more complicated than adding up columns of numbers, you should probably own one. (If you use the spreadsheet tool in Microsoft Works, may we be so bold as to recommend *Microsoft Works For Dummies* by — what was his name again? — David Kay.)

## *Having a look around*

The **Move Up/Down/Left/Right** commands are your best friends when you work with spreadsheets, because they do exactly what you need: move the cursor from one cell to the another. If the currently selected cell is B2, saying, **"Move Right Two"** moves the cursor to D2. If you then say, **"Move Down Five,"** the cursor moves to D7. Unfortunately, the highest number of steps you can move with one command is 20.

For longer trips, **Press Page Up/Down** displays the next/previous screen-full of the spreadsheet. In Excel, **Press Alt Page Up** shows you the next screen-full to the left and **Press Alt Page Down** displays the next screen-full to the right. In some other spreadsheets, **Press Control Page Up/Down** plays this role.

Return to cell A1 by saying, **"Press Control Home,"** and go to the extreme lower-right corner of the spreadsheet by saying, **"Press Control End."**

Go to any cell by selecting it using the Go To dialog box described in the next section.

## Selecting cells

Selecting cells or blocks of cells in a spreadsheet is easy to do by hand with a mouse: You just click the cell you want to select, or drag a selection rectangle over a block of cells. If you want to do the mouse thing by hand, NaturallySpeaking won't stop you, but if you want to use **MouseGrid** to do it by voice, you run into some problems. First, **MouseGrid** is slow and clumsy compared to grabbing the mouse by hand; second, it doesn't do selection rectangles. (See Chapter 11.)

### Using the Go To dialog box to select blocks of cells

One way to select any cell or block of cells while keeping your hands in your lap is to use the Go To dialog box shown in Figure 14-1.

**Figure 14-1:**
Excel's Go
To dialog
box lets you
select any
cell or group
of cells you
can name.

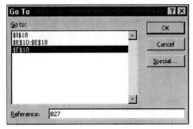

1. **Say,** "Press Control G."

   The Go To dialog box opens. The Excel version of this box is shown in Figure 14-1. Probably a Go To command appears on one of your spreadsheet's menus as well, but there's no predicting which one it will be. The Ctrl+G combination is standard across many spreadsheet applications.

2. **Say the name of the cell or cell range**.

   If you say, "B2," NaturallySpeaking is likely to hear "be to," so we recommend saying, **"Press B, Press 2."** Other numbers are unlikely to cause confusion, so you can say, **"Press D, 37"** to enter D37. If your spreadsheet lets you give cells names rather than designations, you can use that name here; say, "revenues," for example.

   Some of the simpler spreadsheets (like the spreadsheet in Claris Works) may be looking for a single cell address, but most spreadsheets let you select a range. To select a block of cells, say two cell addresses separated by a colon. For example, **"Press B, 5, Colon, Press F, 7"** designates the block whose corners are B5 and F7. The range C2:C10 denotes nine consecutive cells in the C column. If your spreadsheet lets you give a name to a range of cells, you can say the name. For example, you might give the name "Third Quarter" to the block of cells relating to that time period. (Naming works differently from one program to another; check your manual or Help files.)

3. **Say,** "Press Enter."

   The cell or block of cells designated in Step 2 is selected.

The list in the Excel Go To dialog box shows you the cells you have selected previously. You can return to one of these selections by choosing the corresponding element from the list. When you first open the dialog box, the cursor is in the Reference textbox. Move the cursor to the list by saying, **"Press Tab."** Choose an element from the list by using the **Move Up/Down** commands. The Reference textbox changes automatically to match the highlighted element of the list.

### Boxing up a block of cells

In Excel and Microsoft Works, the F8 function key anchors a selection box in the current cell. Moving the cursor to another cell automatically selects the block of cells "between" them — in other words, a block of cells in which these two cells are opposing corners. For example, you could select the C3:E7 cell block as follows:

1. **Move the cursor to C3.**

   Use any technique you want. See "Having a look around" earlier in this section.

2. **Say,** "Press F8."

3. **Say,** "Move Down 4."

   Now the C3:C7 block is selected.

4. **Say,** "Move Right 2."

   Now the C3: E7 block is selected.

If a block of cells is surrounded by empty cells, you can select the whole block in Excel by saying, **"Press Control Shift 8."**

### Selecting rows and columns

To select an entire row or column in Excel, first move the cursor into the row or column. Then say, **"Press Control Spacebar"** to select the column or **"Press Shift Spacebar"** to select the row. How do you remember which is which? The words *control* and *column* both begin with the letter C.

*Do you want column F with that?*

After you select a block of cells, you can extend it by one cell in any direction by saying, **"Press Shift <*direction*> Arrow."** So, for example, if you have selected all of column E, you can add column F by saying, **"Press Shift Right Arrow."** (This command works in many spreadsheets, including Excel, but not all.)

# Inputting and formatting data

Spreadsheets are all about manipulating numbers, so the obvious question is how to get the numbers into the spreadsheet in the first place. The basic idea of how to get a number or date or time (spreadsheets think of dates and times as numbers) into a cell is fairly simple:

1. **Select the cell. (See "Selecting cells" earlier in this chapter.)**

2. **Dictate the number.**

   There are no special commands here, so think of NaturallySpeaking as if it were a keyboard. Whatever you want to see in the cell, say it. If, for example, you want the cell to contain the date 5/17/99, say, **"Five slash seventeen slash ninety-nine."** If you want to see 1.52E+01 in the cell say, **"One point five two Cap E plus zero one."** See Chapter 5, Table 5-2 for more ways to dictate numbers. A good spreadsheet should recognize any of the formats of Table 5-2 as numbers.

3. **Move to another cell.**

Spreadsheets like Excel are capable of displaying numbers, dates, and times in a nearly infinite number of ways. (You'd need a spreadsheet to figure out how many.) Your best bet is not to worry too much about how to format a number in NaturallySpeaking; just get the number into the spreadsheet in any old form, and then reformat it within the spreadsheet.

For example, suppose you were inputting a column of prices. You could dictate them as prices: **"Twenty-six dollars and seventy-two cents."** Or you could dictate them as numbers: **"Twenty-six point seven two."** After you had dictated the column of numbers, then you could convert them to prices as follows:

1. **Select the column. See "Selecting rows and columns" earlier in this chapter.**

2. **Say,** "Click Format, Cells."

   The Format Cells dialog box appears, as shown in Figure 14-2.

3. **Display the Number tab in the Format Cells dialog box.**

   This tab may be on top when the box opens, or it may not. Use the **Press Right/Left Arrow** commands to move from one tab to another.

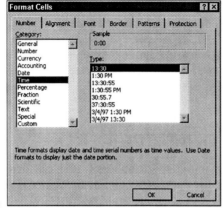

**Figure 14-2:**
A spread-
sheet like
Excel can
format num-
bers, dates,
and times in
more ways
than you
can count.

4. **Say,** "Press Alt C."

   This hotkey moves the cursor into the Category List.

5. **Select "currency" on the Category list.**

   The **Move Up/Down** commands are the easiest way to select items on the list.

6. **Say,** "Press Enter."

   The Format Cells dialog box disappears, and the column is formatted as dollars and cents.

## Improving your vocal functions

Spreadsheets have so many defined functions these days that nobody remembers exactly what their names are and what they do. (Remembering things is for people who *don't* have a computer.) And you really don't want to have to spell out a function name like TANH just because it isn't an English word that NaturallySpeaking recognizes. Don't worry; you don't have to. You can either pick the function out of a list (that the spreadsheet remembers for you) or you add the function name to the NaturallySpeaking vocabulary.

All the popular spreadsheets have a menu command that brings up a dialog box listing all the available functions. In Excel, the command is Insert⇨ Function, and it produces the Paste Function dialog box shown in Figure 14-3.

To use this feature, select the cell where the function belongs, and say, **"Click Insert, Function."** When the Paste Function box opens, the cursor is in the Function Name list. Use the **Move Up/Down** commands to choose any func-tion in the current function category. If you want to choose a different function category, say, **"Press Shift Tab"** to move the cursor to the Function

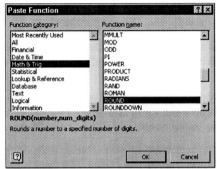

**Figure 14-3:**
A good
spreadsheet
remembers
its function
names so
that you
don't
have to.

Category list. After using **Move Up/Down** to choose your category, return to the Function Name list by saying, **"Press Tab."**

Below the Function Category and Function Name boxes is a description of the function and the inputs it requires. For example, Figure 14-3 tells us that the ROUND function requires two inputs: a number to be rounded, and a number of digits that the rounded number should have.

When you find the function you want, say, **"Press Enter."** A box appears to collect the inputs to the function. Dictate each input into the labeled textbox, and say, **"Press Tab"** to move to the next textbox. When all the inputs have been specified, say, **"Click OK."** You return to the spreadsheet with the function inserted into the proper cell.

If you use the same function over and over again, you can introduce it into the NaturallySpeaking vocabulary. For example, you could introduce the "word" STDEV into the vocabulary and train NaturallySpeaking to recognize its spoken form "standard deviation function." Or you could give the function a pronunciation similar to its written form, like "tansh" for the function TANH. See Chapter 18 for details on how to implement vocabulary tricks like this.

# *General-Purpose Database Applications*

NaturallySpeaking contains no special commands for use with general purpose databases like Microsoft Access or Lotus Approach, and none of these programs are Select and Say. The various database applications are sufficiently different from one another and have such a wide variety of potential uses that we don't have any specific advice to give either. So here's some general purpose advice for using general purpose databases:

✔ **Create macros.** If you have the Professional edition (see Chapter 22), you can create a vocal macro that combines many tedious commands into one simple command.

✔ **Remember that all these forms are just dialog boxes.** Use the techniques described in Chapter 11.

✔ **Replace mouse operations with menu commands whenever possible.** Mouse operations are clumsy to do by voice, whereas menu commands are easy.

✔ **Use hotkeys whenever possible.** Most applications have a list of hotkeys somewhere in their Help files. Check the Help index under *keyboard*. The most valuable voice command you have is **Press *<hotkey>*.**

✔ **You can always fall back on whatever you would have done without NaturallySpeaking.** Take the bull by the horns, the tiger by the tail, the mouse by its paw, or something.

# Special-Purpose Databases: PIMs and Super-PIMs

A general purpose database contains more data-processing power than most people need or can be trusted with. Most of us don't want to design our own data-tracking system; we want somebody to hand us a system that's already designed to track the kind of data that we're interested in.

What kind of data are we interested in keeping track of? Addresses, phone numbers, appointments, and other such stuff. The specialized database applications that take care of such information are called *personal information managers,* or PIMs for short.

If you work in sales or for a company that has a lot of customers to keep track of, you may run into a larger beast that evolved out of the PIM, a sort of super-PIM also known as a *contact manager.*

Dragon Systems has a product especially designed for dictating data into specific PIMs, Dragon NaturallySpeaking Mobile Organizer. It recognizes all the various kinds of entries you can make in your PIM, as well as the various people in your database, and automatically creates those entries for you. (For a price!) For help with that product, see Chapter 15. This section just talks about dictating into and controlling your PIM with NaturallySpeaking.

## Personal information managers

Microsoft Outlook (not to be confused with its younger, less-powerful cousin Outlook Express) is a Select-and-Say application that keeps track of your personal information. (Well, appointments and addresses and stuff. We keep *personal* personal information — old love letters, embarrassing photos, and other memorabilia — in boxes in the backs of our closets.)

Many other PIMs exist, some of which are excellent programs. But Outlook is the only one that NaturallySpeaking currently recognizes as Select and Say. In addition, Outlook has a good collection of hotkeys, which allow you to access features with the **Press *<hotkey>*** voice command. To see a list of Outlook's hotkeys, look in Outlook's Help Index under *keyboard*.

As in Chapter 13, we recommend that you not display the Outlook bar, the column on the left side of the Outlook window that displays icons for the major components of Outlook. This bar is very handy to use with the mouse, but not nearly so convenient with NaturallySpeaking. (The same components are listed on the Go menu, which is easier to access by voice.) Make it go away by saying, **"Click View, Outlook Bar."**

We discuss Outlook's e-mail capabilities in Chapter 13. Now we get around to its other main features: an appointment calendar and a contact list.

### Keeping track of appointments and tasks

Scheduling is handled through Outlook's Calendar window. Bring up the Calendar window (shown in Figure 14-4) by saying, **"Click Go, Calendar."** Opening the Calendar window adds the Calendar menu to the menu bar. Use this menu for all of your calendar-related activities. For example, to put a new appointment on the calendar say, **"Click Calendar, New Appointment."**

Tasks for the day are visible in the Calendar window, but are most easily added and deleted using the Task window. To open the Task window, say, **"Click Go, Tasks."** Opening the Task window adds the Task menu to the menu bar. To add a new task, say, **"Click Task, New Task."**

Whether you add an appointment or a task, a dialog box with a number of fields to be filled in confronts you. When the cursor is in a textbox, you can dictate

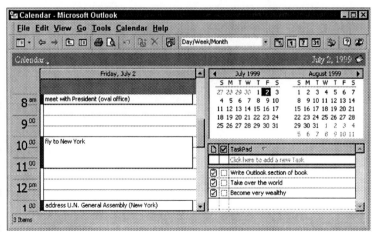

**Figure 14-4:**
Outlook's Calendar utility helps you keep track of your day.

just as you would dictate into a word processor. Don't be afraid to use those Select-and-Say capabilities (see Chapter 10) to edit or correct your entries.

You can move from one field of a dialog box to the next by saying, **"Press Tab,"** or you can jump to any field you want by using the hotkey indicated by the underlined letter in the field's label. For example, in order to check the All Day Event checkbox in the New Appointment dialog box, say, **"Press Alt Y."**

### *Listing your contacts*

We used to talk about *address books*, but Outlook keeps track of so much more than just addresses that they refer to the *contact list* instead. In this context, a *contact* is not one of those clear round things that falls out of your eye during a basketball game, it's a person (or other sentient entity) whom you have contacted at some point in your life.

Outlook handles contacts via the Contacts window, which you open by saying, **"Click Go, Contacts."** As an added bonus, the Contacts menu is appended to the menu bar. Anything you may want to do with your contact list is handled by this menu. For example, to add a new contact, say, **"Click Contacts, New Contact."** Outlook responds by displaying the New Contact dialog box, shown in Figure 14-5.

The New Contacts window looks intimidating because it contains spaces for everything you may know about a person other than hat size, but the only part you really have to fill out is Name. Other than that, you are allowed to skip around, using the hotkeys to pick which field to fill in next. For example, to skip to the Web Page textbox, say, **"Press Alt W."**

The New Contacts window begins with the General tab on top. To switch to another tab, say, **"Press Control Tab."**

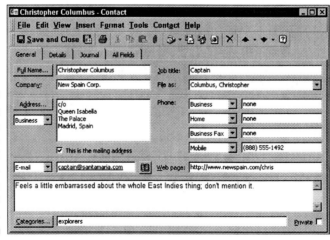

**Figure 14-5:** The modern way to keep tabs on old acquaintances who move around a lot.

# Chapter 15

# Staying Organized on the Move

*A*re you one of those people whose business life is conducted from a forest of sticky notes attached to a day planner? If so, you're undoubtedly excited by the prospect of just being able to dictate all your appointments, memos, and "to do" items into a recorder, and have your PC sort it all out. And that, more or less, is the promise of Dragon's NaturallySpeaking Mobile Organizer.

Well, calm down. If you're a committed sticky-note, day-planner type of person — the kind of person who still, even as we approach the millennium, has not created an address book on his or her computer (tsk, tsk) — you are probably not going to change your ways. (Trust us, we know from personal experience.) For you to use Mobile Organizer, however, you're going to have to deal with a PIM; so unless you have a technology-savvy secretary to stick with your PIM chores, stick to your sticky notes (like you have a choice!).

On the other hand, if you are already a PIM (Personal Information Manager) convert, use your PIM a lot, and would like get data into your PIM more quickly, while it's fresh in your mind, "Moby" (our nickname for Mobile Organizer) may be just the quarry you seek. (Moby is also much more attractive if you have lots of money or someone else is paying.) Sales professionals, in particular, may really enjoy the speed and convenience of simply dictating a few notes into a mobile recorder after a sales contact, rather than hand-entering data into a palmtop. Call us Ishmael, but the future of automated business stuff may lie in Moby's direction, rather than typing on pocket-sized gizmos.

# Getting the General Idea

The general idea of Moby is that, as you are going about your business, you can voice-enter stuff that you would normally hand-enter into your PIM. You carry around Dragon's NaturallyMobile voice recorder, that comes with Moby (the same one that comes with NaturallySpeaking Mobile Edition), and you dictate memos, e-mail messages, appointments, and the like, into it. You excite comment and glances from passers-by, but you don't care. You're a technology-empowered executive, living on the cutting edge without even a styptic pencil.

The next step takes place when you return to your office, hotel, or wherever your PC lives, and have a few minutes to spare. You or your technology-savvy secretary plugs the NaturallyMobile recorder into your PC and runs Moby. Moby sucks your day's worth of dictation into its capacious mouth (okay, window) for your review. It figures out from your dictation which entries are memos, which are appointments, and so forth, and presents them for your review. You review and correct these items, and Moby spews them forth into your PIM.

Moby does its magic by looking for certain words in your dictation. It recognizes certain key words for appointments, e-mail, and notes, for instance. It recognizes words like "to" and when followed by the names of people who are listed in your address book, chooses them as a recipient, if that's appropriate. It recognizes dates and times and durations, and uses them for calendar items.

As of this writing, Moby supports Microsoft Outlook (98) and Palm Desktop (3.0), perhaps the best known PIMs, as well as Goldmine (4.0), Lotus Notes (4.6a), and Symantec ACT! (4.0), which are popular for organization-wide work. You have to have one of the supported PIMs (and the correct version) to get anything useful out of Moby.

# Running and Setting Up Moby

When you install Moby, it checks to see if you have NaturallySpeaking Preferred or Professional. If you have either one, Moby upgrades it; if not, Moby installs NaturallySpeaking Preferred for you. Moby installs its software into a separate folder on your hard drive from NaturallySpeaking.

To run Moby, choose Start➪Programs➪NaturallySpeaking Mobile Organizer from the Windows taskbar. As with all NaturallySpeaking editions, Moby needs a defined, trained "user," and may ask you to choose or create one. In this product, the user needs to have been trained on the NaturallyMobile recorder.

If you've been using NaturallySpeaking Mobile Edition and have defined only a single user (the recorder), Moby simply uses that without asking. If you have several NaturallySpeaking users, Moby asks you to choose one; choose the one trained on the recorder. If you have never trained a user for NaturallyMobile recorder before, follow the directions in the section on Training NaturallySpeaking in Chapter 9.

Whenever you run Moby, it loads in the "contacts" from your PIM. These are the people in your PIM's database of names and addresses.

# Dictating into the Recorder

The trick of using Moby, if there is one, lies in the dictation. (A kind of tricky Dic.?) The Moby dictation trick has three parts.

First of all, NaturallySpeaking has to be well-trained in recognizing your voice, and you have to speak clearly. You do the training when you first set Moby up with a "user." If you haven't created a user, you'll be prompted to do so; see Chapter 9 for instructions. If you've upgraded to Moby from NaturallySpeaking Mobile Edition, Moby continues to use your already-well-trained user from that Edition. You can improve recognition with the tricks in Part IV of this book, or by correcting Moby when you review its work.

Second, you need to know how to use the recorder. See Chapter 9 for information about the buttons, files, and folders of the NaturallyMobile recorder. Each item you dictate should be in its own file. Or, if you want to dictate several items in a single file, you should separate them by dictating the word "jabberwocky" (no kidding!) in between.

Third, you need to know what to say. You need to know how to tell Moby what kind of item you're creating (a memo, an e-mail message), and how to make sure the addressee, the date, or the text you're dictating all go to their proper places in your PIM. For that part of the trick, read on.

## Creating different kinds of entries

PIMs have different kinds of entries. The following bullets list the different kinds of entries and the names for them that your PIM might use.

✔ **Appointment:** Something on your PIM's appointment calendar, with a date and beginning and end times. It could be a meeting or a conference, for instance. Some PIMs also have *Events,* which are similar but last all day.

✔ **Call:** Like appointments, but only recognized in GoldMine and ACT! (Those PIMs are designed largely for sales management, so they know about *calls.*)

✔ **E-mail:** Messages to be sent as e-mail from your PIM.

✔ **To-do items:** The items in a list of things to be done, available in GoldMine, ACT!, and Palm Desktop. They have a start date and time and a duration. Sometimes they are for yourself, sometimes for others.

✔ **Contact:** A person in the PIM database, with name, nickname, position, company, phone and fax number, and so forth.

✔ **Note:** A memo or other snippet of text. (If Moby can't figure out what kind of entry you want, it turns it into a note.)

✔ **Text file:** Plain dictation in a file; sometimes used as an attachment to e-mail.

## Appointments, events, and calls

Most PIMs offer an *appointment* entry. When telling Moby about them, you can use any of those words — regardless of your PIM — or the synonyms *conference, seminar, teleconference, or consultation.* They all mean the same thing to Moby. Outlook, Notes, and GoldMine also have *events,* which are all-day affairs — unlike appointments, which have begin and end times. Instead of *event,* you can say *appointment* or any of its synonyms, if you like, but indicate a duration of one or more days, as in *of two days.*

Your appointment includes a date, a duration, and a contact (a person). You can optionally add a subject, a note, or other frills. Here are the various parts:

1. **To create an appointment, use the commands** Schedule a(n), Set Up a(n), Arrange a(n), Create a(n), Make a(n), **or** Hold a(n) **with the word** *appointment* **or any its synonyms we just listed, as in** Set Up a conference. . . .

2. **Add a person (the contact) involved, such as** . . .With Harry Bates. . . .

   The contact is yourself, if you don't specify anyone else.

3. **Continue the command by saying when the appointment is, and its duration, as in** . . . on September 15, at 3PM, 90 minutes.

A complete command, for instance, would be:

**Schedule a meeting with Harry Bates on September 15th at 9:30 AM, 90 minutes.**

Even though we've numbered the steps, the actual order of dictating most Moby commands isn't very critical. You can say the date and duration anywhere in the command, or even begin with them (**"On November 18th . . ."**). We get the best results by using the order given, however.

Add a subject, if you like. Your meeting could be **"about the you-know-what,"** for instance. Embellish the command by inserting, if appropriate, a priority (**. . . of high priority**), or a follow-up with your contact (**. . . and send e-mail**). To add notes about the appointment, finish your command with the word **Period,** and then continue dictating.

Avoid using durations as adjectives. By that we mean, avoid words that normally would be typed with a dash between them, as in a **two-hour**, **day-long**, or **high-priority** *meeting*. Even if your statement ends up not being very grammatical, use phrases like **two hours**, or **one day** if you want Moby to understand you.

GoldMine and ACT! let you schedule *calls*. Like appointments, calls have a contact, a date and time, and a duration. You can **Schedule a Call** (or a **Phone Call** or **Telephone Call**). You can use any of the synonyms for **Schedule**. You can just **Call** (or **Telephone**, or **Phone**) someone, too.

## E-mail messages

E-mail messages include one or more addressees, a subject, and a message body. You can optionally give a priority to the message (which most people ignore, and not all PIMs offer, but what the heck). Here's how to speak the various parts:

---

# Dates and durations

Moby recognizes dates and times in the usual NaturallySpeaking forms given in Chapter 4: **June 25th**, for instance, or **9:30AM**. (You can leave off the AM and PM for hours between 7AM and 6PM.) Moby also knows what **noon** and **midnight** are, and recognizes times given as so many minutes **past** or **before** a certain hour.

Even more cool than that, however, Moby also recognizes relative dates. You can say **the day after tomorrow**, or **this Tuesday**, and because your recorder records the date and time, Moby can tell what you mean. **This, Next,** and **Last** refer to calendar weeks beginning on Sunday. If today is Monday, **This Sunday** was yesterday.

For durations, giving a number and then a unit of time like minutes, hours or days, usually works best, like **three hours**. Don't bother saying "for three hours," or you're likely to get 43 hours! Remember that Moby does not recognize compound durations like **three-hour**. You can also say durations this way: "**starting at** *<some date/time>* **and ending at** *<some date/time>*."

If you don't give a date or duration, Moby uses today for a date, one hour for an appointment, and ten minutes for a call.

1. **Begin with the command Send or Create, followed by the term E-mail, Mail, or** E-mail Message. **For instance:** "Send E-mail. . . ."

   To set a high priority (if your PIM supports it), you can **Send an Important, Urgent,** or **High-Priority E-mail.**

2. **Say To and list the addressee(s). Say them as they are listed in your address book. For instance:** ". . .To Harry Bates. . . ."

   If the first name is unique, you can leave off the last name. You can also use special nicknames you can set up in Moby. See the sidebar, "In Your Own Words," for details. For multiple addressees, just list them or add them with **and.** For CC's, say, "**Copy** *<addressee>*.**"**

3. **Say About and dictate the subject line. End the subject line with** Period. **For instance:** ". . .About **our mutual friend** Period. . . ."

   To attach a file (assuming your PIM allows it), say **Attach** and dictate the name of the file, such as **friend dot doc.** (If the file has no extension, say **Period** instead.) Moby will, by default, look in the My Documents folder for this file.

   The first time you use the word "About" when dictating any item to Moby, Moby will presume you are done giving it instructions about the item and are now dictating text.

4. **Dictate the body of the message. For instance:** ". . . Do you think Ishmael needs psychiatric help Question Mark."

## Tasks for a "to-do" list

Tasks for your list of things to do have a date and a subject, plus optionally a time, duration, and a contact. (The date is today, the duration is ten minutes, and the contact is yourself, if you don't specify otherwise.)

You can specify a task in all kinds of ways. What works best for us is to begin with the words **To Do, Remind, Remember,** or **Schedule a Task,** followed by **On** and then a day (and, optionally time).

You can specify urgency by including the words **Important** or **High Priority.** Certain PIMs show your action list in order of priority, so setting priority might be important for tasks. Here are a few examples:

**Remember on August 25 to sign the Johnson contract**

**To do on Wednesday, check progress of inventory**

**Remind Katy tomorrow to schedule my salary review — Important**

**Schedule a task for Friday at 1PM to review vendor histories**

## In your own words

Moby lets you define your own terms for people, special days, and certain functions. For instance, although your list of contacts may include the full name of your associate, Werner Apfel Shnitzenkopf, you can set up Moby so you can call him "Werner " to set up a meeting with him or send him e-mail. Also, you can create names for special events, such as "Suzy's birthday" or "International Sales Meeting," and use those as dates in dictation.

Choose Edit➪Special Phrases from the menu bar of the Mobile Organizer window. Click the Contacts tab to enter nicknames, or the Dates tab to enter special events.

On the Contacts tab, type your nickname in the This Word Or Phrase box. Click the down-arrow by the Means These Contacts box to list available contacts, and choose the person for that nickname. Click the Add button to add the nickname to the list.

On the Dates tab, type your phrase for your special event in the This Word Or Phrase box. Then type a date description in the Means This Date box (several examples are already present). Click the Add button.

# Notes, memos, "journal items," and text files

Notes, also called memos or "journal items" by various PIMs, are just that: short chunks of text. To start a note, say **Create a Note, Take (or Record) a Memo,** or just plain **Note.** (We get the best results by simply saying, **"Note."**)

From there, continue to dictate your text. Moby generates a title for your note based on the first words of text.

 For long text documents, create a file rather than a note. Say, **"Create A File Named,"** and then give the file name, such as **Silliness dot text** (silliness.txt). Dictate your text contents. Text files don't take up as much room in your PIM's database as notes do. Moby stores your files in the My Documents folder.

# Changing or adding instructions

You can interrupt your dictation of an item to give additional instructions to Moby, or add modifications to the end of an item. You just have to ask nicely: say, **"Computer Please."**

For instance, if I were dictating an e-mail message and decided, while dictating the message body, to add a CC: recipient, the dictation might look like this:

**"Send e-mail to Katy about the upcoming conference period** Katy comma I hope you can make the conference that we've scheduled for **computer please copy Margy** October period let me know if you will be able to make it period"

The text of the message would read, "Katy, I hope you can make the conference that we've scheduled for October. Let me know if you will be able to make it."

Moby would add Margy to the CC: line of this message. If a CC: contact already existed, Margy would not replace it, just be added to it. I could also have said, **"Computer Please add Margy"** and Margy would have been added to the To: line.

After you say Computer Please, you have Moby's attention until you complete a command. You can command Moby regarding any aspect of the item you're dictating, including contacts, dates, durations, or priorities.

Depending on the kind of information, you change earlier commands if they exist, or simply add information (as in my example). As items generally have only one date, start time, duration, finish time, or priority, anything you add will change the earlier setting. As items can have multiple contacts, your Computer Please statement will add to them.

Use the Pause button on the recorder to gather your thoughts when you need to add an instruction. Avoid making noise with your fingers when you do, though.

# Reviewing and PIMing your work

After you have recorded your dictation, you feed it to Moby. Moby then chews on it, tries to figure out what you had in mind, and regurgitates it to you for review. Here's the process for feeding Moby your dictation:

1. **Launch Moby by choosing Start➪Programs➪DNS Mobile Organizer.**

   If NaturallySpeaking presents a User dialog box, choose the user you trained for the NaturallyMobile recorder.

   Not only does Mobile Organizer appear on your screen, as Figure 15-1 shows, but so does your PIM window. (Moby doesn't, however, have any items in its window yet as Figure 15-1 does.)

   Moby knows about the contacts in your PIM only because it loads the list of contacts from your PIM when you first start it up. If you type new contacts in your PIM, Moby won't know about them unless you choose Edit➪Reinitialize Contacts from Moby's menu, or click the Reinitialize Contacts button on the toolbar.

Transcribed and interpreted item

Download and transcribe     Restore deleted or sent items

Click to choose alternatives | Reinitialize contacts

Play     Send items to PIM | Reinterpret Transcription

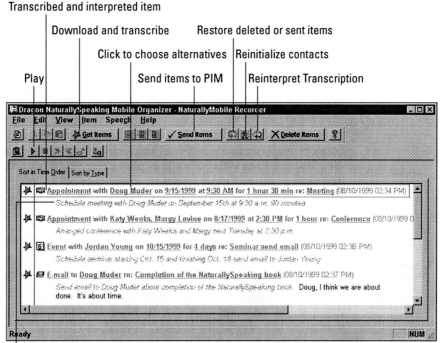

**Figure 15-1:**
Reviewing
your life
with your
pal, Moby.

Your transcribed text

2. **Connect your NaturallyMobile recorder to your PC's serial port.**

   (See Chapter 9 for instructions on connecting the recorder, if you're mystified by this instruction.)

3. **Click the Get Items button on Moby's toolbar.**

   The Get Items dialog box comes to your aid.

4. **In the Get Items dialog box, examine the Select Folder selection box.**

   Make sure it displays the folder where your files are located in the NaturallyMobile recorder. If not, click that selection box and choose the correct folder. (The selection box is a bit slow to respond.)

   If you have recorded items as WAV files using the NaturallySpeaking Recorder or some other utility, Moby can handle those, too. Click the Previously Created Audio Files button, and then click the Browse button to select the WAV file.

5. **Click Start.**

   Moby downloads your files (removing them, in the process, from your recorder) and transcribes your text. Moby's window now looks more like Figure 15-1, with various starred items listed.

If Moby is well-trained, you will be surprised and pleased at the results. If not, you'll be surprised and appalled. In any event, it's time to review the results. Walk this way:

1. **Scroll through the list, checking to see if the transcriptions are correct.**

   Moby displays items in the order dictated, normally. Click the Sort by Type tab if you would rather see all the e-mails together, all the appointments, and so forth.

2. **To change portions that are in red and underlined, such as contacts, dates, times, durations, and subjects, you may click the underlined text. You can then either choose replacement text from a list, or type new text.**

   Use this process only if you change your mind about something. If Moby has made an error, skip to Step 3.

   If you're not quite sure what you said, click the item's icon and then click Play button on the toolbar to hear your dictation.

3. **To correct Moby so that it learns from an error, click the line containing your dictation in gray and black.**

   Highlight the incorrect word and the preceding and following word, and then press the - key on the numeric keypad, or click the Correct button on the toolbar.

   The Correction dialog box appears. See Chapter 5 for details of using it. After correcting Moby, press the F9 key on your keyboard, or click the Reinterpret Transcription button to correct the stuff in red. (Don't forget to save your speech files when prompted about them, when you exit Moby.)

4. **When an item is correct, click its star icon, to change the icon to a checkmark. If you would rather delete the item, click again to replace the checkmark with an X.**

5. **When you have reviewed all the items, click the Send Items button.**

   Moby now transmits all items with a checkmark to your PIM. Any e-mail messages are sent.

   To delete items marked with the X icon, click the Delete Items button. To restore items that have been transferred to the PIM or deleted, click the Restore button on Moby's toolbar.

That's it! From here on out, your PIM is responsible for making things happen.

Be patient! Moby may need additional training and beyond what you did at startup. The Vocabulary Builder and Vocabulary Editor are available to you in the Speech menu.

# Part IV
# Precision Flying

The 5th Wave — By Rich Tennant

"For my finale, Rollo here will flawlessly activate my voice recognition system while I empty this bag of marbles into my mouth."

## In this part . . .

*E*ven the best-behaved dragon drops the occasional fewmet, crashes into a peasant's hut, or eats the occasional prize sheep. If NaturallySpeaking is seriously cutting up (unwilling to go to work, not playing well with others, or breaking the Windows in the Microsoft grass hut) you need to chat with the folks at Dragon Systems about treating the beast for bugs.

If, however, your winged companion is simply not quite as accurate as you think it should be, it may have a good reason. (Or possibly not. Technology is treading awfully close to magic, here, and occasionally NaturallySpeaking just seems to be going through a bad spell. Hey, maybe that's why it has so many wizard caretakers. Maybe it needs a "spell" checker, too.) In this part, we help you figure out what might be limiting your scaly friend's success.

Lots of different things can have an effect on NaturallySpeaking's accuracy. As with any office assistant, training and vocabulary building can make a big difference. It helps to speak to it nicely, too. Also, NaturallySpeaking's magic comes at a cost. It needs the full support and cooperation of your PC: processor power, memory, and disk space. And finally, if you're moving NaturallySpeaking to another PC, upgrading, or otherwise making changes, you need to help your dragon friend cope with change. In this part, we'll show you different ways to achieve and maintain the precision flying you expect.

# Chapter 16

# Feeding Your Dragon: RAM, Disk Space, and Speed

*In This Chapter*

▶ Identifying an underfed Dragon

▶ Budgeting for speed

▶ Budgeting for memory

▶ Budgeting for disk space

▶ Dealing with dragon allergies

*W*e can imagine few more unattractive companions than an underfed dragon. All members of the Dragon family need large-ish chunks of computer power. If your draconian buddy is not the winged wonder you expected, you may try making sure its nutritional needs are being met.

Dragon's needs for computer power can also make other programs, or Windows itself, look sluggish. When NaturallySpeaking runs, it takes away computing power from other tasks that may be trying to run at the same time. It munches your memory, scarfs down CPU speed, digests disk drive space, and then squats, burping and still hungry, on your desk.

Fortunately, most new computers sold today are plump and juicy enough to keep Dragon products happy. If you buy a new PC, get the fastest, highest-memory computer you can afford to make sure you get the best Dragon performance.

Before you buy, however, check the Dragon Systems Web site at www.dragonsys.com. Check their compatibility list, where Dragon Systems indicates which microphones, notebooks, desktop PCs, recorders, sound cards, and other hardware they have tested. Checking laptops is especially important, because you can't change their audio input cards. If you don't have a compatible system, Dragon Systems support may be reluctant to help you.

Besides needing computer power, NaturallySpeaking needs the best quality hardware for audio input. It may not work well at all with the audio system or cheap microphone that came with your computer. See Chapter 19 for more about audio input. This chapter talks only about basic computer resources.

# Diagnosing an Underfed Dragon

Nothing is more sluggish than a draggin' dragon. Some of the specific problems that can crop up include the following:

- ✔ NaturallySpeaking takes a long time to figure out what you said. You dictate, wait, dictate, wait, and so forth.

- ✔ Your other programs run slowly whenever Dragon NaturallySpeaking runs, not just when you dictate.

- ✔ Your PC locks up, crashes, or otherwise gets confused.

- ✔ You simply can't run Dragon NaturallySpeaking and another application at the same time. You get "out of memory" error messages.

If your PC has any of these symptoms, your Dragon could be suffering from any of the following dietary deficiencies:

- ✔ Not enough speed
- ✔ Not enough memory
- ✔ Not enough disk space

# Checking the Pantry for PC Resources

The first step in diagnosing the problem is to find out whether your PC has the right mix of nutrients. Then you can compare that to what your edition of NaturallySpeaking needs. The best way is to check the invoice for your PC, which should tell you the following:

- ✔ The type of CPU (central processing unit).
- ✔ The speed of the CPU given in megahertz (MHz).
- ✔ How much memory (RAM) the PC has in megabytes (MB).
- ✔ The size of the hard disk (given in megabytes, MB, or gigabytes, GB). A gigabyte is 1,000 megabytes.

Another way to check memory and CPU type is to take the following steps:

1. **Right-click the My Computer icon on your Windows 95 or Windows 98 screen.**

2. **Choose Properties from the menu that appears.**

   The System Properties dialog box appears, with several tabs across the top.

3. **Click the General tab, where you should find information about the processor type (for example, Pentium II) and memory (such as, 128.0MB RAM).**

   If not, you can also find information about memory by clicking the Performance tab.

# Coping with the Need for Speed

Dragon Systems says that in order to run NaturallySpeaking Release 4, you need a Pentium II-type processor that must run at a speed of 200 MHz or more. That's true — but in the same way that you need to eat 1,500 calories a day: You can live with that, but you won't be very productive.

Most users seem to find that they're happy with a 300 MHz or higher speed Pentium II. People who have Pentium III computers of that speed are often slightly more cheerful. Dragon now offers Pentium III editions of Naturally Speaking that provide "BestMatch III." This technology makes use of special processor features. The initial releases of this product provide much faster training (about five minutes instead of a half-hour to an hour), but no other performance advantages.

If you don't have all that power, what do you do? You can't just turn a dial to increase you PC's speed. Other than buying a new computer, here are a few things you can do to alleviate speed problems:

✔ Install an accelerator in some PCs, or upgrade to a faster CPU (central processing unit) chip. Speak to a computer supply vendor about CPU upgrades you can install yourself, or go to a computer shop with the details of your PC and ask whether they can upgrade it.

✔ Install more memory. Even if you already have the minimum memory that your NaturallySpeaking product requires, installing more memory can speed things up. (See the following section.)

✔ If your hard disk drive is getting full, it may be slowing you down. Try getting rid of some big files (and don't forget to empty the Recycle Bin), or uninstall some programs you never use. Also try running the Disk Cleanup program. Choose Programs⇨Accessories⇨System Tools⇨Disk Cleanup.

✔ The no-cost option is to try trading off accuracy for speed. In NaturallySpeaking, choose Tools⇨Options, and when the Options dialog box appears, click the Miscellaneous tab. Slide the Speed vs. Accuracy slider all the way to the left, if it's not already there.

# *Serving Up Memory*

Dragons need a lot of memory. (Traditionally, dragons live very long, eventful lives, so that makes sense.) How much memory you need altogether depends on what other applications you run, and which of the many Dragon Systems features you use. Dragon says you need at least 48MB, but on a real-life system, that's very low. In general, we find you should have — at the very least — 64MB of memory in a Windows 95 or 98 system for tolerable performance, and 128MB for acceptable performance.

We find that having 128MB of RAM or more simply makes things a lot better. You can often improve performance with 256MB of RAM, but beyond that, you probably won't notice a difference unless you run several programs simultaneously.

Memory is used up when a program runs, but your PC doesn't run totally out of memory when your programs exceed the RAM your system has. Instead, your PC makes compromises that allow your programs to run, but run slower. Windows gives the currently active program as much RAM as it can afford, and uses disk drive space as "virtual memory" for the rest. Virtual memory is not as good as RAM because it's not as fast. It's okay, though, as long as your disk drive is pretty fast and has plenty of space. For best performance, you should have enough RAM to run NaturallySpeaking (or Word or WordPerfect with NaturalWord, if you're using it) plus about 48MB for Windows.

Several individual Dragon features account for your memory needs. Depending upon which Dragon product you use, you will need more or less memory. Following are some of the features that need memory:

- **Basic Dragon software, such as NaturallySpeaking Essentials:** Requires about 48MB of memory just to run.

- **BestMatch Technology:** Dragon's products offer BestMatch, a kind of model of the human voice that makes voice recognition more efficient. You choose BestMatch, BestMatch III, or Standard when you create a new user. BestMatch requires about 16MB of RAM. If you don't have quite enough memory, the installation wizard, by default, omits BestMatch technology, and NaturallySpeaking will run slower or make more errors.

- **NaturalWord:** This special user interface that's used with Microsoft Word and Corel WordPerfect requires an additional 16MB of memory.

- **Vocabulary:** Dragon NaturallySpeaking 4 uses an "active" vocabulary of 160,000 words (out of 250,000 words, total). It keeps this active vocabulary in memory so that it can refer to vocabulary words quickly. For the full active vocabulary, you need to add about another 16MB of memory to the total you need.

Memory is fairly cheap, so don't skimp. Add up the minimum memory needed by various features in your Dragon product, and we suggest another 48MB of memory to give Windows breathing room. Call a large PC mail-order vendor for the best prices, or shop online vendors such as www.pcconnection.com. You need to tell them exactly what type of memory you have (or if you don't know that, what kind of computer you have) and how much memory (RAM) you currently have.

One solution to a memory problem is to make more of your PC's memory available to NaturallySpeaking. To free up memory, don't run other programs at the same time as NaturallySpeaking. Or, don't use NaturalWord; instead dictate directly into the NaturallySpeaking window.

Your PC may be running lots of little helper programs that start up automatically, in the background. They consume both memory and processor time, although not a lot of either. Generally you will find the icons for these helper programs in the Windows taskbar system tray. (The system tray is a rectangular area at the opposite end of the taskbar from the Start button.) Often these program are minor conveniences such as automatic reminders for Microsoft Money, or a continuously running virus checker. Pause your mouse cursor over an icon to discover what it is for. If you don't need a particular helper at the moment (but don't want to lose it permanently), just shut it down. Right-click the icon, and look for a menu selection that shuts down, exits, or disables. Not all programs can be shut down, however.

To see how much memory each program you're running grabs, run the Windows System Monitor. Choose Start⇨Programs⇨Accessories⇨System Tools⇨System Monitor. In the System Monitor window that appears, choose Edit⇨Add Item. In the Add Item dialog box, click Memory Manager on the left (under Category), and then click Allocated Memory on the right. Click OK, and you see a graph of two things: on top, how busy the processor is, and on the bottom, how much memory all your currently-running programs are calling for. Now exit all programs but NaturallySpeaking (or NaturalWord, if that's what you use) and the System Monitor. If the remaining total exceeds the amount of RAM you have, you're using significant amounts of virtual memory, which is slower.

# Dishing Out Disk Drive Space

Having more disk space available doesn't significantly improve the performance of NaturallySpeaking unless memory is skimpy and your disk is practically full or needs "cleanup."

A shortage of disk space may, however, prevent you from installing certain features. BestMatch technology, for instance, requires 38MB, and it provides a big boost to speed and accuracy.

You need about 240MB of disk space available on your computer to install, train, and run most NaturallySpeaking products. If several people are going to be using the product, or if you use a variety of input devices like different microphones or dictation recorders, you need to budget for about 10–25 additional MB for each of these users or different input devices (10MB minimum, 15MB if the user uses BestMatch, 25MB for BestMatch 64K+).

Some Dragon NaturallySpeaking features are optional. The speech recorder utility program that comes with Dragon NaturallySpeaking, for example, requires 40MB of disk space. The ability to have Dragon NaturallySpeaking read text as speech requires 15MB of disk space.

If you're short on space in your disk drive, you can omit features from your installation. When you install, you can check off various options. If you've already installed NaturallySpeaking, uninstall it (saving your speech files) and reinstall it with fewer options.

# Dragon Allergies

Like the young of other species, Dragon's products are young enough that they have a few peculiar allergies. Certain hardware and software gives them problems. Either they don't work at all, work erratically, or do unanticipated things. For instance, one release of NaturallySpeaking wouldn't work properly if you had installed Internet Explorer 5.0. Later releases, including release 3.5 (actually 3.52) and 4 generally have many fewer problems.

Dragons are particularly sensitive to audio hardware. On a desktop or tower computer, if your audio hardware is a problem, you can generally change it. Not so on a laptop computer, unless you buy a "USB" microphone or use the NaturallyMobile recorder. See Chapter 19 for more about these and other solutions.

All these sensitivities change so often that it doesn't make a great deal of sense for us to write about them here. They would probably have been solved by the time you read this. The best way to check for problems is to scan Dragon Systems' Web site carefully. Two features in particular to look for are the list of compatible hardware and the user forum, where many of these past problems are documented. Bear in mind that a lot of the problems you see there may have been fixed. A call to Dragon Systems may help you figure out whether the problems still exist.

# Chapter 17

# Speaking More Clearly to Your Dragon

**S**ay, "I want a Fig Newton and a glass of milk." Go ahead. Say it the casual way you would in a diner. (Presuming, for the moment, that you like Fig Newtons and milk.)

If you're like us (and heaven help you, if you are), you probably said something like, "Eyewanna FigNew'n 'na glassa milk." You probably skip the final "t" of "want" and slur "want a" ("wanna"), omit the "to" of "Newton," skip the "a" and "d" of "and" ("n"), and don't really pronounce either letter in the word "of."

We North Americans don't waste time or effort, so we ignore short words, initial vowels, and the final consonants of many words. And we unnerstan 'chother perfeckly, raht? Riot. So whah cain't t' dang computer unnerstan goodol 'merican English?

Most Americans would understand the Fig Newton line perfectly because of our vast cookie-and-milk experience. The computer, on the other hand, is rarely fed Fig Newtons and milk, except for what you drop into the keyboard or your kids stuff into the diskette drive for the dog to lick out. The result?

Without direct consumer experience, a computer has to rely on all those little things we normally skip, to tell one word from another. Without them, Dragon NaturallySpeaking may translate the line something like, "I have Fig Newton awesome milk."

That translation may inspire a popular new dairy/fruit beverage but wouldn't be exactly what you had in mind. (It only knows about "Newton," we suspect, because that is the town where Dragon has its headquarters.)

So, should you learn to speak better, or should you train your Dragon to love you just the way you are? As with most things in life, the answer is, "yes."

# Do You Need to Speak Better?

You probably do need to speak a bit better. Improving your speech habits is one of the best and cheapest ways to cut down on errors in NaturallySpeaking.

On the other hand, don't go nuts. For instance, try to pronounce that example sentence about Fig Newtons *without* slurring any consonants or dropping any a's. (Say, "I wan<u>t</u> a Fig New<u>t</u>on an<u>d</u> a glass o<u>f</u> milk," being sure to speak all the underlined letters.)

Hard work, huh? You'd probably get tired of speaking like a BBC announcer after a very short while, or else develop an urge to go to cricket matches. (Not fatal, but often quite painful.) Moreover, Dragon NaturallySpeaking still may not perform perfectly. For instance, you may get, "I want a Fig Newton in a glass of milk." If you try too hard to enunciate phrases like "Fig Newton" you get "Fig a Newton." Go fig ewer.

So, the first question is: Should you try to speak better than you do normally? If you suspect that your speech is naturally a bit sloppy, or if you've never thought about it much, you probably should try to do better.

If you find yourself working too hard to get better accuracy, stop. You will get tired quickly, start making even more errors, and NaturallySpeaking won't ever learn to recognize your natural speech.

If you just have an accent (and who doesn't), don't worry much about it. NaturallySpeaking adapts to your accent during training. What it has most trouble adapting to is missing words and sounds. If your accent is particularly strong, certain words may sound like other words to NaturallySpeaking. (You can correct it using word training, discussed in Chapter 18.)

If you're not sure you'd know good speech if you heard it, listen to some professional news announcers on the radio. But listen to people hired specifically as news readers (as opposed to disk jockeys, "personalities," and retired sports heroes now working as sportscasters). News readers — particularly news readers at larger radio stations or broadcasting companies — are hired partly for their careful speech.

If your speech is pretty clear, but you're still getting recognition errors, consider some of the other remedies in this Part. Training (Chapter 18) and better audio input (Chapter 19) can make a big difference. If NaturallySpeaking is mis-recognizing special phrases, words, or acronyms in your vocabulary, for instance, the solution is more likely to be training or vocabulary work than improving your speech.

# How Do You Do It?

Changing any habit is hard, and speech is one of the most habitual activities any of us do. (Well, besides coffee drinking.) Apart from taking our thumbs out of our mouths, we've been talking the way we do since childhood. How does a person improve his or her speech? Following are some fairly painless tips for speaking better:

- ✔ First, simply try to speak every word, without fretting at first about the enunciation of the word itself. Avoid skipping words. NaturallySpeaking relies on the adjoining words to help figure out a word. If you skip or slur words, it will make more mistakes.

- ✔ Speak long phrases or full sentences, if you can. The more words in an utterance, the better NaturallySpeaking can figure out your words from context.

- ✔ Make sure you pronounce even small words like "a" and "the." If, like most people, you normally pronounce the word "a" as "uh," keep doing so. Don't switch to "ay" as in "hay."

- ✔ Avoid running words together. The tiny breaks between sounds help distinguish one word from another.

- ✔ Focus your effort on pronouncing words differently that *should* sound a little different, and which Dragon NaturallySpeaking may otherwise confuse. Trying to pronounce "hear" differently from "here," for instance, won't gain you much: They are supposed to sound alike. Nor will you benefit from trying to pronounce the "t" in "exactly," because that word won't be confused easily with any other word, even if you pronounce it "zackly." But pronouncing the "th" in the word "the" — even if you do it very lightly — will help NaturallySpeaking distinguish that word from the word "a."

✔ If you're speaking every word and still have problems, work on your enunciation of words themselves. Pay attention to how a word is spelled. Try to speak all the consonant and vowel sounds in a word, especially ones that begin and end the word — unless they make the word noticeably awkward or the word sounds wrong as a result.

✔ If you're getting small words in your text that you didn't say, like "a" or "and," the microphone may be picking up small puffs of breath. Try moving the microphone more to the side. Then run the Audio Setup wizard, choosing volume adjustment. (Also, don't burp.)

✔ Sit with good posture, not bent over. Relax. Breathe freely. Think peaceful thoughts. Visualize whirled peas. You are getting very sleepy. . . .

✔ Don't speak too rapidly. You don't have to speak slowly, but in today's high-pressure environment, many people begin to sound like a chipmunk with a Starbucks habit.

✔ If your throat gets dry or scratchy, take a break and drink some water or warm tea. (Creamy, cheesy, or overly sweet foods or drinks can goo up your throat. They can make you sound murky or cause you to clear your throat a lot.)

✔ If your voice changes volume over time, and errors increase, run the Audio Setup wizard again, choosing to adjust volume. If you have a bad cold or allergies, or any other long-term change to your voice, consider doing some more general training, discussed in Chapter 18.

✔ Speak the way you trained. When you trained NaturallySpeaking, you read text aloud. Use your reading-aloud voice when you dictate text for highest accuracy.

✔ Talk to a voice trainer or singing instructor. A single session with a professional can give you a lot of tips about speaking more clearly. Who knows, you may find a whole new career.

# Shouldn't NaturallySpeaking Meet You Halfway?

Despite all the tips in this chapter for speaking better, NaturallySpeaking is pretty adaptable to a wide variety of speech habits. As best as we can tell, the only speech flaws that can't be compensated for, in some way, are these two:

✔ Skipping words or slurring them together

✔ Pausing between each word (not using continuous speech)

Nearly every other speech peculiarity can be compensated for by training. On the other hand, it may take a lot of training, and maybe you can improve your speech, instead, with less effort. See Chapter 18 for more about word training, general training, and vocabulary work.

For instance, if NaturallySpeaking consistently gets the same word wrong, the problem may be that your pronunciation is a bit unusual. We, for instance, thought we heard a reference to a "9 o'clock chicken" when riding to the airport in New Zealand. We thought it was a colorful Kiwi phrase for a small commuter plane. The speaker was referring to a "check-in." Chickens aside, rather than retrain yourself, you can word-train NaturallySpeaking, or enter a phonetic spelling for the "spoken form" of the word using the Vocabulary Editor. (Of course, if you say "chicken" for "check-in," what will you say for "chicken?")

If something has happened to alter your voice for a while (a cold, allergies, puberty, or some other affliction), consider running general training again. (General training is where you read stories to NaturallySpeaking.)

For the most part, NaturallySpeaking is not very sensitive to how fast you talk. But very rapid or slow speech may require adjusting NaturallySpeaking settings for better accuracy. NaturallySpeaking looks for a pause as a cue that the next text may be a command. Normally it works best using a quarter-second (250 millisecond) pause, but you can adjust it. (Choose Tools⇨Options, and then click the Miscellaneous tab. Drag the slider for Pause Between Phrases to the right for longer pauses, left for shorter.) If this setting is too short, words may get chopped up. If it's too long, NaturallySpeaking may translate commands as text.

# Chapter 18

# Additional Training and Vocabulary Building

*I*f NaturallySpeaking doesn't appear to be quite as bright as you'd like it to be, you can teach it to do better. Dragon gives you several different tools to improve its skills:

✔ **General training:** General training is when you read to NaturallySpeaking, as you did when you first set it up. Try this if you think the quality of your voice, your manner of speaking, or something in your environment may have changed — or changes regularly.

✔ **Vocabulary building:** Vocabulary building is when you let NaturallySpeaking read some of your documents. It adds words to the vocabulary and teaches NaturallySpeaking how you use them in combination.

✔ **Vocabulary editing:** Vocabulary editing lets you add words to the NaturallySpeaking vocabulary (and, optionally, train NaturallySpeaking in how you say those words). It also lets you add *shorthands:* phrases that NaturallySpeaking translates into other text. For instance, you can say, **"my address"** and have NaturallySpeaking type your address.

✔ **Word training:** Word training teaches NaturallySpeaking how *you* say a word. No matter whether you say the word *bear* as "beer," "beyah," or "bayrrr," word training can tune NaturallySpeaking's ear to your pronunciation.

Yikes, what a lot of choices! Nobody said that educating software was easy, but in this chapter we try to sort it out for you: what to do, when, and how.

# Running General Training Again

If NaturallySpeaking seems to be making more mistakes than it used to, ask yourself if *you* have changed since you first trained your dragon. Has your voice, manner of speaking, or working environment changed?

For example, are you getting more experienced at dictation than you were at first? Have you changed your office, or changed something that makes or absorbs sound in your office? If so, try running General Training. (Because you ran General Training once before, when you set up NaturallySpeaking, it is now called additional or *supplemental* General Training in NaturallySpeaking Help files and documentation.) General Training helps NaturallySpeaking get a more accurate picture of your voice and speech habits.

Running General Training after you've had a few days experience with NaturallySpeaking is a good idea. Often, you speak differently after a few days.

To run General Training, choose Tools⇨General Training. The Select Text dialog box appears, listing some choice reading material.

This Select Text dialog box, and all the ones that follow, are the same ones you saw when you first performed General Training to set up NaturallySpeaking. For details on using them, see the discussion of General Training in Chapter 2.

## Checking for hearing problems

Before you assume your dragon is not very bright, make sure it doesn't have a "hearing" problem. Does NaturallySpeaking make errors on lots of different words and phrases, not just a specific few? Your problem could be with speaking clearly, with your microphone position or quality, with your sound card quality, or with the microphone volume set by the Audio Setup wizard.

To rule out a hearing problem, re-run the Audio Setup wizard as Chapter 19 describes. If the Audio Setup wizard thinks your audio is fine, and you still get errors on lots of different words after running the wizard, try the voice tips in Chapter 17.

The plan in General Training is to read something to NaturallySpeaking so that it can figure out how you speak. This time around, you may find some additional reading material in the Select Text dialog box that is shorter to read than the selections that were available when you first set up NaturallySpeaking.

A fundamental problem with General Training is that many people read differently than they dictate. Try to speak the way you would if you were the author and were thinking this stuff up for the first time. Don't laugh too much at the funny stuff. (It's gauche to laugh at your own jokes, if you're an author. We know, we're very gauche.)

Don't say, **"Cap"** or any other dictation commands during General Training. Don't say any punctuation, either. Click the Back Up button if you really mess something up, and try again. Click the Pause button if you need to take a break for the sake of water intake or output.

# Running the Vocabulary Builder Again

If NaturallySpeaking has begun making more errors than before, one reason may be that you're dictating new subject matter. Have you switched from writing about budgets to writing about budgies? It may be time to re-run the Vocabulary Builder and add some words about birds.

Always spell-check any documents you are going to use in the Vocabulary Builder. (Use your word processor's spell checker.) Your dragon prides itself on not making spelling errors, and you don't want to wreck its reputation by adding bloopers to its vocabulary.

## Adding words from documents

To add new words from documents, use the Vocabulary Builder. Choose Tools⇨Vocabulary Builder. Proceed as Chapter 2 describes for the Vocabulary Builder, choosing your new documents, analyzing them, and selecting which words to add. (If you're using multiple vocabularies in NaturallySpeaking Professional, you can add the words to any vocabulary by clicking the Change Vocabulary button, and choosing one of your existing vocabularies. See Chapter 21 for more details.)

When you get to the Adapt To Document Style screen, choose Yes in reply to the two questions there: Do You Want To Adapt To The Document Style Of The New Documents? and (if so) Do You Want To Use The Style Information From Previous Sessions.

If you have two or more very distinct writing styles or subjects, you may get better accuracy if you create a separate vocabulary for each. In NaturallySpeaking Professional, you can actually create multiple vocabularies for a single user. (See Chapter 21.) The lesser editions of NaturallySpeaking only allow a single vocabulary per user. In those editions, you would have to define a new user for each style or subject, perform all the general training that goes with a new user, and do vocabulary building for each new user from the appropriate documents.

## Adding words from somebody else's documents

Normally, you use your own documents to teach NaturallySpeaking about your vocabulary. What can you do, however, for a subject that you, yourself, have not written much about?

You can grab words from documents other people have written. The Web, for example, is full of documents about nearly any subject you can name. The trick is to have NaturallySpeaking pick up on the words, but not the writing style, of this other author (unless you intend to write just like him or her).

To use someone else's documents, first you must get the documents! NaturallySpeaking can read Word or WordPerfect documents if you have Word or WordPerfect installed. It can also read plain text, RTF (Rich Text Format) and HTML (Web) documents. To get documents off the Web, browse to the page you want, and then save the page as an HTML file. In Internet Explorer, for example, choose File⇨Save As, enter a filename in the dialog box that appears, and click Save.

Use these documents in the Vocabulary Builder as you would any other documents. When you get to the Adapt To Document Style screen, however, the Vocabulary Builder asks whether you want to adapt to the document style of the new documents. If you're using someone else's documents, you should choose No for the question, Do You Want To Adapt to the Document Style? If you were to answer Yes, NaturallySpeaking would assume that you write like that other writer and won't be as accurate.

## Fine-tuning the "Add Words or Find Words" process

When you add words using the Vocabulary Builder (or the Find New Words tool), you need to be careful. At first, you see all kinds of stuff that you may not want to add: typos, spelling errors, and capitalized terms (but not the first word of a sentence). You may also *not* see some words you *do* want to add!

In this list of the good, bad, and ugly, the idea is that you checkmark the good words that you want added to the vocabulary, then add them. Figure 18-1 shows you the dialog box that appears when you use either the Vocabulary Builder described in Chapter 2 (where the dialog box is called Add New Words) or the Find Words tool described in the next section of this chapter (where the dialog box is called Find New Words).

**Figure 18-1:**
Adding
*chutzpah*
and *fred*
to the
vocabulary.
This same
dialog box
appears for
both Add
Words
in the
Vocabulary
Builder and
for the Find
Words tool.

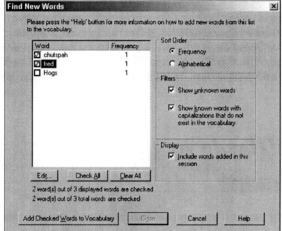

Following are a few tips for adding words by using the dialog box shown in Figure 18-1:

- ✔ Review the list of words to make sure they are real words that you really want. To view the list alphabetically, click Alphabetical in the Sort Order area of the dialog box.

- ✔ Click to check the words you want to add to the vocabulary. When you have checked off all the words you want, click the button Add Checked Words To The Vocabulary.

- ✔ Don't add words that you use very infrequently. This is especially true if they sound like some other word that you do use often. To see how frequently you use a word in the document(s) being analyzed, look in the Frequency column. Words are normally sorted in order of frequency; if they are alphabetical instead, click the Frequency option in the Sort Order area of the dialog box.

✔ Sometimes individual proper nouns that you want from a document are actually common words, except that their capitalization (or lack of capitalization) makes them special for you — a sports team named the Hogs, for example, or an Internet domain named "fred.com." Normally, the Add Words dialog box doesn't show those words. To see those words, click to place a check mark in the checkbox, Show Known Words With Capitalizations That Do Not Exist In The Vocabulary. Now you can click your special capped or uncapped word to mark it for addition to the vocabulary.

✔ The Add Words dialog box ignores phrases of two or more initial-capped words, regardless of what you do. If the Hungry Hogs appears in your document, for instance, it will not appear no matter whether the Show Known Words With Capitalizations That Do Not Exist In The Vocabulary checkbox is checked or not. To add those phrases, use the Vocabulary Editor.

# Finding New Words in the Current Document

The same way you can add words from various documents by using the Vocabulary Builder, you can add words from your current document in the NaturallySpeaking, Word, or WordPerfect window by using the Find New Words tool:

1. **Choose Tools⇨Find New Words from the NaturallySpeaking menu bar or from the Dragon NaturallySpeaking menu choice in Word or WordPerfect.**

   A Find New Words window appears, which Figure 18-1 shows, that looks essentially like the one used by the Vocabulary Builder. It works the same way, too.

2. **Click the checkbox next to each word you want to add to the NaturallySpeaking vocabulary.**

3. **Click the Add Checked Words to Vocabulary button.**

   A confirmation box opens to ask whether you want to train the newly added words. If you click Yes, see the discussion of training words following Figure 18-3 in the upcoming section "Training terms."

4. **After you say all the words on the list, click Done.**

   You return to the Add New Words box.

# *Vocabulary Editing*

You can directly add words to the NaturallySpeaking active vocabulary. The Vocabulary Editor is your tool to add words or delete any you have added. It also has special features that allow you to do any of the following to make your life easier:

✔ Train NaturallySpeaking in your own, personal pronunciation of a word, for better recognition.

✔ Add special words or phrases to the vocabulary, like your company name, properly capitalized or hyphenated, or jargon that you use in your profession.

✔ Give awkward words or phrases a different "spoken form" to make dictation easier, like saying, "my e-mail" for voiceguy@yourcompany.com. These are called *shorthands*.

✔ Come up with alternative ways to say words, punctuation, or whitespace characters, like saying "full stop" for a period.

To launch the Vocabulary Editor, choose Tools➪Vocabulary Editor. You can find it either in the Tools menu of the NaturallySpeaking window or under Tools in the Dragon NaturallySpeaking menu of NaturalWord in Word or WordPerfect. The Vocabulary Editor looks like Figure 18-2.

Although we talk about mouse commands here, you can use voice to control the Vocabulary Editor, too.

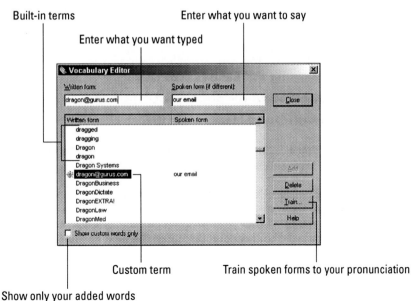

Built-in terms

Enter what you want to say

Enter what you want typed

**Figure 18-2:**
What your parents always wanted to be able to do: Edit your vocabulary.

Custom term

Train spoken forms to your pronunciation

Show only your added words

## Adding custom terms and shorthands in the Vocabulary Editor

To add custom terms to the NaturallySpeaking active vocabulary, launch the Vocabulary Editor (choose Tools➪Vocabulary Editor). Then follow these steps:

1. **Enter the term in the Written Form textbox at the top of the Vocabulary Editor.**

   (Figure 18-2 shows you where to enter whatever you want typed.) In Figure 18-2, for example, we entered our e-mail address, dragon@gurus.com.

   To see what's in the vocabulary, you can either scroll the list in the Vocabulary Editor, or you can type the term in the Written Form box. As you type, the list scrolls to match your typing.

   If you want to speak something other than what's typed, enter it in the right-hand textbox, labeled Spoken Form (If Different). For example, we entered our email there. This is what Dragon Systems calls a *shorthand* — a sort of verbal alias for the typed text. We'll now be able to say, "our e-mail" and have NaturallySpeaking type dragon@gurus.com. If you use a term in the Spoken Form box that NaturallySpeaking doesn't already have in its vocabulary, it pops up a dialog box letting you know that fact and asks whether you want it to "assign an approximate pronunciation." Click OK.

2. **After you enter a written (and, if different, spoken) form of the term, click the Add button.**

   The Vocabulary Editor adds the term to the vocabulary list and marks it with an asterisk.

   You can delete any custom term you add. Just click the term, then click the Delete button. You can also select multiple terms to delete by holding down the Ctrl button as you click.

   For most terms, you're now done.

3. **Click the Close button.**

"Done?" you ask. "But how," you might ask, "does NaturallySpeaking know how this term should *sound?*" Good question, and we're so glad you asked.

NaturallySpeaking has a pronunciation guesser that bases its guess on the spelling of the term (the spoken form, if there is one — otherwise, the written form). If you think that your pronunciation might not match the guesser's guess, you need to train that term. See the next section!

If you have lots of shorthands to add, you can create a list and use the Vocabulary Builder instead of the Editor:

1. **Create a text file in which each line is the "written form" of a vocabulary entry you want to add.**

2. **At the end of any line where you want a different "spoken form," add a backslash and then the shorthand alias you want to speak.**

3. **In the Add Words from a List screen of the Vocabulary Builder (see Chapter 2), read that list.**

## Training words in the Vocabulary Editor

NaturallySpeaking uses a pronunciation guesser to figure out how most terms sound from the spelling. However, lots of jargon, acronyms, and other terms don't conform to standard rules of English pronunciation. Sometimes you can type a spoken form that gives NaturallySpeaking something better to guess from. But, whether you enter a written and spoken form or just a written form, if the pronunciation you're going to use isn't obvious from the spelling, you should train NaturallySpeaking in how you intend to pronounce the word.

For example, you may want NaturallySpeaking to write "Boston and Maine Railroad" when you speak the phrase "B&M." You would enter the written form and the spoken form as the preceding section describes. Then you might say to yourself, "No way is NaturallySpeaking going to recognize the pronunciation of the term B&M." You can use the Vocabulary Editor's word training feature to make sure NaturallySpeaking does recognize your word or phrase.

You can train words without using the Vocabulary Editor, too. Just select a word in your document, and choose Tools⇨Train Words. The same Train Words dialog box appears as the one shown in Figure 18-3.

To train words from within the Vocabuarly Builder, proceed as follows:

1. **Click your term in the Vocabulary Editor's list of words, and then click the Train button in the Vocabulary Editor.**

   For example, we defined the written term "Boston and Maine Railroad" with the spoken form B&M. We thought our pronunciation of the term B&M was unlikely to be guessed correctly, so we clicked the Train button and got the dialog box shown in Figure 18-3.

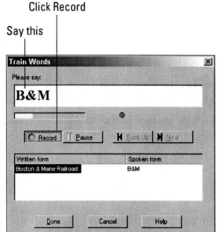

Click Record

Say this

**Figure 18-3:**
Training
train words
in the Train
Words
dialog box.

2. **Click the Record button.**

   The Train Words dialog box displays in large type the spoken form of the term (or the written form if you haven't entered a spoken form).

3. **Speak the term, and NaturallySpeaking remembers.**

   You can repeat the training several times, and in fact, NaturallySpeaking may prompt you to do so in some instances.

4. **Click the Done button after you've spoken the term.**

Sometimes, word training isn't enough. If two terms sound alike, NaturallySpeaking chooses one by looking at how you have used the term before, in context. Your newly added term doesn't yet have any context at all — you haven't used it in a phrase — so NaturallySpeaking is more likely to choose the other term.

The answer is to dictate your new term in context, and then correct NaturallySpeaking with **Correct That** when it chooses the wrong term. If you keep dictating and correcting NaturallySpeaking with the Correction dialog box, it eventually catches on and starts using the new term.

## Creating different ways to say the same thing

The period at the end of this sentence has more aliases (alternative names) than most criminals. The words *period, decimal point, dot, point, stop,* and *full stop* are all valid names for that same symbol in different contexts. NaturallySpeaking doesn't currently recognize all those alternative spoken names, but you can add them to the vocabulary.

If you have an alternative spoken name you would like to use for a word, phrase, or symbol, use the Vocabulary Editor to add that name. (Unfortunately, you can't change any of the existing names, if you don't like them. You can only add an alternative.)

To add aliases, whether for symbols, numbers, or other terms, launch the Vocabulary Editor (choose Tools⇨Vocabulary Editor) and then do the following:

1. **Type the term or symbol that needs an alias in the Written Form textbox.**

    The list scrolls to show the current written and spoken forms.

    To see all the currently defined symbols and dictation commands in the Vocabulary Editor, you must scroll up above the terms beginning with "a."

2. **Type a new term in the Spoken Form box, and then click the Add button.**

    A second copy of the word appears in the vocabulary list, with your new alias, and an asterisk to mark the alias as a custom term. (If the alias doesn't work out, you can delete it. Just click the line and then click the Delete button.)

To add a symbol that's not on the keyboard:

1. **Insert the symbol into a document, and then copy and paste it into the Written Form textbox.**

    For example, in Word you can choose Insert⇨Symbol to insert a symbol into a Word document. Select it, and then press Ctrl+C to copy it to the Windows Clipboard.

2. **Click in the Written Form textbox of the Vocabulary Editor, and then press Ctrl+V to paste the symbol.**

3. **Enter whatever name you would like to speak for that symbol in the Spoken Form textbox, and click the Add button.**

# Training Words

If NaturallySpeaking is having trouble recognizing specific words, word training may be your solution. Word training is most helpful if the problem is that your pronunciation of a word is unique or not at all like its spelling. For example, in Massachusetts, the city of Worcester is pronounced "Wooster." In Boston, it's pronounced "Woostah."

If you pronounce the word as it's spelled and NaturallySpeaking is still having trouble, NaturallySpeaking probably understands how you *say* the word; it just doesn't understand how you *use* the word. Word training won't fix this problem. To fix the problem, use the Correction dialog box (say, **"Correct That"**) whenever NaturallySpeaking gets the word wrong, or do some vocabulary building from your own documents where you use that word.

To train a word, get a leash and a bag of liver treats and take the following steps. (You can also get into word training from the Vocabulary Editor. See "Training words in the Vocabulary Editor," earlier in this chapter, and then skip to Step 4.)

1. **In the NaturallySpeaking menu bar (or in the Dragon NaturallySpeaking menu in Word or WordPerfect), choose Tools➪Train Words.**

   A training dialog box springs up.

2. **Type the word (or phrase) that needs training.**

   (The word or phrase has to be one that NaturallySpeaking already has in its vocabulary. Otherwise, NaturallySpeaking complains and suggests that you use the Vocabulary Editor, instead.)

3. **Click OK after entering the word.**

   NaturallySpeaking gives you the Train Words dialog box. (Refer to Figure 18-3.)

4. **Click the Record button.**

   The Train New Words dialog box displays your word in large type.

   If you got here by way of the Vocabulary Editor, the Train New Words dialog box shows you the spoken form of the term (or the written form if you haven't entered a spoken form).

5. **Speak the term, and NaturallySpeaking remembers.**

   You can repeat the training several times, and in fact, NaturallySpeaking may prompt you to do so in some instances.

6. **Click the Done button after you speak the term.**

Sometimes, word training isn't enough. You'll speak your newly trained word, and NaturallySpeaking still gets it wrong. If two terms sound alike, NaturallySpeaking chooses one by looking at how you have used the term before, in context.

If you have recently added this term (say, in the Vocabulary Editor), NaturallySpeaking has little or no context for the term. You haven't used it in a phrase, so NaturallySpeaking is more likely to choose the term with which it has more experience. The solution is to dictate your new term in context and then correct NaturallySpeaking with **Correct That** when it chooses the wrong term. If you keep dictating and correcting NaturallySpeaking with the Correction dialog box, it eventually catches on and starts using the new term.

# _Training Commands_

If NaturallySpeaking isn't obeying your commands, it may not be recognizing your pronunciation. You can improve its recognition for many commands exactly as you would for word or phrase training. See the steps in the preceding section for instructions. When the Training dialog box springs up in Step 2, type the command you want to train.

Make sure you capitalize the words of the command properly. Check the documentation that comes with NaturallySpeaking for proper capitalization. Most words in NaturallySpeaking command phrases are initial-capped except for articles, prepositions, and other short words.

You can't, however, train "dictation commands" this way. These commands are the ones that control capitalization and spacing, like **No-Caps-On**. To train those commands, use the Vocabulary Editor. Scroll to the very top (above the "a") of the list of words in the Vocabulary Editor. Click a command and then click the Train button.

Before you try command training, check to make sure that you're pausing correctly before and after a command. If NaturallySpeaking gets the words right but types them instead of doing them, pausing is more likely to be your problem than pronunciation. Chapter 4 talks more about solving this problem.

# Chapter 19

# Improving Audio Input

*T*he expression "garbage in, garbage out" takes on a different twist (or perhaps a twist-tie?) when you talk about speech recognition. If garbage goes in, NaturallySpeaking reconstructs it into perfectly good words. It acts like a trash compactor: It makes garbage look better.

Of course, you're not talking trash (unless, maybe, you're at a baseball game). Nonetheless, your words may be trashed on their way to the PC. The microphone or audio hardware may not be quite right. Or the microphone may have moved when you chugged your coffee. Or your office mates, appliances, or kids may be contributing background garbage of their own to your audio. The result may sound okay to your ears if you play it back, but dragons have very sensitive ears.

## Figuring Out Whether You Have an Audio Input Problem

If NaturallySpeaking mis-recognizes lots of words, your second thought is probably, "Something's wrong with my microphone or sound card." (Your first thought is probably uncharitable towards your new dragon. Shame on you.)

NaturallySpeaking may be messing up for lots of reasons, however. As with a puppy that messes up, one reason may be inadequate training. Before you go looking for an audio input problem, make sure you have completed all the training that the New User wizard asked you to. (You'll know if you haven't. When you start NaturallySpeaking and choose an incompletely trained user, NaturallySpeaking warns you and gives you a chance to finish the job.) One symptom of a need for additional training or vocabulary building is that NaturallySpeaking makes the same error repeatedly: cheese for trees, for instance. See Chapter 18 for help with that.

If, however, NaturallySpeaking gives you different text each time you say the same thing (wheeze, sneeze, and breeze for trees), you may have an audio input problem (or allergies). One gut-simple way to test for serious audio input problems is to listen to your PC play back your voice. You can use the NaturallySpeaking Sound Recorder, if you have it (see Chapter 8), or you can use the Windows Sound Recorder. The Windows Sound Recorder is at Start⇨Programs⇨Accessories⇨Entertainment⇨Sound Recorder. Click the red-dot button in Sound Recorder and speak into the microphone to record. Press ◄◄ to rewind and then ► to play. If you hear a lot of noise, or your voice is distorted, you may have an audio input problem.

The most common cause of recognition errors, however, is muttering through your coffee cup, or otherwise not speaking clearly. See Chapter 17 if you may not be speaking clearly. No? Your diction would qualify you for the British Broadcasting Company? Then read on.

# Running the Audio Setup Wizard

If you suspect an audio input problem, the first thing to do is to run the Audio Setup wizard. The Audio Setup wizard can do either a "complete setup" or simply adjust the volume.

If NaturallySpeaking has been working okay to date and only now has begun making errors, your microphone may have moved a bit, or you may be speaking more or less loudly than before. In that case, you only need the wizard to adjust the volume. Choose Tools⇨Audio Setup Wizard from the Naturally-Speaking menu bar and follow the instructions. (For detailed instructions on the Audio Setup wizard, see Step 4 of the discussion of the New User wizard in Chapter 2.)

Some PCs have more than one sound system installed. For instance, you may have installed a better sound card than the one your PC came with, but the original is still present. If you're using a USB microphone, you almost certainly have two sound systems. If you have more than one sound system, the first screen that the Audio Setup wizard displays asks you to choose the sound system. You must choose the system your microphone is connected to: USB Audio Device if you're using a USB microphone, for instance. If the choices you see don't mean anything to you, click Default and proceed. If you choose incorrectly, when the Audio Setup wizard gets to the Adjust Your Volume screen, it will complain that the sound level is too low. Click Cancel to exit the Audio Setup wizard and then restart it and choose the other sound system.

In the Audio Setup wizard, you can skip any screen that you think is unnecessary, except for the Adjust Your Input Volume screen. Just click Next to move on. For instance, you can skip the speaker test.

At the end, the Audio Setup wizard displays a screen that tells you a speech-to-noise ratio and whether that score is acceptable or not. A higher number is better. Anything under 15 is unacceptable and the wizard gives you an error message. If you get a score that's too low, or borderline, try repositioning your microphone. Click Start Quality Check to run the test again.

You engineers and serious audio geeks out there can try pressing Alt+1 when the results screen appears. All kinds of cool, technical displays appear as you talk.

If volume is low, consider speaking a bit louder or moving the microphone slightly closer to your mouth. If you're tired, try taking a break! We have found that our volume varies considerably over the day and is lower when we're tired, sitting with poor posture, or depressed.

# *Checking Your Microphone*

There is many a slip between the PC and the lip. Following are some of the problems you may be having on the microphone end of things, and what to do about them:

- ✔ **Your microphone needs adjustment:** Make sure the microphone is off to the side of your mouth, about a half-inch away from one corner of your mouth. You may have to bend the plastic tube that holds the microphone into an S-shape to get this right. Also make sure that the microphone is facing the right way. One side of the microphone should have a dot, a word, or other marking near the foam ball of the microphone. That mark ought to be facing your mouth. If you can't see the marking at first, try pulling the foam back, or off altogether.

- ✔ **You have chosen the wrong sound system in the Audio Setup wizard:** Read the preceding section, "Running the Audio Setup Wizard."

✔ **You're trying to use the built-in microphone in your laptop computer:**
These rarely provide enough quality, and they pick up lots of extraneous
noise from the laptop and the surface it lies on. Nearly half of all laptops
present an audio input problem to NaturallySpeaking because of their
microphones, sound hardware, or both. One good solution is a USB
microphone — see the following section for details.

✔ **You're trying to use the cheap microphone that came with your PC:**
Give it up! Use the one that came with NaturallySpeaking, or buy a serious microphone from the list of Dragon-certified mikes on its Web site.

✔ **The microphone connection is loose:** Look at where the plug fits the
jack in your PC; make sure it's not wiggly. If you have NaturallySpeaking
Preferred or higher, try playing back some of your dictation. (Select text
and say, **"Play That."**) If it has loud scratchy noises, you may need to
replace the microphone or get someone to test and fix its cable. Some
background noise also comes from the PC (not exactly a high-fi sound
system), and is unavoidable.

✔ **The microphone cable is plugged into the wrong jack in the PC:** If the
microphone is plugged into the *really* wrong jack, like the speaker output,
it won't work at all. If you have no alternative but to plug it into the IN or
LINE IN jack on your PC (you have no microphone jack), it may work but
the volume may be low. If it's plugged into the IN or LINE IN jack and
doesn't work at all, run a complete setup in the Audio Setup wizard as
the previous section describes. On the Choosing Microphone or Line
Input screen that appears when you click the Advanced button, click
Line Input. Volume may still not be high enough, but at least you'll have
a chance.

✔ **You don't have the adapter you need to run your microphone on your
PC's sound card:** On some PCs' sound cards, the microphone jack doesn't
supply enough power to run some microphones. In other cases, the
microphone doesn't provide a good enough match to the sound card.
Some adapters ("battery" or "bias" boxes) only provide the power that
the microphone needs, no sound improvement. Others provide both
power and other adaptation. If you're using a Dragon-supplied microphone and it needs an adapter to operate on certain common sound
boards (like the SoundBlaster 16), a "Universal Microphone Adapter"
that provides both services is provided. If you're using another vendor's
microphone, you can often order an adapter from the vendor.

✔ **You have an adapter, but it's set to the wrong level:** Check the instructions for the microphone or adapter first. If all else fails, check for a
switch and try switching it the other way.

✔ **A battery is failing in the microphone or adapter:** The microphones
that come with NaturallySpeaking don't have batteries, but some microphones do, and we're willing to bet that battery-powered adapters do.

✔ **Windows and NaturallySpeaking aren't getting along:** On some systems, you may have to give Windows a nudge to connect the microphone to NaturallySpeaking. The symptom of this is that no sound gets through to NaturallySpeaking at all. First, turn on the microphone icon for NaturallySpeaking. Then double-click the gold speaker icon at the far end of your taskbar from the Start button. In the Volume Control dialog box that appears, make sure no checkmark appears in the microphone (mic) Mute checkbox. Click to clear the checkmark, if it's present, and then close the dialog box by clicking the X in the upper-right corner.

Should you get a better microphone than the one that came with Naturally-Speaking? Many voice-recognition professionals swear by getting a better microphone, which can run from about $80 to several hundred dollars. A better microphone will generally improve your results, but only up to the limits of your PC's sound card. Both microphone and sound card are links in the chain that brings your voice to your PC, and whichever is the weakest link will limit your sound quality. Those professionals who recommend better microphones also tend to have very good sound cards. Your results will probably not improve in proportion to the money you spend. Check the list of Dragon-certified microphones on Dragon's Web site for options. But before you go laying out big bucks for a new microphone and sound card, read the next section on USB microphones.

# Getting the USB Microphone

One great way to get better quality audio and bypass all this microphone/ sound-card stuff entirely is to get a USB (Universal Serial Bus) microphone. It's probably the best way to deal with a laptop or notebook computer that doesn't have good audio. We love it.

A USB microphone plugs into a USB connector on your PC and delivers digital sound right to the PC. You no longer use the audio input features of your PC's sound card. Because the USB mike removes all the variables that the regular microphone and sound-card system presents, it's one of the better solutions to audio input problems. Some users have even reported that their words are transcribed faster when they use the USB mike. (Your mileage may differ.)

Dragon sells editions of NaturallySpeaking that come with a USB microphone. Or you can buy just their USB microphone, currently a microphone made by Telex, for about 80 bucks. At this writing, the NaturallySpeaking USB microphone doesn't play audio out through the headset. You must use speakers.

What's the catch? Your PC has to have a USB port (connector), and not all PCs do. You can buy a card for your PC that adds a USB port, however, so you or your local PC service shop can add a USB fairly easily. If you have a laptop with a PCMCIA slot, you can buy a card that adds USB ports. Dragon has evaluated one such card from Hi-Val. Most cards cost less than $40.

If you want the very best, Dragon's USB solution may not be the answer. Some users report that the NaturallySpeaking USB microphone isn't as good as the combination of a very good separate microphone and a very good sound card.

A *USB microphone* is really a regular microphone with a tiny sound card (technically, an analog-to-digital converter or ADC) built into a little box in the cable. At this writing, Dragon's USB microphone from Telex provides "16-bit" audio. You can buy better (more "bits") USB converters from microphone vendors, into which you can plug better microphones, if you're really fanatic.

Installing the USB microphone in Windows 98 or later editions of Windows doesn't take much work on your part (if all goes well). In Windows 95, you may or may not be able to use USB. To find out whether your version of Windows 95 runs USB, take these steps:

1. **Go to `www.usb.org` and download the *usbready* product.**

   (As of this writing, you can go directly to the software at `www.usb.org/data/usbready.exe`.)

2. **Download this file (usbready.exe) to a folder on your PC, open that folder, and double-click the file to run the program.**

   If your copy of Windows 95 doesn't run USB, your only choice is to find a very clever computer shop or install Windows 98 (or later).

In theory, you can "hot" connect your USB microphone to your PC. This means you can plug it in while Windows is running. Windows notices and does whatever is necessary, including initial installation. The installation procedure least likely to cause problems, however, is to shut down your PC first, plug in your USB mike, and then turn on the PC.

When you first plug in the microphone and start your PC, Windows starts running the Add New Hardware wizard, which looks for new drivers for the "USB Composite Device." Take the wizard up on its offer to "search for the best driver for your device." The wizard then lists storage devices to look in, including Floppy Disk Drives, CD-ROM drive, Microsoft Windows Update, or Specify a Location. Don't change anything on this screen; just click Next. The final screen, labeled USB Composite Device, indicates that Windows has installed the software that your microphone needs. Click Finish.

After you install the microphone, you need to tell NaturallySpeaking to use it. Because you're using a new microphone, you have to define a new user in NaturallySpeaking. That means reading some more training material to NaturallySpeaking. (Oh, stop whining. Parents, how many times have you read *Good Night, Moon* to your kids?) The process is just like the initial training you did for NaturallySpeaking and goes like this:

1. **In NaturallySpeaking, choose <u>U</u>ser⇨<u>N</u>ew.**

   The New User wizard appears on the scene. Click Next to proceed to the Create User screen.

2. **At the Create User screen, give your USB-microphone user a distinctive name (type it in the top text box), and click <u>N</u>ext to proceed.**

   Continue through the wizard, following the instructions and clicking Next to proceed on to each screen. See the section on running the New User wizard in Chapter 2 if you're fuzzy on these details.

3. **The Audio Setup wizard displays the Choosing Your Sound System screen. Choose the USB Audio Device option and continue with new user training.**

# Playing Your Best Card

Your microphone plugs into a chunk of your PC loosely called the "sound card" or the "audio card." The sound card is responsible for converting what comes out of your microphone into computer bits. Are some sound cards sounder than other sound cards? A resounding "Yes!"

## Being of sound mind, or are you certifiable?

Dragon Systems makes a point of certifying audio (sound) hardware, including microphones and sound cards. Check out Dragon's Web site at www.dragonsys.com for the list of "compatible" products. If you're buying a new computer, make sure that your PC vendor can supply a NaturallySpeaking-compatible sound card already installed and tested.

While you are at Dragon's Web site, explore the user forum in the technical support section. You can search for terms like "sound card" or "microphone" and see what others have said about various manufacturers' products. Some perfectly good hardware has never been certified by Dragon.

## What is a sound card?

Inside your PC is a large board full of electronics that do the essential functions of your computer. Less-essential stuff is on smaller boards, also called "cards," whose rear-ends are typically decorated with various connectors. These small boards are designed so that their connectors stick out the back of your PC cabinet, where you plug stuff in. Depending on the whim of the engineers who built your PC, the sound (audio) features may either be on the big ("mother") board or on one of these cards. If your audio features are on a card, changing to a Dragon-certified card is generally easier than if they are on the motherboard.

How do you know whether your sound card is your problem? It's hard to be certain. Because replacing a sound card is a pain, most people try to improve other aspects of their audio first, like speaking more clearly or adjusting the microphone position. If those efforts don't work, they get a new sound card (or buy a USB microphone). We suggest that route.

If your PC is an off-the-shelf "multimedia PC," it's likely to have either a rather cheap sound card or sound built into the motherboard. It's adequate for running your speakers, and it will let you record your voice, but your Dragon friend may well choke on the result.

If you suspect that's the case, you may benefit by replacing your sound card with a Dragon-blessed sound card. If you haven't installed sound cards in a computer before, buy the sound card at a shop or from a consultant with the expertise to install the card and to disable the existing sound hardware.

The manufacturers of some of the sound cards that get good marks from power users include top-end cards from Creative Labs (SoundBlaster and Ensoniq cards) and Turtle Beach (Fiji cards), but many lower-cost cards do just fine. SoundBlaster cards are the "classic" PC sound cards, and NaturallySpeaking works fine with most of them. A SoundBlaster 16 card, for instance, generally does fine and costs under $50.

Finding out whether you have a Dragon-certified sound card is a good idea. If you have one, and audio input is poor anyway, you'll know to look elsewhere for the cause. (Also, if you do have one, Dragon technical support won't be able to shrug you off when you call or e-mail.)

The best way to see what you have is to check your PC invoice or list of features. Or you could pop the cover off your PC and look at the board with a magnifying glass for a label or printing. That will give you the model number, too.

But that sort of open-cover surgery isn't for everyone, so here's another way:

1. **On the Windows taskbar, choose Start⇨Settings⇨Control Panel.**

2. **In the Control Panel, double-click the Multimedia icon.**

   A Multimedia Properties dialog box pops up.

3. **Click the Audio tab at the top, and see what "Preferred Device" is listed for Recording or Playback.**

   The manufacturer's name or telltale initials of the product line appear there. You may not be able to figure out what it means, but Dragon technical support or your local PC shop may know.

What about the rest of us poor shmucks who don't have a Dragon-blessed sound card, or have no idea whether we do and aren't about to spend the money to get one anyway? The best solution is to try to improve your speaking, run the Audio Setup wizard's volume adjustment regularly, do lots of training and vocabulary building, and make sure you work in a quiet environment.

One slim hope for improving your existing sound card is that you may be able to upgrade the card's software (its "driver" software). Check the Web site for the sound card's vendor (if you can figure out who that is) for information. Dragon Systems notes that if your PC is using a "game-compatible" driver, it's kind of the bottom of the heap. Open the NaturallySpeaking folder on your hard drive (usually C:\NatSpeak), and open the Dragon.log file you see there. (If double-clicking doesn't do the job, open your word processor and then drag the file from the folder to the title bar of the word processor window.) Look (or have your word processor search) for the last instance of the word "Multimedia" — just after that word is the name of the driver being used.

# Ensuring a Quiet Environment

In general, Dragon NaturallySpeaking works best in a quiet environment. Noise from an open window, kids, dogs, appliances, fans, air conditioners, ringing phones, singing modems, blurping coffee pots, or a loudly growling stomach can make it inaccurate. So this is a perfect excuse to go down to the basement, kick out the dog and kids, shut off the phone, drink the last of the coffee, and have a doughnut. If you're at work, it's an excuse to close the door to your office.

Dragon NaturallySpeaking also works best where the environment deadens sound, such as areas with carpets or heavy draperies. (Bring a bean-bag chair down to the basement.) Hard surfaces such as hard floors, glass windows, Formica counters, and metal furniture cause echoes that you don't notice but that Dragon NaturallySpeaking may.

If your environment has become more noisy than when you trained NaturallySpeaking, you may do well to repeat the training. See the discussion of general training in Chapter 18.

The microphones that come with NaturallySpeaking, and most of the ones you may buy, are directional. They are "pointed" towards your mouth. Sounds coming from other directions, especially from locations in front of you, are somewhat suppressed. Sounds coming from behind you, however, may be less suppressed. You may be better off with your back to a fabric-covered cubicle wall than to your cube-mate. (Not turning your back on your cube-mate is probably safer, anyway.)

Besides acoustical noise — noise that you can hear with your ears — you can have electrical noise. Electrical noise is the result of electricity and magnetic fields zinging around near your microphone or sound card. PCs and monitors generate a lot of these fields, so try backing a bit farther away from your PC and monitor when you dictate. It's conceivable that moving your sound card to a slot more distant from other hardware in your PC may also reduce electrical noise.

In environments where you think noise is an issue, and you have money to spend, consider getting one of the better active noise-canceling (ANC) microphones. One such headset mike well-regarded by the power users is the Andrea Electronics ANC-600. It's good for moderate noise environments and runs about $80. Another is the QuietWare 1000 ANC, for higher noise environments, at about $160.

# Chapter 20

# Dealing with Change

## In This Chapter

▶ Adding and deleting users

▶ Moving your user files to a new computer

▶ Upgrading to a better version of NaturallySpeaking

*P*eople used to say that change is the only constant. (But then they stopped — we haven't heard that expression in years.) Computer systems change faster than almost any other part of life: If something works, it must be obsolete. If you become a regular user of NaturallySpeaking, you and your dragon will probably go through a number of changes together — new operating systems, new versions of the NaturallySpeaking software, or even whole new computers. New users may come into both of your lives as family members or officemates decide that they want to start dictating, too.

Some changes have been dealt with elsewhere in this book. In Chapter 19, we talk about hardware upgrades that may improve the performance of NaturallySpeaking: more memory, a better soundcard, and a better microphone. We discuss adding extra vocabularies (in the Professional edition) in Chapter 21. Adding and deleting users is also covered in Chapter 21.

## Moving Your Dragon to a New Machine

Getting a new computer can be a lot of fun. Everything runs faster, the hard drive is bigger, it may have a bunch of fun, new software that you can play with, and the keyboard is cleaner than your old keyboard ever was. But just like moving to a new neighborhood, moving to a new machine means going through a period of uncertainty as you wonder whether all your possessions will make it in one piece or whether you have to leave anything behind.

Or maybe it's not a brand-spanking-new machine. Maybe you've just decided that your dragon belongs on your office computer rather than your home computer, or vice versa.

In either case, the two main possessions that you would like to wrap in bubbly plastic and move to the new machine are your NaturallySpeaking software and your user files.

The first question to answer is whether you need to buy a new copy of NaturallySpeaking to install on the new machine. The answer is maybe.

Owning a copy of NaturallySpeaking entitles you to have it installed on a single machine. (Special rules exist for office networks; let your company's lawyer worry about it.) So if you uninstall NaturallySpeaking on your old machine, you're legally free and clear to install it on a new one. If you want to keep using NaturallySpeaking on two different machines, you're supposed to buy two copies.

The second important question is whether you can transfer your user files to the new machine, so that you can avoid retraining from scratch. The answer, once again, is maybe. NaturallySpeaking itself doesn't create any obstacles to prevent you from doing this, and we tell you how later in this section. But the sheer size of the files may be a problem. The largest single file in our current user folder is 13MB; even compressing it with the WinZip utility (if you don't know what WinZip is, forget we mentioned it) only gets it down to 7MB — roughly five times as big as a floppy disk. A Zip disk or a SuperDisk can handle files of this size with no sweat, and you're also fine if you can transfer the files over a broadband (high-speed) network. You can also transfer files between two Windows computers by using a cable and a program called Direct Cable Connection (directcc). You can read about this approach by choosing Start⇨Help in Windows; on the Index tab of the Help dialog box that appears, type `Direct Cable Connection, overview` and press Enter.

E-mailing the files from your old computer to your new one works if your mail system allows large attached files, but over a 56K modem the process takes forever. If your only way to get files out of your old computer is via floppy disks, you may be stuck with retraining from scratch.

## *Installing NaturallySpeaking on the new machine*

CDs don't remember whether they've been read before, so installing NaturallySpeaking on the new machine is just like installing it the first time. (See Chapter 2.) If you are transferring your user files from the old machine, though, you don't want to redo General Training, so cancel out of the New User wizard just after you select a user name (in other words, right before running Audio Setup). Move on to the "Transferring your user files to a new computer" section.

The only wrinkle in the installation process is if you originally bought one release of NaturallySpeaking and then upgraded to another. Say, for example, that you bought NaturallySpeaking 3.0 and then upgraded to 3.5. The 3.5 upgrade CD may not work on the new machine unless the earlier version of NaturallySpeaking is already installed there. (That's why you shouldn't throw away an old NaturallySpeaking CD when the new release arrives.)

Here's what we recommend:

1. **Try to install NaturallySpeaking from the most recent disk you have.**

   Either it will work (in which case you don't have to worry about this problem) or it will tell you within five seconds that it isn't going to work.

2. **If that disk doesn't install NaturallySpeaking, then find the disk for the earlier version of NaturallySpeaking and install from it.**

3. **Click Cancel to get out of the New User wizard.**

4. **Exit from NaturallySpeaking.**

5. **Remove the disk for the early version of NaturallySpeaking and insert the disk for the later version.**

   Now the Setup wizard should find the old version of NaturallySpeaking and do its upgrade thing. Move on to "Transferring your user files to a new machine."

## *Transferring your user files to a new machine*

The process of transferring your user files to a new machine has a few basic steps, which we explain in detail in the following sections. You have to go through this process for each user that you want to move to the new machine:

1. **Find the right files.**

2. **Copy the files to a folder where the new computer can find them.**

3. **Run the New User wizard long enough to tell NaturallySpeaking your user name.**

   (We suggest that you do this when you install NaturallySpeaking on the new machine — see Chapter 2 — but you can do it now if you haven't done it yet.) This step makes sure that the right folders are created, so that you'll have somewhere to put your user files in Step 4. Cancel out of the New User wizard before you run Audio Setup or General Training.

4. **Move your user files into the right folders on the new machine.**

5. **Run the Audio Setup wizard.**

The next time you run NaturallySpeaking, your user name should appear in the Open User dialog box, and your user files should load just like they did on your old machine.

### Step 1: Poking around in your user folder

If you're going to transfer your user files, you have to find them first. If you installed NaturallySpeaking into the C:\NatSpeak directory, then all of its user files are in the folder C:\NatSpeak\Users. Each user has its own folder, named for the user name. So if your user name is Sue, your individual user files are in C:\NatSpeak\Users\Sue.

Inside an individual user's folder are two folders called *current* and *backup,* plus some other stuff we won't worry about right now. Their names tell you what they are: *Current* contains the user files that NaturallySpeaking is currently using to try to understand what you're saying, whereas *backup* contains an older copy of the same files.

Inside the current folder is a folder called *voice.* This folder contains the file *dd10phat.usr.* (Sometimes this file is called *dd10user.usr,* and it may even have a different name on your PC. In any case, only one super-huge file is inside *voice,* and that's the file you want.) This file is the most important to transfer. It contains everything that NaturallySpeaking has figured out about your voice and how you pronounce the basic sounds that make up the English language.

Also inside the current folder is a folder called *GeneralE*, which is short for General English. (General English is, of course, the high commander of all English majors.) This is the folder where all the vocabulary files are stored. If you have Professional edition and have created any additional vocabularies beyond General English, each of them has its own folder inside the current folder.

### Step 2: Taking user files from your old computer

The files that you want to take from your old computer are dd10phat.usr (which may be called dd10user.usr in some versions) and the contents of the GeneralE folder. We describe in general terms the most likely places to find these files in the previous section. If you installed NaturallySpeaking into the C:\NatSpeak folder, then the most likely address for dd10phat.usr is C:\NatSpeak\Users\YourUserName\current\voice\dd10phat.usr. You can usually find GeneralE at C:\NatSpeak\Users\YourUserName\current\ GeneralE. Figure 20-1 shows where this file and folder are found on our system. (Notice that the individual user folder in this example is Doug, not YourUserName.)

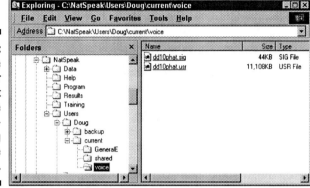

**Figure 20-1:**
Where the
major user
files fit
into the
Naturally-
Speaking
file
structure.

If your dd10phat.usr and your GeneralE are not at these locations, use choose Start➪Find➪Files and Folders to look for it. The name dd10phat.usr isn't a very popular one, so you'll probably only find two of them — one in the current folder and one in the backup folder. You want the one in the current folder.

Copy dd10phat.usr and the entire GeneralE folder to a disk where your new computer can access them. That may either be a high-capacity disk like a Zip disk or SuperDisk (ordinary floppies are much too small to hold these files) or on a network server. If you have set up the Windows direct cable connection we mention earlier, you can copy the files directly to the new PC's hard drive.

### Step 3: Running the New User wizard

You may have already run the New User wizard when you installed NaturallySpeaking on the new machine. If so, then you don't need to do it again. You only need to start it: Choose User➪New.

Don't go through the entire New User process; the point of moving the old user files to the new machine is to avoid retraining. You don't want to train the new user files that the wizard sets up, you just want the file structure to be set up so that you can replace the wizard's generic files with the files you copied from your old machine.

Instead, go through the first step of the New User process (the User Type screen, also labeled "Create User Speech Files" on the left side of the wizard screen). When you get to the User Type screen, click Cancel rather than run the Audio Setup wizard, which is what is about to happen. If the New User wizard then offers to start General Training, click Cancel again. At this point, the wizard decides you are being uncooperative, and NaturallySpeaking exits. No problem — you did just what you needed to do.

If anything about the New User wizard confuses you, look at the more detailed description of it given in Chapter 2.

### Step 4: Installing user files into your new computer

By now we assume that you have moved your user files to some place where your new computer can find them: Either the new PC's hard drive (C:), or a Zip or some other kind of disk drive on the new PC, or some location on a network that the new PC can get to (Step 2). We also assume that the New User wizard has created the appropriate folder structure for your files to go into. Now you just have to put the files where they belong.

Find the folder on the new machine where NaturallySpeaking has been installed (probably C:\NatSpeak). The folder structure under NatSpeak should look like Figure 20-1. Move the copy of the GeneralE that you took from your old machine into the current folder, and move the copy of dd10phat.usr into the voice folder. Files of the same name should already be in those locations; these files are the generic ones that the New User wizard created — don't worry about writing over them. When Windows asks whether you want to replace these files with the ones you're moving, click Yes.

If you have Professional edition, the easiest way to move vocabulary files is by exporting them from your old computer and importing them to your new one. See Chapter 21.

### Step 5: Running the Audio Setup wizard

The next time you start NaturallySpeaking, it knows about the existence of your newly transferred user, but it hasn't calibrated the audio system of this machine for your voice yet. Open your new user from the Open User dialog box that appears when NaturallySpeaking starts. (If you don't see the Open User dialog box, it means that your new user is the only one NaturallySpeaking knows about, so it opened that user without asking.)

NaturallySpeaking will realize on its own that the Audio Setup wizard hasn't been run for this user. When it offers you the opportunity to run Audio Setup, click Yes. For a more detailed look at the Audio Setup wizard and the screens it presents, see Chapter 2.

# Upgrading to a Better Version of NaturallySpeaking

You can upgrade your copy of NaturallySpeaking in two different ways.

> ✔ You can get a newer version of the same edition you already had. For example, you can go from Standard edition 3.5 to Standard edition 4.0.

✔ You can get a better edition of the same release. For example, you could move from Standard edition 4.0 to Preferred edition 4.0.

As you upgrade (in either sense), keep this thought in mind: You're not doing something strange and arcane that nobody else has ever thought of. Dragon Systems *wants* you to upgrade. They try to make it as easy as they can. If the process starts to seem difficult and convoluted, or if you seem to be losing capabilities rather than gaining them, something has probably gone wrong. Don't be afraid to call Dragon's technical support number.

Honesty forces us to admit that we have not tried every conceivable upgrade combination ourselves. However, in the course of writing this book, we've had to juggle a number of different versions of NaturallySpeaking, so we've picked up a fair amount of upgrade experience and can venture a couple pieces of general advice.

✔ **Before you put the upgrade disk into your CD-ROM drive, make a backup copy of your user files.** We've never had to use these backups, so making them is probably a pure exercise in paranoia. But a certain amount of paranoia is considered healthy when you deal with computers. (That's why so many geeks watch *The X-Files*.) Look in the folder where NaturallySpeaking lives (usually NatSpeak or something like it), find the Users subfolder, and (if you have the space) make a copy of it somewhere far, far away from the NatSpeak folder. After you're satisfied that the upgrade has worked, you can drag the copy (the one you put far, far away) into the Recycle Bin.

✔ **Let the Upgrade wizard install the new version into the same folder that the old version was in.** The new version of NaturallySpeaking typically detects the old version and tries to install itself into the same folder. You can force it to choose a different folder if you like, but you shouldn't unless you have some special reason we would know nothing about. Installing into the same folder makes it easy for the new version to find the old user files, which gives you the best chance of a smooth transition. And if anything goes wrong, that's why you made backups. (Now you're in the situation we discuss in "Transferring your user files to a new machine" earlier in this chapter.)

# Chapter 21

# Having Multiple Users or Vocabularies

***

*In This Chapter:*

▶ Creating and managing users

▶ Moving a user to a different machine

▶ Creating custom vocabularies in NaturallySpeaking Professional

▶ Using different vocabularies

▶ Sharing vocabularies with others

▶ Using the legal and medical vocabularies

***

*W*hen we were growing up, our mothers told us not to talk to strangers. Our moms would have loved NaturallySpeaking. It *can't* talk to strangers, because it can't understand what they're saying. NaturallySpeaking understands only folks who have officially introduced themselves as *users* and gone through a training process to create *user files*.

NaturallySpeaking not only can't understand strangers well, but sometimes it can't even understand you well, if something about you changes: the way you use words, or the way you sound. For instance, many people wear several hats. They are doctors and also administrators; they are clergy by day and poets by night; or they are brain surgeons on weekdays and exotic dancers on weekends. Whichever hat they wear (although the exotic dancer is probably not wearing a hat, but we digress) they write very differently in those roles. They may also sound different because of the different environments or microphones they work with.

NaturallySpeaking offers two solutions to solve all of these problems (multiple people, environments, microphones, or hats):

✔ You can create multiple users, either for actual different people or for people who simply sound quite different at different times.

✔ You can create multiple vocabularies (in the Professional edition only) for a given user who wears many hats.

In this chapter, we show you how to use these features for better accuracy. You can keep your day job as clergy and your night job as exotic dancer — at least, as far as NaturallySpeaking is concerned! Hold onto your hat!

# Creating and Managing Users

If you have several people using your NaturallySpeaking software, or if you dictate using different words or writing styles, you may need multiple users. Here's why and how to create and manage those users.

## One person, different users

Here are some reasons why you may want to make more than one user for yourself:

✔ You use different vocabularies or writing styles for different tasks.

✔ You use different microphones for different tasks (say, a cordless and a wired microphone).

✔ You use a portable recorder for dictation. See Chapter 8 (or 9 if you have NaturallySpeaking Mobile).

✔ You want to use different NaturallySpeaking options for different tasks. For instance, you may want to turn off certain features to save memory when using NaturallySpeaking with big applications. See Chapter 3 for instructions. Those option choices are part of the definition of a user.

✔ You have a portable computer and use it in two or more distinct environments (noisy/quiet, outdoors/indoors, in bed/ in the pool, and so on).

The drawback of having more than one user per person is the extra training of NaturallySpeaking that the person will need to do. Each user maintains its own training and experience, starting with the initial "enrollment" training that you'll need to repeat with each user. The same holds true for ongoing training. If you use the phrase "boogie-woogie" in both your personal and professional lives, for instance, not only do you have a very interesting life, but you have to train both users so that Dragon NaturallySpeaking can recognize the phrase.

You can change or broaden NaturallySpeaking's definition of a user, however. You don't have to have a separate user for, say, when you have a head cold. Instead, you run General Training; NaturallySpeaking will add its "head cold" experience to its previous experience of your voice. (See Chapter 18.) It will do better the next time you are sneezy (or grumpy). Likewise, if you run the

Audio Setup wizard, NaturallySpeaking changes the microphone volume to adapt to any change in microphone position. (See Chapter 19.) You can train a single user to broadly cover all the types of writing you do, too. The problem with broadening a user definition is that overall accuracy will go down to the same degree that you have distinctly different situations.

## Adding a new user

Setting up a new user is a lot like setting up the original user: You're off to see the New User wizard. Invoke the wizard's name in any of the following ways:

- ✔ Click the New button in the Open User dialog box when NaturallySpeaking starts up.
- ✔ From the NaturallySpeaking window, choose User⇨New from the menu.
- ✔ When NaturalWord is running, choose Dragon NaturallySpeaking⇨ User⇨New from the Microsoft Word or Corel WordPerfect menu.
- ✔ Choose User⇨New from the NaturallySpeaking Essentials toolbar.

After the New User wizard starts up, it takes you through the same series of steps that you (may) remember from original installation: creating the user speech files, selecting the user type, audio setup, General Training, and Vocabulary Building. Each of these steps is covered in Chapter 2.

---

## What is a user, really?

The NaturallySpeaking idea of a user is probably not quite the same as yours. To you, a user is . . . you. A human being with dreams and aspirations, hopes and fears, and all that kind of good stuff. But NaturallySpeaking doesn't know that. All it knows of users is that they make this wiggly electrical signal in its little electronic ear, and that it is responsible for choosing the right words from a vocabulary to match that wiggle.

If you do anything to change that wiggle, NaturallySpeaking won't recognize you. Or if you try to use a word that's not in the vocabulary that NaturallySpeaking associates with that user, NaturallySpeaking chooses the wrong word.

In other words, a "user" in NaturallySpeaking is more than just you. It's you, plus your microphone or portable recorder, the environment you're speaking in, the sound card in your PC, your PC, and your vocabulary. (In all editions of NaturallySpeaking except Professional, a user has only one vocabulary. In the Professional edition, a user can have several.) It's also the options you've chosen in Tools⇨Options, and the microphone volume set by the Audio Setup wizard.

You may be able to skip over the most time-consuming part of the New User wizard (General Training) if you already have NaturallySpeaking user files that you trained on another machine or with another copy of NaturallySpeaking. See "Adding an old user," coming up next.

## Adding an old user

What if the user you want to add isn't really new to NaturallySpeaking but is just new to *your copy* of NaturallySpeaking? Are this person's user files transferable? Maybe. If his or her copy of NaturallySpeaking is from the same release generation as yours (that is, both 4.0), then you should have no problem. If the files are from an earlier or later generation of NaturallySpeaking, he may have to retrain for your machine. Having different editions of NaturallySpeaking should be no problem; the user files for NaturallySpeaking Essentials 4.0 look just like user files from NaturallySpeaking Professional 4.0, or anything in between. Switch to the new user's point of view and read the discussion of moving your dragon to a new machine in Chapter 20.

## Who are all these users?

If you're not sure what users you have, you can find them listed in the Open User dialog box, shown in Figure 21-1. If your copy of NaturallySpeaking has more than one user, the Open User dialog box shows up spontaneously when you open NaturallySpeaking so that you can identify which user you are. You can also ask to see it by choosing User⇨Open from the NaturallySpeaking menu bar, or Dragon NaturallySpeaking⇨User⇨Open from the Word or WordPerfect menu bar (when NaturalWord is running).

**Figure 21-1:**
The Open
User
dialog box.

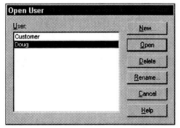

When you look at the Open User dialog box, you may be surprised to realize just how many users you have. Naturally, each separate person who uses NaturallySpeaking is a different user, but you should also have defined separate users for different input devices (like the mobile recorder), different noise environments (like when you're in the shower), or any other circumstance that may make you sound significantly different to NaturallySpeaking.

# Deleting a user

User files take up a lot of space on your hard drive, so deleting user files that are no longer needed makes sense. Whatever your reason for wanting to delete a user, however, don't do it rashly. All the backups for that user get deleted, too, so you can't undo it. If you delete your girlfriend's user files when you break up, she'll have to retrain from scratch when you get back together. (She may get annoyed with you all over again.) Perform the following steps to delete a user:

1. **Choose User⇨Open from the menu in the NaturallySpeaking window.**

   Equivalently, you can choose Dragon NaturallySpeaking⇨User⇨Open from the Microsoft Word or Corel WordPerfect menu (if NaturalWord is installed) or Users⇨Open from the NaturallySpeaking Essentials toolbar. In any case, the Open User dialog box appears, as shown in Figure 21-1 earlier in this chapter.

2. **Select the name of the user you want to delete from the list in the Open User dialog box.**

   You can't delete yourself. That is, you can't delete the current user. Among other things, this safeguard prevents you from deleting the last user on the system. (If you want to do that, you should uninstall NaturallySpeaking.)

3. **Click the Delete button in the Open User dialog box.**

4. **When the confirmation box appears, click Yes.**

# Backing up and restoring a user's speech files

NaturallySpeaking keeps a backup copy of each user's speech files. It automatically makes this copy every fifth time you save NaturallySpeaking's speech files — which most people do when they are prompted to do so, every time they exit NaturallySpeaking. (You can make this backup more or less frequent by using the Options dialog box discussed in Chapter 3.)

The backup speech files lag behind any changes you make by correcting or training NaturallySpeaking. So, if you make a mistake and save speech files when you shouldn't have (perhaps you vocabulary-trained using the wrong documents), you can restore from an earlier version of those files.

You can tell NaturallySpeaking to update the backup copy at any time by choosing User⇨Backup. To restore from the backup copy, choose User⇨Restore. (The files are located in the folder where you installed NaturallySpeaking, in the Users folder there, in the folder that goes with your particular user name.)

# Creating a Custom Vocabulary

If you have NaturallySpeaking Professional, and you have more than one distinct writing style or write about several very specialized topics, you can get NaturallySpeaking to more accurately recognize your dictation by creating specialized vocabularies for each style or topic. Creating a custom vocabulary has two parts. First, you create a vocabulary with a new name, which at first is really just a copy of an existing standard Dragon vocabulary. Then you add your custom stuff to that copy by vocabulary building. (Remember vocabulary building? That was when you had NaturallySpeaking read your existing documents and then you did some cleanup and word training. Read about it in Chapter 18.)

If you have more than one user in NaturallySpeaking, make sure you open the proper user before beginning. For instance, if both you and your secretary use the same copy of NaturallySpeaking, make sure you open your user. Your custom vocabulary will be attached to whichever user is open at the time (although you can export it to another user, later).

Follow these steps to get started:

1. **In the NaturallySpeaking window, choose Vocabulary⇨New.**

   The New Vocabulary dialog box appears. The Based On list box shows existing vocabularies you probably didn't know you had.

2. **In the Based On list box, choose the vocabulary that you want to use as a starting point for your new vocabulary.**

   Depending upon your edition of NaturallySpeaking and how it is set up, here's how to make your choice:

   **Base General English — Standard, BestMatch, BestMatch 64k+, or BestMatchIII:** Anything with "Base" in its name is an original vocabulary that NaturallySpeaking came with. That means it doesn't include any of your training to date. If your new vocabulary and writing style is very different from your old one, (poetry, say, as opposed to sermons) choose a Base vocabulary. That way, you don't get any words or word patterns from your other writing style.

   Standard, BestMatch, and all the varieties of BestMatch give you various levels of speech recognition accuracy and speed to choose from, with BestMatch III being the best. BestMatch III also requires more memory and PC processor speed than the others, about 128MB of RAM, and a 350MHz Pentium II or III processor. The Student BestMatch model is for people with higher-pitched voices.

**General English — Standard, BestMatch, BestMatch 64k+, or BestMatchIII:** This is the vocabulary you created (unknowingly) when you originally set up NaturallySpeaking. It contains all the words you have added so far and it's biased toward the speech patterns you have been using and training NaturallySpeaking to recognize. This is a good choice if your new vocabulary is simply an expanded version of your old one. (Lectures, for instance, as a variation on sermons.)

**Some other vocabulary you created earlier:** If you have already created a specialized vocabulary, this choice lets you specialize it further and add to it. For instance, if you have a biology vocabulary, you could choose that as your base for a veterinary vocabulary.

**A medical or legal vocabulary:** If you have the Medical or Legal Suite, you have the choice of a medical or legal base vocabulary. You can then add your own professional vocabulary to that.

3. **Type a name for your new vocabulary in the Vocabulary Name box.**

   Choose a name that will help you remember the roots of your new vocabulary. For instance, you might use VetBio64K if you were building upon your Biology vocabulary, which in turn was built on the BestMatch 64K vocabulary.

4. **Click OK.**

   The New Vocabulary dialog box closes.

Okay, now what? You're left staring at NaturallySpeaking. What has happened? You've simply created your new vocabulary. You're not using it yet, and you haven't expanded it yet with any new words. It's simply lying about on your PC, an unimproved copy of the vocabulary you chose in Step 2. So, the next phase of the job is vocabulary building.

Before you begin vocabulary building, tell NaturallySpeaking to use your new vocabulary by choosing Vocabulary➪Open. (See "Using Your New Vocabulary" for more details if you need them.) Otherwise, you're still using the original vocabulary, and any building you do will go into the wrong vocabulary!

Now you're using the right user, and you're back in the NaturallySpeaking window again. At this point, you start adding the good stuff — the custom words and writing style — to the new vocabulary.

Building your custom vocabulary is just like building your original vocabulary. You use the Vocabulary Builder in the Tools menu. Because it is the same process, please refer to the description in Chapter 2 where you did vocabulary building when you first set up NaturallySpeaking.

## Using your new vocabulary

You can switch to a custom vocabulary at any time. Here's how:

1. **Choose Vocabulary⇨Open.**

   The Open Vocabulary dialog box appears.

2. **Click your new vocabulary's name in the list in that dialog box.**

3. **Click Open.**

If you've recently used a certain vocabulary, you can switch back to it quickly by clicking Vocabulary, then clicking the vocabulary name from the bottom of the menu that drops down.

Vocabularies are attached to users, so if you switch to a different user than the one you created the vocabulary for, you won't find the vocabulary available. See the next section about exporting a vocabulary to other users.

If you created this new vocabulary based on one of the Base vocabularies that come with NaturallySpeaking, you don't get the benefit of any vocabulary training or correction you have done in the past. You have to repeat that training or correction.

## Exporting your vocabulary to other users

Vocabularies are linked to the user that was in effect when the vocabulary was created. So, if you choose a different user (say, a portable recorder), your custom vocabulary won't be available. You can, however, *export* that vocabulary from the original user and *import* it into a different user on your PC.

Not only can you export a vocabulary to another user on your PC, but you can export it to any Professional edition user, anywhere! If you have developed a vocabulary for, say, worm farming and want to distribute it to your vermicultural colleagues, you can do it. (Vocabularies are big, however, so you can't do it on a diskette. You need to send it by a network or Internet connection, or by using a removable high-capacity storage device like a Zip disk.)

To export a vocabulary, take the following steps:

1. **Choose Vocabulary⇨Open**

   The Open Vocabulary dialog box appears, listing vocabularies.

2. **Click your vocabulary's name in the list.**

3. **Click the Export button.**

   The Save As dialog box appears, where you can choose a disk drive and folder in the Save In box, and enter a filename for your vocabulary in the File Name box. Don't forget what folder you choose! Click Save, and you return to the Open Vocabulary dialog box.

4. **Click Cancel to exit the Open Vocabulary dialog box.**

At this point, you have saved not one, but five files! They all have the name you entered in the Save As dialog box, but each has a different file extension (file type): .To1 through .To4, and .Top. Together, they are the exported vocabulary. When moving the vocabulary to a different machine, you need to get all five files onto that machine.

To import a vocabulary, which attaches it to the current user, do this:

1. **Choose User⇨Open, click the user that you want to receive the imported vocabulary, and then click the Open button.**

   Notice that if you have recently opened a particular user, you can pick that user off the bottom of the User menu. You don't need to choose Open first. This saves you an entire mouse-click of effort!

2. **Click Vocabulary⇨Open.**

3. **In the Open Vocabulary dialog box that appears, click the Import button.**

4. **Browse, if you need to, to the disk drive and folder where you exported the vocabulary files.**

5. **Double-click the .Top file you saved when you exported the vocabulary.**

   The Import Vocabulary dialog box shuffles back onto the scene, with its list of available vocabularies.

If you're ready to use your imported vocabulary at this point, make sure its name is selected in the list, and then click Open. If you're not ready to start making use of the vocabulary yet, click Cancel.

# Legal and Medical Vocabularies

If you have Dragon's Legal or Medical "Suite," what you actually have is NaturallySpeaking Professional plus some specialized base vocabularies for your profession. These specialized vocabularies don't contain all the legal or medical terms you would ever want, but they are a good base to build on. You never use them directly. You always use them as a base from which you create a custom professional vocabulary.

To use these vocabularies, create a custom vocabulary and choose them as the base for that vocabulary. Follow the instructions in the earlier section, "Creating a custom vocabulary." To switch to using that vocabulary, see "Using your new vocabulary."

If, instead of adding a professional vocabulary to an existing user, you decide to create a new user with a legal or medical vocabulary, you use the New User wizard. The Create User screen of that wizard has list boxes in which you choose your vocabulary and speech model. Match the type of legal or medical vocabulary (Standard or one of the varieties of BestMatch) to the type of speech model: choose a BestMatch speech model for a BestMatch vocabulary, for instance.

In release 3.52 and possibly other releases of NaturallySpeaking Legal Suite and Medical Suite, if you add NaturallySpeaking features after installing the base professional vocabularies, you must then reinstall those vocabularies. For example, you may add BestMatch technology at some date, and you would have to reinstall your professional vocabularies afterward. Reinstall the vocabularies from the CD marked Legal Suite or Medical Suite. Insert the CD, choose Start⇨Run, type D:\setup (or substitute the letter of your CD drive for D), and then press the Enter key.

# Chapter 22

# Creating Your Own Commands

## In This Chapter

▶ Creating commands that press keys

▶ Editing custom commands

▶ Creating commands that do more automation

▶ Giving old commands new names

*I*n the Professional edition of NaturallySpeaking, including the Medical and Legal Suites, you can create custom verbal commands (sometimes called *macros*). For instance, if you're a lawyer, you deal with a lot of "boilerplate," text that's pretty standard from one document to the next. You can create a command that automatically writes the boilerplate, or you can create a command that copies a document or selected text from one application window to another.

Creating custom voice commands (macros) can be fairly simple but can also get really, impressively complicated. We will show you how to create only the simpler macros that can be built using the NaturallySpeaking New Command Wizard. These are commands that, for the most part, do anything you could do by pressing keys on the keyboard.

If you want commands much more sophisticated than that, you'll have to get geekier than most *...For Dummies* readers like to do. (See the sidebar "Getting down, getting geeky.") You may have read about or seen some really gee-whiz stuff in NaturallySpeaking: being able to dictate a memo and then say, "Send that to Fred," for instance. However, to pull that off in NaturallySpeaking Professional, you need to master a rather technical programming language. Newer products like NaturallyOrganized have those gee-whiz things built in.

## Getting down, getting geeky

If you're going to tackle the gee-whiz commands, you need a solidly geeky manual. Download the macro manual from the Dragon Web site. You need to be at least slightly familiar with programming to make sense of it. Go to the support page for NaturallySpeaking products, find the download area, and download the Adobe PDF file, VOICECMD.PDF. That file is an Adobe Acrobat file. If you're technically competent to deal with macro language, we're sure you know how to download and view Acrobat files, so we'll leave it to you. Have fun! Check in with the user forum on the Dragon Web site for lots of tips.

If you're technically inclined, you'll want to know exactly where the macro code lives. It is all in the .DVC files in the Data folder, in the NatSpeak folder. These files contain not only the custom commands you create, but also the standard voice commands that come with NaturallySpeaking and NaturalWord. In lower-level editions of NaturallySpeaking, the .DVC files are not readable, but in the Professional edition, they are plain text files.

# Creating Commands That Press Keys

Clear thinking is key to making custom commands, so sit up straight and refill your coffee cup. Stop fidgeting. Spit out that gum. Start with a very clear idea of exactly what steps you want NaturallySpeaking to do when you speak the command. Think it out, click by click and keystroke by keystroke, as if you were giving instructions to someone to operate your computer. For instance, suppose you wanted a command that would adjust the zoom downward (make the page look smaller) in Microsoft Word. Exactly what keys would you press on the keyboard?

Before you start, ask yourself this question: "Do I really want to do this?" No, sorry, wrong question. Try this: "Will I only be speaking this command while using the same application?" For instance, in our example in the previous paragraph, you're only planning on using the command in Microsoft Word. Only two answers are allowed to this question (sorry), Yes or No. Here are the consequences of each answer:

- ✔ If the answer is yes, that you will only be using the command from a specific application window, then your job is going to be easier. You will be making an "application-specific" command.

- ✔ If the answer is no, that you want to use the same command when working in different applications, then you will be making a "global" command. You would make a global command, for instance, if you wanted this zoom example to work not only in Word but also in

WordPerfect. This kind of command is more work to create. You must be very careful about the details, so that it runs any of the programs you may use. Making a global command is not always possible. You may instead have to make several application-specific commands with the same name but that work differently.

Now you're ready to cook. Choose Tools➪New Command Wizard from the menu bar of NaturallySpeaking Professional. The New Command wizard springs into action. (The Old Command wizard presumably has been packed off to the Old Wizards' Home.) The following steps take you through the individual steps of the New Command Wizard and are numbered to match the New Command wizard's screens. Just follow along, clicking Next to advance to the next step.

1. **Is the the command to be application-specific or global? If you choose Global, skip to Step 4 in these instructions.**

   If you choose Application-Specific, the next screen asks you to select "the target application" for your command.

2. **Select the target application for this command from the list of applications, as Figure 22-1 shows.**

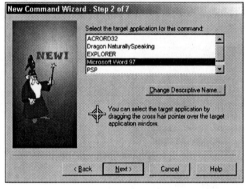

**Figure 22-1:**
Taking aim at the application where you want to run your command.

In plain English, the wizard wants to know which application on the list you're going to be using this command in. (In geek-speak, it wants to know which application will be "current" when you speak the command, indicated by the title bar being colored.) For our earlier zoom-command example, for instance, you would want to specify Microsoft Word here.

The wizard only lists applications that it already knows about, or that are open right now. If your "target" application isn't on the list, launch that application now. Adjust window sizes and positions on your screen so that you can see both the target application and the wizard, and click back in the wizard screen. Click the target application's name, which now appears in the list.

These applications sometimes have cryptic names in the list, so you can't tell what they are. If that happens to you, instead of clicking the name, drag the cross-hair symbol that appears on this wizard screen right on top of the target application's window. (You can change cryptic names by clicking the name, then clicking the Change Descriptive Name button, and then entering a new name in the Change Name dialog box that appears.)

3. **Select a target window or dialog box within your target application for this command. Choose from the suggestions that appear in the list on this screen.**

   This step allows you, if you want, to restrict your command so that it only works when a particular document window or dialog box is open. Restricting the command allows you to have commands with the same name in other places. For example, you may want a "Increase Spacing" command that works in the Font dialog box and in the Columns dialog box, even though they would have to work differently. If you want to restrict the command to a window or dialog box, open that window or dialog box now. Click the title bar of the wizard, and your chosen window or dialog box's name appears in the wizard's list. Click its name in the list.

   If you don't want to restrict the command, choose the application's name from the list. For example, to have the command work in any Word window, choose Microsoft Word. That's what's going on in Figure 22-2.

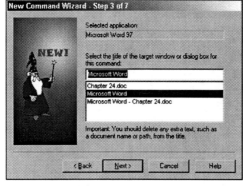

**Figure 22-2:**
No specific
window or
dialog box,
please. Just
Word.

4. **Enter your magic words (the command you will speak) in the Command Name textbox.**

   The command name works best if you use two or more words. For example, you could name the command Zoom Out. For consistency with the NaturallySpeaking commands, initial-cap each word except for small words like articles and prepositions.

   This is not the place to try to modify or replace existing NaturallySpeaking commands. You can create a new **Correct That** command, for instance, but it won't work. You can, however, modify certain commands using the Edit Command wizard, described next, although the job can be pretty technical.

Step 4 also gives you the option of adding a variable portion to the name. For example, you may want to be able to add a zoom-out percentage to your Zoom Out command, as in Zoom Out Ten. This stuff is pretty tricky, so we're not going to touch it here.

5. **Choose how the command is going to do its magic: Will it invisibly press keys on the keyboard, or will it run *scripts,* a kind of programming language?**

   Unless you're already familiar with macro languages, we suggest you stick to the first option: Type Text Or Keystrokes. The other option, Run A Script, lets you do more complex commands, but is harder to learn. Scripts, however, are the only way to create commands that work between applications, not just within applications. So, if you wanted to create something that, say, copied a page from your Web browser to your word processor document, you would need a script. If you choose Run A Script, don't read our next step, but read our discussion of scripts later in this chapter.

6. **Enter the keystrokes that will make your magic happen.**

   These "keystrokes" are the keys you would press on the keyboard to accomplish your end. Your command just plays back those keystrokes like a player piano. If your macro's purpose is just to type some text, enter that text here, complete with any line breaks, spaces, or punctuation you need.

   You can use keystrokes to control menus and dialog boxes, too. That's what's happening in Figure 22-3.

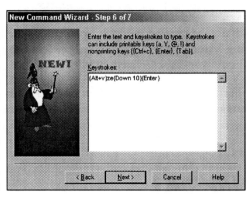

**Figure 22-3:**
Enter the keys to press to zoom out in Word. They form a line of gibberish here.

For instance, to access the Zoom dialog box in Word, you press Alt+V to open the View menu, then press Z to select Zoom. In the Zoom dialog box that appears, you can press E to enter the Percent box and set the zoom factor. Pressing the down-arrow key ten times reduces the zoom factor by 10 percent. Pressing the Enter key closes the Zoom dialog box. That set of keystrokes looks like the following line of gibberish:

`{Alt+v}ze{Down 10}{Enter}`

Enter these keystrokes without spaces or line breaks. Keys or key combinations that normally don't print must be in curly braces, as in `{Alt+v}` or `{Esc}`. Other keys go outside the braces. If you want a key repeated some number of times (10, in this example), put the number in the braces, too. If you want the Enter key pressed, you can either use `{Enter}` or press the Enter key yourself to end the line of keystrokes. You can't, unfortunately, use Alt+Tab or Ctrl+Esc, which allow you to switch between applications in Windows.

Type the letter names of the keys (v, z, and e in this example) in lowercase. Uppercase tells NaturallySpeaking to hold down the Shift key when typing a letter.

If you're writing a global, rather than application-specific, command, you have to make sure that the keystrokes you enter will work properly everywhere you will use the command! For example, Alt+V, then Z will get you into the Zoom dialog box of many applications, but not all of them use E for the zoom factor. In many of them, however, pressing the down-arrow key switches between the preset zoom factors, such as 100%, 75%, and so on. So, for a global zooming command, you may just use `{Alt+v}z{down}{Enter}`.

To find out how to write the names of various keys, click Help. At the bottom of the help text, click Related Topics, and double-click Key Names in the Topics Found dialog box that appears.

7. **The New Command wizard summarizes all the choices you made about the command name, how it works, and where it works. Click Finish.**

Try out your command! If it's application-specific, open the application you designed it for, turn on the NaturallySpeaking microphone, and say the command. If it's global, try it out in several different applications.

If it works perfectly the first time, you're a star! Most mortals mess up a bit. So, what do you do if you mess up? For that, dear friend, we have another tool. Read on.

# *Editing Your Commands*

It seems like everyone is a specialist these days, including wizards. You can't use the New Command Wizard to change your commands. No, you have to use the Edit Command Wizard. (Fortunately, you don't need a referral from the first wizard to the second wizard, and you are covered under wizard insurance.)

The Edit Command wizard works just like its colleague. However, instead of typing in information about what application you want to run in, and what window, you just select that stuff from lists. To launch the Edit Command wizard:

1. **Choose Tools⇨Edit Command Wizard.**

2. **When you get to Step 4, choose your command from a list of commands.**

   Depending upon the application you designed the command for, you may see a lot of commands there. Microsoft Word, for example, has hundreds of them. Where did all those other commands come from? Those are the commands that NaturallySpeaking comes with: the built-in commands and the natural language commands. Yes, if you have NaturallySpeaking Professional, you can edit all the built-in commands!

   But we digress. You want to edit *your* command. Scroll down the list until you find your command, and click it. (If you have decided that this command is beyond hope, you have an opportunity to delete it now. Just click the Delete Command button.)

3. **When you get to Step 5, you have an opportunity to rename your command. Just type a new name in the Command Name box. (Unless you have created a command with a variable portion, you can ignore the Lists Already Defined for This Window area.)**

4. **The Step 6 window is exactly like the Step 6 window in the New Command wizard. Here's where you get to change the keystrokes that you originally entered. Make your changes, click Next, then Finish, and then try your newly revitalized command.**

# Automating Further with Script Commands

The keystroke commands that we talk about in the last sections are nice but are kind of restricted. In particular, you can't use them to switch between different applications. A lot of people want to automate repetitive tasks that their work requires of them, and that often involves using several different applications.

For that job you need script commands. (Like, "Exit stage left, pursued by a macro.") Script commands can get complicated, so we don't go into great detail here. But we would like our more ambitious readers to be able to create commands that juggle different applications.

One nice feature that's simply too complex to go into here is the ability to use variable terms in a custom command. For instance, you might like to be able to give a command like **Email This to Fred.** But using the techniques we've discussed so far, you would have to create separate commands for e-mailing to Fred, Tom, Dick, and Harriet, too. What you would really like to do is be able to create a single command in which you can substitute a different name for Fred. NaturallySpeaking custom commands can do this sort of thing, but it requires some fairly tricky programming.

## Creating a script command

To use script commands, use the same New Command wizard that we describe earlier in this chapter. Choose Tools➪New Command Wizard, and follow the instructions. When you get to Step 5, choose Run a Script.

In Step 6, you create a script by entering commands into the Script box. Figure 22-4 shows the script box. These commands are in the NaturallySpeaking special command language. (This is stuff that you'll find in Dragon's very technical manual, VOICECMD.PDF, that we mention in the sidebar "Getting down, getting geeky.")

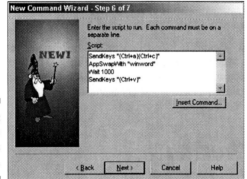

**Figure 22-4:** Where the script is assembled.

If you become fluent in this language, you can just type the commands into the box provided. (You can also have great geeky conversations with the five other fluent speakers of the Dragon script language.) In the meantime, you enter commands by clicking the Insert Command button, which displays the Script Command List dialog box shown in Figure 22-5.

To insert a command from the dialog box into the Script box, just click the command and then click OK. To insert the next command in the Script box, click where you want the command to appear, hit the Insert Command button again, and choose another command.

**Figure 22-5:**
Where
commands
come from:
the Script
Command
List.

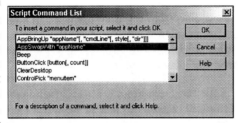

# *Introducing a few key commands for scripts*

We'd like to draw your attention to a few important commands for building scripts — two in particular. As they are listed in the Script Command List dialog box, they are called AppSwapWith "appName" and SendKeys "keystroke text". The words in quotation marks are placeholders. The idea is that, after you insert them into your script, you replace the placeholders with your own stuff.

The SendKeys command is the way you get a script macro to press keys on the keyboard. (Well, sort of. It's *as if* the macro pressed keys; you don't get the nifty "ghost hands" effect of a player piano.) With the SendKeys command, you can type or you can control menus and dialog boxes just as you would with the keystroke macros we discuss in "Creating Custom Commands." After you insert the SendKeys command into the Script box, delete the placeholder words *keystroke text,* and insert the keystrokes you want between the quotation marks. Write the keystrokes just as we describe for keyboard macros in "Creating Custom Commands."

Although AppSwapWith "appName" sounds like a vitamin-enhanced fruit drink, it's actually a good way to switch between two applications. For instance, if you want to copy from one application to another by using a voice command, a nice sip of AppSwapWith "appName" is what you need. You replace the placeholder appName with the name of the program file you want to run. For Microsoft Word, for instance, the program file is winword.exe, so you would enter winword.

You can easily discover the filename for the program you want to run if you have a shortcut icon to that program anywhere on your desktop. Right-click the icon, and then choose Properties from the context menu. In the Properties dialog box that appears, find the Target box, which contains a line of text. At the end of that line, after the last backslash, is the program filename, usually ending in .EXE. Make note of it, and then click Cancel.

A related command to `AppSwapWith` is `AppBringUp` (which doesn't sound like a fruit drink at all — let's not go there). If you just want to launch an application, not switch to it, use the `AppBringUp` `"appName"` command. Delete any brackets and other stuff after the `"appName"` command. As with `AppSwap`, substitute the program's filename for `appName`.

A useful helper command is the `Wait` command. This is useful when you are switching between applications. It causes the macro to wait for some number of milliseconds to allow the new application time to get ready before taking some action. Follow the word `Wait` with the number of milliseconds you want to pause (1000 milliseconds = 1 second).

## Creating an example command

How might you use these script commands? (Sorry, "As blunt instruments" is the wrong answer. Cynicism will never work.) An example will help. Suppose that you want a voice command designed to help you copy documents from Internet Explorer into a Word document. Not that you're plagiarizing for a research paper or anything.

Assume that you start out in Internet Explorer, which will be your "target" application. Launch Internet Explorer. Then launch the New Command wizard and take the following steps, which are numbered the same as the wizard's steps:

1. Choose <u>A</u>pplication-specific.

2. Choose EXPLORER, or drag the cross-hairs to the Internet Explorer window.

3. Choose Microsoft Internet Explorer.

4. Enter the name of the command — for instance, `Grab It`.

5. Choose Run a Script.

6. Enter the script by clicking the Insert Command button and then choosing commands from the Script Command List dialog box that appears:

   Click Insert Command, click `SendKeys` `"keystroke text"`, and then click OK. Replace the words `keystroke text` with `{Ctrl+a}{Ctrl+c}`, leaving the quotes in place. (These keystrokes select all the text of the window and copy it to the Windows Clipboard.) Click to place your cursor on the next line.

   Click Insert Command, click `AppSwapWith` `"appName"`, and then click OK. Replace the word `appName` with `winword`. (This command opens or launches Microsoft Word by having NaturallySpeaking search for and open the Word program file, WINWORD.EXE.) Click to place your cursor on the third line.

Click Insert Command, click `Wait milliseconds`, and then click OK. Replace the word `milliseconds` with 1000. (This command creates a one-second wait.) Click to place your cursor on the fourth line.

Click Insert Command, click `SendKeys "keystroke text"`, and then click OK. Replace the words `keystroke text` with `{Ctrl+v}`. (This command pastes the text from the Windows clipboard into Word.)

The result should look like Figure 22-6.

**Figure 22-6:**
Assembling script commands. These are intended to copy a page from an open Internet Explorer window into Word.

7. **Review what you've done.**

   In this example, the command name is chosen by you (for instance, Grab It). The Action is "run a script." The selected application is EXPLORER, the Target window or dialog box is Microsoft Internet Explorer. Click the Finish button if you have it right. Click the Back button if you need to change anything.

Now, with Internet Explorer displaying some document, you should be able to say, **"Grab It"** (or whatever you named your command) and have NaturallySpeaking copy that document to Microsoft Word. Word doesn't have to be open at the time, but if it is, the copy appears where your document cursor is, in Word.

## NaturallySpeaking commands in other words

If you don't like the words used for the NaturallySpeaking commands, you can, for many commands, create your own command phrases that do the same thing. The HeardWord script command is very useful for that task. Create a script command as in the example, but choose Global instead of Application-specific in Step 1. (Choosing global makes the wizard skip Steps 2 and 3.)

In Step 6, insert the HeardWord script command. Replace the placeholder text "word1" and "word2" with the words of the NaturallySpeaking command you don't like, and delete any square brackets. For instance, you could create a command named Oopsie that used the script command `HeardWord "scratch", "that"`. Whenever you say, **"Oopsie,"** NaturallySpeaking would perform a **Scratch That** command.

# Chapter 23

# Taking Draconian Measures: Workarounds for Problems

*E*very once in a while, you run across a problem that stands head and shoulders above its colleagues. No average, ordinary, run-of-the-mill problem, this one seems to have been unanticipated even by such prescient beings as our distinguished selves. You can't find anything like it in this book, or in the NaturallySpeaking manual. Even when you bring the problem to your local know-it-all, the one who makes you feel stupid even if you only say hello, he just smiles and says "No kidding? It does that, huh?"

In other words, you need one-on-one attention from somebody who isn't just smart in a general sort of way, but who really knows NaturallySpeaking. Where do you find such people? One obvious place to look is at Dragon Systems. You can call or send e-mail to their Technical Support department.

Another place to look is among other NaturallySpeaking users. By posting a question to the discussion forum on the Dragon Web site, or to an e-mail list that specializes in voice-recognition systems, you can get your question to the attention of NaturallySpeaking users all over the world. Some of them are pretty darn smart, and a few of them may have seen exactly the same problem themselves.

# Calling, Faxing, or E-Mailing Dragon Systems Technical Support

Dragon Systems maintains a technical support department to answer your questions and help you solve problems that you run into. You can talk to a real, live person on the phone, or you can submit a question by fax or e-mail. You can even use the U. S. Postal Service if you're in no hurry. See Table 23-1 for addresses and phone numbers.

The phone call is at your own expense, so getting your question answered by fax or e-mail (if possible) is definitely cheaper.

| Table 23-1 | Where to Find Dragon Systems' Technical Support |
|---|---|
| *To Contact Them Like This* | *Try This* |
| Telephone | 617-965-7670 |
| Fax | 617-527-4576 |
| E-mail | support@dragonsys.com |
| Mail | 320 Nevada Street, Newton, MA 02460 |
| Web | www.dragonsys.com |

## Getting help through fax or e-mail

In general, the better defined your question is, the more likely you are to get satisfaction from a fax or e-mail message. If you can say, "When I do this and this and that, I get this error message," the technical support person has half a chance to figure out what's wrong and give you a written answer. They also can do a good job with "How do I make NaturallySpeaking do X?" questions, though we believe we have answered almost all of those in this book. And questions like "When is the next upgrade coming out?" can be easily handled in writing.

The fax number and e-mail address of Dragon's Technical Support department is given in Table 23-1. You can also send e-mail to technical support by using a form on the Dragon Systems Web site. See "Using the Dragon Systems Web site" later in this chapter.

But if NaturallySpeaking is doing something you really don't understand and have a tough time explaining, or if it's doing something very simple that gives you no information to work with (like failing to install or refusing to respond), you're going to need to talk to a person on the phone.

If you do send e-mail to report a problem, be sure to attach the file Dragon.log, which you can find in the folder where you installed NaturallySpeaking (usually C:\NatSpeak). This file is a record that NaturallySpeaking has been keeping of all the error messages it has sent.

## Talking to technical support on the phone

Calling Dragon Systems' technical support department is free except for the cost of the phone call, which (unless you happen to live in Newton, Massachusetts) is a long-distance call. See Table 23-1 for the phone number.

### Preparing before you call

A conversation with technical support proceeds much more efficiently if you gather together the significant information before you call. (Being well-organized has the added benefit of establishing that you're not a complete idiot and therefore that you may be facing a real problem.)

The most important thing to have handy is the text of any error messages that are related to the current problem. If you don't remember and can't reproduce the problem to generate a new error message, check the file Dragon.log, which lives inside the folder where you installed NaturallySpeaking (probably C:\NatSpeak). Dragon.log is NaturallySpeaking's record of what it has been up to, including any error messages it has sent. It's a text file, and you can open it with WordPad. More recent events are recorded near the end of the file.

You should also know what version of NaturallySpeaking you have, both the release number (4.0, say) and the edition (Standard, Preferred, and so on). This information should be displayed whenever you start NaturallySpeaking. Or you can find it by selecting Help⇨About NaturallySpeaking in the NaturallySpeaking document window.

A large percentage of the real problems people have with NaturallySpeaking (as opposed to the apparent problems caused by using the product wrong) have to do with mismatches between the user's hardware and the hardware Dragon had in mind when it created NaturallySpeaking. For this reason, the technical support person is likely to be interested in the following information:

✔ **Computer name and model.** We once called a computer Jennifer, but that's not what they want to know. They're looking for an answer like Compaq Presario 420 or Gateway G6-200. It's probably written on the front of your computer somewhere.

✔ **Processor type and RAM.** The processor type is something like Intel Pentium II, for example, or AMD K-7. RAM is given as some number of megabytes. Both are probably displayed in that text that you never read when your computer is booting up. Or you can right-click My Computer and choose Properties to display the System Properties dialog box. The processor type and RAM should be on the General tab.

✔ **Operating system.** Windows 98 or NT4, for example. Restart your computer and you can't miss it.

✔ **Free hard disk space.** Find your hard drive (C, usually) in either My Computer or Windows Explorer. Right-click it and select Properties. On the General tab of the Properties dialog box, you'll find Free Space and some number of megabytes.

✔ **Sound card name and model.** This is something else to check for in the System Properties dialog box. Right-click My Computer and choose Properties, and then select the Device Manager tab. Click the + next to Sound, Video, and Game Controllers. Your sound card should be listed there.

✔ **Microphone name and model.** The obvious place to look is on the microphone. Ours says Parrott VXI.

### Finding your product serial number

The first thing that Dragon Systems wants to establish when you call their technical support department is that you are a bona-fide customer who actually paid them money for this software, not some freeloader who picked up a black market disk in Shanghai for $10. This is why they instruct their technical support people to ask for your product serial number. It's not a foolproof method, but it does eliminate some of the most egregious abuse.

Where can you find your product serial number? It's on a sticker on the bottom of the box that your software came in. It was also probably on the paper or plastic case that the NaturallySpeaking CD was in. Do you still have any of that? In Chapter 2, as part of our installation instructions, we tell you to write the serial number on the inside cover of this book or the inside cover of the manual. Maybe you did — go look.

Assuming that you have the number, the call proceeds. (We didn't have the heart to call technical support without a serial number to see what they would do.)

### During the call

Take notes. In particular, write down any changes that the technical support person has you make. If these changes don't solve the problem (or at least make it better), you may want to undo them later. A difficult problem can take several phone calls to straighten out, and you may end up dealing with more than one person. This process goes much more smoothly if you can tell the new person exactly what the previous person had you do.

Take very, very good notes if you end up doing something to the Windows Registry. (You'll know because you start using a program called RegEdit.) The Registry is a labyrinth that very few people understand well. (We are not among them.) Like prescription drugs, Registry changes often have unexpected side effects, and it's difficult to undo a change to the Registry unless you know exactly what was done.

# Getting Help through the Internet

The Internet opens up many channels of information, both official and unofficial. Dragon has its own Web site, which contains much technical and troubleshooting information that they didn't want to bore you with in the manual. (They guessed — probably correctly — that you don't want a ten-volume manual.) Other Web sites also exist that give you information about NaturallySpeaking, including one maintained by a Dragon engineer, apparently in his spare time.

In addition to making expert opinion and information available to you, the Internet also gives you ample opportunity to trade information with other users. Dragon maintains a user discussion forum on its Web site, and there are also independent user newsgroups and e-mail lists about speech recognition products. Through these media, you can find out what problems other users are having; ask questions of your own; answer other users' questions; share experiences; commiserate; speculate about the motivations, intelligence, ancestry, and personal hygiene of the people who wrote whatever part of NaturallySpeaking you're currently having trouble with; and (most important of all) tell everyone about what a wonderful, readable, insightful book you have found.

## They didn't do it

The people who answer the phones in technical support departments are the infantry of the software business. They may not be standing in muddy trenches, but they probably are sitting in windowless cubicles with nothing but a phone, a computer, and some reference manuals. They spend their days talking to people who are at best frustrated and at worst totally irate.

Chances are, the person you talk to when you call tech support had nothing to do with designing the product or with creating the mistake (if any) that you are suffering from now. He or she may well be as annoyed with the design of this particular feature of the product as you are, though it would be unprofessional of him or her to say so.

We know it's difficult, but try to be pleasant and patient. Figuring out why software does what it does takes time, and they're trying to solve in a few minutes something that has probably had you pounding your head against the wall for hours. We don't doubt that if they could solve it faster, they would.

Information you get on the Internet — especially from other users — comes without warranty. The vast majority of the users who post messages to discussion groups are well-meaning people who just want to help, and a few of them are downright brilliant. But you should only trust them to the extent that they are making sense. You have no way to verify that they know what they're talking about.

## Using the Dragon Systems Web site

Dragons and webs don't seem to go together, but don't let a metaphor get in the way of using an important resource. The Web provides an excellent way for companies to make large quantities of technical information available to their users without printing thick, expensive manuals. Dragon Systems has taken advantage of this possibility. From its Web site (at www.dragonsys.com), you can search for technical information, join a discussion forum of other NaturallySpeaking users, send a message to the technical support department, learn about new Dragon products, register your copy of NaturallySpeaking, or order upgrades.

Murphy's Law dictates that companies will reorganize their Web sites as soon as anyone writes about them, so don't be terribly surprised if particular features of the Dragon Web site are not exactly where we say they are. Still, the trend is for Web sites to acquire more and more information with time, so odds are that the features we mention are still there somewhere. On the whole, Dragon does a pretty good job of structuring its Web site, so if you look around you should be able to find things, even if they've recently moved. You can get to the page shown in Figure 23-1 from the front page of the Dragon Web site by clicking the Support and Services link and then choosing NaturallySpeaking.

### Finding technical information

If you're the kind of person who likes to look things up yourself rather than ask for help, the Dragon Web site provides ample reference sources you can look through. If the particular problem you're facing isn't absolutely unique to your system (and most problems aren't), chances are somebody has asked Dragon's tech support people about it before. Or someone has posted a question about it to the User Discussion Forum and maybe gotten an answer.

**Figure 23-1:**
The
Naturally-
Speaking
Support and
Services
page of the
Dragon
Systems
Web site.

If someone has, you can look it up. When the technical support department runs into a new problem, they like to write down their solutions in "technotes," so that their own people can look it up rather than solve the same problem over and over again. Those technotes are on the Dragon Web site. So are the archives of the Discussion Forum. Best of all, you can search them both by filling out a single search form.

### Scanning technotes

Whenever the technical support people at Dragon figure out how to solve a problem with NaturallySpeaking, they write a "technote." Follow these steps to scan the lastest technotes:

1. **From the front page of the Dragon Web site, click Support & Services.**

2. **Click the Latest Technotes link.**

What you'll find is a list of technotes arranged by date, with the most recent on top. It reads like a long troubleshooting guide, with the title of the note being the statement of a problem, such as "Dragon Software slow in Microsoft Word 97."

### Searching for technical information

Looking through the technotes or the Discussion Forum messages in order can be like searching for a needle in a haystack. Unless you know that the note you want has been posted to the Web site in the last few days, you can look at a lot of message titles without finding what you're looking for. Fortunately, Dragon provides a very convenient feature for scanning both the technotes and the messages on the User Discussion Forum.

Before going to the Dragon Web site, try to state your question concisely, and then look at your question and pick out the important words. These are your search terms.

1. **From the left column of the Support And Services page (refer to Figure 23-1), click the Search for Technical Information link.**

   A page appears that explains what database you're searching.

2. **Click the Open the Search Form link.**

3. **Fill out the Technical Search form (see Figure 23-2).**

   (See Figure 23-2.) List terms that seem relevant to your search in the Search For the Following Words box. You may also, if you like, fill out the Search Constraints and Sorting portion of the form, but they are not necessary.

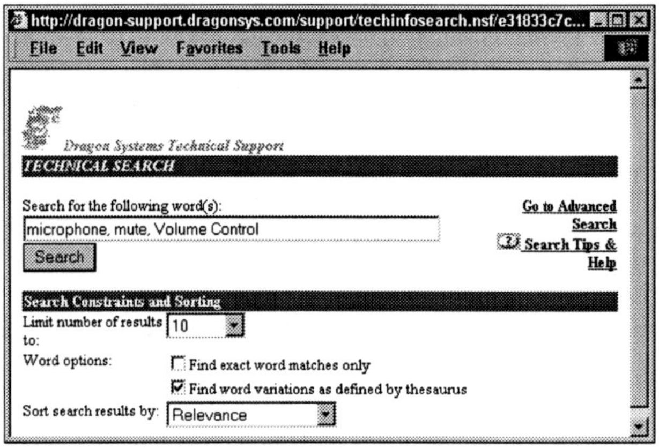

**Figure 23-2:**
The Technical Search form.

4. **Click the Search button.**

   A set of links to documents in the support database that contain the terms you listed appears.

### Accessing the Hardware Compatibility Guide

If you're buying a new system or looking to upgrade part of the system you have, you can also use the site's Hardware Compatibility Guide to check whether Dragon Systems has tested its performance with NaturallySpeaking.

To access the Hardware Compatibility Guide from the Dragon home page (www.dragonsys.com), select it from the drop-down list and click the Go button. You can also go there directly by using its URL: www.dragonsys.com/support/techsupport/compatibility.

When you arrive at the Hardware Compatibility page, click the name or picture of the kind of hardware you want to check out: microphones, notebook computers, desktop computers, recorders, soundcards, or miscellaneous to see a list of devices that Dragon has evaluated in its compatibility labs.

## Sending a message to technical support

In essence, using the Dragon Systems Web page to send a message to technical support is no different than sending e-mail to technical support in any other way. It all goes to the same place. However, if you're already looking for something on the Dragon Web page, you may find it handier to send a message from there than to open your e-mail program and compose a message. Also, the form on the Dragon Web page reminds you to provide all the relevant information about your system.

To send a message to technical support:

1. **Click the Contact Tech Support link on the table of contents in the left column of most pages of the Dragon Web site.**

2. **Click the Submit a Support Request Online link.**

   A new browser window appears explaining the process for submitting a support request.

3. **Click Continue.**

4. **Enter your contact information into the form provided.**

   Only fields marked with an asterisk are required.

5. **Click Continue.**

6. **Fill out the form requesting information about your computer hardware.**

   If you don't know the information requested in fields marked by an asterisk, you can't continue. Send an ordinary e-mail message to support@dragonsys.com or call technical support on the phone.

7. **Scroll down to the bottom of the form and type your message into the Message window.**

8. **Click Continue.**

   Your message is sent and you're given a Technical Support Issue Number. Copy down the number in case you need to refer to it in future communications with the technical support department.

9. **Click Finish.**

### The User Discussion Forum

In school, we noticed that sometimes other students could explain things to us better than the teachers could. The same thing happens with software: Sometimes the explanations from the manual writers and the technical support people go right over your head, but a user who has had about a week's more experience than you is still speaking your language. For this reason, you may find it useful to discuss any problems you're having on the User Discussion Forum that Dragon makes available on its Web site.

The Discussion Forum consists of messages written by NaturallySpeaking users who have visited the Dragon Web site. The messages are organized into topics and put into chronological order, with the most recent topics at the top of the page, as shown in Figure 23-2. Each title in Figure 23-2 is a link to the corresponding message.

You can go to the Discussion Forum from the Support and Services page shown in Figure 23-1.

Even though the discussion forum is on the Dragon Systems Web site, Dragon takes no responsibility for any bad advice that you may get from other users. Occasionally, Dragon employees participate in a discussion and answer a question or two, but they're under no obligation to do so. If you want a response from Dragon technical support, you should contact them directly.

#### Reading messages on the Discussion Forum

The main page of the User Discussion Forum is shown in Figure 23-3. Across the top is a "toolbar" of five "buttons." The first button on the left lets you create a new main topic, which we discuss in the next section. The next three buttons are ways to display the messages: by date, category, product, or author.

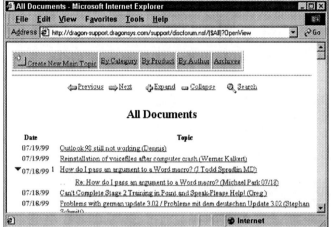

**Figure 23-3:**
The main
page of the
User
Discussion
Forum.

"But wait!" you say. "That makes four ways to display the messages, not three." The buttons allow you to *change* the way the messages are displayed; they don't need to give you a button to leave things the way they are. So, in Figure 23-3, messages are displayed by date (the default), and the buttons correspond to category, product, and author. When the messages are displayed by author, the buttons represent date, category, and product.

The final button on the toolbar takes you to the Discussion Forum Archives, which were under construction when we were last there.

However you display the messages, you can scroll through the titles until you find one you find interesting, and then click it to display the message. At the bottom of the window displaying the message is a miniature version of the main window, showing you the messages in this topic, with a You Are Here sign next to the message you're reading. Click any of the other messages in the topic if you want to read them. You can click the Previous Main Topic or Next Main Topic links if you want to read the topics in order, or you can go back to the main window by clicking an All By Date/Category/Product/Author link.

### Sending messages to the Discussion Forum

You can participate in the discussion either by adding a message to an existing topic or by starting a new topic. To start a new topic:

1. **Click the New Main Topic link on either the main page of the Discussion Forum (refer to Figure 23-3) or in a message window.**

The next thing you should see is the form shown in Figure 23-4, where you're asked to give your name and e-mail address, and to choose a product, category, and subject for your message. (Don't worry about giving your e-mail address, it won't be posted with your message unless you include it in the body of your message.)

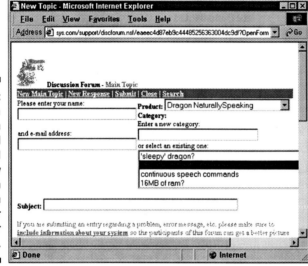

**Figure 23-4:**
Starting a new main topic. Scroll down to find the window into which you can dictate or type your message.

2. **After you fill all that out, scroll down to find the Message window (not pictured in Figure 23-4).**

3. **Type (or dictate if you're using NaturalWeb) your message into this window and then click the Submit button.**

If you want to add something to an ongoing discussion, you should submit a response to the existing topic rather than creating a new topic:

1. **Open a message in the topic you want to contribute to, and click the New Response link at the top of the window.**

   An abbreviated version of Figure 23-4 appears. The topic already has a designated category and product, so the boxes for choosing those are not needed.

2. **Enter your name and e-mail address, and then type your message into the message window.**

3. **Click the Submit Response button.**

# *Other sources of online information*

In addition to the resources that Dragon Systems makes available, you can find other Web pages, newsgroups, and mailing lists that give you information on NaturallySpeaking and how to use it.

# *Comp.speech.users*

Comp.speech.users is a newsgroup that lets you trade information with other users of speech-recognition products, including NaturallySpeaking. It's a good place to post questions about using NaturallySpeaking, particularly have-you-ever-tried-this or does-this-ever-happen-to-you questions. You can also read the newsgroup to find tips, to see what problems other users are having, or just to commiserate.

You can read comp.speech.users with a newsgroup reader like Outlook Express or Free Agent, or you can read it at the Web site of Deja.com with your Web browser.

### *NaturallySpeaking Unofficial Information Pages*

These Web pages may be unofficial, but they do come straight from the dragon's mouth. This Web site is written and maintained by Joel Gould, the architect of NaturallySpeaking and its ancestor Dragon Dictate.

At this writing, the Web site hasn't been updated in about nine months, so some of the information is out of date. But even so, we found it useful and learned a trick or two from it. Maybe Joel has been a little busy with Version 4.0.

### *VoiceGroup*

VoiceGroup is an e-mail list for sharing information among users of speech recognition systems. It's hosted by OneList, who charges you nothing but requires you to register at their Web site, www.onelist.com. For information about VoiceGroup, write to the group's moderator, listed on the Web site.

### *Searching for new sources of online information*

New Web pages, newsgroups, and e-mail lists are created every day. You can type "Dragon NaturallySpeaking" into any of the popular search engines and be inundated by a list of Web pages — probably not what you want. Instead, we recommend that you let someone else filter the Web for you. Go to any of the popular Web guides — Yahoo.com and About.com are two of our favorites — and drill down through the category system. See Table 23-2.

Look for new newsgroups at Deja.com and new e-mail lists at Liszt.com. Again there are category systems; see Table 23-3.

| Table 23-2 | Where to Find Speech Recognition in Popular Category Systems |
|---|---|
| Yahoo! | Science > Computer Science > Artificial Intelligence > Natural Language Processing > Speech Recognition |
| About.com | Computing & Technology > Software > Artificial Intelligence > Speech |
| Deja.com | Computing & Tech > Productivity Software > Speech Recognition |
| Liszt.com | Computers > Speech Recognition |

| Table 23-3 | Web Sites Mentioned in This Chapter |
|---|---|
| Dragon Systems | www.dragonsys.com |
| NaturallySpeaking Unofficial Web Pages | www.syapseadaptive.com/joel |
| OneList | www.onelist.com |
| Deja.com | www.deja.com |
| Yahoo! | www.yahoo.com |
| Liszt.com | www.liszt.com |

# Part V
# The Part of Tens

"I'm using the 'Cab Driver's' edition of NaturallySpeaking, so it understands words like '☉✳✦✠⅍' and '✓⌘☉✦!'."

## In this part . . .

"The Top Ten Salads of Summer!" "The Ten Top Ski Resorts of Anhedonia!" "The Ten Best-Dressed Nudists of 1999!" Judging by the popular magazines, it seems like no publisher can resist the number ten. Well, IDG Books Worldwide, being no slouch itself in the popularity department and never too proud to follow a trend, is happy to offer you its own decimal delineation: The Part of Tens.

Just as in the magazines, here is where we cut through the clutter for you and focus on the top ten things in various categories: dictation problems, command problems, mistakes, and boo-boos. As an extra special bonus in this issue only, we include ten fun ways to torture your dragon. (Fun ways to torture. . . ? Hey, just check it out.)

Mind boggled by the other 300-plus pages of this book? Here's the place for you. The Part of Tens. You saw it here first.

# Chapter 24

# Ten Common Problems

**D**id you ever own something that worked perfectly as soon as you took it out of the box, and never gave you a lick of trouble during its long, productive life? Neither have we. Problems are just part of the experience of owning something. And software problems . . . let's just say that the phrase "bad software day" has replaced "bad hair day" in our households. (Our hair isn't bad, it's just independent.)

So, without further ado, here are our ten favorite NaturallySpeaking problems.

## Nothing Happens When You Dictate

The words are leaving your mouth, but they aren't appearing on the screen. Obviously, they must have taken a wrong turn somewhere. Suppose we follow the path the words should have taken, and see where they may have gotten diverted.

But before we take that trip, are you sure that *nothing* is happening? Say a few words into the microphone and see whether the Results box changes. Even a <<???>> appearing in the Results box tells you that *something* is happening. Okay, back to following the words after they leave your mouth.

**First stop: the microphone.** Is it connected to the computer? In the right socket? (The red socket is usually the correct one.) Try using the microphone for something else, like the Windows Sound Recorder. If you can record a sound through the microphone, then it isn't the cause.

**Second stop: the sound card.** Having a poor sound card would make for poor recognition, but even poor recognition is a far cry from nothing. The sound card would have to be broken rather than just poor in order to cause NaturallySpeaking to stop dead in its tracks. Seems unlikely.

**Third stop: Windows.** Double-click the loudspeaker icon on the taskbar and look at the Microphone Balance. Is the little Mute box checked? Uncheck it.

Another possibility is that Windows (for its own unfathomable reasons) has changed your device settings — redefined your microphone to be a printer or something equally helpful. (We think we're exaggerating, but it's hard to be sure.) Running through a complete setup with the Audio Setup wizard will either fix the problem or give you a more specific complaint to take to Dragon Technical Support. (See Chapter 23.)

**Fourth stop: microphone icon.** Is NaturallySpeaking asleep? Check the microphone icon on the Windows taskbar or on the NaturallySpeaking toolbar. Is it lying flat on its back? Click it so that it stands at an angle.

If you're trying to dictate directly into the NaturallySpeaking document window, those are all the obvious steps. But if you're dictating into a different application, there are some more places to look for problems.

**Fifth stop: NaturalText.** Check that the NaturalText sound bubble on the Windows taskbar is blue and not gray. If it's gray (with tiny Zs), click it to wake it up.

**Sixth stop: the application.** Maybe you don't realize which window is active, and text is actually piling up somewhere that you're not looking. Click in the window you want to dictate into to make sure that it's active. If you use the keyboard to type something, does it appear where you expect it? If not, the problem has nothing to do with NaturallySpeaking.

Still stumped? That's about as much help as we can give you from this distance in time and space. You need some one-on-one help either from Dragon Technical Support or from other NaturallySpeaking users. See Chapter 23.

# NaturallySpeaking Doesn't Type What You Say

If NaturallySpeaking just doesn't get it right when you dictate, you're having what's called recognition errors or accuracy problems. Now, don't you feel better, having an official diagnosis of your problem?

No? Then turn to Part IV of this book. So many different things can affect accuracy that we have an entire Part about them. If that sounds too wearisome, try the following first-aid:

✔ Make sure you actually speak each word fully and speak entire phrases. Don't pause between words, and don't skip them, clip them at the end, or slur them to other words.

✔ Make sure your microphone is positioned off to the side of your mouth, about one-half inch away.

✔ Run the Audio Setup wizard again: Choose Tools⇨Audio Setup Wizard.

✔ Choose Tools⇨Options, and in the Options dialog box that appears, click the Miscellaneous tab. Drag the Speed vs. Accuracy slider you see there more to the right. Click the OK button.

If your problem is that NaturallySpeaking repeatedly gets certain words wrong, make sure you use the Correction dialog box so that NaturallySpeaking learns about its errors. (Say, **"Correct That"** after NaturallySpeaking errs.) If you just select the erroneous text and dictate over it, NaturallySpeaking will never learn.

# Commands Get Typed as Text

Few things are more frustrating than to select the most important line in your document and say, **"Italicize That"** only to watch the whole line disappear and be replaced with the words *italicize that*. (A quick **"Undo That"** or two usually gets back what you lost.)

This kind of thing can happen for a number of reasons. Here are some things to check or try:

✔ **Is the command supposed to work in this application?** We're not sure how many times we've threatened to reprogram our computers with a sledgehammer, only to discover that we had been dictating (well, yelling actually) a Select-and-Say command at an application that wasn't enabled for Select and Say, or a NaturalWord command when NaturalWord wasn't running.

✔ **Get your pauses right.** On multi-word commands like **Italicize That** or **Format That Arial Bold 16 Point**, you should pause briefly before and after the command, but not at all in the middle.

✔ **Is NaturallySpeaking hearing you correctly?** Watch the Results box, or pay attention to what NaturallySpeaking types instead of doing what you want. If it's hearing "Italy sized hat" then it's not going to italicize anything. If this keeps happening, you should do Word Training on the particular commands that NaturallySpeaking misinterprets. See Chapter 18.

✔ **Hold down the Control key.** Holding down the Control key while you dictate is a way to say "Hey, dummy, this is a command I'm saying!" (If you actually say this, NaturallySpeaking just types it. Trust us, it's not very satisfying.) If this doesn't work, it's time to try to accomplish your purpose another way. For example, you might try **"Press Control I"** instead of **"Italicize That."**

# Select and Say Doesn't Select What You Say

The most common reason why Select and Say doesn't work is that the application you're dictating into isn't a Select-and-Say application. See Chapter 10 for the complete list. One especially tricky case: If you start Microsoft Word or Corel WordPerfect and then start NaturallySpeaking some way other than the Dragon NaturallySpeaking⇨Use NaturalWord menu command, NaturalWord doesn't automatically start. Consequently, when you dictate into Word or WordPerfect, you're at the NaturalText level rather than the NaturalWord level. The solution here is to start NaturalWord. See Chapter 12.

# NaturallySpeaking Inserts Extra Little Words

Some days you find your documents littered with little words like *in* or *to* or *and*. You're sure you didn't say them — NaturallySpeaking just seems to have an overactive imagination today.

These little extra words come from two places. The most likely explanation is that your microphone is positioned badly. If the mike sits in front of your mouth rather than to the side, your words are being punctuated by little bursts of air. Those puffs hit the microphone and make a short, sharp noise that NaturallySpeaking interprets as a short word. It's also possible that the breath coming down out of your nostrils is blowing across the microphone. In either case, move the mike further to the side of your mouth.

The second possibility is that you're trying too hard to enunciate your consonants. For example, maybe you had trouble a few lines ago getting NaturallySpeaking to recognize your **Format** command. It heard *formal, form, for Matt,* or some other phrase that wasn't **Format.** The next time you need to format something, you try too hard to make it hear the *t* at the end. And NaturallySpeaking does hear it — a little too well — and so it types *format to.* The only solution here is just to relax; go back to speaking the way you naturally speak. (That's why they call it NaturallySpeaking, you know.)

# Dictation Is Slow

You dictate something to NaturallySpeaking, and then you wait. How long is it going to take to figure out what you said? Did it even hear you? Should you repeat? Finally, the words show up.

You can deal with slow response time in the following ways:

- ✔ **Ignore it.** We're serious. Don't wait around for the words to show up on the screen. Just keep dictating. NaturallySpeaking remembers as much as a half hour's worth of dictation, so don't worry if you get a few lines ahead of it.

- ✔ **Change the settings.** From the NaturallySpeaking window say, **"Click Tools, Options."** When the Options dialog box appears say, **"Click Miscellaneous"** and then **"Press Tab"** to select the Speed vs. Accuracy slider. Move the slider towards Fastest Response with the **Move Left <*number*>** command. When you have the slider where you want it, say **"Click OK."** (You can also do all those steps with your mouse, if you prefer: Choose Tools⇨Options, click the Miscellaneous tab, drag the slider left, and click OK.)

- ✔ **Liberate some RAM (memory).** Close any programs you don't need, and turn off background features of those you do need, like automatic spell checking.

- ✔ **Exit all your applications and restart the computer.** If you've been on the computer for several hours and have opened and closed a number of applications, Windows' bookkeeping may have gotten tangled. Restarting may give the computer access to resources it had forgotten about.

- ✔ **Install more RAM.** This isn't going to do you much good in the next five minutes, but in the long run it's the best solution.

✔ **Turn off natural-language commands.** If you don't need the natural-language commands, just regular old dictation and the dictation commands that work in the NaturallySpeaking window, you can turn off natural-language commands. Choose Tools⇨Options in the NaturallySpeaking window (or from the Dragon NaturallySpeaking⇨ Tools menu in Word). In the Options dialog box that appears, click the Dictation tab. On that tab, click to clear the check mark labeled Use Natural Language Commands in Microsoft Word. Click OK. A dialog box warns you that you'll have to restart NaturallySpeaking. Click OK, and then exit and restart NaturallySpeaking.

# Menu Commands Don't Work

When you say, **"Click"** and nothing happens, probably the problem is that your Use Active Accessibility for Menu and Dialog Control box is unchecked. To check it:

1. **From the NaturallySpeaking window, select Tools⇨Options. (There's no point in telling you how to access this by voice, because that's exactly what isn't working!)**

2. **When the Options dialog box appears, click the Miscellaneous tab.**

3. **Find the Use Active Accessibility checkbox and make sure it gets checked.**

If that wasn't the problem, here's another possibility: Some of the very early versions of Internet Explorer 5.0 also interfered with Active Accessibility. Go to the Microsoft Web site (www.microsoft.com) and update your copy of Internet Explorer.

# Natural-Language Commands Don't Work

If the natural-language commands we describe in Chapter 12 don't seem to work, check out the following possibilities. The two most likely possibilities are

✔ **You aren't dictating into Microsoft Word.** Natural-language commands don't work in WordPerfect or anyplace other than Word. They don't even work in versions of Word earlier than Word 97.

✔ **NaturalWord isn't running.** If you can dictate text, but the natural-language commands don't work, one possibility is that you launched NaturallySpeaking separately, after launching Word (not from within Word). NaturalWord is off. (The reason you can dictate is that NaturalText is running.) Go to Chapter 12 to see how to launch NaturalWord.

Another possibility is that someone has turned off natural-language commands. To turn them back on:

1. **Choose Dragon NaturallySpeaking⇨Tools⇨Options from the Word menu bar.**

2. **In the Options dialog box that appears, click the Dictation tab.**

3. **On that tab, check to make sure the checkbox labeled Use Natural Language Commands in Microsoft Word 97 has a checkmark. If not, click that checkbox, and then click OK.**

   A dialog box warns you that you will have to restart NaturallySpeaking.

4. **Click OK, and then exit and re-launch Word.**

# Undo That Doesn't Undo

Often — particularly in Word — **Undo That** doesn't fully undo (an underdone undo?). It partially undoes. For example, suppose you highlight some text, speak the command **Format That Arial 14,** but instead of NaturallySpeaking changing the format, it types *Format that aerial for teens* over your selected text. Not what you had in mind. (And who wants a teen-formatted aerial? Teens, we suppose. But we digress.) So you say, **"Undo That"** and NaturallySpeaking removes the offending text — but the original text is still missing!

In that event, you need to repeat the **Undo That** command. Many NaturallySpeaking actions are actually made up of several Word actions, and **Undo That** only undoes one Word action at a time.

# Start Doesn't Start

You say **"Start America Online"** or **"Start Microsoft Works"** or **"Start Quicken"** and nothing happens. What's the deal?

The **Start** command will start any application that's installed on your machine and has either

- ✔ A shortcut icon on the desktop, or
- ✔ An entry on the Programs menu

The catch, however, is that you have to say the name exactly as it appears on the shortcut or menu entry. So if the entry on the Programs menu is Microsoft Works 4.5, then you need to say **"Start Microsoft Works four point five."**

If the name on the icon or menu entry is too much of a mouthful to be worth pronouncing, or if you can never remember exactly what it says, you can rename it. Rename a desktop icon by right-clicking it and choosing Rename. You can do the same thing to the Program menu entries, but you have to find them first. They live in the folder C:\Windows\Start Menu.

# Chapter 25

# Ten Time-and-Sanity-Saving Tips

### In This Chapter

▶ Use hotkeys in dialog boxes

▶ Position the microphone the same way every time

▶ Change your mouse habits

▶ Drink with a straw

▶ Turn off your word processor's automatic spell checking

▶ Work on small pieces of large documents

▶ Use dictation shorthands

▶ Turn the microphone off when you walk away

▶ Select or correct longer phrases

▶ It's okay to use the physical mouse and keyboard

**S**ometimes the difference between doing well and just getting by is a well-placed piece of advice from a wiser and more experienced mentor. Go West, young man. Don't take any wooden nickels. Look before you leap — that kind of thing.

We looked all over for a wiser and more experienced mentor, but we came up short. That's the problem with cutting-edge software: "more experienced" means somebody who installed his copy last Thursday. Anyway, here are ten things we wish somebody had told us last Thursday.

## Use Hotkeys in Dialog Boxes

We've become big fans of hotkeys in general, but they really shine in dialog boxes. The varied features of dialog boxes, the radio buttons and checkboxes and the like, respond unevenly to voice commands. In some dialog boxes, you can say, **"Click *Never Ask Me This Question Again*"** and have a check show up in the Never Ask Me This Question Again box. And in other dialog boxes it doesn't work. But saying **"Press Alt S"** works every time.

# Position the Microphone the Same Way Every Time

Misplaced microphones are the number one cause of error. NaturallySpeaking learns best when you sound the same way every time you say a word. And even if you actually *say* the word the same way every time, it *sounds* different if your microphone isn't in quite the same location.

Develop your own precise way of knowing that the microphone is in exactly the right place. Maybe you can just fit a finger between the microphone and the corner of your mouth. If all that is too much trouble, get in the habit of running the Audio Setup wizard whenever you put your microphone on: Choose Tools⇨Audio Setup Wizard from the NaturallySpeaking menu bar.

# Change Your Mouse Habits

No, we're not talking about altering the headgear of a rodent religious order. We're talking about all those things that you might be in the habit of doing with your computer's mouse: clicking toolbar buttons, using scrollbars, dragging and dropping, clicking links on Web pages, and relocating the cursor.

NaturallySpeaking has mouse commands, which we described in Chapter 11. So you *could* keep all your same mouse habits, but just use mouse voice commands instead of grabbing the physical object next to your keyboard. But that's not a great idea. The mouse commands (like **MouseGrid**) are usable in a pinch, but they get tedious if you try to do everything with them.

Instead, learn to do the same actions with other commands. Use the NaturalWeb commands with Internet Explorer. Say, **"Press Page Down"** or **"Press Page Up"** instead of clicking the scrollbar. Use menu commands instead of toolbar buttons. Cut and paste with hotkeys instead of dragging and dropping. Use the **Move** and **Go** commands to put the cursor where you want.

# Drink with a Straw

Dictating is thirsty work. You can maintain a clear, steady tone of voice and avoid doing damage to your throat if you keep something to drink close at hand and sip it occasionally. But there is no way to raise a cup to your lips without moving the microphone.

The solution is to drink through a straw! We admit, hot coffee or cold beer through a straw is a weird experience, but most drinks are just fine.

# Turn Off Automatic Spell Checking in Word Processors

NaturallySpeaking is incapable of making a spelling error (unless you introduce a misspelled word into its vocabulary through the vocabulary-building process). So spell-checking is a waste of your computer's resources, (which NaturallySpeaking may already be stretching near the breaking point). If NaturallySpeaking seems a bit sluggish when you're using a word processor, turn off that word processor's spell-checking.

In Word, choose Tools⇨Options from the menu, and then click the Spelling and Grammar tab. Make sure the Check Spelling as You Type box isn't checked.

While you're there, you can save some more RAM by making sure the Check Grammar As You Type box is unchecked as well. In WordPerfect, select Tools⇨Proofread⇨Off.

# Work on Small Pieces of Large Documents

This tip is another RAM-saver. Large documents take up a lot of your computer's memory, memory that could be better applied to improving the performance of NaturallySpeaking. Don't make your computer keep your whole novel in memory if you really only need to work on one scene. Put the scene in a separate file and work on that file instead.

# Use Dictation Shorthands

You can save a lot of time by teaching NaturallySpeaking some shorthand. Teach your dragon to type "the Honorable Judge James J. Hackelgruber" when you say "the boss," or to reproduce your full street address when you say "my address." See Chapter 18 for details.

You can also use shorthands to gain some privacy for yourself. If, for example, you have a pet name for your spouse that you would rather not have overheard in the next cubicle when you dictate e-mail, substitute some dull-sounding shorthand.

# Turn the Microphone Off When You Stop Dictating

NaturallySpeaking and the microphone that comes with it are usually good enough that they don't pay attention to random noises. The microphone doesn't, however, know that you have just picked up the phone or are talking to the person who just came into your office. We've had some interesting and lengthy gibberish result from such interruptions. We find that the habit of pressing the + key on the keyboard (or clicking the microphone icon) when we're interrupted or otherwise done dictating is a good one to get into.

# Select or Correct Longer Phrases

When you dictate "a hippopotamus" and NaturallySpeaking types "the hippopotamus," don't just say, **"Correct *the*."** NaturallySpeaking may mishear it again, and there's bound to be an "a" in your document somewhere that it will try to correct instead.

Instead, say, **"Correct *the hippopotamus*."** Chances are good that only one occurrence of "the hippopotamus" is currently displayed and that NaturallySpeaking will pick it out for you right away. Select an even longer phrase, if you can: **Correct *tickle the hippopotamus*,** for example.

# Don't Be Afraid to Use the Physical Mouse and Keyboard

In theory you can do just about anything with the NaturallySpeaking voice commands. Voice commands like **MouseGrid** and **Click** give you a virtual mouse, and the **Press** command gives you a virtual keyboard, so you should be able to do without the gross, physical mouse and keyboard — in theory. (Theory is a nice place, and we're thinking about relocating there. We hear they have an average temperature all year long.)

Sometimes, however, doing something by voice is simply a pain. Give it up. If you know in your heart that you can do it in three clicks of a mouse's tail, do it. You'll have better days, and you can figure out how to handle the situation with voice commands then.

# Chapter 26

# Ten Mistakes to Avoid

* * * * * * * * * * * * * * * * * * * * * * * * * * * * * * * * * * * * * * * * * * *

### In This Chapter

▶ Don't run a lot of other programs simultaneously with NaturallySpeaking

▶ Don't tell NaturallySpeaking to shut down the computer

▶ Don't correct what you ought to edit

▶ Don't edit what you ought to correct

▶ Don't cut corners on training

▶ Don't forget to re-run Audio Setup when the environment changes

▶ Don't sign on with somebody else's user name

▶ Don't speak into the back side of the microphone

▶ Don't create dictation shorthands or macro commands that sound like single common words

▶ Don't forget to proofread

* * * * * * * * * * * * * * * * * * * * * * * * * * * * * * * * * * * * * * * * * * *

*E*verybody makes mistakes, and some people make really big and entertaining mistakes. We made a gob of mistakes with NaturallySpeaking, and probably you'll make some, too, from time to time. Here's all we ask: Don't make these ten obvious mistakes that we were able to guess ahead of time. Be original. Be creative. Go out there and make brand-new mistakes that no one else has ever thought of before.

## Don't Run a Lot of Other Programs and NaturallySpeaking Simultaneously

Dragons are greedy beasts and, true to type, NaturallySpeaking will grab lots of memory. It grabs even more when NaturalWord runs, and then your word processor has its own memory greed. The same thing happens when you browse the Web: NaturalWeb takes up a certain amount of memory, and Internet Explorer wants its own hoard of RAM. If there's not enough RAM for everybody, everything slows down, and you could even freeze the computer.

So shut down programs that you aren't using. Plan your activities so that you don't have to run NaturallySpeaking and Word and Internet Explorer all at the same time. Don't leave DOOM or a big spreadsheet or a giant graphics program running in the background if you don't need them.

# Don't Tell NaturallySpeaking to Shut Down the Computer

Certainly you can imagine an operating system that gracefully handles a shutdown request from one of its applications. *Get real, people.* This is Windows we're talking about. Saying, **"Click Start, Shut Down, Click OK"** is more-or-less equivalent to saying "Send me the Blue Screen of Death." Most likely you won't even get that; the computer will just freeze and you'll have to turn it off manually. And then you and some techno-gypsy will have to hold a cyber-seance to contact the files you were working on.

# Don't Correct What You Ought to Edit

You should use the Correction process described in Chapter 5 only when NaturallySpeaking has made a mistake that you don't want it to make again. If you just said the wrong thing, edit it.

Suppose, for example, that you're writing an e-mail to tell a friend about the bonus that your officemate just got. But your Freudian subconscious gets the better of you, and you say *bogus* instead of *bonus*. If you then say, **"Correct bogus,"** you are in effect blaming NaturallySpeaking for your own error.

NaturallySpeaking is a diligent little dragon, and will strive mightily not to make the same "error" again. And so it may start typing *bonus* when you really do mean to dictate *bogus*. It may even change its settings to reflect the possibility that sometimes your *n*'s sound like *g*'s. And then it starts turning *go* into *no*, and making other similarly mysterious mistakes.

# Don't Edit What You Ought to Correct

NaturallySpeaking's performance will never improve if you don't tell it that it has made a mistake. Sometimes it seems easier just to say, **"Scratch That"** and repeat the phrase again, but in the long run it just costs you time because you'll see that same mistake again in the future. See Chapter 5 for detailed instructions about correcting NaturallySpeaking's mistakes.

# Don't Cut Corners on Training

You can, if you're so inclined, skip out on the New User wizard after the first part of General Training. This avoids the second (longer) part of General Training, and the Vocabulary Builder. NaturallySpeaking will never be more than a toy if you do this.

There is only one corner we recommend cutting: If you're using NaturallySpeaking on a new machine and you already have user files on another machine, you should move the files over rather than retraining. See Chapter 20.

# Don't Forget to Run Audio Setup Again When the Environment Changes

So you get a great new microphone that you expect to improve NaturallySpeaking's accuracy, and instead it gets worse. What happened?

Maybe you forgot to tell NaturallySpeaking that anything had changed. Maybe your dragon is sitting there saying "That's not my master's voice! Where are the pops and clicks? Where is the background roar?"

The way to tell NaturallySpeaking that something has changed is to run Audio Setup again. (See Chapters 2 and 19 for details.) You should also run it again if your voice volume changes (maybe you're tired) or if you move your computer to a new location. Anything that would make you sound different is an occasion to run Audio Setup again. If that change is permanent or likely to be a recurring event, run General Training again, too. See Chapter 18.

# Don't Use Somebody Else's User Files

You might say "We sound alike. Why should I bother to train my own user? It won't make any difference." Trust us, it will make a difference. The performance will be poor, and if NaturallySpeaking starts adjusting to your voice, it will start performing badly for the user whose identity you're borrowing.

# Don't Speak into the Back Side of the Microphone

The microphone that comes with NaturallySpeaking is a noise-canceling directional microphone. That means that it has a front side and a back side. It tries to pay attention to what comes in the front side, and tries to cancel out what comes in the back side. The front side has a little mark indicating that it's the front.

# Don't Create Shorthands or Macros that Sound Like Single Common Words

One of the dumbest things a person could do with NaturallySpeaking would be to create a macro command called **The** that deletes the entire current document. No one would be able to dictate for more than a sentence or two without accidentally invoking **The** and deleting their document.

Dictation shorthands can get you into trouble, too. What if you defined "two" to be a dictation shorthand for the numeral 1? Great confusion would follow.

Instead, make sure that any command or shorthand that you define consists of at least two words. **Trash the Document** would still be a dangerous macro to have lying around, but the danger would derive from rash decisions rather than accidental usage.

# Don't Forget to Proofread

NaturallySpeaking doesn't make spelling mistakes, so spell-checking is useless. But that doesn't mean that your documents are perfect. They just have *correctly spelled* mistakes in them.

In some ways, that is worse. When you mis-type a word, you usually wind up with nonsense. Your readers can deduce that a mistake has been made, and can probably even figure out what you meant to say. But when your document has correct English words that only sound like what you meant to say, your readers may think you are trying to be clever. When Mr. Jiro sees his name written "Mr. Zero," he may think you mean something by it.

# Chapter 27

# Ten Stupid Dragon Tricks

**D**ragon Systems created NaturallySpeaking to handle dictation in contemporary English (or French or Italian or German or Spanish, if you have one of those versions). The idea was to make it easier for you to write letters or memos or detective novels or reports or newspaper articles. The vocabulary and word-frequency statistics are set up for this kind of contemporary writing.

But when people first sit down in front of a microphone to test NaturallySpeaking, what do they almost inevitably start dictating? Something from memory, which usually means something they had to memorize in school. Something archaic, in other words — Shakespeare, the King James Bible, or the Declaration of Independence.

NaturallySpeaking wasn't designed to understand this kind of stuff, and it makes lots of mistakes — downright hilarious mistakes sometimes. This causes people to laugh at their poor, abused dragon, and to start feeding it stuff it couldn't possibly digest: nonsense rhymes, text in other languages, you name it.

This is cruelty, plain and simple. The folks at Dragon Systems have encouraged us to condemn such behavior in no uncertain terms, and so we will: It is bad. Bad! Bad! Bad! Bad! Bad!

Got that? It's also quite a bit of fun, but most bad things are, aren't they? Nobody has ever had to make a rule against putting hot coals in your mouth, after all.

So, purely out of humanitarian concern (or dragonatarian concern, or something), and so that you won't be tempted to do something like this yourself to your own poor, helpless computer program, we are (with great sorrow) publishing the results of our own dragon torture. Remember: We're professionals. Don't try this at home.

In the unlikely event that you're the kind of person who would ignore our stern moral condemnation (bad! bad! bad! bad! bad!) and torture your own dragon with archaisms and nonsense and the like, you need to take two simple precautions to make sure that you don't screw up the NaturallySpeaking training (you don't want NaturallySpeaking to *expect* you to talk like Shakespeare, do you?):

- **Don't correct any mistakes that NaturallySpeaking makes while you're torturing it.** If it interprets "forsooth" as "fort's tooth," leave it alone. Who knows, you might really want to say "fort's tooth" someday.

- **Don't save your speech files when you're done.** If you don't save your speech files, it's as if the whole session never happened. You're like the stage hypnotist who says "When you wake up you won't remember any of this."

*Note:* If you really, seriously want NaturallySpeaking to learn to recognize archaisms — say if you're a Shakespearean scholar or you frequently quote the Bible — it can, given time and training. Creating a new user for this kind of talk (or a new vocabulary if you're using NaturallySpeaking Professional) is best. You'll want to use Vocabulary Builder to introduce mass quantities of that kind of writing, and then just correct NaturallySpeaking whenever it gets something wrong. Forsooth, in a fortnight or so, your dragon will be a veritable maven of the bardly tongue.

## *Dictate Jabberwocky*

NaturallySpeaking is forced to interpret whatever you say as words in its active vocabulary. If you aren't saying words at all, it just has to do the best it can. Turning "Beware the Jabberwock, my son!" into "Be where the jab are walk, my son!" has to be seen as a heroic effort on its part. Ditto for turning "Callooh! Callay!" into "Colder! <colon> a!"

Twist drilling, and a slightly to those
did Dyer and Kimball in the law:
all names he were the Borg wrote us,
and a moment as out crowd.

"Be where the jam are walk, my son!
The John is that bite, the clause that catch!
Be where the job show bird, and shunned
from the a spend your snatched!"

He took his for full so Word in hand:
long time the Mac so faux he sought
so rested feed by the time down tree,
in and stood awhile in thought.

And, as in a fish thought he stood,
the jam are walk, with eyes of flame,
King with thing through the told the wood,
and durable as it came!

1,2! 1,2! And through and through
before full blade what sticker snack!
He left it did, and with its head
he way to go along thing back.

"And pastel slain the jam are walk?
Come to my arms, might be mission boy!
Over fret just day! Colder!: a!"
He chore told in his joy.

Twist drilling, and the slightly to those
to John Eric and Kimball in the while the:
all names he were the Borg wrote us,
and the moment acts out crowd of.

# Dictate The Gettysburg Address

We dictated this immediately after General Training, when the system was most likely to misunderstand. The mistakes have a certain prescience to them: "government over the people, buying the people" has a ring to it, don't you think?

We picture Lincoln on the train to Gettysburg, dictating into his portable recorder:

"*Or* score and seven years ago *homeowners* brought forth on this continent *emu* nation, conceived in Liberty and dedicated to the proposition that *old* men are created equal. Now we are engaged in a *Greek* Civil War, testing *weather* that nation or any nation so conceived and so dedicated *Campbell into work.*

"We are met on a *Greek* battlefield of that war. We have come to dedicate a portion of battlefield as a final resting-place for those who *hear* gave their *law is* that that nation might live. It is altogether *hitting* and proper that we should do this. But in *the* larger *cents,* we cannot dedicate, we cannot *concentrate,* we cannot *Howe of* this ground. The brave men, living *in* dead who struggled here have *concentrated* it far above our *war* power to add or detract. The world will *Littleton to normal* remember what we say here, but *he* can never forget what they did here.

"*Each use* for us *to* living rather to be dedicated here to the unfinished work which they *won't* here have thus far *sewn openly* advanced. It is rather for us to be here dedicated to *decree* task remaining before us — that *control* these honored dead we take increased devotion to that *callers* for which they gave the last full measure of devotion — that we here *Hialeah* resolve that these dead shall not have died *evening,* that this nation *undergone* shall have a *rebirth* of freedom, and that government *over* the people, *buying* the people, for the people shall not *parish* from the earth."

# Dictate Shakespeare

NaturallySpeaking did rather badly when we dictated Romeo's speech under the balcony, starting with "What light through yonder window breaks?" But most of the mistakes are due to simple archaisms: "yonder window" becomes "the under Window," and "vestal livery" turns into "us delivery."

"What light through the under Window breaks? It is the East, and Juliet is the son. Arise, fair son, and kills the in the us Moon, who is already sick and pale with grief, that now her mate art far more fair that she; the not her mate, said she is envy of; her us delivery is but sick and green and non-but fools to where it; casting off."

But it did even worse with Juliet's reply. The biggest problem here is that in the alpha-bravo-charlie way of saying the alphabet, "romeo" is the letter R. Stranger still, "Capulet" is interpreted as "Cap period." Because there is no capital period, NaturallySpeaking produces an ordinary period instead.

"O. r, r! Wherefore art that r? Deny the high father and refused I name; or, if now will cannot, be but sworn my love, and I'll no longer be a."

The bard's poetry fared no better. Dictating, "Full fathom five thy father lies" resulted in "Full phantom 555 their lives."

Antony's speech over the body of Caesar is at least recognizable, possibly because, as he says: "I am no orator, . . . but . . . a plain blunt man." But who is this Barry Caesar character, anyway?

"Friends, Romans, countrymen, land need your here is; I come to Barry Caesar, not to praise him. The evil that man to lives after them; the good is often incurred with their bones; so let it be with Caesar. The noble purchase have told you Caesar was ambitious: if it were so, it was a previous fault, and previously have Caesar answered it."

Hamlet *is* an orator, but the NaturallySpeaking rendition of his speech just needs a good editor. And don't we all wish for "no blur in the mind?"

"To be, or not to be: that is the question. Whether to is no blur in the mind to suffer the swings and arrows of outrageous fortune, or to take arms against the Sea of troubles, and by opposing and them?"

# Dictate from The Bible

Okay, we admit it. We chickened out on this one. We are relatively certain that putting, say, *Genesis* through NaturallySpeaking would result in text that (at least in certain circles) would be considered hilarious. However, we will allow this theory to remain untested.

We are well aware of the statistics reporting that the incidence of blasphemy these days is rather high, and the incidence of death-by-lightning-bolt is rather low. But after considerable thought and consultation with spiritual advisors, we decided not to take the chance.

Remember, though, that this chapter is a list of things *not* to do. So we couldn't very well leave this one off the list, could we? Dictate *Genesis* at your own risk, and keep your lightning rods in good repair.

# Dictate Limericks

Well, actually this one isn't so bad. We tried to dictate:

"There once was a man from Peru,
Who dreamed he was eating his shoe.
He woke up in the night
With a terrible fright
To find it was perfectly true."

NaturallySpeaking almost got it. If only we could have told it that the lines were supposed to rhyme.

"Their once was a man from Peru,
Who treat he was eating his should.
He woke up in the night
With a terrible frightened
To find it was perfectly true."

# Dictate "Mairzy Doats"

This one more-or-less speaks for itself:

"Mayors he doubts,
And does he doubts,
And little land see tiny.
Get lead 92, would you?
Get lead 92, we can you?"

# Turn NaturallySpeaking into an Oracle

You do this by abusing the Vocabulary Editor. The idea is to be able to ask NaturallySpeaking a question, and have it provide the answer. For example, you want to be able to ask, "What is the answer to life, the universe, and everything?" and have NaturallySpeaking answer: 42 (or whatever you think the answer is).

The trick is to enter the answer as the written form in the Vocabulary Editor, and enter the question as the spoken form. So, for our example, do this:

1. **Choose Tools⇨Vocabulary Editor**

   The Vocabulary Editor eventually makes the scene.

2. **In the Written Form box, type** 42.

3. **In the Spoken Form (If Different) box, type** What is the answer to life, the universe, and everything?

4. **Click Add, and then click Close.**

You're done! Try asking NaturallySpeaking the question.

# Sing

Singing doesn't sound like speech at all. Not only does the tone jump around, but the pace is all wrong, too — at least from the NaturallySpeaking point of view. It wants to insert extra words or syllables to account for those extended vowels, especially at the end of lines. There's also no room in the song for you to insert punctuation, capitalization, or line breaks, so what you wind up with looks pretty weird.

Everyone who saw the movie *2001: A Space Odyssey* remembers the computer HAL singing *Bicycle Built for Two* to his human colleague Dave. We trained NaturallySpeaking until it could recognize the spoken lyrics of *Bicycle Built for Two*, and then we sang the first verse. It came out looking like this:

> "A. easy day easy to video around CERT true hot and the half crazy all for the love of you move it won't be a stylish narrated shy can do for the carriage but you'll look sweet upon the seat of a bicycle build afford to"

# Dictate in Foreign Languages

We dictated (and didn't sing) the French verse of the Beatles song *Michelle*. We got something you can actually sing if you know the tune:

> "Michelle, mob they'll
> Solely Mall key home trade BN owned song,
> Trade BN owned song."

# Use Playback to Say Silly or Embarrassing Things

Certain things just sound hilarious when they are said by an artificial voice. Anything passionate or whimsical takes on a Kafkaesque absurdity when proclaimed in Playback's prosody-free manner.

The SciFi Channel sometimes takes advantage of this phenomenon with its artificial announcer. After reading off the evening's schedule, the SciFi announcer has been known to say things like "I am living *la vida loca.*"

# DragonSpeak: A Glossary

Dragons speak an ancient and cryptic tongue. Dragon Systems uses a terminology that is newer but sometimes nearly as cryptic. We try not to rely too much on its terminology. But, if you wander through its literature and help files, or browse any of the user dialog on the Internet about NaturallySpeaking, you'll hear DragonSpeak. And we sometimes have no choice but to resort to DragonSpeak ourselves. So, if "it's all geek to you," here's the translation.

**Acoustic model:** A mathematical description of the sound of your voice created during General Training and individual word training. NaturallySpeaking maintains one such description per user.

**Active vocabulary:** The database of words in your PC's memory from which NaturallySpeaking draws when it's guessing what you said. To ensure that it contains the most words you're most likely to use, NaturallySpeaking swaps words into and out of active memory from the backup dictionary when you correct NaturallySpeaking.

**Audio Setup wizard:** A wizard that can test the microphone and sound card and modify sound card settings, especially input volume.

**Backup dictionary:** A collection of nearly all words known to NaturallySpeaking. Words are placed in the active vocabulary from this dictionary, based on how often you use them.

**BestMatch:** A piece of Dragon Systems gizmology that increases accuracy and speed, but takes additional memory and processor power. BestMatch 64k+ does it even better, and requires yet more memory. BestMatch III is the current top of the heap, and is intended for a Pentium III PC, but as of this writing only gives you a shorter enrollment period.

**Correction:** The process of pointing out an error to NaturallySpeaking and giving it the correct text, using the Correction dialog box. When you use NaturalText, you can correct only your most recent utterance. In Select-and-Say applications, you can correct any text you select.

**Custom command (or macro):** A set of actions that you have chosen to be performed automatically for you by NaturallySpeaking, possibly including typing of text. You cause NaturallySpeaking to execute the actions by speaking a word or phrase that you have chosen. (Custom commands are only available in NaturallySpeaking Professional.)

**Custom words:** Words you add to a vocabulary. You may also add phrases or dictation shorthands.

**Dictation commands:** Commands that control capitalization, line and paragraph endings, tabs, and spacing. You can substitute your own commands by changing the "spoken form" for these commands, listed in the Vocabulary Editor.

**Dictation shorthand:** A spoken phrase that results in a different, typically longer, phrase being typed. You create shorthands (also sometimes called shortcuts) by using the Vocabulary Editor.

**Enrollment:** Initial training to set up a user.

**Finding new words:** Having NaturallySpeaking scan the current document for words not in its vocabulary, and then optionally adding them to the vocabulary currently in use.

**General Training:** Teaching NaturallySpeaking about your speech patterns by reading to it.

**Language model:** A statistical model kept by NaturallySpeaking of how frequently a user uses various words alone or in combination.

**Macro:** Another name for a custom command.

**MouseGrid:** A tool for verbally positioning the mouse pointer on your screen. You speak a number from a numbered grid of squares that is overlaid on the screen. A new grid then appears on that square alone. Right-click, left-click, and other commands allow simulating mouse actions.

**NaturalText:** A feature of NaturallySpeaking that allows you to dictate into nearly any Windows application. Its formatting and selection features are limited compared to those available in the NaturallySpeaking window itself. NaturalText is automatically launched when you launch NaturallySpeaking, and is switched on and off by clicking a "balloon" icon on the Windows taskbar.

**NaturalWord:** A feature of NaturallySpeaking that allows you to launch and control NaturallySpeaking from the Word or WordPerfect menu bar. NaturalWord also imparts a larger command set to Word or WordPerfect than you would otherwise obtain by using NaturalText.

**Play back:** To play back the audio from dictation. Found only in NaturallySpeaking Preferred or Professional.

**Read back:** To convert text to speech. Found only in NaturallySpeaking Preferred or Professional.

**Select and Say:** The ability to select text visible on the screen by speaking the **Select** command and then the text. Select and Say only works in specific applications.

**Speech files:** Files defining a user's speech patterns, updated by NaturallySpeaking as you make corrections or vocabulary changes, or perform additional training.

**Text-to-speech:** A feature of NaturallySpeaking that uses a computer-synthesized voice to read text aloud. Found only in NaturallySpeaking Preferred or Professional.

**Tracking:** The ability of NaturallySpeaking to click on menus.

**Transcribe:** To convert speech to written text. In NaturallySpeaking, the Transcribe command specifically converts recorded speech to text.

**User:** A setup of NaturallySpeaking that is adapted to a particular person, environment, microphone, and sound card. It includes that person's settings in the Options dialog box, and any custom voice commands they may have created. A user has a only one vocabulary in most products; in NaturallySpeaking Professional, a user can have alternative vocabularies.

**Vocabulary building:** Having NaturallySpeaking read documents you have created previously, to learn new words and learn how you use words in combination.

**Vocabulary:** A database in NaturallySpeaking that records the written and spoken form of words, plus statistics about how those words are used in combination. NaturallySpeaking comes with base vocabularies from which a user obtains an initial vocabulary that you can expand and customize.

**Word training:** Teaching NaturallySpeaking how you say a word. Normally, NaturallySpeaking guesses pronunciation from the spelling. Word training gives it the actual pronunciation.

# Index

**• E •**

# Notes

# BUSINESS, CAREERS & PERSONAL FINANCE

0-7645-5307-0

0-7645-5331-3 *†

**Also available:**

- Accounting For Dummies †
  0-7645-5314-3
- Business Plans Kit For Dummies †
  0-7645-5365-8
- Cover Letters For Dummies
  0-7645-5224-4
- Frugal Living For Dummies
  0-7645-5403-4
- Leadership For Dummies
  0-7645-5176-0
- Managing For Dummies
  0-7645-1771-6

- Marketing For Dummies
  0-7645-5600-2
- Personal Finance For Dummies *
  0-7645-2590-5
- Project Management For Dummies
  0-7645-5283-X
- Resumes For Dummies †
  0-7645-5471-9
- Selling For Dummies
  0-7645-5363-1
- Small Business Kit For Dummies *†
  0-7645-5093-4

# HOME & BUSINESS COMPUTER BASICS

0-7645-4074-2

0-7645-3758-X

**Also available:**

- ACT! 6 For Dummies
  0-7645-2645-6
- iLife '04 All-in-One Desk Reference
  For Dummies
  0-7645-7347-0
- iPAQ For Dummies
  0-7645-6769-1
- Mac OS X Panther Timesaving
  Techniques For Dummies
  0-7645-5812-9
- Macs For Dummies
  0-7645-5656-8

- Microsoft Money 2004 For Dummies
  0-7645-4195-1
- Office 2003 All-in-One Desk Reference
  For Dummies
  0-7645-3883-7
- Outlook 2003 For Dummies
  0-7645-3759-8
- PCs For Dummies
  0-7645-4074-2
- TiVo For Dummies
  0-7645-6923-6
- Upgrading and Fixing PCs For Dummies
  0-7645-1665-5
- Windows XP Timesaving Techniques
  For Dummies
  0-7645-3748-2

# FOOD, HOME, GARDEN, HOBBIES, MUSIC & PETS

0-7645-5295-3

0-7645-5232-5

**Also available:**

- Bass Guitar For Dummies
  0-7645-2487-9
- Diabetes Cookbook For Dummies
  0-7645-5230-9
- Gardening For Dummies *
  0-7645-5130-2
- Guitar For Dummies
  0-7645-5106-X
- Holiday Decorating For Dummies
  0-7645-2570-0
- Home Improvement All-in-One
  For Dummies
  0-7645-5680-0

- Knitting For Dummies
  0-7645-5395-X
- Piano For Dummies
  0-7645-5105-1
- Puppies For Dummies
  0-7645-5255-4
- Scrapbooking For Dummies
  0-7645-7208-3
- Senior Dogs For Dummies
  0-7645-5818-8
- Singing For Dummies
  0-7645-2475-5
- 30-Minute Meals For Dummies
  0-7645-2589-1

# INTERNET & DIGITAL MEDIA

0-7645-1664-7

0-7645-6924-4

**Also available:**

- 2005 Online Shopping Directory
  For Dummies
  0-7645-7495-7
- CD & DVD Recording For Dummies
  0-7645-5956-7
- eBay For Dummies
  0-7645-5654-1
- Fighting Spam For Dummies
  0-7645-5965-6
- Genealogy Online For Dummies
  0-7645-5964-8
- Google For Dummies
  0-7645-4420-9

- Home Recording For Musicians
  For Dummies
  0-7645-1634-5
- The Internet For Dummies
  0-7645-4173-0
- iPod & iTunes For Dummies
  0-7645-7772-7
- Preventing Identity Theft For Dummies
  0-7645-7336-5
- Pro Tools All-in-One Desk Reference
  For Dummies
  0-7645-5714-9
- Roxio Easy Media Creator For Dummies
  0-7645-7131-1

* Separate Canadian edition also available
† Separate U.K. edition also available

Available wherever books are sold. For more information or to order direct: U.S. customers visit www.dummies.com or call 1-877-762-2974.
U.K. customers visit www.wileyeurope.com or call 0800 243407. Canadian customers visit www.wiley.ca or call 1-800-567-4797.

 **WILEY**

## SPORTS, FITNESS, PARENTING, RELIGION & SPIRITUALITY

0-7645-5146-9

0-7645-5418-2

**Also available:**
- Adoption For Dummies
0-7645-5488-3
- Basketball For Dummies
0-7645-5248-1
- The Bible For Dummies
0-7645-5296-1
- Buddhism For Dummies
0-7645-5359-3
- Catholicism For Dummies
0-7645-5391-1
- Hockey For Dummies
0-7645-5228-7

- Judaism For Dummies
0-7645-5299-6
- Martial Arts For Dummies
0-7645-5358-5
- Pilates For Dummies
0-7645-5397-6
- Religion For Dummies
0-7645-5264-3
- Teaching Kids to Read For Dummies
0-7645-4043-2
- Weight Training For Dummies
0-7645-5168-X
- Yoga For Dummies
0-7645-5117-5

## TRAVEL

0-7645-5438-7

0-7645-5453-0

**Also available:**
- Alaska For Dummies
0-7645-1761-9
- Arizona For Dummies
0-7645-6938-4
- Cancún and the Yucatán For Dummies
0-7645-2437-2
- Cruise Vacations For Dummies
0-7645-6941-4
- Europe For Dummies
0-7645-5456-5
- Ireland For Dummies
0-7645-5455-7

- Las Vegas For Dummies
0-7645-5448-4
- London For Dummies
0-7645-4277-X
- New York City For Dummies
0-7645-6945-7
- Paris For Dummies
0-7645-5494-8
- RV Vacations For Dummies
0-7645-5443-3
- Walt Disney World & Orlando For Dummies
0-7645-6943-0

## GRAPHICS, DESIGN & WEB DEVELOPMENT

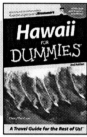

0-7645-4345-8

0-7645-5589-8

**Also available:**
- Adobe Acrobat 6 PDF For Dummies
0-7645-3760-1
- Building a Web Site For Dummies
0-7645-7144-3
- Dreamweaver MX 2004 For Dummies
0-7645-4342-3
- FrontPage 2003 For Dummies
0-7645-3882-9
- HTML 4 For Dummies
0-7645-1995-6
- Illustrator CS For Dummies
0-7645-4084-X

- Macromedia Flash MX 2004 For Dummies
0-7645-4358-X
- Photoshop 7 All-in-One Desk Reference For Dummies
0-7645-1667-1
- Photoshop CS Timesaving Techniques For Dummies
0-7645-6782-9
- PHP 5 For Dummies
0-7645-4166-8
- PowerPoint 2003 For Dummies
0-7645-3908-6
- QuarkXPress 6 For Dummies
0-7645-2593-X

## NETWORKING, SECURITY, PROGRAMMING & DATABASES

0-7645-6852-3

0-7645-5784-X

**Also available:**
- A+ Certification For Dummies
0-7645-4187-0
- Access 2003 All-in-One Desk Reference For Dummies
0-7645-3988-4
- Beginning Programming For Dummies
0-7645-4997-9
- C For Dummies
0-7645-7068-4
- Firewalls For Dummies
0-7645-4048-3
- Home Networking For Dummies
0-7645-42796

- Network Security For Dummies
0-7645-1679-5
- Networking For Dummies
0-7645-1677-9
- TCP/IP For Dummies
0-7645-1760-0
- VBA For Dummies
0-7645-3989-2
- Wireless All In-One Desk Reference For Dummies
0-7645-7496-5
- Wireless Home Networking For Dummies
0-7645-3910-8

Printed in the United States
71766LV00005B/75-104

9 780764 506383